The Institutionalised Transformation of the East German Economy

Contributions to Economics

Christoph M. Schneider
Research and Development Management: From the Soviet Union to Russia
1994. ISBN 3-7908-0757-5

Bernhard Böhm/Lionello F. Punzo (Eds.)
Economic Performance
1994. ISBN 3-7908-0811-3

Lars Olof Persson/Ulf Wiberg
Microregional Fragmentation
1995. ISBN 3-7908-0855-5

Ernesto Felli/Furio C. Rosati/Giovanni Tria (Eds.)
The Service Sector: Productivity and Growth
1995. ISBN 3-7908-0875-X

Giuseppe Munda
Multicriteria Evaluation in Fuzzy Environment
1995. ISBN 3-7908-0892-X

Giovanni Galizzi/Luciano Venturini (Eds.)
Economics of Innovation: The Case of Food Industry
1996. ISBN 3-7908-0911-X

David T. Johnson
Poverty, Inequality and Social Welfare in Australia
1996. ISBN 3-7908-0942-X

Rongxing Guo
Border-Regional Economics
1996. ISBN 3-7908-0943-8

Oliver Fratzscher
The Political Economy of Trade Integration
1996. ISBN 3-7908-0945-4

Ulrich Landwehr
Industrial Mobility and Public Policy
1996. ISBN 3-7908-0949-7

Arnold Picot/Ekkehard Schlicht (Eds.)
Firms, Markets, and Contracts
1996. Corr. 2nd printing 1997.
ISBN 3-7908-0947-0

Thorsten Wichmann
Agricultural Technical Progress and the Development of a Dual Economy
1997. ISBN 3-7908-0960-8

Ulrich Woitek
Business Cycles
1997. ISBN 3-7908-0997-7

Michael Carlberg
International Economic Growth
1997. ISBN 3-7908-0995-0

Massimo Filippini
Elements of the Swiss Market for Electricity
1997. ISBN 3-7908-0996-9

Giuseppe Gaburro (Ed.)
Ethics and Economics
1997. ISBN 3-7908-0986-1

Frank Hoster/Heinz Welsch/Christoph Böhringer
CO_2 Abatement and Economic Structural Change in the European Internal Market
1997. ISBN 3-7908-1020-7

Christian M. Hafner
Nonlinear Time Series Analysis with Applications to Foreign Exchange Rate Volatility
1997. ISBN 3-7908-1041-X

Sardar M.N. Islam
Mathematical Economics of Multi-Level Optimisation
1998. ISBN 3-7908-1050-9

Sven-Morten Mentzel
Real Exchange Rate Movements
1998. ISBN 3-7908-1081-9

Lei Delsen/Eelke de Jong (Eds.)
The German and Dutch Economies
1998. ISBN 3-7908-1064-9

Mark Weder
Business Cycle Models with Indeterminacy
1998. ISBN 3-7908-1078-9

Tor Rødseth
Models for Multispecies Management
1998. ISBN 3-7908-1001-0

Michael Carlberg
Intertemporal Macroeconomics
1998. ISBN 3-7908-1096-7

Sabine Spangenberg

The Institutionalised Transformation of the East German Economy

With 5 Figures
and 28 Tables

Physica-Verlag
A Springer-Verlag Company

Series Editors
Werner A. Müller
Martina Bihn

Author
Dr. Sabine Spangenberg
Richmond College
The American International University in London
School of Business
16 Young Street
GB-London W8 5EH, Great Britain

ISBN 3-7908-1103-3 Physica-Verlag Heidelberg New York

Cataloging-in-Publication Data applied for
Die Deutsche Bibliothek – CIP-Einheitsaufnahme
Spangenberg, Sabine: The institutionalised transformation of the East German economy: with 28 tables / Sabine Spangenberg. – Heidelberg; New York: Physica-Verl., 1998
(Contributions to economics)
ISBN 3-7908-1103-3

Softcover Design: Erich Kirchner, Heidelberg

SPIN 10675514 88/2202-5 4 3 2 1 0 – Printed on acid-free paper

To Ian, Lena and my parents

Preface

"It is, perhaps, worth stressing that economic problems arise always and only in consequence of change. So long as things continue as before, or at least as they were expected to, there arise no new problems requiring a decision, no need to form a plan." (Hayek, 1945, p. 523)

This book is based on my research for the degree of Doctor of Philosophy which I received from Lancaster University, England in the second half of 1997. It is an analysis of the structural transformation of the economic system in East Germany and the behavioural relations these changes imply. The approach of institutionalised transformation (not the least by the creation of the Treuhandanstalt) is examined with a theory-based framework which is derived from system-theoretical, evolutionary and constitutional-ethical considerations as well as from the newly developed adjustment model which has been constructed as a dynamic transformation approach. A relationship between norm changes, the new institutional framework of the economic system and the compatibility of the latter with changes of the remaining partial societal systems is recognised. Rigidity factors in the system's flexibility to react as well as the adjustment of economic behaviour to structural changes are analysed. The "marginal product of system change" is defined (section 2.8.2). These factors help to explain why the internalisation of particular system changes has not been achieved and the analysis of this is given by a combination of empirical research and an application of the relevant theoretical framework. The study argues that the East German transformation approach applied a previously defined behavioural selection function as its privatisation strategy and the study suggests causes for deficiencies in economic adjustment in its particular structural form as well as recognising a time-lag of behavioural adjustment. The study portrays that economic structures and economic behaviour are not sufficiently described by mechanical approaches. Rather these structures are socially designed (not necessarily commonly though) and the study of the organisational and institutional framework needs to go beyond the study of the existence of structures. It needs to analyse the distribution of rights which are derived from these structures. The thesis presents a theoretical-empirical analysis of institutionalised transformation which adds knowledge to the fields of system transformation, institutional economics and property rights theory.

I would like to take the opportunity to thank those people who have helped and supported me throughout the accomplishment of my research and the transformation of the thesis into a publishable book. Firstly I would like to express my deepest gratitude to my husband Ian Sempers without whose support - especially since the birth of our daughter Lena - it would have been difficult to reach the stage of completion and publication. Secondly a very big thank-you to my parents who I consider to be the ones who made all this possible with their loving and educational upbringing. I would also like to mention my sister Barbara and thank her and my close friends whose interest and reassuring words have been reassuring.

The subject of this thesis was not chosen at random and it has been very fulfilling to carry out research in and write about a field which has been close to my heart. I would like to thank all those with whom I studied and worked at the Department of Economic Policy at the University of Duisburg (Germany) for introducing myself to the field of comparative economics and the various aspects of political economics during my time as a student. I thank the Department of Economics at the University of Lancaster for allowing me to carry out this research and would like to thank my former colleagues within the Department of Economics for the support I have received since my arrival as a "Fachlektor" at Lancaster. I am in particular grateful for the friendship I have received from Dr. Robert Reed whose moral support has been highly appreciated. I am grateful to the German Academic Exchange Service who in 1991 made it possible for me to start teaching at a British university and thereby provided the solution to the search of finding the work environment I had sought until then. After having tought at various British universities I am currently lecturing at Richmond College, The American International University in London, who have been extremely supportive with regard to this publication and I would like to thank the School of Business and the University for their financial support.

TABLE OF CONTENTS

CHAPTER THREE
THE INSTITUTIONALISATION OF THE EAST GERMAN SYSTEM TRANSFORMATION

CHAPTER FOUR
TRANSITIONAL PRIVATISATION POLICY: OBJECTIVES, INSTRUMENTS AND THEORETICAL IMPLICATIONS

CHAPTER FIVE
ECONOMIC IMPLICATIONS AND POST-INSTITUTIONALISATION POLICY

CHAPTER SIX
APPLICATION OF THE ADJUSTMENT MODEL TO THE EAST GERMAN TRANSFORMATION

CHAPTER EIGHT
SYNOPSIS AND CONCLUSIONS

Chapter One
Research Objectives, Methodology and Layout

1.1 Field of Analysis and Research Objectives

The research project is undertaken to contribute to the comprehension of system change and its process. This field of analysis is wide in nature and a definition of the research project is achieved by aiming to investigate the economic system within a societal framework. This definition necessitates the analysis of the place of the economic system within the societal system as well as the derivation of elements and structures to classify economic systems. Economic transformation is conceived as the change of system structures and it is intended to establish a framework to provide a method of distinguishing its features. Any analysis of change, however, needs to go beyond the classification of structural changes and has to focus on the process of change. This process of change is described by the term "transformation" and is juxtaposed to the term "evolution". Both forms of change are based on human action and a humanistic view is thereby accepted. The objective is to extend a system-theoretical static approach, focus on human action within a framework and establish some fundamental features about human behaviour. Questions are raised with regard to why system changes happen, how they materialise and why the term "adjustment" is factually relevant. Can we consider system change to happen without any behavioural adjustment and what are the reasons for the lack of internalisation of structural change? Does any need exist to alter fundamentally a system's constitution and why can we conceive such pressure? And even if this change is implemented, can there be various forms of implementation which can achieve different levels of acceptance and internalisation? Historic evidence shows that even the introduction of theoretically approved elements (i.e. forms of market mechanisms) into economic systems do not necessarily achieve the expected transferral onto the level of human behaviour and the economic output. The objective of comprehending transformational changes focuses on two levels: a) the institutional level of system structures and elements and b) the actions and rights of action assigned to individuals.

The case study of East Germany has been chosen as the empirical phenomenon of this research thesis because its societal system has been undergoing substantial institutional changes within the last six years since the demise of the East German Democratic Republic (GDR, see list of abbreviations). Throughout the existence of the Democratic Republic the economic system was committed to the institutional structure of a planned and centralised economy which sustained its existence within the securing borders of Socialist Eastern Europe. With the demise of real existing socialism at the end of the 1980s the former Republic united with the Federal Republic of Germany (FRG) and adapted its societal forms. Not only did the institutional framework of the economic system change, but also the foundations of the remaining societal systems such as the political and legal systems. The particular objective of this thesis is the analysis of why the previously existing system proved to be unsustainable, which new order and form of change has been intended and to what degree this intended order has materialised.

The thesis intends to understand the entity of an economic system in the form of its structures and elements and to identify particular features which can be employed in the classification of economic systems undergoing transformation. The static approach of identifying dichotomous systems restricts the analysis of the process of change and the aim is to develop a dynamic approach which contributes to the comprehension of changing economic systems in the form of the origination of change, its materialisation and effects. The analysis expects to extend the critical appraisal of existing theories which are identified as relevant in their focus on evolutionary developments of structures and features, and their interpretation. In particular, the structure of property rights is important as it will be established that the structure of ownership has traditionally been accepted as a feature for classifying systems. The issues of whether a private property rights structure is *per se* synonymous with best usage and whether scope exists for differentiation are addressed. Structural elements and features of the economic system are focused on in their classifying nature and the question is raised whether any structure exists which is better than any other one. Is it possible to design a best order and do factors exist which have so far not been academically acknowledged to contribute to a good performance of the economic system? If this argument is accepted, structures and elements might need to be defined in a new manner.

1.2 Methodological Discussion

The field of analysis is plentyfold in its methodological basis, in its theoretical relevance, in its phenomenological features and in its potential as a basis for the development of new ideas and methods of analysis. The multiplicity of methodological approaches can be limited by the definition of the field to be studied and the selection of methods of logic. The thesis aims to contribute to the understanding of changes of and within economic systems, regarding the economic system as a social system. This presumes the acceptance of the social scientific assumption of human action with the individual playing an active role in bringing about some process of action and state of economic output. The particular economic field of analysis is thereby categorised as a science which intends to find functional explanations.

The philosophy of science applied to economics generally distinguishes between inductive and deductive methods of analysis. The inductive method which has been widely supported during the 19th century (for example Mill, 1843) tends to observe facts in an allegedly free and unprejudiced manner and to form some universal laws about these facts by the means of inductive inference. In contrast the largely accepted hypothetico-deductive model is based on the explanation and prediction-axiom, i.e. an explanandum is derived by the rules of deductive logic from some event whose explanation one seeks. It follows the hypothetical syllogism of an abstract calculus in a deterministic form in the form of the covering-law model of scientific explanations (Blaug, 1980). The explanation "like it should be" is thereby juxtaposed to historical explanations which can be described as not in fact being truly scientific because they do not provide definite predictions. A strictly deductive methodology has not been accepted for the analysis because no previously defined method exists for the study of changes and neither does economic theory contain any relevant hypotheses concerning what makes systems change which could be tested. The research method is thereby deductive-inductive. It is deductive in collecting system-related and evolutionary theories to form a theoretical framework of some previous observations and tested theories, and inductive in the aim to establish facts about the transformational changes of economic structures and individual economic behaviour. It is thereby acknowledged that the field of study has not yet been undergoing any scientific progress in the form of the identification of previously defined hypotheses which can be tested. Rather theories can be selected out of various economic fields of thought which can provide an understanding of individual economic features of change. The mixture of deductive-inductive methodology can be further exemplified by this study of theories and the culmination of this study in the development of a logically constructed model. This model will be utilised to explain some of the inductively established phenomena of the factual transformation.

A functional explanation for the causation of change and the effect of certain economic behaviour is thus sought in some form of necessary relationship. Of course the term "necessary relationship" - meaning to describe a causal and functional conjunction - needs to be treated with care because any model can be limited and constrained in setting appropriate assumptions and thereby potentially expose the model to the critique of not being scientifically purposeful. Here I rather agree with Kuhn's argument of scientific revolution in that paradigm change always contains non-rational elements which go beyond mathematical or logical substantiation (Kuhn, 1962). Scientific progress will be continued by the formation of further arguments which will advance the new paradigm. This of course exposes the methodological debate to Popper's demarcation criterion of science being a body of synthetic propositions about the real world which can principally be falsified by empirical observations (Popper, 1959 (1965)). The falsifiability criterion is clearly opposed to the covering-law model of scientific explanation (telling "like it should be" rather than "like it is") in the already mentioned form of constrained setting of assumptions which rarely occur in the real world such that the model is thereby not open to any empirical test. The use of non-observable entities has not been employed here because it contradicts logical positivism which necessarily implies the operationalism of scientific progress. Operationalism is conjectured to exist if features can be observed, although empirical quantifiability is not accepted as a necessary prerequisite for science. This thought is based on the one hand on v. Mises's *Verstehen*-doctrine (1949) and on the other hand on the principle of methodological individualism (Popper, 1957). Although I do not go as far as accepting v. Mises's concept of praxeology and radical apriorism in the form of rejecting any openness of economic science to verification or falsification with reason being the ultimate yardstick, it is here agreed that economics is a social science whose dominant unit of analysis is the individual human being and it is surmised that the assumption of a rationally behaving individual is merely an assumption for the operationalism of this particular science. It is thereby believed that the observation and explanation of a certain (even non-rational) behaviour can scientifically be approved as contributing to the understanding of the real world. The definition of economics as a social science implies methodological individualism in the construction and analysis of sociological models in terms of individuals, their attitudes, expectations and relations. Methodological monism is rejected because methods for analysing physical and chemical relations are strictly mechanical and social science seeks to understand human behaviour within the conceptual limitation of factual individualism.

The identification of economics as a social science opens the debate as to whether this field of science is normative or positive and of which nature the applied research methods should be. Myrdal (1970) identified economics as a value-impregnated science because it does not contain any ethically neutral, factual assertions. This does not necessarily contradict Weber's value-free science *(1947, Wertfreiheitspostulat*) because it is still possible to discuss values without value judgements. In particular the intended analysis does contain value considerations and they are subject inherent. The classification of economic systems traditionally chooses particular structures and elements as classifying features on the basis of these features bringing about a certain behaviour and some predictable final states of economic outcome. The identification of particular scientific fields to be analysed goes beyond objectivity because it is carried out by individual selection. It would be erroneous to maintain that the frequency of individuals selecting the same features and outcomes makes the analysis positive. The same can be applied to the socialist economic science which itself is opposed to neoclassical economic theory because of inherently assigning different weights to different features. It is therefore a fallacy to ascertain that for example neoclassical theory is positive and Marxist price theory is normative. The acceptance of economics as being a value-impregnated science does however not imply that the means of analysis need to be normative, it is however essential to realise the existence of values[1]. Comparison of the economic relations and outcomes of the former socialist structure with those of a market-based one has therefore been rejected on methodological grounds. This has been expressed in the acceptance and definition of a social goal function which represents values and their implications for economic life. Conclusions can however be drawn as to whether structures of the economic system are congruous with those of other social systems and objectives of the social goal function. Bergson's (1938) view, however, of any definition of a social goal function implying a ranking of states of the economy is not accepted because it is possible to analyse functional relations without imposing a value judgement. Welfare economics is normative-utilitarian and neither does the consideration of redistributive possibilities of the New Welfare Economics make the analysis positive. It is the analysis of welfare in itself which needs to be value free. Within the penultimate chapter I summarise the applied East German transformation approach in a welfare model and it will be shown that the modelling itself is not normative rather the approach is identified as being normative by the means of modelling. A value-free analysis is here maintained to be achieved if the existence of values and the objectives of some economic policies are identified. This sets the methodological prerequisite of not assessing economic-political means with anything but the evaluation of the achievement of these goals and objectives with the chosen means and instruments, and this requires a stringent application of the chosen methodology. It is therefore rejected that the chosen methodology is normative in any dominant form: it aims to deal with values and norms in a positive way because it accepts the existence of a normative and institutional constraint. It is aimed to achieve this with a deductive-inductive methodology, i.e. a compilation and observation of facts which are tried to be explained by the creation of causal links. This methodology is often influenced by phenomenological features since some causal links are difficult to measure quantitatively but are still observable. The notion of observability is methodologically on the border to phenomenologism because some of the causal links will be developed on the basic assumptions that structures and elements of economic systems assign certain rights of action to individuals and that this assignment bears some behavioural implications. The transformation of any system's structures implies a preceding process of constructing (formal-consciously or informal-evolutionary) some new order and this represents that any real state of economic life in this respect is socially created. The observation of a certain phenomenon does not deny the observer's independence and value-freedom in Weber's sense and allows the establishment of behavioural laws which can undergo scientific observation in the form of testing the law's scientific quality. The phenomenolistic methodological influence can be further substantiated if the aim is not to merely define and measure behaviour, rather the analysis aims to explain it. A holistic and integrated approach is thereby pursued in the analysis of the transformation of the economic system. The assumptions about the institutionalised transformation are positively constructed and the transformational approach is analysed within a system-theoretical and non-deterministic evolutionary-theoretical framework. The analysis goes beyond testing a prior existing theory because no such appropriate theory exists and the deductive method aims at the understanding of features within the theoretical framework. It is aimed to provide further explanations and predictions about system changes in an inductive-phenomenological way.

1.3 Structure of Analysis

The structure of a research project which contains scientific quality needs to be discussed and the requirements of doctoral theses need to be identified in order to put the researcher in the position to meet these demands and justify his particular analysis. Firstly, any research analysis in its generally accepted structure has to take the following form: The project originates in the definition of the problem or question which it is intended to answer. This problem identification is followed by a literature review to select theories which are subject relevant or by the identification of a preliminary study. A conceptual theoretical framework is constructed in an inductive or deductive way, concluding with a hypothesis which is assumed to resolve the identified problem. This hypothesis is then tested by the means of information gathering and an analysis of the attained information. An evaluation is to be accomplished in the form of conclusions about the acceptance or rejection of the hypothesis, an identification of the limitations of the applied test methods and suggestions in the form of another hypothesis or different solutions. Secondly, doctoral theses which take the described form need to contribute to the research area in an original way and this original contribution can take the form of new knowledge, new theories and ideas or new methods of investigation, and ideally should provide a combination of these three forms (Easterby-Smith *et al*, 1991).

This above structure has been consented to and adopted in its form for the structure of the research project. The identification of transformational economics in its origins, features and outcome is identified as the research objective which is followed by the literature review of system-theoretical, evolutionary and constitutional-ethical theories in Chapter 2 (until section 2.6). This literature compilation is followed (in Chapter 2, sections 2.7 and 2.8) by a theoretical evaluation of the relevant theories in the form of a contribution of knowledge. In particular the limitations of the identified approaches are pointed out and this process culminates in the finding that no dynamic theoretical framework exists for the analysis. The necessity of the progress of science in this field is recognised and this lack of theory has led to the logical creation of the adjustment model (Chapter 2, section 2.8) based on the evaluation and recognition of the limitations of the existing theoretical framework. This model, which can be classified as a hypotheses because of its status of original formation, will be tested by a) identifying the transformational approach applied and b) collecting data describing the real effects of the approach. Chapters 3 and 4 identify the chosen transformational approach, at the same time reflecting on the empirical evidence and testing some of the theories which were recognised as relevant, in particular the property rights approach. Within these chapters the theories which are proven to lack empirical support are amended, which qualifies as a further contribution to the field of transformational economics. Chapter 5 intends to present data on the economic implications and also identifies transitional policies which have been employed to mediate some of the adjustment deficiencies recognised. The empirical and phenomenological analysis culminates in Chapter 6 into the application of the hypothesis in the form of the adjustment model which will then be identified as operationally explaining transformational adjustment and its potential deficiencies in a dynamic system-theoretical approach. Chapter 7 contains a Pareto-analysis of the transformation approach applied in East Germany. The design of this model is justified because if one intends to evaluate the effectiveness of any method one has to be aware of the intended objectives (which are not those of the author, but those of the transformation approach identifying group; existence of normative constraint) and has to apply a synonymous methodology. Once the approach has been modelled in a value-free way the researcher is in a position to assess its effectiveness with regard to a) the achievement of the (institutionally) intended objectives and b) reflect on the appropriateness of the chosen approach and its quality. This and general conclusions and limitations of the research project are portrayed in Chapter 8. The compilation and evaluation of a theoretical framework, the design of a new model, the assembly of empirical evidence and the application of the developed model satisfy the criteria of providing new knowledge and ideas to the field of transformational research as well as offering new methods of investigation.

Chapter Two
Theoretical Approaches to System Analysis and the Institutional Framework

2.1 Introduction

Until recently the analysis of economic systems has concentrated mainly on comparisons of different economic systems and explanations of economic processes within a particular system. The comparative approach was essentially static and hardly any attempts were made to make the analysis dynamic. Events in Eastern Europe in the late 1980s and the subsequent economic transitions from the centrally planned economies into free market economies require the application of dynamic theoretical models to the transformation of economic structures, explaining their origins and developing an analysis of implications of the implementation of particular economic frameworks.

Before attempting to identify the most efficient institutional framework and to analyse the political economy of transformation, a review of the "classic" analysis of economic orders and processes in different systems will be discussed. This will provide a methodology to clarify the prevailing circumstances from which the transformation process originates. The review contains a static comparison of the institutional frameworks and the implications for the economic process of action and performance. It should be noted that the general theory of systems and the theory of comparative economic systems have been established against a background of differences in structures and functions of opposed economic systems, i.e. market and command economies. A dynamisation of these existing theories leads to the possible derivation of policy recommendations concerning the setting of a new institutional framework and economic order. A particular aim of this dissertation is to ascertain the structural differences between East Germany prior to and after the economic and national unification as well as to establish the intended and actual changes of the institutional economic order and the implications for the economic process.

The analysis of system differences mainly concentrates on the economic structures against the background of existing political environments. An analytical framework has to be constructed which takes into account the assumption that the economic structure is part of the wider social system and the analysis therefore becomes an approach of political economy. The aim is to find a general framework for analysis within which it is possible to establish structural features prior to the economic transformation and changing or newly established structural elements. Elements of the economic structure have to be evaluated with reference to the general societal structure. The interest is thus not in the collection and listing of differences between economic systems but in the functional relationships within particular systems. The close link between the economic system and other social systems must be realised and the distinguishing parameters of different systems must be established.

Distinguishing parameters as well as boundaries between different systems must be identified on the basis of a theoretical classification of different and identical elements and structures in contrasting systems. Some of these identified elements and structures have to be given classifying values in order to appraise fully any transitional processes. The recognised distinctive features can then be applied to investigate particular behavioural relationships within the societal system.

The objective of the theory of system analysis is therefore the explanation of the relationships between the classified structural orders and the economic processes of action and performance. The structural order includes the entity of all regulations and conditions that determine human behaviour and are of a permanent nature, e.g. the constitutional acceptance of free markets. Process on the other hand portrays the entity of human and especially economic behavioural relations, e.g. profit-maximising behaviour.

It is assumed that the structural elements influence the economic behaviour of individuals so that those structures can be said to determine the economic process and performance. It is necessary to define the economic system and distinguish it from other social systems. Various economic systems must be differentiated according to their structural elements and the functional relationship must be found between those structures, economic behaviour and performance with the help of general economic theory. Those theoretical findings can subsequently be applied to the case of East Germany.

The theoretical findings identify certain structural changes which necessitate an analysis of property rights structures in particular and the distribution of decision-making authority which evolved from the East German transformation. Within this chapter the property rights theory is referred to in its neoclassical character and will be appraised by an application of democratic theory. Motivational implications of property rights structures are given special interest because behavioural assumptions can be derived. Economic behaviour will then be analysed by a decision-theoretic approach as part of the general framework of political economy. Sections two and three are intended to give a theoretical overview of the general institutional transition and transformation of the societal and economic systems. Sections four to six analyse the control structure within the economic firm and aim to establish the ethical foundations of the firm, appraising them from a constitutional viewpoint as well as explaining their relevance in view of the particular German participatory structure.

2.2 General System Theory

2.2.1 System Segmentation

This thesis is concerned with the transformation of economic systems and before any analysis can be undertaken, basic assumptions must be outlined and definitions of the terminology used must be made.

Social and economic systems consist of a multitude of elements which interrelate with each other. A system is generally defined as the entity of elements and their characteristics, e.g. fairness, redistribution and democracy, which are in relation to each other (Leipold, 1985). Elements are components of the system and serve to achieve the system's objectives. The elements are to be defined as partial objectives, principles and methods which are themselves determined by a given norm. The norm is a prevailing feature of a set environment of a particular historical stage and is a behavioural rule or interdiction. This relationship can be exemplified by the system of feudalism, elements of this being large-scale land-holding and vassalage and the norm being the rule of obedience.

Systems analysis is characterised by distinguishing a combination of certain elements so that the unlimited number of possible character elements is reduced to a limited number and thus complexity is avoided. Elements outside the defined systems can be called environmental factors. Since there is a deterministic link between the elements of the system and the environment, a system has to be qualified in such a way that it can react to external influential factors. Only those systems which are able to meet the requirement of flexibility are going to survive because a necessary possibility of reaction must be given (Ashby, 1956). Referring to the above example of the feudal system, it lacked the flexibility to adapt to changing economic and political forces and the system was unable to sustain itself because the system elements and the norm had changed. A high grade of the system's order (for example dictatorship) is synonymous with a low reaction flexibility to external influential factors. A deterministic statement can be made in that the norm determines the elements and they condition the system. Leipold (1985) declares that social systems are systems of organised complexity which work together in a mechanical way.[2]

The preceding deterministic statement appears rather sterile, since it disregards the involvement of any human beings in the framework of a system. It has therefore to be clarified that norms, elements and systems are created by human beings (North, 1990) and none of those features are necessarily static in the long-term since human action and behaviour adds a dynamic pattern to them and renders them changeable. Once this principle of thought has been set the evolutionary character of societal systems is ascertained and behavioural relations can be analysed.

Certain rules organise the behavioural coexistence and those rules can either be spontaneous or be set centrally. According to Hayek (1963) any behaviour according to rules reduces the scope of action and the behaviour can be called "ordered". The effect on a system caused by uncertainty about future events is reduced if the scope of action of the elements, i.e. the actual possible and allowed design of the elements, is minimised. If the elements are highly ordered it becomes easier to predict the effects of certain events. The relationship between order of a system, freedom of behaviour and uncertainty about future events can be expressed as follows: If there is low scope of action for elements the lack of information and therefore uncertainty about future events is reduced and there is a high knowledge about behavioural possibilities. This behavioural knowledge increases the predictability regarding processes and final situations. If freedom of certain elements is identical with a wide scope of action, so is freedom - to behave in a certain individually desired way - associated with a high degree of uncertainty about the behaviour of elements and final situations. A wide scope of action of elements implies a high degree of uncertainty about the future final state of a system.[3] It is not typical for social systems to have no order present as this would be synonymous with chaotic complexity and hence impossible to draw any conclusions about behaviour within the general system.

As a result of defining classifying elements different partial systems can be identified. Social and economic systems are part of the general societal system and can be analysed once they have been defined. A definition of systems can be undertaken according to a differentiation between the institutional and organisational framework.

2.2.2 The Institutional Framework

2.2.2.1 The Economic System as a Partial Social System

Society has to be understood and analysed as a complex of partial social systems and the human being is the basic element of this system (Thieme, 1984). The human being is this central subject because he participates with his particular behaviour and social systems are therefore systems of human action. The traditional assumption of rational behaviour is that individuals do not act without any thought so that social systems comprise meaningful and purposeful actions. Meaningful actions follow a certain order and this order might be in the form of norms and institutions, norms becoming rules and interdictions in a factual context.

Institutions are rules which shape human interaction and determine the opportunities of a society (North, 1990). Norms and institutions preform the scope of behavioural possibility, reduce complexity and structure social relations and behaviour and therefore the process and final state of action. Rules, norms and institutions create partial social systems, e.g. the legal system, and constitute their order and structure.

The economic system is conceived as a partial social system and the economic order can be defined as the evolved or consciously established (e.g. commanded) legal and institutional regulations which influence the economic actions of human beings. In the sense of the system theory economic actions follow the aim to satisfy wants so that needs become the central point of any economic behaviour (as in traditional consumer theory and the theory of the firm), whereby philosophical needs (e.g. individual's perception of economic justice) are not taken account of. Thus in an utilitarian sense every particular economic system comprises any actions that evolve around the supply of goods and services in order to satisfy the need for their consumption with respect to the underlying problem of scarcity (Thieme, 1984).

The economic partial social system is the centre of the theory of comparative economic systems which concentrates on the comparison of organisational arrangements which are designed to serve previously defined economic functions. This concept of an economic function assumes that particular organisational arrangements serve particular ends.

Economic systems can be described as interactions of

participants: individuals and groups of individuals,
orders: the transmission of information which demands a certain response of one individual,
rules: predefined actions of a set of participants,
organisations: group of individuals in which the members' actions are connected to a chain of interactions, the hierarchical structure of organisations is described by the concept of supervision and subordination, and the
legal framework of the economy: the set of laws which defines the scope of economic action.

The economic process takes place within the above described institutional framework, i.e. the economic order, but since the economic system itself is a partial social system it becomes part of a wider behavioural function. The economic outcome is characterised by an interaction of the environment, i.e. elements outside the classified economic system, the political system which defines the prevailing decision-rule for political decisions and the economic system itself. According to Koopmans and Montias (1973, p. 35) this relationship can be expressed in the following way:

$$Q = f(E, S_e, S_p) \qquad (2.1.)$$

where Q is the economic outcome, E the environment, S_e the economic system and S_p the political system. This relationship sets the political system beside the economic system and implicitly sets the assumption of a correlation between the two systems and constitutes the basis for the comparative analysis of economic systems.

Individual behaviour within this institutional framework allocates resources in the course of economic process. The societal goal function also defines the variables upon which the distribution of income and wealth depends.

2.2.2.2 Social Goal Functions

The relationship between the partial social systems raises the question of the origination of the different systems and their establishment. The organisational arrangements and the economic functions themselves are part of a social goal function which constitutes the national choice of economic objectives (Koopmans & Montias, 1973). A social goal function is defined here as comprising the ultimate objectives of a society. Not being able at this point to analyse or question the existence of any such society within a philosophical context, a society is conceived here by its regional boundaries and thus is identical with nations. Societal objectives origin in the society's political and institutional framework, i.e. the objectives within a democratically constituted nation are decided upon by political elections or in the case of autocracy by the present ruler.

Since the economic goal function is defined by the total societal system, it also characterises the decision rule available to the individual. Individual choice is a function of political, economic and social institutions, legal structures and traditional rules. Individual decisions are normative and it should be noted that they are taken within a specific societal framework which defines the scope and range in which the choice can be made. The decision made implies a certain individual behaviour which itself may influence the environment. The economic environment can be divided into effects of endogenous interactions between individuals or groups of individuals (such as a change in technology or the creation of a new product) or exogenous conditions, such as the resource and initial technology endowment[4]. Economic interaction based upon individual or collective decisions leads to a certain economic process of action.

The aim of the comparative analysis is to improve the understanding of the economy's productivity and performance under the institutional and normative constraint. This normative constraint is described here as derived from the setting of the societal environment. From the definition of this aim it follows that the analysis is static and does not intend to give policy recommendations concerning institutional changes. The environmental and political framework is assumed to be given and a maximisation of performance within the defined structure, which will be described and explained, is the main objective of the comparative approach. The purpose of the comparison of economic systems is to find ways of improving the performance of any given economy or system within the established and adopted form (Koopmanns & Montias, 1973).

Certain social and normative objectives which are common to all economic systems and particular objectives which are unique to certain ones can be specified as:

-the efficient use of resources,
-a high level of *per capita* consumption of goods and services or steady economic growth,
-stable employment and income,
-distributional equity of income, wealth and opportunity or the maintenance or extension of individual power,
-social security, and
-the provision of orderly change in a system to allow adjustment to environmental changes.

With respect to the latter objective it should be noted that changes are not perceived as fundamental societal alterations which endanger this system's integral continuity and further existence. This notion prevails as many reforms in Eastern Europe failed to achieve their aims because no radical changes were allowed. An analysis of the institutional organisational framework explains the origins and foundations of individual decisions, their motivational psychology and the coordination of individual decisions to results which are generally acceptable.

2.2.3 The Organisational Framework

2.2.3.1 Hierarchical Organisational Structures

If the area of system change was to be narrowed as the field of analysis, one has to investigate changes within a smaller unit, the organisation. The limits within which decision makers operate depend on the organisational structure of the system. The organisational structure characterises the participants' interactions via the degree of mutuality, i.e. mutual benefits from co-operation. The degree of mutuality forms one differentiating characteristic of economic systems because it prescribes the form in which economic activities are coordinated. It can be conjectured that partial - or no - mutuality entails costs due to the efficiency loss created by X-inefficiency or shirking. In the case of a mutual agreement, economic activities are mainly coordinated by the price system. The organisational structure of the system also predefines the variables which enter the individual's utility function. "The precise response of a decision-maker to an informational action will be conditioned by his motivation, which [is] ...defined as a function associating with each course of action the utility of the outcome of the probability mixture of expected outcomes" (Koopmans & Montias, 1973, p. 61).

The degree of motivation depends on the incentives offered to an individual. Since the scope of action might be limited in a subordinately organised structure, the range of utility-influencing elements is constrained. Moreover preferences are likely to be imposed by superiors and the effectiveness of this depends on the information superiors hold over the subordinate's desired outcome and the degree to which his behaviour is sanctioned. The imposition of preferences is often surmised to be linked with either cultural indoctrination or the degree to which certain behaviour can be forced on somebody by orders. If compliance with orders is not unconsciously adopted by indoctrination the individual behaviour has to be controlled and such activities involve costs and an efficiency loss in terms of the possibility of an alternative use of resources. The lack of information in a highly hierarchical organisation and the suspension of mutually beneficial agreements cause high transaction costs due to the necessity to establish information channels. Furthermore motivational factors have to be introduced to enforce decisions which are not mutually taken and beneficial, such a motivational factor could be a bonus rewarded for the number of units sold. Since those costs could have otherwise been used within the production process, this type of coordination is inefficient.

In the case where the organisational utility function - defined by superiors - diverges from the subordinates' utility functions, conflicts of interest occur. If the outcome of all participants' actions within the organisation is defined centrally and without any consultation with subordinates these conflicts of interest might hinder the successful exercise of predesignated economic activities.

The aspect of mutuality and supervision determines the degree of centralisation of the organisation. The degree of centralisation is a system characteristic since it defines the coordination of the economic process. Referring to hierarchical organisational structures it has to be realised that coordination by a superior involves the cost of collecting the relevant information from the subordinates regarding their actions. Thus the gathered information becomes the main focus for the decision to be taken towards the assignment of activities and duties. The hierarchical organisational structure thereby influences the efficiency of the use of resources and the coordination of economic activities.

The degree of centralisation can be analysed by referring to the hierarchical structure of the organisation. A hierarchy prescribes the behavioural functions of individual subordinates depending on the information transmitted to them by the superior. In the case of central planning the superior is not autonomous in the decision concerning the transmitted orders, he himself receives information and orders from his superior. Hurwicz (1973) uses the preceding authority concept to define a command economy where the directing group is a subset of the hierarchy and the units outside the hierarchy lack autonomy and cannot influence their own actions. A hierarchy is centralised "when all its members are under the order of one member..." (Hurwicz, 1973, p. 96).

2.2.3.2 The Coordination Structure

The structure of information and coordination has been analysed by Hurwicz (1969, 1973), who divides the economic process into two phases, thus employing time. The first phase is the exchange of information by economic agents. In the second phase information is transmitted into plans of actions via the coordination process of decision making. Phase One consists of a sequence of stages which contains initial messages and responses, whereby the latter flow of information initiates the succeeding stage. The response function depends on the initial message and the responding individual's environment. Since the individual's environment is assumed to be known only to the individual himself in its entirety, the exchange of messages also leads to an exchange of environmental perceptions.

In a decentralised economic process the response function only depends on the immediately preceding messages, whereby messages of all previous stages are gathered by one agency in a centrally planned economic process. The factual and temporal interdependence of partial decisions was recognised by the Lausanne School[5] in a general equilibrium model. The factual interdependence characterises the correlation between individual decision-makers with regard to content and the temporal interdependence denotes the sequence of the decision stages.

The universal economic process leads to the necessity to coordinate individual and partial plans of action. If a decentralised decision-making process is not possible the individual plans have to be coordinated by a central plan.[6] The central planning authority accumulates information from the economic agents and the exchange of information differs here from the decentralised one in the way that the messages of preceding stages are also at its disposal. The flow of information is therefore predetermined with respect to its final direction.

The structures of economic process thus define the information and coordination functions within the organisation. The chosen economic process depends on the institutional framework, which defines a specific behavioural rule, i.e. individual actions within the economic process. The coordination of economic activities can be analysed by applying game theory on the basis of the neoclassical motivational assumption of the utility function (tables 2.1 and 2.2).

Behavioural incentives have to be introduced which can be described as elements of an individual's utility function. Since it is generally surmised that the utility function is to be maximised by the individual, a utility function which is compatible with the behaviour rule of the organisation accounts for a Nash equilibrium (Hurwicz, 1973).

This can be demonstrated by a one-off game, played by two subordinates, individuals A and B (table 2.1). Both individuals define their utility functions which they wish to maximise. They are involved in a joint team production process whose output is countable. Both receive income (I) according to the amount produced each day, input material is given. The two individuals are tempted to be lazy and some substitution possibility between idleness, which is further denoted as leisure (L) and income exists. Nevertheless both individuals value income higher than leisure up to a certain point of utility. Although they might be tempted not to cooperate and be idle, income is more important than leisure since work is their only source of income, so that an ordinal ranking of preferences can be surmised. Both value joint coordination highest (value 4) since it will maximise their individual income. If Individual A is tempted to behave non-cooperatively his own utility will decrease, but since he gets some satisfaction from leisure he gains some utility out of the foregone income (value 3). Individual B who wishes to cooperate suffers an income loss due to individual A's behaviour which is not compensated by extra leisure time (value 2). The game is symmetric. If both individuals fail to cooperate they will suffer an income loss and this is the worst outcome (value 1).

The individual utility functions can be written as $U_A = U_A$ (I,L) and $U_B = U_B$ (I,L), and constant homogeneous preferences are assumed. Since the production of output is within the behavioural domain set by superiors a Nash equilibrium is achieved by cooperative behaviour.

Table 2.1: Cooperative Behaviour as Nash-Equilibrium

		Individual B	
		cooperation	non-cooperation
Individual A	cooperation	(4,4)	(2,3)
	non-cooperation	(3.2)	(1,1)

If the scenario was altered in a way where both individuals have identical utility functions but they do not coincide with the behavioural rule, a different dominant strategy would emerge (table 2.2). Both individuals still engage in the same production process, but they detest the machines they have to work with. Individual A thus attains the highest utility from not working himself whilst his team partner works (value 4). Both individuals receive an hourly wage rate and their income does not depend on the output quantity (value 3). The production process is still team production but the scenario changes. Either individual is affected with regard to his utility which will fall if he desires to work but cannot do so to his fullest satisfaction due to the non-cooperative behaviour of his partner (value 1). The following one-off-play matrix emerges, where non-cooperative behaviour is the dominant strategy and the Nash equilibrium.

Table 2.2: Non-Cooperative Behaviour as Nash-Equilibrium

		Individual B	
		cooperation	non-cooperation
Individual A	cooperation	(3,3)	(1,4)
	non-cooperation	(4,1)	(2,2)

Since the solution "not to cooperate" is sub-optimal the superior can either adjust the behavioural rule or try to influence the utility functions. The behavioural rule might be unchangeable because it is set by a central authority within the institutional framework. The individual utility function can be adjusted by imposing normative changes, which also brings in the notion of convention and follow-up games will eventually lead to the desired equilibrium of dominant cooperative behaviour. If no such intervention takes place or is unsuccessful, the situation will evolve into a super-game in terms of an indefinite sequence of ordinary games. Both individuals will realise that by playing the above game over and over again that they will gain from cooperative behaviour in the long run, since both of them can expect punishment and retaliation in every subsequent game by not cooperating in the first game. The decision depends on the temptation ratios and the individual's value of the parameter to discount future benefits to present values.

Axelrod (1984) defines a collective stable strategy by extending the two individuals game to a n-person compound game as a strategy which enables the society to further exist and protect itself from external risk factors. Here it can be interpreted as the strategy to neither change the economic system nor the structure of organisation. To always not cooperate is a stable strategy since the loss from cooperating is due to every other individual choosing not to cooperate. Whether the tit-for-tat strategy is stable depends on the discount parameter which represents the degree to which the pay-off of every move is discounted in relation to the previous move. For a stable strategy the discount parameter has to be greater than the temptation ratio.[7]

The stability of the organisation therefore depends on the choices individuals make and if a trade-off exists between the individual and the organisational utility functions, the collective strategy chosen might jeopardise the centrally designed functioning of the unit. The adaptation of a collectively stable strategy within an organisation stabilises the participants' expectations and if the strategy is known to outsiders the organised behaviour will stabilise their expectations too. An organisational change within a stable environment will cause externalities especially for those who did not originally participate in the decision to adopt changes. This notion certainly has to be extended in the way that the actual decision might have been derived from a majority rule so that further deficiencies are to be expected. This problem of the coordination of individual decisions will be further dealt with in the section on democratic theory (section 2.5).

2.2.3.3 The Decision-Making and Information Structure

In addition to the central or decentral hierarchical coordination of the economic process, central and decentral informational structures can be distinguished. The coordination is informationally centralised, if at least one economic agent attains the entire relevant information about each individual's environment. Informational decentralisation allows dispersion of information between several economic agents and is indicated by the choice of every economic agent regarding the gathering of information. This is due to the inherent difficulties in gathering information and the impossibility of one agent attaining all the relevant information. The central planning system is deemed to fail even if the concept of an altruistic and well-meaning dictator were to be adopted.

The DIM-approach (decision, information, motivation) originates in the neoclassical school of thought in the sense that is focuses on decisions as the main element of the study. The structure of the economic system is conceived as being divided into the decision-making, the information and motivation structures, whose structures are highly correlated. The close link between the decision-making, information and motivation structure was shown in Neuberger and Duffy's decision theoretic approach of modern economic theory applied to the study of economic systems (Neuberger & Duffy, 1976). The analysis focuses on the interrelationship of the system elements and on the uncertainty within the decision-making process. It endeavours to understand the correlation between the economic system, efficiency and performance of the economy, implications of economic growth and the relationships between economic systems, political systems and human welfare. In particular the latter element is of significant importance and although the interrelationship between societal and political systems was recognised in the general system theory, the aspect of human welfare and the implications a certain economic system has for the distribution of income and wealth was widely neglected in comparative economics.

Economic systems can be distinguished according to the allocation of decision-making authority, its origins, form and content. Decision-making authority can be defined as the power to choose a certain action from a given set of choices. The power is defined as legitimate and derived from the societal structure and its granting of the possibility to gain and attain decision-making authority.[8]

Some sources of decision-making authority are ownership, performance and the ability to use coercive force - possibly due to political loyalty - and legal regulations for codeterministic decisions.[9] These origins emanate from the societal structure and predefine how derived decision-making authority can be awarded to secondary authority holders.

The range of authority sources is restricted and only applicable to modern industrial economies. Tradition and totalitarian power are neglected since all countries analysed refer to human rights and dignity of the individual human being. Authority derived from tradition although still present in certain political decision-making processes is becoming increasingly unimportant within the economic process.[10] The aspect of ownership is investigated within the property rights theory and some approaches to derive authority from performance are attempted in section 2.6.3. The legal regulations to apply codeterministic decision-making will be studied mainly with reference to the mandatory system in the FRG. Decision-making authority derived from political loyalty and performance will be applied in the case of the former GDR.

The distribution of decision-making authority implies the classification of centralisation and decentralisation following the hierarchical structure within the decision-making organisation. The application of the neoclassical school of thought assigns each individual a utility function which is to be maximised. Decisions which affect the economic process in terms of the chosen economic activity are based on utility maximising behaviour and essentially on the analysis of the variables of the utility function. Furthermore it must be considered that interrelations between individuals exist and that decisions may not be made by only one economic subject. As decision units consist of different individuals, a group's utility function may have different objectives to each individual's utility function and the group's utility function is not simply the summation of individual ones. The coordination of economic activity depends on the degree to which utility functions differ and the actual distribution of decision-making authority.[11] The distribution of decision-making authority is the degree to which superiors influence and control actions of subordinates. The hierarchical structure of the organisation produces a certain control pattern concerning the allocation of resources. Since every economic action follows a plan of action - the plan might still be spontaneous -, planning can be seen within the scope of centralisation and decentralisation and the degree to which authority is exercised by the centre. Levine (1973, p. 141) describes the centre as "the ruling group and its central bureaucracy..., that is, more than a single ruler or executive board but less than the entire state bureaucracy". According to Levine (1973) a classification of the degree of centralisation can be expressed by referring to the action plan.

The plan itself is divided into three categories:

1) The Plan
2) Construction of the Plan
3) Implementation of the Plan

The plan itself is described based on the following elements:
a) periodicity of the plan (long term - short term)
b) scope of the plan (small part of the economy - entire economy)
c) plan coverage of investment (none - entire)
d) plan coverage of distribution of materials (none - entire)
e) level of plan detail (highly aggregate - very specific)

A high degree of centralisation is considered to exist if the plan covers a long time period, a large part of the economy and the economic activities (i.e. investment, resource allocation) and if this coverage is very specific.

The construction of the plan is classified on the basis of who is responsible for the plan creation, according to the criteria detailed below:
a) extent of participation by the periphery (high participation - no participation)
b) extent of participation by the periphery in the construction of the investment plan (high participation - no participation)
c) type of participation by the periphery (authority to initiate proposals - information only)

With regard to plan construction the degree of centralisation is greater, the fewer peripheral authority units there are within the decision-making process.

The third classification comprises the attempts and methods to implement the plan:
a) attempt to implement the plan (no attempt - strong attempt)
b) means of implementation (manipulation of parameters - issuing of parameters)
c) number and detail of directives (low - high)
d) centre's plan adjustment mechanism (weak - strong)

e) implementation incentive mechanism (low pressure - high pressure)

The centralisation of authority is greater, the stronger the attempt to implement the given plan and the lower the possibility of modification, the higher the use of directives and coercive power and the less discretion is left to subordinates regarding the execution of directives. In addition high centre authority is surmised to be given if the successful plan implementation is rewarded with material and non-pecuniary bonuses (non pecuniary awards circumscribe mainly power and reputation).

The above classification is useful in differentiating economic systems according to the degree of central planning. Nevertheless it has to be surmised that even a system classified as a decentralised planning structure contains elements of concentrated decision-making authority. If it is generally assumed that decision-making authority in decentrally planned systems originates in ownership, participatory rights serve useful to further classify hierarchical structures. This aspect will be further taken into account in the property rights theory, its leakages and cases of codeterministic approaches (section 2.3.1.2 and section 2.4).

Whilst the distribution of decision-making authority and the motivation structure can be called upon to explain non-economic principles (societal), the information structure determines the efficiency of resource allocation within a certain system (Neuberger & Duffy, 1976). The information structure serves the purpose of informing economic agents and units about their environmental perceptions and environmental changes. The ever-changing nature of the environment leads to the constantly repeated flow of information, since the individual economic agent's knowledge and information is restricted by his own perception. The coordination of economic activity requires information and therefore becomes an element of the production function whose usage involves costs, and in order to maximise utility marginal costs and benefits should be equated.

The informational structure can be used as a classifying element with regard to economic systems mainly in the form of the direction of the information flow. The vertical transmission of information between superiors and subordinates is highly associated with centrally planned economies, whereby horizontal transmissions are used in decentralised market economies. This broad conjecture neglects any overlapping structures within this classical dichotomy. The information structure though is mainly determined by the distribution of decision-making authority and the associated hierarchical structure of any organisation, since the decision-making economic unit itself initiates the flow of information. Any exogeneously initiated information flow will be assessed on the basis of the marginal benefit the information produces and the costs it involves. Since information is essential for the coordination of economic activity it enters the production function and the decision about its necessity is subject to every decision made in the economic process and therefore it must be surmised that the decision-making structure also defines the information structure. Informational externalities cannot be excluded and can be analysed with transaction cost economics.

2.2.3.4 The Motivation Structure

The decisions taken by the authority-holding economic unit have to be executed by subordinated economic agents. The degree to which those decisions are carried out depends on the motivation structure, which can be characterised as the means of control and incentives exercised by the superior in order to secure compliance with decisions. The degree to which actions are exercised successfully depends on the homogeneity of the economic agents' objectives, i.e. whether the objectives are mutually tolerable and do not exclude each other. Various views have been expressed on the issue of the unanimity of participants' objectives within an organisation. The viewpoints span from the Weberian compatibility of objectives to Leibenstein's X-inefficiency. The analysis of any motivation and incentive structure depends on the underlying assumptions regarding organisational and individual objectives.

The Weberian assumption is that all economic agents behave rationally under the distinction between *Zweckrationalitaet* and *Wertrationalitaet*, i.e. they behave rationally towards the attainment of subjective goals and their behaviour serves an *ex-ante* defined purpose. Weber (1968) distinguishes four types of social action and suggests that this differentiation applies to every kind of human action. Action is explained with regard to its underlying motives, which can be described as:

1) instrumental-rational

This rationale is determined by the expected behaviour of the social environment and the individual's objectives and purposes which he tries to attain. Every action is based on the expectations that construct conditions or means towards the materialisation of certain purposes.

2) value-rational

Individuals are aware that any behaviour originates in values attributed to different forms of behaviour and the decision to behave in a specific manner depends on the subjective values added to behavioural options. The action and rationale of action is entirely independent of any perceptions of outcome, but is rather determined by the chosen behavioural form itself.

3) affectual and traditional.

Affectual and traditional orientation circumscribes action which originates in the actor's emotions and framework of socially accepted routines.

Although Weber describes the motives as applicable to any kind of action, he clearly distinguishes between individual and social action. Action is denoted social only in the case where the acting individual appraises the behaviour of other individuals and if a social relationship exists in the probability of social action (Weber, 1947). In this sense economic behaviour is defined as social action if the behaviour of one individual or a group of individuals takes account of the behaviour of somebody else. According to the underlying motives of social action, social relationships are considered to be either "communal" or "associative" (Weber, 1947, p. 136). A communal relationship is based on affectual or traditional motives, whereby the associative form applies to the types of rationally motivated forms of actions. The associative social relationship originates in a rational agreement by mutual consent.

Since economic action aims at the attainment of certain objectives, it can be classified as rational action and economic organisations are one particular form of associative social relationships based on mutual agreement. The economic organisation is herewith defined as a corporate group, a social relationship that is closed or limited to outsiders by regulations. It seems possible to keep still the assumption of mutual agreement especially in relation to the formation of the group. But since the legally-established order of this corporation or of this corporate group originates either in a) a voluntary agreement, or b) in an imposed regulation, scope for different motivation structures is given. Economic activity within different forms of economic systems is based on the individual utility functions and no further explanation regarding the homogeneity of different agents' objectives and preferences is offered in the Weberian theory of organisation.

The notion of motivation and its implications for economic actions and results were referred to and elaborated in Leibenstein's X-efficiency concept (Leibenstein, 1966). The empirical studies carried out to portray the implications of improved allocative efficiency on economic growth suggested small magnitudes of welfare gains. Ineffective allocation was mainly referred to in cases of imperfect market structures and trade restrictions or interventions, and the benefits from the elimination of allocative inefficiency were unexpectedly low. The small degree of welfare gains is expected to have been caused by restricting the analysis of firm's decisions to the equating of marginal costs and benefits. Since microeconomic theory investigates economic decisions as decisions taken by an organisational unit, it does not take into account qualitative factors of efficiency. Qualitative factors of inefficiency can be envisaged as deficiency within the prevailing motivation and incentive structure. Qualitative factors such as payment by result, affiliation, superior labour selection methods and psychological factors - small working units, homogeneity of workers, general rather than strict personal supervision and improved informational flow - represent improved incentives and the derived increased motivation accounts for better proficiency by the organisation's participants.

According to Leibenstein (1966, p. 406,7) X-efficiency is determined by the following three elements:

1) intra-plant motivational efficiency (form of organisation, level of hierarchy, working conditions, etc.),
2) external motivational efficiency (e.g. wage negotiation), and
3) non-market input efficiency (ethos, culture).

Qualitative motivational factors gain importance because the relationship between production factors and output is not predetermined, because

i) labour contracts are not complete,
ii) not every input factor has an assigned price,
iii) the production function is incomplete, and
iv) firms' behaviour may be tacitly cooperative rather than competitive due to interdependence and uncertainty.

The first three factors point out the heterogeneity of the segmented labour force and the lack of knowledge regarding the individual's maximum proficiency. This accounts partly for the lack of awareness of the production possibilities as the production function is not entirely known and thus production takes place within the production possibilities frontier.[12] Another finding of the Leibenstein interpretation was the cost reduction due to X-efficiency improvement which leads via the increased residual to economic growth. Knowledge dissemination was surmised as one important factor of cost reduction, and the expansion of information might have improved the incentive structure.

A close relationship between innovation and cost reduction was conjectured in his study based on the evidence that firms operate sub-optimally and do not attempt to produce at minimum cost because of a failure of the motivation system. Improvement in X-efficiency increases the firm's residual and influences economic growth. Motivation and competitive incentives determine via the concept of X-efficiency, the position of the firm's unit cost function and the place of the firm on it. An improvement in X-efficiency leads to the movement of a production situation within the production possibility curve towards a point on or closer to the frontier.

Within the general system theory an attempt has been made to identify classifications of systems on the level of the entire economic system and on the level of the organisation and the individual. These classifications will be vested further with a dynamic nature referring to evolutionary theories. Deterministic approaches as well as non-deterministic approaches will be explained in the forthcoming section.

2.3 Evolutionary Approaches of System Transformation

2.3.1 Non-Deterministic Approaches of System Transformation

A non-deterministic evolutionary process can be defined as a process where structural elements inside a system produce evolution and this complexity is identical with an expansion of choice. The system receives signals from the environment and by letting those signals become elements of the system itself it widens the scope of action and reaction. The system can react directly or indirectly, consciously or unconsciously.

The changes can take place in the form of variation, selection and stabilisation. A variation changes the structure of a system violently or non-violently, so that the system can take in new elements. Selection lets those structures survive which are more successful than others and stabilisation is aimed at the future existence of the selected new structural elements. Non-deterministic approaches conceive a system as open, i.e. it is not static and is thus changeable. The elements inside the system can alter and are able to react to changing environmental factors. The system is defined as flexible and no definite conclusions about the economic outcome can be drawn.

2.3.1.1 The Ordo-Liberal Theory of Economic Systems

2.3.1.1.1 The Morphological Methodology of the Approach

The methodology applied by Eucken (1950) to analyse the economic system can be described as a morphological synthesis of the inductive and deductive methods of economic theory. Following the historical school - mainly at the beginning of his career - he collected and classified facts found at different historic stages to derive regular occurrences on the basis of a particular area and time. The deductive method of deriving individual cases from theoretical constructions and models was also valued because he acknowledged the existence of a limited number of pure economic forms of which past and present economic systems consist. This morphological method aims to establish the pure forms of economic systems and to provide a theoretical framework which analyses the course of the economic process on the basis of these pure forms. Eucken thereby accepts the conception of the historical school that economic behaviour can be interpreted on the basis of the institutional framework, i.e. the economic system.

The "great antinomy" exists in the necessity to grasp economic reality on the basis of the individual-historical approach and the requirement of general-theoretical study in order to provide scientific experience. The economic process can only be analysed by applying abstract methods of economic theory subsequent to the recognition and identification of the structural elements of the economic system. The aim is to comprehend economic life, i.e. the economic system and the course of economic action, at a certain time, its development and its adjustment to changing elements.

Economic life is characterised by a variety of forms and historical processes and the classical theoretical analysis does not do justice to the constantly changing range of economic orders or systems and thus fails to understand the "great antinomy". Eucken also criticises approaches which construct stages of economic development because of the great variety of economic systems which existed in the past and the impossibility of epitomising this variety in a single stage or style of development. Furthermore styles of development are surmised to be accidental and a classification of economic systems according to development stages would represent an over-simplification.

2.3.1.1.2 The Pure Forms of Economic Systems

The economic system is defined as the entity of the respectively realised forms in one country within which the economic process takes its course. Economic plans and economic actions by individuals take place within this framework of a historically given economic system. The institutional framework of the economic system builds the basis of the economic process and the process can not occur without such foundation. The economic system is not necessarily determined by the economic constitution (i.e. the construction of general principles) which render it efficient, but rather it depends on the determining economic facts and the elementary forms within which the economic process takes place. The determination of the economic system by the legal system (e.g. the law of property and contract) is thus denied although its influential importance is acknowledged.

Eucken chooses the form of the plan according to his collection of historical facts as the criteria for the classification of different economic systems. A general occurrence in every economic system at every point in historic time is that individuals act according to economic plans. Following this classifying form two different types of pure elemental forms of economic systems are extracted, that of the exchange economy and that of the centrally directed economy. The exchange economy is characterised by the existence of two or more independent economic units - households and firms - which specify and realise their economic plans. Within the centrally directed economy the economic life of the society is centrally controlled and follows a plan defined by the central authority.

2.3.1.1.2.1 The Exchange Economy

The pure form of the exchange economy is identified by the existence of independent economic units - households and firms - which are in exchange with each other. The economic process consists of many individual partial plans and each economic unit has to take account of other units' plans. A mutual interdependence between the economic units exists and the coordination of the different plans takes place according to the form of the market and the monetary system. The different combinations of market forms and monetary systems produce a number of possible variants of the exchange economy which exceeds the varieties of the centrally directed economy.

The market forms are distinguished according to the number of individual plans on the supply and demand sides, the openness of the market and the nature of the facts which enter the individual plans as data, e.g. the price or the consumers' demand. On the basis of this systemisation Eucken derives five basic market forms: perfect competition, partial oligopoly, oligopoly, partial monopoly and monopoly.

Any form of exchange economy comprises exchange values which guide the economic units. The main forms of the monetary economy are distinguished as to whether this exchange value is also the unit of account. Different types of the monetary system are classified on the basis of the origination of money: a) money originates with some commodity which is used as money, b) money is created as a return of a good or service, and c) money originates in the granting of credit.

2.3.1.1.2.2 The Centrally Directed Economy

Two forms of centrally directed economies are differentiated, that of the totally centralised economy and that of the simple centrally directed economy. The totally centralised economy prohibits any form of exchange and the employment of productive resources. The distribution of goods follows a plan formulated by the central authority. All economic actions are covered by central orders and only one planner exists. The simple form of centrally directed economies is mainly found within an independent economy or economic unit. This form is characterised by the facts that it allows the free exchange of goods but centrally plans the production process and the distribution. Whereas the totally centralised economy does not produce scarcity indicators, the simple form might assert that individual demand reflects requirements and that these needs might be taken into consideration for the formulation of the central production and distribution plans.

2.3.1.1.3 The Course of Action on the Basis of the Economic System

By means of abstracting the significant characteristics the pure forms of economic systems, the elementary market forms, types of monetary system and of centrally directed economies are derived. By applying the morphological approach and employing theoretical considerations, such as the assumption of the desire to satisfy needs and the theorem of diminishing marginal returns, real economic life can be understood (Eucken, 1950). The given economic system preforms the course of economic events and the recognition of the economic system at a certain period of time and place allows the understanding of the course of the economic process. The uniqueness of the economic world at a particular economic stage is recognised by this approach as well as the never constant nature of the form of the economic system. It is thereby concluded that the economic environment is dynamic and any development takes place in two ways, namely either in a change of the economic system itself or in a change of the economic process. A change in the economic system implies a change in the economic process, but not every change in the economic course of action brings a change in the economic system.

The coordination of economic plans and the entire economic process of action takes place differently according to the form of the market, the monetary form and the type of monetary system (Eucken, 1950). This assumption allows for the derivation of economic policy recommendations in a way that any political actions, in order to influence the course of economic events, have to focus primarily on the economic policy of systems (*Ordnungspolitik*). The role of economic policy in the exchange economy or market economy is in the construction of an economic system which allows for the effective functioning of forms of the market and the monetary system (Eucken, 1952).

The evolutionary thesis of the ordo-liberal conception is thus that only the efficient economic systems will survive in the real world. The recognition of the scope for economic policy nevertheless recognises that the development of efficient economic systems is not of a spontaneous nature: it is rather designed and the result of decisions of economic policy. Within the scope of economic policy, forms of economic systems are set and these forms are the object of the analysis.[13] The theoretical analysis of the economic system focuses on economic efficiency and thereby adopts the traditional economic theory. The morphological approach allows a comparison of economic systems, the courses of economic action and their outcome and performance as well as offering the opportunity to draw conclusions about the stability of certain economic systems.

2.3.1.2 The Property Rights Theory

The property rights theory is similar to Marx's evolution theory (see section 2.3.2.2) since the evolution of societal structures is surmised to be characterised by the economic structure, i.e. the ownership of the means of production on the one side and the structure of property rights on the other side. It nevertheless qualifies as a non-deterministic approach because it does not specify whether or when a transformation of inefficient forms of economic systems will occur. The property rights approach and the theory of institutional change are closely linked to the ordo-liberal theory. Certain institutional structures are analysed with respect to their behavioural economic implications. The approach stresses the influence of legal and institutional structures on the development and establishment of forms of economic systems. This is the main difference to Eucken's approach which more strongly accentuates determining economic facts and elementary forms than the constitutional framework as influencing the economic process and classifying the economic system.

2.3.1.2.1 The Structure of Property Rights and Transaction Costs

The institutionalist property rights theory originates in the criticism of traditional production and price theory which led to a new analysis of property rights structures and in particular of the interrelation between ownership structures, incentives and economic behaviour (Furubotn & Pejovich, 1972). The traditional theory has been extended by three main aspects:

1. The tight relationship between the structure of property rights and economic behaviour and the notion of different existing property rights suggests that the aim of profit maximisation might not always be met.
2. Individuals within the organisational structure look after their own self interest and seek to maximise their utility, whereby the organisational structure influences the way in which the self interest can be materialised. The traditional assumption of profit maximisation is modified and widened.
3. The existence of transaction costs essentially determines the development of institutional structures.

The first aspect has mainly been expressed by Alchian and Demsetz (1973) who, as the main protagonists of the school of institutional change, criticise the conventional discussion concerning the production of goods and their consumption within the society by noting that social systems are characterised by certain societal structures. Decisions about the use of scarce resources are made within this social system. Societal structures are conceived as certain techniques and rules, i.e. norms and institutions. These structures specify how conflicts of interest due to the scarcity of resources are solved. The analysis of these conflicts focuses on property rights and in particular on the historic existence of the property rights structures at a certain time, how they evolved and which particular behaviour in terms of the resolving of social problems these structures lead to.

According to Pryor (1973) property rights have two fundamental characteristics: ownership and control. Ownership is defined as the right to use a resource and this right is socially acknowledged. The ownership of a right of action can be classified as a degree of realisation of the owner's determination about the use of this right and it also includes the right to retain income from the owned capital assets. Income can be received either through profits from the current use of assets in the production process or through changes in the asset's value. It can be positive in the form of gains or negative in the form of losses. Control can be described as the right to decide about the utilisation of the asset.

The property right can be owned entirely by one person or be shared by several individuals: each person might own the right of a particular use of the resource or several individuals might own the right commonly. In accordance with this the use of the property right and the final determination of the use can be distinguished and statements can be made about the structure of property rights. Characteristic elements of the property rights structure are the existence of property rights and the identity of the property rights owners. The existence of property rights is defined as the degree to which the use of this right is socially recognised and accepted. The identity of owners entails the possible ownership structure, i.e. the distinction between private, communal or state ownership. The distinctive element of the owner's identity opens scope for societal implications such as state ownership which, for example, unavoidably involves the matter of state control by which social systems can be distinguished *inter alia*. Exclusive property rights are connected to a high intensity of control of social interactions by the state.

The classical dichotomy of private and state ownership is here widened by the communal rights ownership. Communal rights follow the definition of public goods in terms of non-exclusion (except for prior and continuing usage), but the aspect of rivalry may still be persistent.[14] Communal rights do not take into account the true costs of usage because they are not incorporated into the individual's decision making process. The costs of the supply of the right to use or the cost of the resource itself is not a variable in the individual's behaviour function, the function's variables are self interest and utility.[15] Without the existence of a market clearing system the proper evaluation of the property right is hardly possible and changes in the value of the property right are neglected. Devaluation of a property right through over-usage and non payment leads to an increase in transaction costs and an alteration in the allocation of resources.[16] The property right structure implies certain economic behaviour. The right of action consequently necessitates specific behaviour by individuals according to the allocation of resources and social systems can be distinguished by the structure of property rights. The property rights theory suggests a close relationship between property rights structures and the allocation and the use of resources, and therefore a systematic relation between property rights and economic choice.

The second aspect of the critique of conventional economic theory concentrates on human self interest. The analysis of the identity of property rights owners is a benefit analysis assuming that human beings act according to their self interest. The emphasis laid on utility rather than profit maximisation encourages the analysis of an individual's behaviour within different institutional structures and systems. The optimisation axiom of utility depends on the structure of property rights and the identity of property rights owner. Each individual creates his own utility function and his action is motivated by self interest in such a way that he tries to achieve the highest possible level of utility. Thus the model of utility optimisation focuses on the behaviour of the individual decision-maker rather than on the behaviour of the firm (Furubotn, 1985).[17]

The property rights theory is based on neoclassical assumptions and focuses as its third major pillar on the belief that the transaction of resources or commodities, production and utilisation takes place within a certain structure of order. This order determines the process and quality of production. The exchange of goods and services is based on contracts which are formed due to the costs of using markets. The emergence of these contracts leads to associated costs of transaction defined as external costs associated with exchanging property rights. The magnitude of transaction costs depends on the structure of property rights due to the assumed internalisation of external costs under a private property rights structure (Coase, 1960).[18] An equilibrium condition is expected if the utilisation of resources cannot be improved by any further transactions of property rights. Although it has been recognised that transaction costs are hardly ever zero, it is assumed that a reallocation of property rights with negligible transaction costs does not affect the optimisation of the most useful utilisation of the resource (Demsetz, 1964).[19] Positive transaction costs have a potential negative reallocative effect on resources because of the divergence between the prices and values of the rights exchanged.

Within the New Economic History Approach, associated with institutional economics, the development of economic eras is analysed with reference to the system of property rights in relation to transaction costs, based on the neoclassical assumption of the individual's pursuit of his self interest. North and Thomas (1971) suggest in their study of newly evolving institutional structures, referring to the manorial system in England, that if it is impossible to account for external effects (i.e. because certain actions cannot be assigned to particular individuals or groups) no economic initiative can be expected due to non-existent incentives. This implies that the structures of the economic system change if they do not satisfy the individual needs due to altered circumstances. The property rights structure has to meet the requirements of the actual economic desires of the individual economic units and it is surmised that only a private property right structure enables the internalisation of external effects. The incongruity between private and social effects follows insufficiently defined property rights. Insufficient structures which certainly evolved during history are the result of positive transaction costs and political deficiencies.

The structure of property rights arranges a certain order which determines the economic initiative and performance. Institutional change and varying property rights structures are accompanied by transaction costs so that the evolution of the supposedly efficient property rights structure might be hindered by a cost-benefit analysis. A positive institutional change can be expected if the benefits are higher than the costs of transaction, *et vice versa*. The implications of the identity of the owners for transaction costs and resource allocation make the property rights model dynamic.

2.3.1.2.2 The Evolution of Property Rights

The Property Rights School assumes that different private owners respond to market incentives in the same way. It is assumed that they always use their property right in the most profitable way and it is expected that this is being well realised. Perfectly competitive market structures are implicitly assumed in all the discussions as well as the corresponding behavioural relations. An essential link is hereby created between the structure of ownership, the owners' behaviour and the performance in terms of production and output mix. Private ownership and negligible transaction costs will lead to an allocation of resources which ensures the most valuable use of resources. On the other hand an alteration of the ownership structure of the property rights might prevent this useful utilisation if transaction costs are positive and high. The allocation of resources according to certain property rights structures is extensively influenced by the magnitude of transaction costs. Transaction costs affect institutional changes of property rights and the resulting allocation of resources.

A framework for a theory of ownership can be created by referring to the distinction of ownership as an exogenous or endogenous feature (Demsetz, 1988). Ownership as an exogenous feature analyses the identity of owners and the truncation of ownership rights. By altering certain elements of the exogenous ownership structure the relationship between the assignment of ownership rights to individuals and the definition and extent of these rights and economic behaviour can be analysed. The endogenous character of ownership implies the allocation of the property by individual and collective action. Endogenous changes of property rights induced by cost-benefit perceptions can be created via individual or cooperative action depending on the degree of exclusiveness of the right and the right to reassign ownership. According to this distinction it is possible to define property rights as private, communal or state property rights. Furthermore the scope of cooperative action depends to an important extent on the size of the society (Olson, 1977). The larger the size of the group or society the more preferable is individual action and the more difficult it becomes for cooperative action dependent on the particular decision-making process.

The development of property right structures is perceived as follows: Any communal right system will eventually develop into a private ownership structure because every communal right once materialised becomes a private one and only private rights ensure a useful utilisation of resources in the individual's conception of self interest.[20] If transaction costs are negligible, private rights are suggested to be socially preferable since they internalise external costs and as such account for total social costs (Coase, 1937, 1960).[21] A development towards a communal rights system is not perceived as stable once it has been established because it does not provide incentives to use the resource in the most useful way. Often the problem of shirking becomes an issue and this problem can only be dealt with if the individual's behaviour is controlled by a central authority (Alchian & Demsetz, 1973; Demsetz, 1988). The central authority has to influence the individual's behaviour to make them contribute to the society, a possible means of order being cultural indoctrination. The second major problem within the communal rights structure is the responsiveness towards external changes, e.g. innovations. Such external elements alter the value of utilisation of a resource and a new system of private property rights will eventually be established.

A communal right can not be exercised by one individual but requires the action of all community members. In contrast to private ownership no one can be excluded from exercising this right. State owned property rights might imply discretion by the state for the exclusion of the right. Considering communal ownership, evolutionary externalities that imply necessary changes are connected with high costs of negotiation due to the largeness of the community. Another factor which increases the difficulty of negotiation and decision-making process is the problem of the perception of costs and benefits. The individual's conception of necessity tends to be smaller, the larger the group is and inherent conflicts of interests might occur. The subsequent cost of an individual's action is difficult to assess and to take into consideration. This negotiation problem leads to high externalities and costs. As for private ownership external costs associated with communal ownership are internalised due to the owner's right of exclusion. Negotiation costs are considerably lower.

The property right which is assigned to a particular object or resource influences the value of it. Any exchange of property rights is therefore subject to the value in terms of property rights because it represents an element of the individual's utility function. Any exogenous change of the property right consequently affects its value. An attenuation or truncation of the property right possibly induced by a governmental restriction of the use of the right of action will decrease the value of the property right. In this case it follows that income effects are present and not only will the allocation of resources change but also the distribution of income (Buchanan & Stubbleline, 1962).[22] Particular rights of usage or action are removed by truncation and "a change in the general system of property relations must affect the way people behave and, through this effect on behaviour, property right assignments affect the allocation of resources, composition of output, distribution of income, etc." (Furubotn & Pejovich, 1972, p. 1139).

The main function of property rights is to internalise externalities and the evolution of property rights can therefore be followed by the analysis of underlying social benefits and costs. Externalities are also perceived as evolutionary or revolutionary changes of elements and structures of the economic environment (technological changes, innovations, wars, etc.) which affect production functions and therefore cause alterations in cost-benefit structures. These effects lead to the emergence of new property rights which have to be assigned. If the benefit of internalisation is greater than the cost of creating new property rights which internalise externalities, new creation will occur. In this respect a close relationship between the development of property rights and externalities is ascertained. Property rights which develop in turn can be of different forms, namely communal, private or state. On the basis of this development approach the property rights theory favours an economic policy which ensures exclusive property rights and the existence of a competitive market structure.

The property rights theory offers a valuable approach in explaining institutional changes that certainly can be applied to transformation processes. It claims that efficient forms of economic systems evolve if perfect information is given (i.e. no transaction costs and perfect competition with all the relevant sub-assumptions). The application of these rigid assumptions and the insufficient critique in the neoclassical school of thought, however, renders the evolution approach inapplicable as a valid transformation approach. This will be elaborated further in the subsequent critique.

2.3.1.2.3 A Critique of the Transaction Cost Approach as Part of the Property Rights Theory

Applying the Coasian theorem of externalities (1960), changes in the identity of private owners will not change the efficient output mix if transaction costs are zero and income effects are absent. The output will be identical within a competitive market structure regardless of the assignment of ownership rights and the absence of income effects implies no alteration of the individual's marginal rate of substitution. Assuming linear homogeneous production functions, constant consumption preferences and price relations, the unchanged combination of goods produced and supplied leaves consumers' utility unaffected. The theory does not give any information as to why such exchanges of property rights should take place. It should rather be expected that the original competitive equilibrium was stable and that no necessity to exchange existed in this Pareto-optimal situation.

A wide scope for criticism and further investigation appears with reference to the above notion. The Coasian suggestion of the absence of income effects has been criticised by Demsetz (1988), who argues that changes in the assignment of ownership indeed affect production and the output mix because not all individuals have the same preferences. He assumes that those who produce also consume these goods as well as defining ownership as wealth. A change in ownership thus alters the distribution of wealth and this consequently implies an income effect. The suggestion of a wealth effect seems to be erroneous, since individuals within a competitive structure will not exchange voluntarily if Pareto-suboptimal effects are expected. An exchange of rights can only take place if the two producers exchange along their contract curve. This implies no change of the individual production possibility curve which can be derived from the contract curves.

However the assumption of no income effects due to changes in the assignment of property rights under perfect competition has to be doubted. Within a general equilibrium framework any movement along the production possibility or transformation curve will result in an alteration of the price relationship and, if constant consumer preferences are assumed, income and substitution effects are to be expected. Any exchange according to the market value of the exchanged resource will leave the distribution of wealth unaffected but will change the composition of wealth. But nevertheless if the assumption of linear homogeneous production functions is disregarded and different economies of scale as well as differing production and managerial knowledge were assumed, both an alteration in the output mix and consumption possibilities are to be expected. Even if the production functions were homogeneous, the optimisation of the production possibility may not be met due to insufficient knowledge. It seems that if some of the very rigid competitive market assumptions are rejected, a change in private property right assignments will affect the production mix and consumer's utility.

It follows that if transaction costs are zero every individual whose initial endowment position allows an exchange of resources is in the position to alter the output mix. Individuals without original wealth who might nevertheless have a profound production knowledge are entirely unable to participate[23]. The initial endowment and assignment of property rights combined with individual knowledge determine the output mix. The attainment of optimal production and consumption depends also on knowledge in addition to property rights assignments. This factor is totally neglected within the ownership rights theory. Although changes in the assignment of property rights keep the macroeconomic production function constant, the optimisation problem of the microeconomic production function prevails. The conclusion that different ownership rights assignments do not change the output mix depends elementarily on the assumption of linear homogeneous production functions with constant economies of scale. Different scale elasticities will change the output mix, which can be sub- or hyper-optimal in the case of imperfect market conditions and inconsistency between the marginal rate of substitution and the marginal rate of transformation.

Furthermore a major assumption of the property rights theory is that private property entails incentives which lead to a "good" utilisation of the resources. This seems very superficial since good utilisation is not defined, neither in terms of producers' nor consumers' surplus. Self interest implies good utilisation of resources and this self interest can only mean profit maximisation. The authors (Alchian, Demsetz, 1972, 1973) do not take account of possible imperfect market structures where no adequate supply is provided and no market clearing system exists. The evolutionary approach does not give any indication of how to evaluate different structures and systems, it merely states that communal rights have to imply authoritative control or cultural indoctrination if they are to survive. The adaptation of externality economics to the explanation of the development of property rights seems problematic since it only explains the evolution with the assumption of existing external costs. Furthermore the evaluation process is logically lacking since no care has been taken in the development of communal rights other than being associated with primitive societies. The evolution of a communal right system as being the basis of the evolution theory is not explained sufficiently since it is only assumed to continue in existence if regulated. Therefore the entire development seems to be impossible because no communal system could ever exist without regulation which prevented changes towards a private property right system.

2.3.1.3 Liberal Economics

2.3.1.3.1 The Natural Order of Freedom and Evolutionary Competition

The issue of how societal systems of orders (orders are to be understood as a form of constitutional basis of organising partial societal systems) develop and change was analysed within a theoretical framework by Smith in the Wealth of Nations (1776). His theory of orders links three fundamental systems: ethics, market and state. Based on these systems it is attempted to explain the origins, orders and principles which constitute how individuals and societies attempt to achieve the subsistence of existence and wealth (Recktenwald, 1985). The methodology is threefold: it is positive in trying to explain the origins, normative in asking what the optimal order can be and prescriptive in deriving principles for economic policy.

Originating in the ideas of the natural order (Hume, 1739) the human being is the central focal-point of his study. The driving force of any economic, political and cultural development within a society is the natural desire of the human being to improve his actual situation. He tries to secure his existence and place in society, increase his comfort and expand his ease and tranquillity. This welfare function is based on human self-interest, i.e. the societal order is based on self-esteem rather than on selfishness. Personal development which is derived from self-esteem ensures the welfare of the society without any intervention, such as the design of an order, being necessary. Any individual behaviour which suggests selfishness on the one side and idleness on the other is morally disapproved of and thus does not enter the welfare function. Based on this assumption of individual behaviour and personal development the welfare of society is secured.

This belief in human nature is the basis of the system of natural liberties. This system of natural liberties serves to benefit the entire society directly but without the individual necessarily being aware of it and actively trying to contribute to society. Smith is nevertheless aware of the necessity to guide human behaviour in order to safeguard this system. Four corrective forces which are designed to regulate human behaviour are introduced: sympathy, ethical rules, legal norms and competition (Smith,1926). Under these assumptions all individuals led by their self-interest benefit from the free exchange of goods and services. Evolutionary competition and rules of justice facilitate the division of labour and the achievement of values of exchange which are beneficial for the entire society. This theory of the invisible hand has been mathematically formulated by Arrow and Debreu (1954).

Smith combines three fundamental models in the wealth of a nation: the historical model explaining economic and social developments, the system of the circular flow of income and the system of growth. The analysis of historical developments places particular emphasis on the significance of economic forces which influence political and social structures. Depending on the production process from which the human being earns his living and particular forms of ownership which generate appropriate institutional structures of hierarchy or subordination, four stages of development are epitomised in the historical theory: hunting, herding, agriculture and trade (Smith, 1776). The driving force of the process of development is found in the continuous desire of the human being to improve his material, social and intellectual situation. This momentum leads to the development of productive forces which induce the improvement of the wealth of the community.

Although Smith produces a theory of the stages of development, his theory is not deterministic. It is noticed that the normal development can be interrupted. It is therefore possible to find relicts from former systems in newly developed ones. Feudal dependencies can for example be identified in orders of market economies because behavioural patterns change slowly. The theory of change is thus open although a clear basis for an equilibrium is elaborated and found in the correcting rules and the evolutionary competition. The analytical model of the market economy is grounded on the division of labour and the human self-interest, the combination of both enabling specialisation and trade. Exchange on the market produces values and flexible prices and competition is attributed particular significance. The forces of evolutionary competition continuously change the structures of the system and the concept of dynamic competition does not produce a zero-sum-game.

The system of natural liberties maintains that freedom in the sense of economic and political liberty includes the ability of individuals to act in their own self-interest and to be guided by morality. Individual behaviour which aims at the realisation of personal wealth is limited and guided by feasible rules of justice. The extent of the rules depend on the efficiency of moral self-control and evolutionary competition.[24]

2.3.1.3.2 The Concept of Spontaneous Orders

The theory of natural order of freedom was further targeted in the theory of spontaneous orders. The concept of spontaneous orders, which has been mainly expressed by Hayek (1945, 1949, 1969) was closely linked to the theory of the invisible hand. The invisible hand approach suggests that societal orders are the result of individual and separate actions and this is further explored by Hayek analysing the construction of a rational economic order (1945). The design of a rational economic order is characterised by the problem that if an optimum solution is sought it can only be found on the basis of an analysis which assumes certain data to be given. The methodological problem inherent in this analysis is that no analyst possesses the entire knowledge about the data. The knowledge does not exist in concentrated form, rather the data has to be perceived as available to individuals only. Thus no optimum economic order can be constructed, it can merely call for an order which secures the best use of resources and utilisation of individual knowledge.

The construction of a rational economic order is herewith redesigned into the construction of a framework of an economic system which secures the efficient use of the knowledge available to individuals and takes into account the fact that this knowledge in its importance is only known to individual human beings. Since the economic process is a process of planning and coordinating these plans, economic planning is given a classifying character so as to distinguish economic systems. Planning can be undertaken by a central authority or decentrally by many individuals (Hayek, 1945). This classifying element leads to the differentiation of three major forms of planning:

1.) Central Planning: The entire economic process follows one central plan.
2.) Competition: Separate individuals make independent plans.
3.) Monopoly: Some organised industries are authorised for planning and this structure includes features of the first and second case.

It is conceived that individual planning data is only available to separate human beings, no rational economic system can be constructed and economic policy can only focus on the insurance of a system which makes efficient use of this knowledge and the utilisation of the resources. The term "efficiency" is made operational by employing the information flow. The information flow as efficiency criterion can be described as the question of which of the three systems can be expected to make the best use of the existing knowledge. This represents the above dichotomy of central and decentral planning, i.e. is it more efficient to put the knowledge which is to be used at the disposal of a single planning authority or to enable individuals to coordinate their individual plans with the plans of other individuals?

Knowledge is believed to be unique in terms of time, place, person and quality, and economic problems arise as consequences of change. The economic process does not follow the principles of mechanical functioning, it is characterised by a process of continuous adaptation to changing circumstances (Hayek, 1945). This societal problem of changing circumstances has to be solved on a decentralised basis of dispersed knowledge, i.e. decisions within the changing environment have to be taken by those individuals who posses the intimate knowledge about the changing factors and resources. The knowledge about changing circumstances is further qualified by the relative importance of knowledge, that is the knowledge about changes which also includes the information which needs to be channelled to the decision-maker. The problem of relative importance is solved by the price system which also serves the coordination of individual actions. The price system allows the participants to receive the necessary information about changing circumstances and on the basis of this knowledge actions can be planned separately from and coordinated with the plans of other participants.

The two fundamental beliefs of Hayek are expressed in the nature of the price system. The price system is not a design of the human mind and the participants in the price system are not consciously contributing to the benefit of society. These evolutionary characteristics represent the close nature of thought to the invisible hand approach of Smith. The main social theoretical thesis is that all orders evolve spontaneously as results of individual interests and actions unaware of their social implications. Although evolved orders can be characterised as spontaneous they are human developments of civilisation. Furthermore there is no need for conscious control and secondly conscious control could not be successful because of the limitation and imperfection of knowledge (Hayek, 1949, pp. 33 - 57).

The approach has been elaborated further by Schotter (1981). He insinuates that social institutions develop because they have proved to be efficient in solving recurring economic and social problems which demand particular solutions. The development of these institutional solutions is based on the fundamental societal belief that cooperative behaviour is more favourable than non-cooperative behaviour. This assumes a structure of interests which allows all participants to benefit from cooperative behaviour and to create a structure of commonly preferred combinations of action. The evolved economic order thus qualifies as spontaneous because participants act upon their separate knowledge and also as desired. Economic orders are herewith established spontaneously as best suited and desired but by no means consciously designed (Hayek, 1947; Schotter, 1981).

The approaches which have been summarised under the section of liberal economics offer a comprehensive approach to the explanation of transformation processes. They are designated as evolutionary changes from inefficient economic orders to more efficient structures once the more efficient one has been identified. Although some of the non-deterministic approaches hardly give any explanation of why inefficient structures evolved originally, the approach of evolutionary competition and spontaneous orders certainly define these reasons in changing circumstances. These influential factors make changes necessary through the dispersion and unfolding of knowledge and make adaptation to these changes possible through the evolution of a new institutional framework or economic order.

2.3.2 Deterministic Approaches of System Transformation

2.3.2.1 The Schumpeterian Theory of Economic Development

Joseph Alois Schumpeter, who was mainly influenced by Eugen von Boehm-Bawerk and Friedrich von Wieser, identified the individual as the basis of any historical processes and followed the Austrian School in this respect. He greatly admired the work of Karl Marx because of its dynamic nature, although he criticised the Marxist labour value theory, the theories of exploitation and the particular approach to the decline of the capitalist system. He called the dialectic materialism "the so-called Economic Interpretation of History,... one of the greatest individual achievements of sociology to this day" (Schumpeter, 1976, p. 10).

Schumpeter's development theory is a theory of economic process which aims to explain the functioning of capitalist and socialist economic systems. He distinguishes five cases of economic development (Schumpeter, 1926):
a) the production of a new consumer good or the improvement of an existing one,
b) the introduction of a new production method,
c) the opening of a new market,
d) the discovery of new raw materials, and
e) the realisation of new organisational structures and economic institutions.

The theory can be divided into two main areas: The first theory of business cycles is directed at the theoretical explanation of changing methods of production and how these alterations affect the economic process of action. This analysis includes deterministic elements, because the appearance of these development factors is not continuous and thus does not qualify as a theory of the development of specific combinations of production. This part of Schumpeter's development theory can be characterised as the transformation according to the criteria of efficiency. The second field of analysis is the deterministic prognosis of developing economic and societal structures. The development is persistent because it explains the inevitable decline of the capitalist system and the establishment of a socialist structure.

2.3.2.1.1 The Theory of Creative Destruction and Business Cycles

Schumpeter's analytical starting-point in Business Cycles (1939) is the question of why periodical disruptions of stationary equilibriums develop and exist. An economic equilibrium is characterised by a relative constancy of prices and costs over a more or less long period of time. Such an equilibrium is disrupted by either the introduction of new combinations of production or an endogenous shock (e.g. war). The new productive combination is an innovative act which destroys old structures and substitutes old for new and which thereby becomes a creative destruction. The economic business cycle follows this endogenous character of the innovative act. A successful innovative act initiates imitations and thus the equilibrium is not only disrupted by a single push but by a series of similar ones. This will cause a general change of price and cost relations.

A high number of innovators and entrepreneurs is the foundation of an economic upswing (Schumpeter, 1926). Economic rent is increasingly eroded by imitation and increased costs. The business cycle reaches the point of return which is linked to a decrease in commercial transactions. This initiates the phase of recession which does not necessarily lead to a depression (Schumpeter, 1939). The phase of upswing is accompanied by an opposite development of prices.

Since all industrial and labour capacities are fully used in the equilibrium state, new investments can only be financed by a withdrawal of resources from their old usages. This can only be achieved through the utilisation of the banking system and this system stands between those who want to carry through new production combinations and those who own the factors of production (Schumpeter, 1926).

Schumpeter's concept of Business Cycles is an attempt to make static concepts dynamic. The economic fluctuations as organic components of the capitalist development process are distinguished into three cycles depending on the length of the time duration: 1.) Kontradieff-cycles, sixty years, 2.) Juglar-cycles, ten years, 3.) Kitchin-cycles, fourty months. Kontradieff- and Juglar-cycles are explained by the introduction of new production combinations which cause disruptions in the existing equilibrium. The shorter Kitchin-cycles are interpreted as adjustment processes due to secondary waves (Schumpeter, 1939).

Schumpeter's methodological approach in Business Cycles can be described as the analysis of selected individual actions within a given institutional structure and the deduction of consequences for the system, the economy and society. He predicts the failure of capitalism and the subsequent inevitable establishment of socialism due to the self-destructiveness of the capitalist system. The self-destructiveness is hypothesized to follow the economic success of capitalism which develops social institutions which are unable to be sustained (Schumpeter, 1976). Schumpeter himself points out that this development qualifies as a prognosis rather than a desirable evolution towards socialism, but this development is nevertheless of a deterministic kind.

2.3.2.1.2 The Inevitable Transformation of the Capitalist System into Socialism

The inevitable transformation of the capitalist system into a socialist structure is based on the analysis of the economic process. Economic performance of the capitalist system is suggested to be measured by total output changes and in particular in terms of output available for consumption. Available output - total production corrected by the change in durable industry equipment - is conjectured to rise at two per cent per year. This capitalist growth process, due to the introduction of new methods of production, progressively increases the standard of living by making a larger number of products available for more people and this phenomenon is historically referred to as the industrial revolution having produced more goods and services for the masses of consumers.

The increase in output available for consumers and the alteration of the production methods coincide with an increasing number of social problems. Although Schumpeter rejects the problem of unemployment being an unsolvable matter and thereby criticising his contemporary Keynes (Schumpeter, 1976, p.

69) he stresses the necessity to provide for the unemployed. Unemployment is an unavoidable effect of the phase of adaptation which follows the prosperity phase in the business cycle and the true danger of unemployment is the destruction of the human self-value and self-esteem.

The capitalist system with the structural element of private enterprises allows for a selection process according to individual ability and performance. Since performance is not guarantied by the social selection process - in contrast to the biological selection methods - the capitalist structure proves to select successfully by means of ability and ensures the economic survival of those who meet this requirement. Socialist structures do not follow this selection mechanism and are thus deemed to fail with respect to economic performance. In spite of this acknowledgement the capitalist selection creates unfavourable social structures due to monopolistic and oligopolistic market structures. The latter development is substantiated by the evolutionary character of capitalism and the notion that it can never be stationary and will always be changeable.

Capitalism is an evolutionary process following human creativeness and developing new methods of production, markets, goods and industrial organisations. This evolution is accompanied and conditioned by changes in the environment, those changes influencing the economic data itself and thus affecting the set of possible actions available to the individual. Evolutionary capitalism can be described as a "history of evolutions" (Schumpeter, 1976, p. 83), each evolution initiating long waves within the business cycle. Economic revolutions are the main element and reasoning of Schumpeter's description of capitalism as a process of creative destruction. New products, markets and forms of industrial organisation revolutionise endogenously the existing economic arrangements and thus destroy old economic structures.

Due to the evolutionary character and the organic process of the capitalist form Schumpeter stresses the necessity to analyse economic performance by a dynamic rather than a static method. The methodology can only be undertaken within long-term periods and this is necessary to enable the analyst to take full account of the ultimate performance of the capitalist system. In particular it is surmised that the outcome of the full utilisation of all available possibilities proves in the long run to be situated below a system where such possibilities are not given or utilised at any point of time. Capitalist structures can only be successfully analysed if the origins of existing structures, the capitalist creation and also the destruction of those structures are taken into account. In this sense the classic approach to competition has to be amended so that it implies the creation as well as the threat of creation of new production combinations.

The capitalist process of creative destruction brings monopolistic units into existence and the mechanism of perfect competition appears to be too weak to lead to a new competitive equilibrium.[25] Monopolistic tendencies due to the capitalist evolution produce depressive catastrophes. The output is thereby reduced and the acquisition of supernormal profits indicates a social waste and the utilisation of resources will be well below optimum.

Alongside the developing monopolistic units Schumpeter conjectures a general decline in investment opportunities on the grounds of the declining rate of growth in population (effects on demand and supply side), the reduced scope to open up and acquire new land and countries, the unforeseeable future of technological advance and general satiation, so that investment possibilities mainly remain in the continuous renewal of capital. Complete human satisfaction of economic wants and a perfect state of production methods would lead to a stationary economic state and capitalism would cease to exist as an evolutionary process. The societal structure, the methods of production and the industrial and organisational institutions are visualised to develop into a socialist system. Bureaucratic organisations and the mechanism of the production process may evolve under the above conditions. The entrepreneurial function as the core of the economic process in capitalist society will be jeopardised and the capitalist order tormented. The social function of the entrepreneurial human being loses importance since innovation has been reduced to routine. Rationalisation, specialisation and mechanisation depersonalise the economic process and "bureau and committee work tends to replace individual action" (Schumpeter, 1976, p. 133).

The role of the industrial bourgeoisie and entrepreneurship is replaced by a system of labour wages. The automisation of the production process, due to the capitalist industrialisation, leads to the vanishing of the capitalist enterprise and thus capitalism itself. Capitalist industrial organisations become large-sized enterprises comprising steadily repeating production processes which reduce the necessity of innovative entrepreneurial action since the on-going existence of those institutions is secured by their monopolistic size. The market structure of perfect competition and the capitalist role of creative destruction lose their reason and the achievements of capitalism themselves make the decline of the entrepreneurial bourgeoisie inevitable.

Alongside this development the capitalist process also undermines the necessity of private property and freedom of contract in its final state. Private property often takes the form of absentee ownership and contracts are mainly agreed in the form of impersonal and bureaucratic work contracts. Thus the capital system depersonalises itself and a gradual development towards socialist structures is identified. This inevitably influences the social atmosphere and becomes a major impediment on the original functioning of the capitalist system. Depending on the political system public policy becomes hostile to capitalist interests and capitalism eventually ceases to function.

The entrepreneurial function and motivation is threatened by this development. The modern industrial organisation socialises the entrepreneurial intrinsic motivation and the importance of entrepreneurship decreases due to absentee ownership and the work contract. The capitalist mechanism decomposes by its internal forces and the system tends towards self-destruction. The capitalist process destroys its own institutional framework (i.e. private property and free contracting) and thereby creates a framework for the establishment of the socialist system. Schumpeter uses the term "transformation" for this development since it does not only imply the destruction of capitalist institutions but also the transformation of "things and souls" (Schumpeter, 1976, p. 162). Acknowledging Marx, the economic process is granted the prime origin and determining variable of the social transformation.

2.3.2.1.3 The Economic Order and the Feasibility of Socialism

The evolved socialist system is described by Schumpeter as a blueprint using commercialist terminology, e.g. distribution, markets and prices are explained by reference to vouchers, plans of production, etc. This enables him to point out that the case of socialist planning in a stationary economic environment where everything is properly foreseen is the only way in which the results of perfect competition can be achieved (Schumpeter, 1976, p. 183).

By attributing to the socialist system a central authority for the determination of the relative significance of consumer goods and the subsequent production process with the allocation of resources, the logical theoretical justification of centralised socialism is achieved. The notion of practical impossibility is disposed of by referring to the existence of an administrative bureaucratic apparatus with sufficient information concerning the adequate quantities demanded and the output to be supplied. Furthermore complete knowledge and a constant nature of resources are assumed.

Setting the above assumptions enables Schumpeter to express the similarity between the socialist and capitalist[26] theoretical approaches and the point of view that both systems could function rationally and proceed towards optimal situations. Nevertheless the attempt is made to stress the superiority of the socialist system within the economic sphere, having already indicated the comparatively higher ranking in terms of cultural energies of the latter. The socialist system should not be compared with the capitalist model of perfect competition. It should rather be juxtaposed to the monopolistic case, whose development was asserted in the development theory. The dialectic nature of the development itself indicates the superior efficiency of large-scale units with respect to technological and organisational possibilities.

Schumpeter defines economic efficiency as productive efficiency and the superiority of either system lies in the long-term production of larger streams of consumer goods (Schumpeter, 1976). The socialist superiority holds in so far as it is compared with the final state of the capitalist evolution, i.e. the downward swing of the system accompanied by imperfect market structures. This is expressed in the deterministic nature of socialist prices and output as opposed to the capitalist indeterminate ones and in the absence of uncertainty. Socialist planning and coordination eliminates any severe cyclical changes as progress is consistently planned and the destructive nature of capitalist creative evolution does not exist.

Socialist management contains a higher level of rationality and thus proves superior to big-business capitalism, the latter being the only form of long-term relevant capitalism. An example of this superiority is the reduction in unemployment due to the elimination of cyclical depressions. Another major disadvantage of the capitalist system is expressed by the structural differences and the impossible coordination (by nature) between private and public activities. Public economic activity (e.g. taxation) which interferes with the private economic process entails waste. The productive process is harmed on the one side and on the other side the public administrative apparatus is more self-protecting than efficiently functioning. "No such conflict, consequently no such waste, would exist in socialist society" (Schumpeter, 1976, p. 198).

Criticisms with respect to human nature and thus the small feasibility of socialism are rejected. Such criticisms would methodologically confuse the ideal system with the real systems. Nevertheless it is stressed that no advocation of socialism is sensible without reference to the given social conditions. Any criticism with respect to the impossible compatibility of socialism and human nature is put aside by the construction of the "change by reconditioning" (Schumpeter, 1976, p. 202). Changes in the social environment alter human behaviour but do not affect the fundamental human nature. The social environment is therefore understood to influence behavioural patterns and those patterns are referred to as propensities to feel and act and are summarised under the term "habits" (i.e. the human behaviour in a particular environment). The potential of human adaptability is given credit by allowing the basic pattern of humanity to be affected by either the elimination of substantial and stubborn features or by group dynamics making it impossible for certain elements of human nature to continue to exist (e.g. selfishness). Since the change by reconditioning has been recognised the adjustment of habits is claimed to be a sufficient condition for social practicability and thus no change of human nature is necessary.

The defence of a socialist system has to take account of the following:

1.) Capitalist reality is referred to as the stage of big-business capitalism.
2.) The irrelevance of how this particular historical stage has developed must be recognised, i.e. development by the capitalist process itself or by external factors.
3.) Socialism is mainly envisaged in terms of the chances this structure offers.

A successful adaptation of socialism involves the utilisation of the human resources partly gained within the capitalist system. The bourgeois class which destroys itself should be employed according to its managerial qualifications and the method of the survival of the fittest, i.e. the capitalist selection process of performance is proposed to exist still. A requirement derived from this selection mechanism is the individual employee's freedom to act under his own responsibility. This requirement in particular might be jeopardised by the increasingly inevitable bureaucratisation of economic life - inevitable due to the historic stage and regardless of whether a socialist or capitalist organisation of economic life exists. The bureaucratic influence may be eliminated when the full socialisation and moral acceptance of the socialist order is achieved. Any socialist concept based on altruistic human nature is deemed to fail and a well-functioning system of rewards and stimuli in the form of the acceptance and recognition of proficiency has to be implemented or created, because it is conjectured that self-interest and self-assertion are fundamental human characteristics. The socialist system emphasises the need for moral allegiance and this reinforces self-discipline as well as group discipline in socialist society. This form of self-motivated discipline alleviates the need for authoritarian practice.

2.3.2.1.4 The Phase of Transition and the Role of Democracy

An aspect of major importance is the transition from capitalism to socialism. Mature socialisation where the economic process socialises itself contains the following elements:

-large-sized bureaucratically organised businesses,
-depersonalisation of property and management,
-absentee ownership,
-interest rates converge towards zero, and
-decreasing investment opportunities and capitalist motivation.

At this historic stage of society and economy the new socialist order is assumed to evolve and this will happen - neglecting the unlikely case of revolution - in a peaceful way by a change in the constitution. The transitional period of time involves possible expropriations, restructuring of companies and concerns, the gradual implementation of a central bank and the re-employment of human resources which had been employed in occupations which no longer exist. Superior performance of the socialist system over the capitalist one is expected if the above described mature transition is successfully completed.

In the case of premature socialism, transitional policy has to concentrate on the value of money and socialisation itself. Inflation is expected to expropriate effectively and private enterprises will cease to function since supervising committees will have been established. A successful realisation of the phase of transition ensures a fruitful socialist system.

Having finally achieved the socialist structure the question is asked whether socialism is compatible with democracy (Schumpeter, 1976). Democracy in 19th century philosophy is defined as an institutional arrangement for political decisions and this arrangement serves a common good which the people choose via electing individuals who carry out the particular vote. The common good of democracy is the common will and this is carried out by specialists or committee (parliament) in the sense of representing the will of the electorate.

Schumpeter disapproves of the above definition by rejecting utilitarianism and pointing to the impossibility of defining a common good in the above sense, since rationality is not given due to the lack common wants. Furthermore even if this rationality was ensured it is unlikely that the choice made represents the true will of the people. The likelihood of a compromise raises in the Schumpeterian point of view the possibility of arriving at a more acceptable outcome if a decision was imposed by a non-democratic institution.

The hypothesis of rationality appears to become increasingly invalid if conglomerate (class or group) actions are analysed and the evidence suggests that individual actions are neither as individual nor as rational as suggested from a utilitarian stand-point. Individual action is open to external factors of influence (e.g. persuasion) and is thereby not guaranteed to be definite and rational. Rationality is substituted by the sense of reality, familiarity and responsibility (Schumpeter, 1976, p. 259). These senses, which may be said to converge into habits, express relatively definite individual wills. If responsibility is reduced, political ignorance will be executed and thus no such thing as a common will is going to develop. The individual becomes an object open to influence from all sides. This lack of rationality increases the opportunities for certain groups of individuals to determine the public mind.

These groups are exemplified by professional politicians and lobbies and these individuals produce the common will by manufacturing political decisions since particular information is channelled into the desired directions. The individual hereby becomes the victim who is entirely defenceless in the short-run. This political analysis makes Schumpeter come to the conclusion that utilitarian rationalism is dead and democracy cannot be analysed by referring to rationality. Instead the methodology has to focus on collective group actions. Thus the democratic apparatus serves people to form a national executive institution for political decision and this government is elected following a process of competition for political leadership. Following this definition of democracy it is surmised that no incompatibility between socialism and democracy exists.

The transition from capitalism to socialism with its process of political and institutional change can thus successfully be managed by the political method of democracy. The method of competitive leadership is seen as a product of a capitalist society. Democratic socialism is expressed to be possible, since the extension of the range of public management does not necessarily imply an extension of the political management range. Certainly if extension of the latter was the case, democratic socialism is deemed to fail. A clear distinction between public and political management is essential and the economic management must be realised independently from any political bodies so that the only inefficiencies of the system can be described by the inherent bureaucracy. Another further requirement - as already mentioned - for the success of socialist democracy is the mature state of the capitalist society at the stage where socialist democracy is introduced.

Although the transformational prognosis of the failure of capitalism and the inevitable creation of socialism has to be falsified with reference to the developments in Eastern Europe in the late 1980s, the theory contains valid and useful elements for explaining transformational developments. In particular the acknowledgment of the importance of the transitional phase and the democratic process of decision-making serve a better understanding of the issues.

2.3.2.2 The Marxist Law of Motion

According to Oakley (1984, p. 189) Marx's evolutionary theory was mainly influenced by three factors:

-Hegel's dialectic philosophy of history,
-the empirical study of the temporary instability of capitalist activity and
-an analytical treatment of the dynamics of the system.

2.3.2.2.1 The Philosophical Basis of Dialectic Materialism

In the preface to the first German edition of Capital (1867) Marx identifies his objective of analysis as the clarification of the economic law of motion of modern society. Economic development is conjectured as a process of natural history and he aims for the creation of an evolutionary law on the basic assumption that the formation of social systems follows natural historic processes. He believes and thereby follows Hegel's philosophical notion that the individual human being is subordinated to the historic fate (Aster, 1932).[27] Referring to Hegel's metaphysical law of history in the Feuerbach Critique (1845) Marx sees the basis of society in materialist foundations. He criticises Feuerbach for neither acknowledging the social product of the religious sentiment nor that every abstract individual belongs to a specific society as a historic fact (Marx, 1845, p. 405). Individuals are not responsible for the circumstances in which they live and this has been expressed in his belief that his stand-point "... can less than any other make the individual responsible for relations whose creature he socially remains, however much he may subjectively raise himself above them" (Marx, 1867, p. 451). The individual is a subject in the economic system until the revolutionary stage when he can actively shape the evolution. In the 11th thesis on Feuerbach he announces that the philosophical aim has to be the change of existing circumstances rather than their pure explanation (Marx, 1845).

2.3.2.2.2 The Basis-Superstructure-Theorem as Methodological Foundation

Marx sets himself the task analysing particular situations under which human beings produce their individual existence and life in the form of work and production. The aim of the investigation is to find out which factors influence the existence of social systems and their dynamic changes.

The economic structure of society is constituted by the relations of production, i.e. capital and labour. These relations of production conform with a particular stage of development of the material productive forces. The human being is part of these productive relations but does not design them and it is surmised that they are not designed by the productive forces. This stresses the materialist foundation of the law of motion indicating that the human being is part of a natural law, here material law, which is beyond his own control. The economic structure of the productive relations is conceived as the foundation of the legal and political superstructure. The economic system as the basis defines forms of social consciousness and conditions the social, political and intellectual life. Since the relations of production are not of human design and because they also define the general societal life and structure, the economic system is seen as the basis of any societal system. This indicates that it is the human consciousness that is a product of social life and that economic and social life are not a product of human consciousness and design (Marx, 1859). It is assumed that revolutionary pressures begin to exist at an historic stage where the productive relations are no longer in harmony with the human conscience, i.e. the material productive forces come into conflict with the relations of production (Marx, 1859). The revolutionary pressures will change the economic system and because this implies a destruction of the general social framework the entire superstructure is altered and transformed.

Human life is mainly determined by his productive work, which is conceived as being alienating until the revolutionary change has been initiated. The means of production are the essential factors in determining social life. Due to the economic forces of nature specific socio-economic situations develop and those are understood as production relations. The latter can either be creative or alienating depending on the allocation of those means of production. A particular allocation leads to a particular "consciousness of society" (Angresano, 1991, p. 360.) regarding the social relations between individuals. The unity between natural and socio-economic conditions implies that the allocation of production means determines a person's position in society, i.e. whether he has any right of disposal or not. Ownership in this sense constitutes the right of disposal and is the product of labour, and it is therefore the essential structural element of the social system.

The same is argued in the basis-superstructure-theorem, which suggests that economic conditions are the foundation of the political, cultural and legal system superstructure. Hereby Marx sets a definite relationship between the economic partial system with its essential structural element of the allocation of the means of production and the other partial social systems. The entire superstructure is determined by the basic economic system.

This leads to the conclusion that the evolutionary process has to be based fundamentally on a conscious society and has its origins in the economic system. The evolutionary theory of social change finally leads to the inevitable working-class revolution with the aim of abolishing any private property and the "right of personally acquiring property as the fruit of a man's own labour" and the dynamic process is manifested in the "antagonism of capital and wage labour" (Marx & Engels, 1848, p. 47).

2.3.2.2.3 The Historic Development of Communism

The dialectic correlation between productive forces and conditions of production implies rules of societal development. The dialectic and historic materialism is the methodological basis of the political economy of Marxism-Leninism. The development of production conditions, its interrelations with the means of production and the superstructure are conceived as the creation, development and resolving of dialectic contradictions. This evolutionary and revolutionary process leads to changes in the relations of production and hereby to stages in societal development.[28]

The origins of the development of historic stages and any social system are seen in primitive society. This primitive society is characterised by collective work and joint ownership of primitive means of production. With the rising sophistication of the means of production and the division of labour, private property came into existence and primitive society changed into the form of slavery. Slavery is inferred to be the result of the "second great division of labour" (Engels, 1884, p. 312) which induced an increase in labour productivity, the value of labour and the overall production output.

The increasing production and productivity is accompanied by a further specialisation of labour. The steadily rising surplus product results in the establishment of classes and the distinction between physical and mental work. The antagonism of the relations of production - here slavery - leads to the decay of the system and the transition into the feudalistic state. Basic structural elements of this economic and societal system are private property of land and the villeinage of landowners.[29] International trade and large scale production lead to the un-sustainability of feudalistic production and the creation of industrial and capitalist ways of production. Capitalist processes of production are defined to have begun as a production method when the same amount of capital employs comparatively more labour (Marx, 1867, p. 212).

The transition to capitalist production reflects a process of entire separation of production and ownership of the means of production and the abolition of the identity between labour and property. Capitalist production aims at the production of surplus value, workers don't produce for themselves but for the capital, i.e. the capital owner rents and employs labour (Marx, 1867, p. 287). Marx analyses the dynamics of the capitalist system at this stage of development and has in this respect basically been influenced by his studies of A. Smith and D. Ricardo. Referring to the general theory of development and the relationship between growth and distribution he concludes that policies aimed at solving the recurring and immanently generated crisis within the capitalist structure were finally limited.[30] At this stage of evolution the antonym exists between the social character of production and the private and capitalist appropriation as well as between the surplus value and the exchange value of the good or service. In the Critique of the Gotha Programme (Marx, 1875) it is indicated that the economic and political transformation from the capitalist system into the communist can only be achieved by the revolutionary dictatorship of the proletariat.

Having set out the means of how to achieve a communist state in the Manifesto (Marx & Engels, 1984) the final societal system is one where the socialist productive conditions are formed by everyone's work for society and by the accumulation of the entire product of labour by society. The stable and final aim of the evolution is achieved because of the unity between human beings, the means of production and the production relations. This situation is stable because of the assumed indivisibility of nature and socio-economic conditions.

The Marxist development theory manifests a deterministic development of the societal process which results from the class struggles between the established class (which is conditioned by the means of production) and the class of the proletariat (which desires to free itself from the conditions of production). The dialectic process is a constant struggle of transformation in which the class of the productive forces succeeds and thus determines the superstructure of the entire society. This is achieved when the ownership structure coincides with the structure of the conditions of production, which is the stage in which capitalism is abolished.

2.3.2.2.4 A Methodological Critique

A review and critique of the Marxist evolutionary theory must start with his basic assumption concerning the Hegelian philosophy. Thesis and antithesis produce a synthesis, which creates a new historic situation and which is always of a higher order than either of the previous ones. This positive evolution must be justified if the law of motion is to be verified. The inevitable establishment of a classless society cannot be justified by referring to a law of history, it might only be justified in explaining past historic epoches. This is further clarified by noting that Marx employs *ex-post* explanations for the historic development until the stage of capitalism and *ex-ante* explanations - nevertheless deterministic - for the stages following the beginning of capitalism.

The definition of a social system by referring solely to the structural element of the means of production is certainly too narrow. It may though historically be applied to the stages from feudalism or early capitalism to communism in the sense of expropriation but it hardly coincides with the movement from primitive society to slavery. In the latter example it also fails the supposedly higher order of the synthesis and Marx even states a negative development from feudalism to capitalism. Furthermore the necessary movement from capitalist structures to communist ones must be doubted in the light of the background of factual developments, namely the evolution of socialist structures out of feudalistic systems rather than highly industrialised ones.

There is no methodology for analysing the direction of a development, it rather seems that the abolition of the surplus value held by the capitalist owner is the sole objective. Even if this was the sole objective Marx does not account for any factual positive developments regarding the workers' situation in capitalism, namely the activities of trade unions, regulations concerning working hours, etc. Any changes within the capitalistic system are analysed against the background of crisis management in the way of the process of development towards socialism. Rather there must be an individual analysis of the individual's situation in either case unless the individual is conceived as a means to achieve a certain societal order. Referring to history Marx points out that human beings are slaves of historic situations but he gives no explanation why it had to take thousands of years of unsatisfactory economic orders to achieve the final good order. He suggests the necessity of a revolution and does not give sufficient explanation why this revolution could not have happened earlier. The dialectic materialism suggests a human being who lacks awareness and surely an antithesis in the form of a civilised society with common property can be found in earlier history (Eucken, 1950).[31] The Marxist application of the Hegelian dialectic philosophy of history interprets productive relations as not being a human design. If the Hegelian philosophy is accepted, no productive relations create themselves and Marx ignores the notion of identifying ownership with power at this relevant stage in history.

Furthermore no explanation is given as to why the structural element itself does not give way to other structural characteristics. This closed system is highly unlikely as in an open complexity, such as that assumed here, there might be new incoming values and structures which replace old ones. Many other elements besides economic structures influence the development of a societal system as even geographically close nations develop in different directions. Cultural, political, ethnical and religious factors must not be neglected. Another major criticism is the moral evaluation of the strict movement to a higher societal order, where each stage is superior to the previous one. The theory of historical change becomes a theory of inevitable historic progress, for its development however no positive - rather than normative - standard of evaluation is given. As last point of critique, Marx's theory of labour might be scrutinised from the viewpoint of neoclassical price theory. The surplus value does not exist if the marginal product of labour is equal to the wage rate in a perfect labour market with flexible wages. The argumentation of surplus value is even less convincing if a Pareto-situation is assumed where the marginal cost of production equals the marginal utility and price.

The Marxist Law of Motion alongside the Schumpeterian Development Theory is not applicable as an approach for explaining the transformation processes in Eastern Europe due to its wrongly proven deterministic character and some methodological inconsistencies. Nevertheless it has to be credited that the institutional theoretical basis of this approach is very close to the one of the property-rights theory and it offers insight into the relationship between the economic and other partial social systems, which if not accepted, opens the field for debate.

2.3.2.3 The Development Theory of Rostow

Clearly opposed to the Marxist Law of Motion are the assumptions applied in the Stages of Economic Growth by Rostow (1971). Although he is concerned with the development of societies he denies the assumption that societies are a mere superstructure based on economic structures. He views societies as interacting organisms and economic change as a result of political and social as well as economic forces. The basis-superstructure dialectic is thus rejected and, whereas Marx identifies the productive forces as the revolutionary class, he indicates that economic changes are the result of mainly non-economic factors and human motives.

2.3.2.3.1 Stages of Sectoral Growth

Rostow declares a possible identification of all societies according to their economic dimensions within the following classifying range:

-the traditional society,
-the preconditions of take-off,
-the take-off,
-the drive to maturity and
-the age of high mass-consumption.

The traditional society is characterised by limited production functions due to the ceiling on the productivity of their economic techniques. This also implies a limitation of the attainable output per head because science and technology were not available to extend these limits. This stage is described as a pre-Newtonian world which allocates a high proportion of their resources to agriculture. The creation of new production functions in agriculture and industry in the late seventeenth century due to the development of modern science introduces the phase of transition, i.e. the preconditions for take-off. The development of modern science is surmised to have created a shock which made the existing societal structure obsolete and thus having initiated a process of constructing a new one. This new society is characterised by a whole expansion of growth and increases in incomes. This expansion in terms of a steady growth rate is assumed to last for about two decades and sixty years after the beginning of the take-off general maturity is attained. The stage of maturity is indicated by complex production processes and functions (beside others, international trade). The final stage of high mass-consumption is represented by consumers' goods which are durable and this stage is conjectured to have been mainly achieved by societies within the twentieth century.

The analytical structure of a dynamic theory of production is the methodology of classifying different stages in economic development. The process of economic growth has to be examined within a flexible, disaggregated production theory, i.e. aggregates have to be decomposed into sectoral components and theoretical sectoral equilibriums can be identified (Rostow, 1971, p. 13). These sectoral optimum positions are determined by different factors of the demand and the supply side of the economy. The demand side determines the level of total output via the levels of income, total population and the taste of consumers. Science and technology, entrepreneurial knowledge and innovative potential modify the capital stock as such and define the supply side's determination of economic growth.

Acknowledging that these sectoral optimum positions can hardly ever be identified in history, Rostow indicates the necessity of analysing the factors which cause these disequilibriums. Imperfections in the private investment process, public policies and exogeneous factors, such as war, are made responsible for deviations from the equilibrium path. A path of economic development can nevertheless be identified if economic growth is considered to be characterised by certain sectors. Leading economic sectors, i.e. those that have rapid growth rates, enable the sequencing of economic development in terms of stages of sectoral growth.

2.3.2.3.2 An Incomplete Analysis of the Transitional Phase

Factors outside this economic system such as general societal decisions are also taken into account as interacting with the economic dynamic forces. The cultural and political system determines the particular content and capacity of the sectoral and thus economic development. The important transformational issue of the interaction of these partial societal systems is thereby addressed. Potential boundaries of economic development are identified in the incompatibility of economic development forces with cultural and political norms and institutions.

The interpretation of the transitional phase which is placed in the stage of the preconditions for take-off, is twofold. It is interpreted as either the preparation of society for endogeneous economic development or the adjustment of society to growth which is induced by external forces. The observation of historic developments allows Rostow to differentiate two kinds of developments, the special and the general case of transition. The special case of transition was mainly introduced by economic and technical factors and he exemplifies this process with the development of railways. The transitional phase was founded by social groups and endogeneous factors established pressures for a fundamental change of the traditional structure of society. Technical developments are surmised to have created incentives to increase economic growth and is in this respect assumed to have been self-creative.

The second, general case of transition requires fundamental changes in the social and political structure of society as well as changes in the production techniques. The necessity of transition is derived from the deterministic nature of Rostow's economic development stages and thus has its origins methodologically in his historic observations. He does not identify the forces which make this transition necessary or induce it, he rather deduces the transition compulsion from his own development theory which is deductive in nature. Since a deductively derived theory can only be based on the observation of historic facts, his methodology of explaining transitional processes has to be vehemently criticised because he does not explicitly identify the elements which effectuate the transition and make the development from one stage to the next inevitable. The basis of his deductive methodology is incomplete observation and he thus theorises on transition as a general case which is not factually perceived. The nature of transition (Rostow, 1971) becomes a "must-theory" without fundamental qualification. The societal structure has to change to meet his stages of development and the structural changes are expressed as general changes of societal values and production techniques. This explanation of the general case of transition can only be assessed as a theory which tries to explain economic growth with the necessity of economic growth but not identifying why this necessity is inevitable.

Rostow claims that these stages are not merely descriptive but that they represent a high grade of abstraction and generalisation. Although the deductive methodology of deriving theories from historic experiences in transformational matters is applicable, he fails to set a clear task of the analysis and merely classifies stages of history which match economic conditions (Delhaes, 1971).

2.3.2.4 The Convergence Theory

Another deterministic approach which is of relevance for transformation processes is the thesis of the convergence of socialist and capitalist economic systems (Tinbergen, 1966; Galbraith, 1971; Wiles, 1977). The existing convergence theories or prognoses can be distinguished into closed and open approaches, depending on the degree to which the authors allow factors outside the defined system to influence the future development of institutions and societies. The approaches differ with respect to the emphasis placed on the relevance of geographical, international and inter-system elements indicating and initiating diffusion and convergence.

2.3.2.4.1 The Open Approach

Following Wiles (1977) convergence of systems is defined as the adoption of foreign production techniques and management methods by a nation and its economic units. The forces determining diffusion of knowledge are distinguished into competition, imitation and inner necessity. Competition and imitation are both considered to be internationally initiated, competition symbolising participants of the society being compelled by their government to imitate new foreign technology or institutions and imitation representing the belief of a decision-making authority that this new technology is beneficial to society. This differentiation is not very clear and represents the methodology chosen in this approach which is a description of sectoral historic development and its likely future state.

The inner necessity of convergence is conjectured to lead to an organisational change which is either spontaneously necessary or imposed by technological progress. Although the inner necessity is surmised to be self-moving, in accordance with Wiles's critique of the Hegelian dialectic, statements are only made with respect to the development of the economic system and no convergence is indicated concerning the political system. The chosen separation of the economic system and the political system is nevertheless not explicitly qualified.

The convergence following competition and imitation is assumed to be rather pro-capitalist whereas the inner necessity indicates a more socialist development. Wiles (1977) derives the state to which each society will converge from a sectoral description which does not necessarily follow his methodological framework of competition, imitation and inner necessity. The prognosis of all societies being advanced and rather centralised with state planning, high minimum income but unequal distribution, equality in capital holdings, worker participation, hierarchical organisations with high specialisation etc. seems to be derived from the existence of mixed-economies. The appearance of Western style market techniques in Eastern formally planned economies and state interference and public policies in market economies are extrapolated to a final convergence. Since he does not offer a profound methodological basis and argues that some developments are caused by "ill human nature", the approach can only be evaluated as merely vague. Despite these criticisms the openness of the economic system towards international and outside influences is certainly to be appreciated and it is important in any analysis of institutional change and transformation processes.

2.3.2.4.2 The Closed Approach

2.3.2.4.2.1 The Necessity of Planning in the Industrial Society

Galbraith (1971) identifies technology as the elementary factor which induces a necessary development of the economic and social structure of society. Advanced science and technology require capital and the necessary specialist skills and these requirements can only be met by large business organisations. The development of industrial bureaucratic organisations is interpreted as being inevitably generated by technological and industrial progress. This progress has definite implications for production and income and will change the social structure of society into industrial affluence. The affluent society is characterised by the substitution of basic physical needs by the human want for power and prestige. This implies a considerable change in the structure of the demand and supply sides of the economy. Consumers no longer make their consumption decisions based on prices and needs, they are becoming subject to influence by the suppliers. Suppliers are conjectured to not meet consumer requirements but rather control the markets through their bureaucratic business organisations. The technological sophistication on the other hand entails large capital requirements for further research and development as well as for new investment, which accrues a high risk involvement and might thus hinder further progress. These developments lead to and require an increased state involvement and political regulation of economic areas. The newly evolved societal structure of the industrial bureaucracy induces the necessity of state policy, the growing function of the modern state is derived from technological progress that eventually leads to the unreliability of the market mechanisms (Galbraith, 1971).

The established power of large business organisations has disrupted the market forces and increases the power of bureaucracy so that economic life becomes subordinated to industrial planning and control. This power and control over markets has important societal implications in that it affects values and beliefs. This industrial development shapes the economic society and is inevitable. The necessity of this development indicates the convergence between industrial societies and thus destroys the antinomy between market economics and social planning. The newly established economic system is a system of controlled planning by industrial bureaucracy. Advanced technological production takes up time and employs sums of capital which can then not be employed in another productive form and thereby reduces productive flexibility. Economic planning becomes inevitable and necessary due to this inflexibility and the indispensability of foresight and anticipation of consumers' needs. Anticipatory strategies modify market behaviour by corporate planning. Corporate planning includes, as part of the industrial planning, the authoritarian determination of prices and quantities produced. Industrial planning which can be exercised internally through vertical integration of supply units and externally by market control and inter-firm contracts is juxtaposed to state planning. Economic state planning is identified in public markets, agriculture and in the setting of diverse norms, standards and international arrangements.

Galbraith interprets the co-existence of socialist planning and large industrial organisations as societal awareness of the necessity of planning. The indispensable convergence of the two economic systems is identified by the following indicators:

-the large size of organisations,
-the control over the supply of savings and capital,
-technical knowledge and management is assigned with decisive power,
-organisations are led by the techno-structure,
-corporate exercise replaces entrepreneurial governance and
-individuals within the organisation are sustained by the organisation.

Industrial progress and technological advancement has created large bureaucratic business and planning organisations. Corporate savings within the industrial society and the formally planned society exceed consumers' savings many times over and investment is thereby mainly financed by the corporation's own capital availability. Capital planning is furthermore supported by state capital planning, i.e. fiscal and monetary policy. The abundance of capital and the assumption that power is always appointed to those factors of production which have the greatest inelasticity of supply lead to the change of the assignment of power away from capital. Capital is replaced by organised intelligence which comprises technological knowledge and managerial expertise. Galbraith designated this specialist knowledge as "techno-structure" which eventually takes the place of the entrepreneurial function of corporate governance and this stage is called the "mature corporation". The transferred power in the organisation represents the increasingly minor importance of the individual whose distinctive decision-making authority is transmitted to group decisions because the individual does not have the necessary knowledge at his disposal due to the advanced technological structure.

2.3.2.4.2.2 The Convergence of Industrial Societies

The above economic and societal indicators have transformed society and a further proceeding transformation is deduced. Galbraith (1971) derives a particular development of economic and social life which originates in the technological progress and he particularises the following characteristics of the industrial society besides the structural change in the labour market and the reshape of the union's significance:

-societal goals are derived from organisational goals,
-price control, and
-organisational and macroeconomic demand management.

The mature corporation and the formal plan-society identify an increased importance of the motivational incentives of identification and adaptation. Identification represents the case where the individual values the goals of the group higher than his own previous ones and adaptation reflects the individual's motivation to conform to the organisation's goals more closely than with his own preferences - and thereby following them. The societal implications of this motivational structure are thus twofold. Societal goals are created by the acceptance of organisational aims and at the same time by individual preferences influencing the goals of the organisation. However the values and standards of behaviour in the industrial society are subject to the organisational goals. The organisational goals are represented by the pursuit of the techno-structure's objective of its self-survival. The survival is secured by the autonomy in decision-making power and the protection of a minimum level of return which serves this objective. Since the industrial society consists of these large business operations or planning bureaucracies the motivational structure supports this target and economic growth becomes the accepted societal goal.

Economic growth and the seeking of minimum levels of return serve the techno-structure's goals and they are achieved through price controls and demand management. The unreliability of the market necessitates the control of prices and the management of demand with the support of the government in order to ensure the managerial autonomy and the societal goal. The producer thus controls and shapes the market and consumer behaviour to accommodate for the performance of the industrial system and his own purposes.

According to Galbraith the current state of industrial societies symbolises similar developments in capitalist and socialist societies where planning eventually replaces the market. Planning, government control and state socialism are common features. Consumer sovereignty is replaced by corporate and bureaucratic autonomy and the industrial society relies on the control of demand and on state policies so that the industrial system becomes a comprehensive part of the government apparatus. The mature industrial society is methodologically proven to be stable because of the transformed motivational structure which eventually leads to the acceptance of the organisational goals as societal goals.

Although the increasing corporate and bureaucratic power can be identified and the approach does not lack major logical inconsistencies with regard to the transformation of the large business organisation following technological progress, Galbraith overlooks the historical reasoning of the establishment of socialism. Since political pressures are more likely to be made responsible for the socialist formation, the eventual societal acceptance of economic growth as being derived from organisational goals can only be identified with difficulty. If on the other hand he identifies - though lacking clarity - the identity and acceptance of societal and bureaucratic goals in political purposes (and power according to political rather than technological features) he clearly disregards the openness of the two systems. His approach is a closed-system approach where no exchange of information can take place. The human individual is interpreted as part of a closed organisation with no knowledge, identification and adaptation of other societies' objectives. Had he acknowledged the effects of societal over-spilling, his scenario which necessarily had to be amended might not have factually proved to be invalid. The methodological basis of the closed society is made explicit with reference to the poor within the industrial society which Galbraith identifies as "outside the industrial system...who cannot qualify" (1971, p. 317).

Nevertheless he succeeds in analysing dynamically the structures of economic systems, their foundations and implications for societal structures. His motivational approach is not to be disregarded despite his lack of belief in human morale.

2.3.3 Classification of the Two German Economies and Theoretical Relevance of Dynamic Approaches

In the last two sections (2.2 and 2.3) static approaches of identifying different economic systems along with dynamic approaches of analysing and explaining system transformation were presented. The economic system has been identified as a partial societal system interacting with other societal systems. Different economic systems have been identified by referring to their organisational framework. The DIM-approach was chosen to categorise comparative economic systems in the traditional dichotomy of market and planned economies. Based on this static comparison an attempt was made in section 2.3 to identify approaches addressing the dynamic nature of economic system changes. The approaches were divided into non-deterministic and deterministic ones. The non-deterministic approaches were chosen with regard to their descriptive validity and their analytical foundation with respect to its applicability to the process of economic transformation. All the approaches descriptively identify certain elements as characteristic for the classification of economic systems.

The ordo-liberal approach focuses on the plan as classifying indicator and thereby differentiates between centrally directed and exchange economies. The same classifying element was recognised by Hayek. The analysis of economic systems via the plan as classifying element leads to the system categories of central planning, competition and monopoly. The latter two being two particular forms of Eucken's exchange economy. Once again the classical dichotomy of central and decentralised planning is established, here by reference to the information flow. The property rights approach uses a categorisation according to the identity of property owners and the holders of control over property, which culminates in the categories of private, communal and state ownership according to the degree of ownership exclusiveness, the right to reassign ownership and the possibility of allocating the property by individual or collective action.

A synthesis of these major categories describes the former East German economy as a centrally planned economy with no private property and the West German economy as a decentrally planned exchange economy with private property. East German partial societal systems were highly ordered in the form of a socialist constitution whereas the West German society can be described by a democratic constitution which does not contain a specific economic constitution. Economic actions were coordinated by central plans - utilising scarcity indicators - in the former GDR, individual plans and competition being the basis for economic coordination in the Federal Republic. Within the German Democratic Republic no private property was allowed by constitution and the state exclusively held control over the means of production (the utilised term "people's property" was a rather euphemistic description of state property).

The non-deterministic approaches address the dynamics of systems as either a spontaneous or a consciously designed development. In the ordo-liberal belief efficient economic systems do not develop spontaneously, they are the result of conscious decisions taken to create a stable institutional framework. This notion is contradicted by liberal economics. No rational economic order can be formulated due to the lack of knowledge and the existence of a common will. However Smith advocates the safeguarding of an institutional order which allows the best use of resources and utilisation of individual knowledge, whereas Hayek goes one step further and interprets economic orders as spontaneously established as best suited. The democratic upswing in the former GDR in the late 1980s (in the form of public protests and demonstrations by various groups of interest) can be interpreted as such a spontaneous evolution, the spontaneity of the final state however, i.e. the economic unification and transformation, must be doubted due to its institutionalised design of specific features and elements of the economic system (see chapter 3). The evolution of property rights finds applicability to the transformational process and the particular East German development of private propeny rights and the implications for welfare will be explained later (chapter 4, section 4.4). Despite the apparent failure of the selected deterministic approaches to forecast the recent breakdown of East European socialist and communist societies the methodologies with regard to the analysis of system changes are valid. Structural features such as large-scale bureaucratic organisations, wage labour, absentee ownership, technocratic structures and the increasing depersonalisation of the work environment were correctly anticipated. The Schumpeterian approach identifies superior efficiency of certain structures (e.g. large-scale business organisations) as the dialectic method of the development process of changing systems. The creative destruction in this sense is closely linked to the Hayekian advocation of the spontaneous unconscious evolution. Social and economic partial system changes affect the global social system. A more detailed influence relationship between the partial societal system is given in Rostow's development stages, the convergence theory and the Marxist law of motion. Marx as well as Galbraith identify factors of the economic system as determining the development of the entire society. The ownership of the means of production and the specific production relations condition the state of the superstructure and social goals on the other hand are derived from organisational goals. In both approaches social values and standards of behaviour are made subject of the economic system. In contrast to these notions, Rostow interprets the economic development as initiated by non-economic factors and human motives. The partial societal system determines the economic development.

Both interrelative connections can be historically proven and here a synthesis is to be assumed: Political, social and economic system are highly interrelated and no mono-directed relation is to be presumed. The political and legal system impose boundaries on the economic system, e.g. permission of property rights influences the use of resources and thereby affects the economic performance. The economic system does not leave social values untouched, e.g. a monopolistic market form influences consumers' choice. This notion will be addressed in the adjustment model (in section 2.8) which advocates harmony between the partial social system to allow efficient change and a sound transitional period.

The structural differences within economic systems have been established and section 2.4 is intended to examine theoretically the institutional structures with respect to existing forms of decision-making and behaviour inside a firm as well as to look at the empirical evidence regarding efficient organisational structures. Types of organisational structures of firms are linked to the classification of economic systems according to the identity of the planning and controlling agent and the allocation of property rights. The relationship between selected structures and elements of economic systems, i.e. those which have been identified as classifying, and the economic outcome will be analysed.

2.4 The Institutional Structure of Control Inside the Firm and Organisational Efficiency

The institutional structure of a firm entails a certain distribution of decision-making authority and has implications for motivation, individual behaviour and organisational as well as economic outcomes. The distribution of decision-making authority is analysed in this section with respect to two factors which are the main elements within the property rights theory: ownership and control. The relevance of ownership and control for the analysis of organisational and institutional patterns was realised with respect to the problematic nature of the principal agent which was first recognised by the Property Rights School (Coase, 1937).

The control by the owner over the manager who pursues interests which are potentially different from the owner's interests may involve costs. The existence of such costs of control can be seen as a system-comprehensive fact, since the necessity of control emerges for the private stockholder as well as for the owner of a state firm (Leipold, 1985).[32] Nevertheless private property in association with a perfectly competitive market structure is suggested to be more efficient than communal or state ownership since the private property right owner is entitled to the residual income and the benefits of control are higher than its costs (see section 2.3.1.2.1). Different property right assignments lead to different production processes, allocation of resources and output. This behavioural relationship implies that a change in the content of property rights concerning the use of resources alters the individual's behaviour and actions. Once this relationship is assumed different types of organisations can be analysed according to the ownership of and control over resources under the assumption of utility-maximising behaviour.

2.4.1 The Organisational Form and Input Factor Monitoring

The economic organisation of the firm is conventionally based on a contractual agreement in order to arrange inputs in a cooperative and specialised production process. Input factors in a decentralised capitalist firm are rewarded according to the value of marginal productivity. Productivity and rewards thereby have to be measured. Multilateral contracts between all the input owners are replaced by a combined and central bilateral contract and this mitigates the achievement of an efficient organisation of team production. This contractual form builds the basis for the institution of the firm. The correct measurement of productivity is essential for a stable production process, since a positive correlation between rewards according to productivity and forthcoming productivity is assumed.

A particular problem is the assessment of the correct marginal productivity of one input factor in a team production process. Within a team production process the last produced output unit cannot be separately assigned to the individual input factors and consequently the costs of assessing the marginal productivities of the input factors are increased. Factor productivities have to be metered so that marginal products equalise marginal factor costs. The team production function cannot be defined as the sum of separate production functions because the team production process is assumed to yield a higher output than separate production functions combined. Cooperative production will be used in a capitalist firm if there is a net increase in productivity due to team production. Thus the benefit yielded by the extra output has to be greater than the costs which are created by team production (Alchian & Demsetz, 1972). These costs arise from the necessity to control and discipline team members.

The difficulty in discovering shirking and the impossibility of attributing a reduction in output to a particular team member allow the private cost of this counterproductive behaviour to be less than its true social costs if detection costs are positive. According to Alchian and Demsetz (1972, p. 783) the shirking problem is reduced if the monitor owns the following rights:

"1) to be the residual claimant,
2) to observe input behaviour,
3) to be the central party common to all contracts with inputs,
4) to alter the membership of the team and
5) to sell the right, which defines the ownership of the classical... firm".

Different types of organisational contracts (profit-sharing firms, socialist firms, cooperations, non-profit firms, partnerships and employee unions) have been analysed by the above authors with respect to the degree of shirking which was to be expected. The following results were found: Incentives to shirk in a profit-sharing firm are fewer the smaller the optimal size of the team. A small team size will increase the individual benefit from the reduction of shirking. Socialist firms are assumed to be profit-sharing but residual sharing is politically rather than economically motivated. These firms have a lower residual compared to the capitalist firm because of the monitor's shirking resulting in a loss which is greater than the gain from shirking reduction through profit-sharing. Within a stockholder corporation (public stock company) decision authority is widely transferred to a managerial group. Thereby the initial shirking problem by the actual stockholders caused by the large number of asset holders is reduced and cooperative activity tends to be more effective. Within this structure stockholders keep their rights to sell their shares, to control and alter the management team and to participate in fundamental decisions concerning the structure and further existence of the corporation. Although stockholders' shirking has been eliminated, managerial shirking evolves. The control of negative motivation is enforced indirectly by potentially replacing managers from inside or outside the corporation as well as directly by the stockholders' power to terminate managerial contracts. If the capitalisation of future benefits is not materialised the structure of ownership will eventually change. The emergent structure is characterised by the stockholders' rights to managerial decision-making and to the residual. The saleability of shares and the consequent blocking option of stockholders increases their monitoring power in terms of the possible reaction to unsatisfactory managerial performance. Within a non-profit firm no capitalisation of future benefits as a result of an efficient management is possible and therefore any motivation to deter shirking is absent. Partnerships as small self-monitoring organisations prevent shirking to a high degree. Employer's shirking can be decreased by an employees' union as a monitoring institution.

The existing analysis of the different types of firms leads to the emphasis which has to be placed on the organisational and contractual form of the firm. The firm receives a flow of information about the productivities of input factors and the costs of achieving this information and transforming it into an efficient production process depends on the structural type of the firm. The firm itself becomes an efficient market and input factors compete with each other through this institution rather than through the conventionally assumed factor market, since the information employees receive within their firm is less costly than the acquisition of information from outside the firm. The study of different contractual structures leads to the suggestion that the problems the markets suffer are as a result of the defects of communal property rights in organising and influencing the use of resources.

Ownership and control structures within firms are thereby identified as having motivational and efficiency implications. Chapter 3 will identify the introduction of corporate firm structures and private property rights as the predominant organisational transformation in the former East Germany. The adaptation of the German contractual law, in particular the participatory law "*Tarifgesetz*", necessitates at this point the analysis of the participatory form of contract and the implications for decision-making and efficiency.

2.4.2 The Codeterministic Form of Participation and Input Factor Productivity

The organisational form of codetermination as a participatory firm was analysed by Furubotn (1985) with respect to implications on efficiency and productivity as well as on the distribution of income. Industrial democracy is expected to increase productive efficiency because direct labour participation is supposed to increase the degree of self-fulfilment of labour. A corporate reform towards direct participation of the labour force will result in a Pareto-optimal situation. This situation once achieved will only be changed if further welfare improvements are expected having been initiated by endogenous or exogenous changes within the economic environment (e.g. innovation, technological change).

2.4.2.1 Mandatory Codetermination

A mandatory codeterministic structure is defined as a legally imposed codeterministic system where wages are independently set by negotiations between industry and employee representatives. The agreed wage consequently has to be accepted as a fixed wage for the firm. No further wage negotiation costs are expected for the firm, since they do not have to engage in any money-wage discussions. Employees and stockholders have equal supervising and decision-making rights which are legally mandatory. A special judicial process allows each party to veto suggested reorganisations, so that structural and organisational changes can be expected to be successful only if they are welfare-improving (Pareto-efficient).

Furubotn (1985) operationalises the workers' welfare conception by employing a community's utility function, which assumes identical preferences and the same levels of income for each employee. The presently agreed wage rate as well as the work environment (non-pecuniary income) enter as the defined variables into the utility function. A positive behavioural relationship between non-pecuniary income and utility is assumed and the environment is suggested to provide greater utility the less hierarchically structured the organisation and thus the decision-making process is. Given the exogenously agreed wage rate, labour's utility function depends on the existing environment characteristics. The stockholders' utility function is entirely determined by profits and thus by variables and actions which increase the firm's profits. Besides the given product prices and market and agreed prices for the input factors capital and labour, the production function which enters the stockholders' utility function is determined by the technical parameters of the employees' utility function. The technical parameters represent the internal organisation. An alteration of the technical parameters will cause a technological change. If the values of the technical parameters increase the workers' utility improves, but the effect on output might be twofold. It can increase the firm's productivity and thus the stockholders' utility, but it can also imply increased necessity to control the employees and this control entails costs which potentially decrease profits.

The analysis shows that capitalist firms without any form of codetermination and with technical parameters lower in value than their optimal sizes cause sub-optimal efficiency since no knowledge is present about the employees' utility function and efficient reorganisational structures. This lack of awareness causes positive information costs which prevent efficient production. An organisational change towards participation can nevertheless improve productive efficiency - if assumed not to be fully optimised - if codetermination is accepted as organisational structure. The improvement in efficiency is due to the reduction in transaction costs because the quality and extent of information flows within the firm have been improved. If a positive relationship between codetermination and incentives and motivations is accepted, an organisational change towards industrial democracy (here synonymous with codetermination; see section 2.5) increases efficiency. Thus "industrial democracy may offer benefits that give the participatory firm some advantages the traditional (hierarchically organised) firm does not possess" (Furubotn, 1985, p. 31).[33]

The essential argument that knowledge about employees' utility functions and the use of this knowledge increase utility implies the task for firms is to obtain this knowledge. The information is obtained at zero costs in the industrial democracy model of legally mandatory codetermination. The information can also be gained by creating different participatory organisation structures or strategic information centres.

Although the costs of internal wage conflicts are reduced by the separation model (outside determination of wages), the gains may be offset by limits to reward payments according to individual productivity. Furthermore the individual worker's scope of decision to fulfil his own work-leisure concept is reduced. The exogenously negotiated wages might thus prove to entail drawbacks on efficiency gains which are created by the codetermination model. But nevertheless the model of industrial democracy focuses on the ability of changes of the institutional organisation to create Pareto-improvements, because it can be assumed that decisions within a codeterministic institutional form are only taken if they are mutually beneficial.

The static analysis shows that the participatory reform creates welfare gains under restrictive assumptions. A technological change, within a dynamic system, may offset welfare gains by welfare losses in the next period due to conflicts arising about the distribution of losses or benefits. The distribution that occurs depends on the actual internal decision-making process and legally imposed regulatory codetermination. If the implementation of a new technology does not create mutual benefits, thus improving either the stockholders or the employees' utility, the technological innovation will not be introduced. This assumes that preferences are constant and both parties have legally enforceable control rights. The long-term existence of the firm within the market might therefore be jeopardised through participation. The need to make compromises is high and stockholders as well as employees should be aware of this if the firm is to exist in the long-run.

2.4.2.2 Voluntary Codetermination

Furubotn (1988) argues further that institutional changes towards intensified labour participation in corporate policy have been motivated by political rather than economic consideration. The legally imposed codetermination structure with labour control rights and a joint-decision-making process between capital and labour has been analysed as less efficient than the organisational structure of voluntary codetermination, the joint investment firm. The structure of property rights is of significant importance since only the shareholders of a firm's assets are suggested to bear the risk and uncertainty and only the bearing of risk justifies the carrying out of control rights (Alchian, 1950). Workers who are taking the investment risk "are significantly affected by [the firm's] economic performance [and] should be guarantied a share in the firm's residual or granted authority in decision-making" (Furubotn, 1988, p. 171). The worker's property right should not be saleable since it might end the codeterministic structure of the firm. It is the property right to the residual which the worker retains that allows codetermination with the aim of maximising profits. Incentives and motivations to increase the firm's productivity are created by the workers' participation in the decision-making process on the grounds of their interest in maximising productivity and their future income stream. (The technical parameters of the workers' utility function may be partly replaced by the profit-share variable if a trade-off exists between profit and the work environment. This depends entirely on the individual values attached to the variables of the utility function.)

The workers' utility function (U_w) becomes a function of wage-income (I), non-pecuniary income (NP) and profit-related income (PI),

$$U_w = U_w\,(I, NP, PI) \qquad (2.2)$$

The stockholders' utility function (U_{st}) depending on profits (PR) can be written as

$$U_{st} = U_{st}\,(PR) \qquad (2.3)$$ where

$PR = pq - c + aNP + bPI$ (2.4) with p denoting price, q quantity and c costs.

Non-pecuniary income (NP) and profit-related income (PI) thus also enter the stockholders' utility function, since greater productivity is expected from a work environment with which the worker can identify as well as from profit related income. The degree to which profits are increased depends on the magnitudes of a and b and whether these parameters are complementary or substitutional. In the case of substitutional variables, the degree to which profits increase due to a profit-sharing structure depends on the ratio of a/b (the propensities to increase profits due to higher productivity according to the assumed positive influence of work environment and profit-sharing). Since it should be expected that profit-sharing and participatory decision-making power improve the work environment and the degree of fulfilment (loss of alienation), an overall increase in productivity can be expected purely on the grounds of a voluntary joint-investment and joint capital structure.

The common property rights structure of the voluntary codeterministic firm leads to the following results compared to the legally imposed codeterministic structure:

1.) Conflicts over corporate policy and thus costs of negotiation are reduced since workers and stockholders share the same motives and incentives.
2.) Profits are allocated according to previously agreed property rights schemes, which lower the costs of profit distribution.
3.) Workers' cooperation and motivation increase due to the benefit achieved from increased efficiency and productivity.
4.) The codeterministic structure tends to be stable because property rights can not be sold to outsiders.

Although the positive implications of the joint-investment model appear obvious, the share of profit-related income related to workers' income is important to consider. Since profit-related income bears risk, wage income can still be expected to remain the main income stream. A positive impact of profit or performance related income on productivity has to be assumed, but it has to be regarded as unlikely that workers overall start to behave as stockholders (the most important factor is the transformation of incentives and motivation). Negotiations about wage adjustments are still important and since wage income represents the main and most secure part of income, workers might regard wage increases as a prime objective within the negotiation process. The consideration of risk adverse behaviour leads to the improbability of a worker's willingness to take on a full property right. A positive performance related income with attached control rights would rather be more effective than a *per se* control right.

2.4.3 Empirical Studies of Participatory Organisational Forms - Misinterpretation and Lack of Differentiation

2.4.3.1 Existing Empirical Studies

Control inside the firms of participatory organisational forms has predominantly been restricted to empirical research in the areas of former socialist forms of participation, mandatory codetermination and on a wider scale has been addressed by the analysis of the relationship between institutional frameworks and economic growth on a macroeconomic level. From this small field of empirical research studies have been selected which - even though they might have been carried out a long time ago - are appropriate to the case study and will allow a critical reflection on these studies.

The organisational structure of the former Yugoslavia and its implications for efficiency and innovation was analysed by Pejovich (1987). The structure of self-management contains state ownership of all capital, employees govern the business firm through workers councils and retain all returns from the firm's capital. Economic change is here understood as innovation and analysed according to different institutional arrangements. Since "innovation is individualistic in its origin and social in its consequences" (Pejovich, 1987, p. 463) economic change enlarges the set of choices and alters the institutional structure. Within a private property rights structure with freedom to contract and innovate the innovator retains the residual or the market value if an exchange contract is agreed. The self-management structure proves to be inefficient since no full property rights are assigned to employees, and bureaucracy and overall economic problems connected with a socialist economic system are created. The specific decision-making process within the self-management structure has decreased the number of innovations in comparison to a private property rights structure because no capitalisation of future benefits of efficacious inventions is possible. An institutional change following an innovation and an expansion of choices is thus encumbered by the rigid property rights structure and the restriction of the innovator's freedom.

The mandatory organisational structure as practised in post-war West Germany is also widely considered as efficiency decreasing. Svejnar's empirical study (1982) of the legally imposed codeterministic structure and its efficiency shows no significant efficiency-increasing effects from the implementation of the German Codetermination Laws of 1951 and 1976 (*Montan-Mitbestimmungs-gesetz*) and the Works Constitution Acts (*Betriebsverfassungsgesetz*) of 1952 and 1972. These participatory laws (Codetermination Law and Works Constitution Act) complement the basic law of coalition (Art. 9 Clause 3, Basic Law) which allows everybody to form coalitions in order to safeguard and promote economic conditions.

This basic law secures the position of unions and employers' federations and ensures the free collective bargaining (Hesselberger, 1990). Wage and salary negotiations are hereby taken independently by employee unions and employers' federations without any state interference. This law is certainly juxtaposed to the participatory laws which were introduced later. The Codetermination Law and the Works Constitutions Act were inaugurated to prevent uncontrolled economic concentration and to protect political democracy (Claessen *et al*, 1989).

Implications of the institutional framework for economic growth were studied by Scully (1987, 1988). One hundred and fifteen market economies were analysed over the time period 1960-1980 and the institutional framework was qualified by measures of political, civil and economic freedom and the national economy was described by a linear-homogeneous production function (Scully, 1988). The institutional framework spanned from intervening and regulating state governments to individual mutually beneficial choice in a structure of forming contracts. Scully (1987) concluded that a secure system of rights which grants the rights to liberty and property reduces transaction costs and leads to greater individual wealth. In particular the secure capitalisation of future benefits increases the investment and thereby, other things being equal, economic progress.

Since the allocation of resources is determined by the structure of property rights, economic efficiency and process become a function of the institutional framework. The institutional framework is thus considered as exogeneously given, with individual choices being made within the given framework. The choice of institutional framework of the economy is then surmised to have consequences for the allocation of resources in the economy.

The ranking of the different institutional frameworks is derived from political and civil liberty measures. They cover the democratic control by individuals over the governing institution and the relative rights between individuals and the state. The empirical analysis proves a significant positive relationship between the degree of political, civil and economic liberty and the national economic growth rate. Liberal societies grow on average three times faster than societies with restricted freedom. The liberty constraint can be interpreted as a "67 percent tax" on the wealth of the individuals in liberty-restricted societies (Scully, 1988). This study leads to the suggestion that exclusive property rights and liberty rights increase economic efficiency. On a more general level it is concluded that the choice of the institutional framework has essential implications for economic progress.

A further general policy suggestion can be made according to these empirical results. Policy-makers should be concerned with the creation of an institutional framework within which individuals can cooperate efficiently through contracts and decentralised decision-making processes. Social welfare can not be optimised centrally since no knowledge about individual values and utility functions exists and individualism has to be maintained. Hayek (1949, p. 16) expresses the following opinion on the subject:

"From the awareness of the limitations of individual knowledge and from the fact that no person or small group of persons can know all that is known to somebody, individualism also derives its main practical conclusion: its demand for a strict limitation of all coercive or exclusive power."

The relationship between the structure of property rights and economic growth has recently been analysed empirically by Torstensson (1994). Differences in countries' growth rates are partly caused by differences in the property rights structure. The structure of property rights is quantified by the degree of state ownership of property and the degree of arbitrary confiscations of property by central authorities. The study suggests that well-defined private property rights lead to allocative efficiency and will produce a higher gross domestic product *per capita.* If an institutional change originates from better enforced private property rights, an overall increase in gross domestic product *per capita* can be expected. Furthermore well-enforced private property rights ensure the possession of future benefits from investment already undertaken and have thereby a positive indirect effect on long-term economic growth.[34]

Torstensson's study proves the following direct effects of private property rights on economic growth:

a. more efficient use of human capital and
b. higher efficiency of investment.

A more efficient use of human capital is assumed because private property rights guarantee the allocation of human capital in its most useful way. The structure of private property rights creates incentives for individuals to use their human capital for productive purposes because the existence of a secure private property structure is expected to pay for this use. Technological progress and innovation are enhanced due to the security that the individuals can retain the residual from their productive undertakings. Private property rights cause investment in sectors where a high capitalisation of future benefits is expected and the return of capital is certain to be retained by the investor. Since high (private) returns of capital in a perfectly competitive market structure without any externalities reflect social values, allocative efficiency is created by private property rights. Investment in sectors with high social returns enhances economic growth. The empirical analysis verifies the expected positive relation between private property rights and economic growth. Although no significant negative relationship between state-ownership and economic growth could be ascertained, a significant negative correlation between a high degree of arbitrary confiscation and economic growth was noted. It has been suggested that a one percentage point increase in economic growth could be attained through a negation of arbitrary confiscations - other things being equal (Torstensson, 1994). The empirical analysis states once again that poorly defined and insecure property rights lead to an inefficient allocation of resources and in particular inefficient allocation of human capital and investment funds.

A brief review of reforms in East European countries towards the creation of market socialism from the 1950s to 1980s was given by Schroeder (1988). Although the emphasis was placed mainly on the introduction of market processes in order to increase efficiency, full private property rights were denied until the 1990s. The initial reforms he refers to did not create competitive markets and the problems associated with bureaucracy and central planning persisted. Ownership behaviour was not created because rights were not transferable and a formal subordination to the respective governments due to a restricted decision-making process was not abolished. It was generally concluded that the reforms aiming to create some form of "market socialism" did not achieve the outcomes desired. Due to the ambiguous attitude towards the introduction of private ownership no increase in economic efficiency could be found.

2.4.3.2 The Need for Differentiation within the Analysis of Codetermination

2.4.3.2.1 Self-Management as Opposed to Ill-Defined Property Rights

The different empirical studies suggest a close relationship between the institutional framework of the economic system and the performance of the organisation and the economy. The efficiency of participatory firms may be restricted through an ill-defined property rights structure and the low economic performance of socialist societies is substantiated with the lack of individual freedom and choice. The performance of the economy is measured by either growth rates and efficiency measures in terms of profits or utility. Although the evidence seems to suggest a positive behavioural function between private ownership and well-defined control rights, it has to be realised that the participatory firm itself is defined as an organisation with a particular distribution of decision-making authority and does not define a certain property rights structure. Although participatory firms were predominantly identified in so-called mixed economies, they are certainly not identical with common property rights structures.

Within the framework of the former Yugoslav system, the participatory firm is analysed within an order of decentralised decision-making and state or common property. The weak innovative and growth performance should not be used to suggest that participatory organisations are inefficient. Pejovich misinterprets the small number of innovations as an effect of the self-management form of codetermination. In contrast his analysis only indicates that the non-existence of private property rights implies the impossibility of the capitalisation of future benefits of successful innovations and that this is hindering economic growth. Often the participatory structure is identified with common property rights, but this does not necessarily have to be the case. Clearly a separation of ownership rights and decision-making authority within the analysis has to be undertaken. The codeterministic form with common property can not be analysed under the profit-maximising behavioural assumption, from which an economic growth creating motivation is supposed to be derived. In the Yugoslav case participation can not lead to profit-maximising behaviour because the social structure and system does not allow any such behaviour. This is a misinterpretation and a logical neglect of the behavioural relationship and the framework itself is misjudged. Economic performance can not be qualified in terms of profits and no neoclassical assumptions can be applied to the participatory case within a socialist structure.

2.4.3.2.2 Constraints of Codetermination within the German Participatory Laws

With respect to the German participatory laws (*Montanmitbestimmungsgesetz* and *Betriebsverfassungsgesetz*, section 2.4.3.1) Svenjar (1982) seems to falsify Furubotn's (1988) model of profit-increasing codetermination due to the technical parameters. No negative relationship was realised and it should be kept in mind that institutional patterns should be judged according to their desired objectives.

In its original form the Codetermination Law (*Montanmitbestimmungsgesetz*, introduced in 1952) applied to joint-stock companies of the coal and steel industry. In 1976 this law was extended to include all joint-stock companies (public stock companies) which employ more than two thousand people. This regulation provides for the equal representation of employees and capital owners in the supervisory board of the company and requires that a certain number of the employees' representatives has to be employed by the respective company itself (representatives are often union members). The chairman of the board has to be elected by a majority of two thirds and in the case of an unsuccessful election the procedure has to be taken solely by the capital representatives. The equal decision-making authority is hereby undermined and the codetermination has also been circumvented by the formation of supra-national concerns and by the vertical integration of the primary industry and the processing industry. Performance measures and the study of efficiency effects of codeterministic structures have to take account of these facts and it is also essential not to neglect the structural change the economy was undergoing, i.e. the decreasing significance of the coal and steel industry and the diminishing share of contribution to the German gross national product.

The Works Constitution Law (*Betriebsverfassungsgesetz*) also introduced in 1952 is relevant for the majority of companies and constitutes the formation of the works committee. The revision in 1972 and the amendment in 1988 authorise the works committee to codetermination in social matters, to a right of cooperation in personal issues and to a right of information in corporate affairs. The representation of employees in the supervisory board is designed to be one third. The main objectives of the Works Constitution Law are twofold. "Employer and works committee work together...in order to achieve the welfare of the employees and of the company" (translated by the author). The aim of company welfare which can be circumscribed as the aim of high profits is likely to interfere with the aim of a high wage ratio. The mere elaboration of the laws' design, the area of application, the field of the works committee's competence and the design of the vote on resolutions within the supervisory board represent the limits of participation. Svenjar's study (1982) should thus be evaluated against this background of constraint of German mandatory codetermination.

These two cases of participation - self-management and mandatory participation - clarify the necessity to differentiate between participation alongside state property and participation with private property. Any empirical analysis which intends to examine the efficiency of an institutional structure should not confuse the intended aims of the structural element. Since the Yugoslav model can not claim to aim at profit-maximisation it can not be valued by this means of judgement. Certainly if such conflicts are realised they can be dealt with. Nevertheless no analysis should condemn a structure for pursuing an objective by which it is not judged. This would produce a major lack of logic.

Although difficulties inherent to any evaluation of codeterministic structures are appreciated the constraints of the codeterministic application have to be realised in order to not draw general conclusions about the efficiency of certain institutional structures. Furthermore the neoclassical methodology of pre-defining the company's objective as profit-maximisation and evaluating the participatory scheme on this basis requires additional differentiation.

The problem of input factor monitoring and the weakness of the legally imposed participatory system emphasise the necessity to consider organisational improvements of the control structure. The German economic unification and the breakdown of the GDR system necessitate the contemplation of the ethical foundation of democratic capitalism. Once the ethics of the property rights structure are analysed with respect to democratic theories an alternative structure of the allocation of control inside the firm will be developed.

2.5 Constitutional Economics and the Theory of the Democratic Firm

2.5.1 The Conventional Employment Contract and Ethics

2.5.1.1 The Rights-Based Versus the Utilitarian Normative Theory

Constitutional economics and the theory of the democratic firm (mainly represented by Ellerman, 1986, 1988, 1990) criticise fundamentally the conventional employment contract as describing the relationship between the production factors capital and labour. The theory of the democratic firm advocates a negation of this convention to a scenario in which labour rents capital. This notion is based on rights-based theories as opposed to utilitarian normative theories which are predominantly represented by welfare economics (Bergson, 1966).[35] The theory of the democratic firm is rights-based in that it refers to the Kantian principle of treating the individual as an end rather than as a means. The categoric imperative (Kant, 1781) defines a just society as one in which each individual is treated equally in law and is subject to equal concern by, and is of equal interest to, society. The same moral principle is applied by Rawls (1973) where justice is interpreted as fairness and a society can only be justified on the Kantian principle and not on utilitarian grounds.

This ethical principle stipulates respect for other individuals because they are rational human beings and any treatment of human beings as a means to achieve a set objective ignores exactly this status of rational individuals. Conflicting interests between human beings must therefore be dealt with in consideration of each individual's equal value. The Kantian ethics and thus the categoric imperative is rights-based on account of the equal treatment of individuals in law. As human beings behave rationally they are subordinated to the Kantian absolute rule of morale that is unconditionally binding and an obligation. The categoric imperative is used to operationalise this moral thesis since good or wrong can not be defined *per se*. The moral is self-creative since it develops out of respect towards this law, respecting oneself thus implies respecting other human beings. Moral behaviour develops out of self-respect and if this principle is followed, morale is ensured.

The Kantian principle can be applied as a critique towards the conventional employment contract (Ellerman, 1988). Voluntary self-enslavement as a basic individual right (Norzick, 1974) contradicts the Inalienable Rights Theory (section 2.5.1.4) and implies a treatment of individuals as things in terms of the fulfilment of the contract. The inalienability of personal rights also applies to the self-rental contract. The employment contract does not assign positive decision-making authority to the employee neither does it grant legal responsibility to the fruits of labour and the worker is thus treated as a thing in the Kantian sense and the contract of a person taking on a non-person's role is invalid (Ellerman, 1988).

2.5.1.2 Positive and Negative Control Rights

Ellerman (1990, 1992) analyses the given structure of democratic capitalism by referring to the question of employer-employee relationships or self-employment in the workplace. The debate between capitalism and socialism is transferred from private or public ownership and employment of workers to the acceptability of the typical employer-employee relationship (i.e. the renting of human resources) and the issue of general self-employment of people in the workplace in a private property market economy.

If a contractual role is assigned to firmhood, the property right becomes a negative control right and the employment contract is a positive control right. This positive management right is not part of the property ownership, it is derived from the renting contract and implies decisions based on other people's behaviour and activities. Thus ownership does not immediately undermine any rights within the production process, the use of factors of production is controlled by contractual hiring agreements. Capital ownership hereby defines a negative control right over other individuals' behaviour (e.g. to deny the use of a machine in a factory) and any positive right (e.g. to command an employee to use a machine in a certain way) is allocated by an employment contract. By defining control rights in this way the classical use of the term "ownership" is revised in the sense that ownership traditionally defines property rights and these determine the production process via control rights. Only the negative control rights are implied by "firm" or "capital" ownership and management rights are derived from contractual agreements.[36] Private property ownership and negative control rights are not the centre of Ellerman's critique - in contrast to the Marxist opposition to private property of the means of production. Rather it is the employment contract and thus the short-term renting of human labour is analysed following an application of democratic theory.

The entire property rights theory is fundamentally criticised as being invalid in the sense that ownership of the production factors does not immediately and without any further investigation imply the claim of the residual (i.e. the output) nor the bearing of the costs involved by the utilization of input factors in the process of production. The bearing of the costs and the claim to the residual are defined as a contractual agreement. The appropriation of ownership originates in a contract or legal agreement (e.g. the transaction of property) and thus ownership does not *per se* define property rights. Property rights are defined by specific contractual agreements and so are the rights to the residual and the duty to bear the cost of input factors. (A separation between ownership and property right is given in any leasing or renting contract and thus ownership and residual claimancy and input cost bearings are divided.) The firm is thereby the legal institution whose activities, rights and duties are assigned by contracts and not necessarily by *per se* ownership. The productive activity, the right to claim the residual, the duty to bear certain costs are derived from contracts and not from property rights. Since property rights are contractual control rights and not ownership rights the question of property appropriation in terms of the residual claimancy has been neglected in political economic theory and in particular in the economic theory of property.

A property right is described by the term "whole product" and this is the net outcome of the positive and negative product of the right to the output asset and the obligation of input liabilities (Ellermann, 1992, p. 28). The acquisition of a property right can either be by the initial creation of an asset or by the transfer of an asset within a contractual exchange by gaining the legal right to it and the initial creation is defined as "appropriation" and assigns a property right to an asset. The appropriation of the whole product (i.e. the net outcome) follows the laissez-faire market mechanism. The input purchasing body - the firm - bears the cost of the consumption and utilisation of the input factors within the production process and thus the firm becomes simultaneously eligible for the whole product of this production. Thus the input hiring party appropriates the net outcome and the composition of the firm depends on who the hiring body is, i.e. capital hiring labour or labour hiring capital. The form of input contracts determines the cost bearing and only the cost bearing justifies the appropriation of the whole product. This is in stark contrast to the property rights theory where ownership in itself is the justification for residual claimancy.

2.5.1.3 The Labour Theory of Property

The notion of product claimancy of the party bearing the input cost raises the issue of where to place labour within the concept of input factors and this issue can be analysed by pursuing the labour theory of property. The labour theory of property is a non-utilitarian approach and does not comprise of any utility and preference ordering because it is neither based on measuring values of certain activities nor on the desire to maximise any defined objective function. This theory of property applies the juridical principle of imputation and is grounded on the clear separation of labour from other input factors due to responsibility *inter alia* (Proudhon, 1966). The juridical principle of imputation epitomises that the whole product of the production process should be appropriated accordingly by labour following a humanistic view of production. This humanistic view expresses the human responsibility and active role in the production process which makes use of other input factors. The labour theory of property is based on the notion that labour's product consists of the whole product plus the labour services. This is opposed to the classical labour theory of property, which defines the whole product consisting of the positive product - excluding the negative product (Thompson, 1824; Hodgkin, 1832). Thus labour is not a given input factor, it is rather produced by people involved in the process of production.

The responsible agents in production are eligible to appropriate the whole product and these agents' (i.e. labour) product and since only human beings are assumed to be responsible the concept of labour's product should be followed. No other input factors can be claimed responsible for any action and thus capital suppliers' appropriation of capital's product is rejected regardless of their efficacious utilisation and productivity. Since the juridical principle of imputation is accepted, the responsible party in the production process is labour and this active party is liable for the utilisation of input factors and is eligible to the appropriation of the produced output (including labour's product).

The theory implies fundamental criticism and non-acceptance of the neoclassical theory and is also opposed to the Marxist theory of making the ownership of capital (i.e. the means of production) responsible for specific historic stages and procedures in production. The negation of capital's juridical responsibility and active role within the process of production places emphasis on the human force and self-determination. This viewpoint places the human being in the centre of the economic and societal entity and is in this respect strongly opposed to the basis-superstructure theory and Hegelian philosophy of the human being subordinated to his historic fate.

Although capital and natural resources are productive whilst being used in the production process only labour is responsible for the positive and negative products of production, and the classical labour theory of property only accounts for the positive output (Thompson 1824, Hodgkin 1832). Juridical imputation and responsibility implies that the active labour force is liable for the produced output, since labour created the output itself. Labour creates the net (whole) product and the labour service itself and the subtraction of the cost of labour services leaves the labour product which is the positive output minus the cost of the use of input factors except labour. The relationship has been expressed by Ellerman (1992, p. 70) as the following vectors:

$$(Q,-K,-L) - (0,0,L) = (Q,-K) \qquad (2.5)$$

where (Q,-K,-L) denotes the whole product, (0,0,L) the produced labour service and (Q,-K) the labour product.[37] The labour theory of property insinuates the appropriation of property rights as well the appropriation of obligations. The application of the juridical responsibility of labour is in disagreement with the marginal productivity concept since no marginal product can be produced by input factors other than labour. The human utilisation of inputs (e.g. capital and land) is responsible for the usage and its produce.

The conventional employee-employer relationship is based on an employment contract and the employee has no responsibility as to the liabilities within the production process and thus is not eligible for the appropriation of the property right of the output. The employment contract can be seen as a "quitclaim deed" (Ellerman, 1992, p. 78) where the employer releases the workers from any obligations towards the utilisation of other input factors and the workers voluntarily give up any claims to the positive output.

The employment contact is conjectured to build the basis of capitalist appropriation of the property right to the output and the obligation to cover liabilities. Ellerman uses the labour theory of property to vote for the abolition of employment and voluntary labour hiring contracts and thus for the democratic firm where workers rent non-labour input factors and thus appropriate the property rights to the positive and negative product they produce and are responsible for. He does not object to capital or other input factor owners drawing income from renting out their property since rent or interest rate are not identical with the appropriation of the produced net product. In contrast he objects to companies' shareholders receiving income from this ownership if they themselves are not actively responsible for the production since this represents appropriation of workers' produce. The renting out of capital is an exchange for usage rather than an appropriation.

2.5.1.4 The Inalienable Rights Theory

The employer-employee relationship represents the major organisational obstacle according to the labour theory of property and thus the proposed alternative structural organisation of the production process is the concept of economic democracy (democratic worker ownership, universal self-employment). The concept of economic democracy and the democratic worker-owned firm are characterised by labour renting capital and being self-employed. This is opposed to the classical "employment firm" where capital hires workers' labour within the employment contract relationship and capital can either be privately or publicly owned. The classical debate between capitalism and socialism uses the latter employment firm and concentrates on the capital ownership itself.

The labour theory classifies capitalism as capital employing labour indicated by the employment contract without public or private capital ownership having any significance in this definition. The criticism of the employment contract is its fundamental juridical invalidity in its aforementioned form of not realising the juridical responsibility of labour. The notion of its involuntary nature in the sense of the coercion-or-contract tradition can here not be employed as a critique (Friedman, 1962). Within the involuntariness critique it is argued that inherited property and human capital constrain choices and consent is thereby socially involuntary. The employment contract would herewith be accepted in its validity.

The refusal of the involuntariness critique is based on the inalienist tradition such as the democratic tradition of liberal thought. The inalienability of people's basic and human rights causes contracts which alienate these rights to be invalid. Voluntary contracts which involve the democratic selling of basic rights in a "pactum subjectionis" (Hobbes, 1651) are supported by the alienist tradition of liberal thought and claim employment contracts as the institutional foundation of capitalist production acceptable and valid. The alienist school interprets human rights as property rights and the full assignment of property rights to human basic rights also includes their saleability. Voluntary consent in form of a contract enables the transfer and alienability of basic rights and this includes the transfer of the property right in the labour product as part of the employment contract. The labour theory of property follows the inalienist and democratic tradition of liberal thought and advocates political democracy in the form of a democratic government and economic democracy in the form of a democratic worker ownership. The *de facto* inalienability argument is derived from the fundamental inalienability of indispensable human characteristics. These human characteristics are exemplified as responsibility and decision-making (Ellerman, 1992, p. 127).

Human responsibility is divided into *de facto* and legal responsibility and this separation is applied in the employee-employer relationship. Whereas the workers are jointly *de facto* responsible for the produce according to the labour theory of property, legal responsibility for the positive and negative product is only granted for capital owners who are characterised in shareholding companies by absentee ownership.

The arguments of the imputed legal responsibility and the inalienability of fundamental human rights, such as self-determination, are combined in the proposal for democratic worker-ownership business in opposition to the private or public employment enterprise. Only workers who are actively working in the organisation are eligible to be members of this firm. *De facto* responsibility is an inalienable human characteristic and the impossible transferability identifies *de facto* responsibility with legal responsibility.

The democratic firm is herewith based on the following theories:

1.) Labour Theory of Property (imputed legal responsibility due to inalienability of *de facto* responsibility),
2.) Democratic Theory (governance system, individual decision-making) and
3.) *De Facto* Theory of Inalienability.

The democratic argument for worker ownership is the inalienability of individual decision-making and the classical employment contract legally alienates decision-making. The democratic firm is characterised by delegating decision-making authority to a unified centre, the democratic management and workers thus jointly instead of individually govern the enterprise (Ellerman, 1992).

The inalienable rights theory is strongly opposed to transaction and externality economics, where efficiency demands that the transaction of property rights is permitted if transaction costs are zero and no externalities exist. Since neoclassical theory does not include the time aspect in its analysis of the labour market, labour today is as alienable as labour tomorrow (Ellerman, 1992, p. 158). The general acceptance of the employment contract due to voluntary consent allows the alienability of labour and the transferability of private and political rights with respect to an increase in efficiency and welfare. Ellerman (1992) refers to Tobin's welfare increasing voluntary transaction in political votes (Tobin, 1970). Although political vote-selling is generally rejected, the neoclassical theory allows the transfer of corporate votes and gives no reasoning for the separation of the two.

For clarification it should be noted that the inalienable rights theory focuses on the right of action which is not transferable and not on the final service or product. A self-employed hairdresser does not sell his private right by offering the service of cutting hair where he sells the intangible product and possesses the entire decision-making authority and carrying-out of the action, i.e. the service is at his disposal and he is also entirely responsible for his action. Thus he is *de facto* responsible and also eligible for the negative and positive results of his action in terms of the legal responsibility.

The legal validation of the employment contact as the institutional foundation of the employee-employer relationship assigns the legal responsibility for the positive product and the negative obligations to the capital-owning employer and the factual responsibility of the workers' action to the employee. The dictionary's explanation defines the employer to be always capital owning and individuals who are not owners of the company's capital can only sign employment contracts *on behalf* of the company. Applied to the responsibility school capital is assigned with the legal responsibility. "The employment contract is a contract where the employee puts his service at the employer's disposal. The employer is not always human but always a company. The employee-status excludes self-employed, civil servants and those helping in family businesses." (German Encyclopaedia, Der Neue Brockhaus, Mannheim 1991, translated by the author)

2.5.1.5 The Appropriation Critique

The appropriation critique concentrates on
-the economic capital theory and
-the competitive equilibrium theory.

Conventional capital theory imputes the whole product and its profits to capital rather than recognising that the whole product is a return to a contractual role and not a return to capital. The whole product is not pre-owned because its existence is materialised in the future and the ownership of the original resource (i.e. capital) does not simultaneously include the ownership of this property. The property of the whole product is therefore appropriated by the capital owner since the property appropriated in the future does not have a present owner. The return on capital to be the return to property is conjectured in the critique, i.e. the renting or selling price of capital. The capital theory envisages the return as "net productivity" (Samuelson, 1976, p. 661) or as "marginal efficiency of capital" (Keynes, 1936) and these definitions include the whole product.

The property appropriation critique on the competitive equilibrium theory with positive pure profits (Arrow & Debreu, 1954) finds its basis in the negation of any production function ownership. The production opportunity set shows different combinations of input factors (e.g. capital and labour) and the actual output is assigned as property to the firm. The terminology of firm ownership is fallaciously used, since capital ownership is not necessarily equivalent to the ownership of the whole product due to the responsibility theorem (section 2.5.1.4) and also its dependency on the nature of the hiring contract. Ownership of resources is not an entitlement to property of the "production unit" (Arrow & Debreu, 1954) and the property of the whole product is to be seen as expressed in the input-renting contract. Therefore the property-theoretic assumption of ownership of a corporation being ownership of a firm is erroneous since the corporation's production process could be entirely based on rented input factors. Furthermore the ownership of production possibilities would jeopardise the existence of production arbitrage between input- and output-markets since only the owner could demand the use of the input factors (Ellerman, 1992). As long as free input factor markets exist the Arrow-Debreu-model does not hold in the case of positive economic profits, i.e. decreasing returns to scale and production arbitrage.

The preceding arguments support the general opposition to the system of wage payments in the way suggested by the marginal productivity theory. Human responsibility for actions and objects' lack of responsibility do not allow the application of marginal productivities as values of contribution. The marginal productivity of capital (i.e. the additional output produced when one extra unit of capital is added whilst the other input factors remain constant) is not created by the extra capital but by labour using this additional factor unit. The marginal product of capital can thereby be expressed as the ratio of labour's extra positive product over its extra negative product (Ellerman, 1992).

The fundamental theorem of property theory states that a valid transfer of property implies no conflict between legal and *de facto* responsibility. Within the production process legal responsibility is assigned to the last buyer of the input factors and the first seller of the output. *De facto* responsibility is held by the last possessor of the input factors and the first possessor of the output. The market mechanism of proper appropriation is jeopardised if the two responsibilities are assigned to different parties. The labour-renting capitalist enterprise produces a mismatch of responsibilities in the legal and factual sense (due to the above outlined arguments) and thus endangers and violates the system of property and contract.

2.5.2 The Theory of Economic Democracy and the Firm

2.5.2.1 General Democratic Principles

Economic democracy is defined by Ellerman (1990) as a market economy where the majority of firms are democratic worker-owned firms. This system is fundamentally characterised by private property, free markets and entrepreneurship and the characteristic that employment contracts are replaced by a democratic structure of the firm. The democratic firm is characterised by labour renting capital and the latter being legally and *de facto* transferred to labour and the output for which labour holds the factual responsibility is legally sold by it. The application of the fundamental theorem of property transfer and the "natural system of property and contract" (Ellerman, 1992, p. 238) is the basis for the worker-owned self-managed enterprise. Legal responsibility is correctly imputed due to factual responsibility in the appropriation system under self-employment. The natural system of property and contract is followed and fulfilled in economic democracy or general self-employment. In contrast absentee ownership does not involve any factual responsibility and the mismatch between legal and *de facto* responsibility is given.

Individuals involved in the firm can be divided into two groups: the group of governed people and the group of affected people (Ellerman, 1990). The governed group takes orders from the enterprise management and is under managerial authority, i.e. the workers of the firm. The affected group comprises those individuals whose property or person is affected by the enterprise's activity and are not under authority or control by the enterprise's managers, i.e. the shareholders, the input suppliers and consumers. This classification does not coincide with the assignment of control rights in the employment firm. Direct control rights in the form of positive decision-making authority are held by shareholders and the group of governed people as well as suppliers and customers conventionally have indirect control rights in the way service or purchase can be denied.

Democratic theory is based on the two elementary pillars of the affected interest principle and the democratic interest principle. The affected interest principle suggests that those whose rightful interests are affected by decisions of an organisation should be given an indirect control right in order to protect their interests. Indirect control rights are usually consummated by the market mechanism, where imperfect conditions and externalities are neglected. This principle is concerned with the assignment of indirect negative decision-making authority to the outside affected interests. The democratic interest principle claims the direct control right over an organisation to be assigned to the people governed by the organisation. Within the organisation of the firm the group of governed people includes only the workers and they are thus entitled to the positive decision-making authority, i.e. the right to make decisions of the enterprise.

The affected interest principle and democratic interest principle assign indirect control rights to outsiders of the organisation. Direct control rights are to be realised without jeopardising third parties' interests, i.e. within the constraint of the outside affected interests. The democratic framework applied to an enterprise recommends economic self-determination and self-governance, i.e. workers self-manage the enterprise, suppliers and consumers self-govern their supply and demand.

2.5.2.2 The Democratic Firm

A democratic firm is characterised by the fact that those who manage the firm are responsible to those who are managed, i.e. the workers inside the enterprise. The governed workers in a democratic firm elect the managers, i.e. those who govern, on a one-person-one-vote-basis. Membership in a democratic firm can only be obtained by a person's work in this firm and this membership is synonymous with ownership. The democratic firm implies a general institutional change (with reference to the conventional firm) and alters the conventional ownership structure but does not abolish private property.

The theory of the democratic worker-owned firm is based on two principles (Ellerman, 1990):
-property structure: people have a natural and inalienable right to the output of their labour and
-governance structure: people have a natural and inalienable right to democratic self-determination.
These principles define the rights to vote and to the residual and should be assigned to the workers to achieve democratic self-governance and rightful appropriation of the output.

2.5.2.2.1 Property Rights and Personal Rights

The labour theory of property (section 2.5.1.3) expresses the untouchable right of people to appropriate the output of their labour. The structure of property rights being transferable profit and control rights within the conventional employment enterprise with absentee ownership violates any personal rights assignments. Profit and control rights should be assigned according to functional roles within the organisation if the democratic theory is applied and membership rights are personal rights. Personal rights are defined as extinguishable when a person dies whereas property rights are transferable, either by inheritance or marketability.

The membership in an organisation should be based on personal rights rather than on property rights if the democratic principle and the functional role principle are applied to the economic firm. Following the labour theory of property and the inalienable rights theory (section 2.5.1.4) a conversion from a property based employment firm to a person based worker-owned enterprise changes the property rights system and restores the labour basis of appropriation (Ellerman, 1990, p. 59). The critique of the classical capitalist firm does not concentrate on private property as opposed to public property, it focuses on the owning individuals. Private property is to be assigned to those who have functional responsibility within the enterprise and this simultaneously implies the abolition of the employment contract which is to be replaced by the firm-membership status.

2.5.2.2.2 The Democratic Principle of Self-Governance

The democratic self-governance principle illustrates the inalienable right of people to self-govern their activities. The right to elect is ascribed to those who are governed, i.e. the group of governed people attains the positive decision-making authority. Indirect control rights in the form of a veto are attributed to the affected interest group who has no direct right to decide who will govern and manage the firm. The direct control right coincides with the residual claimancy right and the members of the enterprise are eligible to cover the liabilities and the positive product produced. Direct control rights are personal rights and are not transferable because they are assigned to the functional role of being governed. Those who hold positive decision-making authority elect the board of directors which consists of insiders of the firm.

2.5.2.3 The Financing of Democratic Worker-Owned Firms

The democratic considerations necessitate a discussion of the financial structures of worker-owned firms, in particular structures which allow the efficient utilisation of resources as well as meeting democratic principles. The factual financial operationalibilty of this organisational form will now be considered.

2.5.2.3.1 The Net Asset Value of the Firm and Internal Capital Accounts

The net asset value of a corporation is defined as the value of the corporation's assets minus its liabilities. It originates in the initial capital endowment corrected by the corporation's retained profits and losses over the time of its existence. Present workers might not be responsible for the net asset value and it is therefore not considered as a personal right. The net asset value of a corporation is not linked to any right to vote or to claim the residual and it is described as "social property" (Ellerman, 1990, p. 78).

The problem of the potential unwillingness of the members to retain profits within the corporation (which then become social property) can be avoided by the creation of internal capital accounts. Retained profits are credited on workers' savings accounts in the firm and these accounts may be used to finance the necessary input factors. Workers thus rent capital and receive interest on their pseudo-loans. The internal capital account hereby symbolises debt capital which is owed to the workers and represents internal capital creation.

The internal capital account is also used to finance losses, i.e. each member has a share in the losses during the time of enterprise membership and the respective share is subtracted from each member's internal capital account. This function epitomises the individual worker's entitlement to the whole product and the obligation to cover costs of the input factors as the personal right of appropriation. The utilisation of internal capital accounts is a lien method where debt is paid by debiting the members' internal savings accounts. Although the internal capital account has a property right attached to it, it cannot be resold since the enterprise has a lien against the capital account to cover the workers' future share of losses.

Each new member has to pay their contribution-share into the capital account. The Mondragon-example (section 2.5.2.4.3) is that each member is not allowed to own more than five per cent of the total capital and a share of the capital contribution is required as an initial down-payment (Oakeshott, 1973). Profits are allocated according to the member's labour which is measured in wages or hours worked and not with respect to individual capital accounts. The accumulated values in the account should be paid out after a fixed time period rather than with retirement or work termination in order to share risk-bearing more equally. A "roll-over scheme" (Ellerman, 1990) is characterised by cash payments after the accounts have been debited to cover losses and thus by equalisation of the capital account balances of different members.[38] Roll-over capital or closing balance capital could be paid out by using consols, i.e. issuing perpetual debt instruments which pay interest but which do not have maturity dates (Ellerman, 1990).

2.5.2.3.2 External Financing

Research in external financing of democratic firms is rare which necessitates the turn to external financing of participatory firms which contain some of the classifying features of democratic worker-owned firms. A theoretic analysis of the financing pattern of participatory firms was formulated by Vanek (1971). Comparative failure of cooperative firms is put down to the fact that these corporations have mainly been internally rather than externally financed. In the case of constant returns to scale self-financing and collective membership leads to self-extinction forces. The workers try to reduce the number of members in order to increase the income per worker at given capital. Thus having increased the capital-labour ratio and arrived at a situation with diminished marginal productivity of capital a new force will tend to move to the initial equilibrium through dis-investment and capital consumption. This self-extinction force has thereby reduced the labour capacity and capital capacity - although finally removed to the initial capital-labour ratio. Self-financing in the above case of constant returns to scale is likely to produce under-investment since the marginal efficiency of capital tends to be higher than the members' time preference and thus cause an effect where members are adverse to the employment of new workers because this would reduce the capital-labour ratio and thereby the income per worker.

In the case of first increasing and then decreasing returns to scale, self-financing of a corporate firm leads to both inefficient production at a low output level and to under-investment if compared to external financing. These effects are due to an equilibrium position in the range of increasing returns to scale because here the average product of labour is maximised and this fulfils the main objective of participatory firms. The maximisation of every member's income proves to be technically inefficient causing under-investment and under-production.

Vanek uses his findings to explain the rather unsuccessful operation of cooperative organisations and prescribes increased external funding as a remedy. External financing leads to higher output and the workers retain the accumulated savings in the internal capital account. His analysis lacks comparison of cooperative and capitalist operation and an explanation of how exactly external funds are raised without capitalising the organisation. He nevertheless concludes that the participatory firm with external funding is superior to all existing forms of productive organisation.

An economy which consists of democratic firms does contain an equity market since the workers' shares are not marketable. The equity market's function of efficient allocation and risk diversification can be fulfilled by private markets for physical and financial capital and a public capital market. The scarcity values of physical and financial goods are represented by the private market which prepares for efficient allocation of non-labour input factors. The public capital market is a market for the negative debt instruments such as debentures issued by the democratic firm. The payout to these debentures is mandatory in the form of interest rates and also variable and thus risk-sharing. A major characteristic of the debt instruments is that they do not assign any rights to vote. Non-voting participatory securities are a form of external financing.

An example of this external funding and risk spreading is given by Ellerman (1990) who suggests mutual funds for participating securities. The shares in the mutual funds can be sold on the public capital market and schemes like this might increase the overall performance of democratic and cooperative firms. This type of external funding is expressed in the Model of a Hybrid Firm (Ellerman, 1990).

2.5.2.4 Examples of Worker Ownerships

The following paragraphs discuss different forms of existing worker-owned enterprises. Existing worker-owned companies can be analysed according to

a) the voting rights,
b) the profit and residual rights and
c) the net asset rights.

These elements represent elementary deviations from the conventional property rights bundle.

Common to all different forms of worker-ownerships are a voting pattern on a one-person-one-vote basis and the allocation of the residual to the member workers according to their labour. The workers' labour is often called "patronage", the term describing different kinds of measurement of the members' productive efforts, e.g. hours worked or number of units sold.

2.5.2.4.1 Traditional Worker Stock Cooperatives

Membership shares within the traditional worker stock cooperative are bought by workers. The membership is not acquired on the basis of labour, it is based on the purchase of the share. The share carries membership and capital rights. It therefore does not qualify as a labour-based cooperative because membership is not assigned according to the functional role of working in the firm.

2.5.2.4.2 Yugoslav-Type Worker Cooperative

The Yugoslav type of self-management consists of no command planning over production as in conventional socialist economies. The workers in each enterprise elect the workers' council which selects the enterprise's director. The net asset value within this type of cooperative is treated as common or social property. Any recoupable claim on the fruits of labour, i.e. reinvested profits, are denied to the workers. The common ownership equity structure is characterised by all investment being financed by external debt. It is best suited for small-sized, labour-intense and service-oriented cooperations.

Workers have no individual rights to claim the asset value of the enterprise and the social equity structure implies negative incentives for efficiency and motivation. The original property rights deficiency causes problems due to different time horizons and these negative incentives are often referred to as horizon problems (Ellerman, 1986). Horizon problems arise in labour-managed firms where the net assets of the corporation can not be reclaimed by the workers because they do not hold any property rights. The financial autonomy of the enterprise and the fact that the manager is elected by the workers' council suggest that individual interests are met in paying out most of the residual which then in turn becomes private property. Short-term private rights can be assumed to be stronger than long-term social rights although the individual's workplace depends on the existence of the firm.

The social property implies financing investment with external debt and the increased demand for loans can be inflationary. The property rights structure of social property leads to workers trying to recoup their assets through higher wages. This leads - as in the internal financing case (Vanek, 1971) - to a rejection of new workers in the corporation, the so called "no-employ-effect".

The two major deficiencies of Yugoslav self-management have been expressed by Nove (1983, p. 217) as follows:

1.) Workers have no interest in expanding the labour force because it would reduce their income.
2.) Workers lack a long-term interest in their enterprise because they do not benefit from the company's assets since they are social property and can not be individualised.

2.5.2.4.3 Modragon-Type Worker Cooperatives

The industrial Mondragon cooperation was first established in 1956 and currently contains 106 industrial cooperations. More than 20 000 workers are engaged in the production of consumer durables, computerised machine tools and high technology products. The financial centre of the cooperation is the Caja Laboral Popular, a cooperative bank of which all worker cooperatives are members.

The Mondragon-type worker cooperative is a labour-based cooperative with internal capital accounts. The members start off with paid-in membership fees which accrue interest. The labour-based patronage of retained profits and losses is allocated to the individual capital accounts, which are paid out over several years. The value balance on the capital account is a property right representing the value of the member's paid in membership fee, reinvested values of the fruits of labour and accumulated interest. Alongside the internal capital accounts a collective account exists which receives a portion of the retained profits and losses. This account is not paid out, it is passed on to the next generation.

Membership shares are personal rights and they are not transferable. If a member leaves the cooperative the membership share is retained in the company and the internal account's balance is paid out over a period of years. Since the membership share is a personal right it remains with the cooperation if a member dies, whereas the balance on the capital account is a property right and passes on to their heirs.

Major points of critique of this type of corporation are the reduction in labour mobility and the impossibility of risk diversification, because capital is accumulated within one corporation.

2.5.2.4.4 The Employee Share Ownership Plan

Employee share ownership plans are often used as redistributive instruments following the two-factor theory of Kelso (Kelso & Hatter, 1967). The theory assigns labour and capital individual productivities. It claims that capital is more productive than labour and hereby tries to explain maldistribution between income and wealth. In order to achieve a smoother distribution workers are assigned capital ownership which will in turn increase total income through creating or increasing capital income.

Shares in this ownership plan are indirectly owned through a trust and each employee is assigned an account which keeps record of individually-owned capital. Shares cannot be sold and employees receive the shares when they leave the company or in the event of retirement. Varying numbers of shares can be owned and votes are assigned according to the numbers of shares. Voting and profit rights are thus distributed to workers according to their capital and not according to their patronage. Employee stock ownership plans do not qualify as following the democratic principle as the functional role of cooperative membership is replaced by ownership. This system does not differentiate between property rights and personal rights. The right to govern remains a property right and does not become a democratic personal right assigned to the functional role of working in the corporation. Political democracy assigns the right to vote on the basis of a personal right (as opposed to a property right like in a monarchy, where the landowner is the ultimate decision-maker). The implications for corporate governance of following this approach are that there is a positive decision-making authority for those who are governed and have a functional role of working in the corporation. Self-governance and self-determination by electing representatives in political democracy as a one member-one vote principle is not applied in this type of plan which follows a one share-one vote principle.

2.5.2.4.5 The Chinese Responsibility System

The Chinese forms of cooperative enterprises can be divided into the family contract responsibility system and the factory manager responsibility system. Under Deng Xiaoping's agricultural reform, collective farms established under Mao were broken up into family-sized units and those units leased the land from the local government. The physical lease of the land is close to ownership because it is a long-term lease and all negative and positive profits are owned by the family. The factory manager responsibility system tries to adopt the physical lease of land to the physical lease of the means of production either to the workforce of the enterprise or to a private individual who employs workers. Several minority stock ownership programmes exist for workers and the economy is diversified in that state-ownership, collective ownership and private ownership exist alongside each other. In the majority of cases in the Chinese system the workers are employed by the government and do not have definite property rights in the enterprise since the companies are state-owned.

2.5.2.4.6 Hungarian New Economic Mechanism-Reforms of 1968

The objectives of the enterprise responsibility reforms of 1968 in Hungary were to gain more financial autonomy for firms and to decentralise the process of production. Within the framework of state regulation a partial market environment was created. Markets were created for consumer goods, productive goods and bonds. The Hungarian reform process followed the Lerner-Lange-model of state-socialist firms simulating decentralised, profit-maximising firms in the respect that autonomous firms were supposed to be self-accounting by covering their own losses from their revenues. The programme proved successful within the agricultural cooperative sector.

The persistent state regulations softened incentives and risks of the enterprises, i.e. a profitable firm was levied with taxes or other charges and if the enterprise made losses a "soft budget constraint" was applied (Kornai, 1986). Workers had no capital accounts and thus tended to maximise their short-term payout. Horizon problems existed, such as in the Yugoslav case (section

2.5.2.4.2). The reforms were not very successful because they did not give the enterprises ownership rights and ownership by everybody functioned as ownership by nobody (Schroeder, 1988).

2.5.2.4.7 Soviet-Type Cooperatives

The Chinese system of leasing contracts (section 2.5.2.4.5) was adopted by Gorbachev's reform programme where the people lease land and the means of production for a certain period of time. Under the State Enterprise Restructuring Law of 1987 enterprises in the USSR were supposed to gain more financial autonomy whilst the enterprises remained state firms and the workers were still employed by the government. Although the retained income had to be reinvested a certain portion of this income was allowed to be distributed to the workers on a profit-sharing bonus. No ownership rights were given to the workers and only participatory election rights to choose the managers were assigned. The idea of increasing the financial autonomy was similar to that of the Hungarian New Economic Mechanism in 1968 (section 2.5.2.4.6) and the East German Reform Programme of the 1970s (chapter 3, section 3.3.2.5).[39]

2.5.4 Reform Suggestions

Physical leasing contracts give those who use the land or means of production the right to the residual without assigning them the ownership of the physical assets which are used in the production. Physical lease contracts of depreciable assets such as means of production can prove rather inefficient if maintenance, replacement and new investment are considered. Financial lease contracts rather than physical ones are more efficient with respect to capital maintenance. Here labour rents the financial rather than the physical capital. This suggestion appears to be a valid reform programme for the reconstruction of state-owned companies towards democratic worker-owned firms. State-residual claimancy is transferred into worker-residual claimancy and this could be realised either step-by-step or at once.

In order to achieve worker ownership of the enterprise the company could provide capital accounts for each worker in order to fulfil the ultimate objective of worker-residual claimancy. In the case of a gradual transition workers could be endowed with a certain percentage of the ownership according to their past labour within the enterprise. In order to attain full ownership a loan could be taken from the government which would in turn be used to pay the enterprise's equity from the government. The loan would then be paid back over a certain period of time (worker buy-outs).

The most significant reform seems to be the enterprise lease practiced in the former Soviet Union since it changes the residual claimant. The disadvantage of this reform is that the workers have little interest in the maintenance of depreciative capital if it is government-owned and this provides a serious problem in this kind of lease arrangement. It also involves high transaction costs for the government to maintain the means of production.

The horizon problems can be solved by implementing internal capital accounts as a means of self-financing and the workers will retain their rights to the net asset, i.e. their reinvested earnings. This capital structure is not simply a theoretical construction, it has been exercised over many years by the Mondragon-type cooperative (section 2.5.2.4.3, Oakeshott & Wiener, 1987). Ellerman (1986) has explained by using an accounting method that labour-managed firms with internal capital accounts do not provide any residual horizon problems (which were identified by Jensen & Meckling, 1979). Voting rights and the stream of economic profits, the economic net income which is the value of the whole product, are generally assigned as personal rights to the members of labour-managed firms and internal capital accounts also assign the property right of the net book value to current members. Members of the corporation have property rights to the present whole product but not to the future whole product and thus there is no residual horizon problem.

Only firms with definite ownership autonomy can achieve the efficiency of a decentralised market economy (Ellerman, 1990). The ownership increases the X-efficiency through increased worker motivation. The financial lease and worker buy-outs seem to be the right way to implement democratic principles in the economic process and could have been followed in the East European transformation process. Keeping the conventional socialist ideology of common or social property, or the conventional neoclassical theory in mind this appears to be rather radical.

Within the East European decentralisation reforms workers have become more autonomous and decapitalisation pressures (negation of social property) more relevant. However, the worker-members of a democratic firm with internal capital accounts attain the wealth in the form of retained profits which are added to their account balances and those profits paid out are subtracted from the accounts. Internal capital accounts reduce depreciation pressures since the enterprise's and thus the workers' subsistence would be jeopardised if the net asset value of the corporation was reduced. This argument is supported by Ellerman's two pockets (in one pair of trousers) principle (1990). Decapitalisation of a corporation is prevented if dividends which are paid out to an individual come out of his pocket (i.e. the corresponding loss in the capital value of the company) which would thereby represent a transferral from one pocket into the other. Although the conventional capitalist firm as well as the democratic firm apply the two pockets principle, the capitalist employment firm proves to be motivationally inefficient since it makes use of the employee-employer relationship. The employment contract causes X-inefficiency since absentee ownership does not provide the required motivation for the workers and managers in the firm. The same lack of interest in the company's future applies to socialist state enterprises and to some degree to cooperative firms without any property rights assigned to the workers to the residual and the net asset value of the corporation.

The implementation of motivational means by the absentee owner in the capitalist firm proves to involve agency costs and this problem has been academically addressed by the principle-agent-theory. Similar motivational problems are present in socialist state-owned firms where no property rights are assigned to anybody involved in the enterprise's actions. The "collective incentive" of a socialist firm is added to an individual incentive in the democratic self-managed firm. The divergence between collective and individual interests in democratic organisations was analysed by Downs (1957).

2.6 An Alternative Allocation of Control within the Codeterministic Firm and the Democratic Firm

Taking the analysis of participatory schemes and the democratic firm into consideration it is possible to develop an alternative structure of control inside the firm. This structure is not designed to be a radical change, rather a gradual step towards the establishment of a democratic firm.

The analysis of codeterministic control structures (in section 2.4.2) led to the necessity to place emphasis on the negative implications of a legally imposed mandatory participatory system. A *per se* assigned control right without performance related income will increase the costs of negotiation and the possibility of block votes might lead to the adaptation of a corporate policy which jeopardises the firm's existence in the long run (e.g. steel companies in Germany during the late 1980s). The analysis has so far concentrated on the aim to maximise profits, but it should be noted that employees within the current economic environment are concerned about keeping their individual employment and thus the mobility of labour cannot be expected to be perfectly flexible. Therefore a profit related joint investment scheme might not fulfil employees' prime objectives.

In contrast the theory of the democratic firm principally allocates control as a property right to all members of the firm. The personal right of appropriation and the right to vote are constituted as membership rights according to the functional role within the firm. Although direct control rights are not transferable the principle of self-governance should nevertheless take care of the interests of the firms as long-term existing organisations, the interests of suppliers and consumers as well as the members' free choice of participation which must be guarded. Since it can be assumed that the members on the one hand have non-identical preferences and varying inclinations to get involved in the company's policies and on the other hand have different managerial abilities and knowledge the allocation of control rights has to be differentiated. The suggested control structure should distinguish between primary and secondary control rights to be allocated to members inside the firm. The differentiation between primary and secondary control rights enables an increase in efficiency in the codeterministic firm as well as in the democratic firm. The implications of these rights will be explained in section 2.6.2 and section 2.6.3.

2.6.1 Individual and Corporate Objectives

The analysis of the codeterministic structure within the conventional employment firm tends to generalise aims of stockholders and workers. Care has to be taken with regard to different aims of the corporation's workers. The profit maximising aim has a tendency to hold for stockholders and only to a limited degree for the managerial labour force. The democratic firm on the other hand internalises the corporate objective - e.g. profit-maximisation - through the utilisation of internal capital accounts and protects the distribution of the company's profits to the members of the corporation. Whereas the objectives of the workers within the conventional firm are dependent on the contractual agreement concerning performance related income, it is suggested within the structure of the democratic firm that the profit distribution follows the allocation of control rights. A *per se* profit-maximising behaviour shall not be assumed since behaviour in practice is either determined by a specific performance indicator within the conventional firm or by the assignment of control rights in the democratic firm respectively.

Performance can not always be measured by only one indicator and performance measurement tends to involve costs. If the costs of quantifying and qualifying results exceed its benefits an analysis of the individual's action will not be implemented. The analysis' benefits are such that once the indicator determines additional non-wage income, the indicator becomes a variable in the worker's behavioural function. Since performance related non-wage income is part of the individual's utility function and this utility is expected to be maximised, the indicator itself becomes an optimisational parameter. On such grounds the indicator has to be part of the worker's behavioural function and should be individualisable. Company's profits can only be split up at very high costs and assigned to individual workers. Since profits are the result of non-separable actions of more than one individual (section 2.4.1) they tend to be a very weak indicator. Indicators have to focus on individual action and the particular aim the single worker has to fulfil.

The impossibility of defining individual indicators reduces the worker's utility function to wage-income and a non-pecuniary income which constitutes itself from the work environment within the conventional employment firm. If a positive relationship between the variables of the utility function and performance is assumed, participatory rights can be expected to have a performance-enhancing effect (Furubotn, 1985). The assignment of the possibility of influencing those work-environmental factors by the employees themselves becomes a sufficient condition in order to increase labour utility and thereby performance. Participatory rights should consist of rights to take part indirectly in wage and work condition negotiations in a company (rather than industry) and at a departmental level respectively. If labour productivity is separable at low cost, indicators should be directly assigned to workers and thus become part of the utility function. Control rights on a corporate basis should only be assigned once target values for indicators are met.

2.6.2 The Principle of Free Choice of Participation and Primary Control Rights

The suggested control structure within the capitalist firm coincides with the distribution of control rights within the democratic firm concerning the principle of participation and free choice of involvement. The conclusive control structure should be a flexible organisation where the degree of participation depends on performance and commitment. The structure must be flexible in the sense that each individual worker in the employment firm and in the democratic firm can decide for himself whether he wants to take part in codetermination and primary control respectively. Since every worker has the basic right to participate he is in the position to influence his individual utility function. Workers' preferences are not homogeneous and a consistent indifference map which meets every worker's marginal rates of substitution can not be found. The substitutionability is impossible to measure and the decision about the assignment of marginal utilities should remain at the worker's level. Individual choice is granted and each worker can optimise the utility function himself. At the corporate level an awareness about the factors which constitute the utility function is necessary and this information should be channelled through by a workers' committee or a representative board of primary control rights holders.

Primary participatory rights are obtainable for workers within the conventional firm for whom no performance indicators exist. The option of taking part in the decision-making process gives workers the opportunity to decide whether or not to involve themselves in departmental policy negotiations. Membership of the work committee is purely voluntary and can be terminated by the worker resigning from the company or by terminating his membership. The voluntary participatory structure leads to workers' behaviour according with their individual utility function; this behaviour is expected to increase productivity within the team production process. Since the work committee is designed to participate through representatives in corporate policy decisions, information costs (to obtain knowledge regarding departmental performance) will be reduced.

Furthermore the work committee attains information about shirking behaviour, which reduces the utility of those workers overall who place high value on the work environment (see section 2.2.3.2 and section 2.4.1 on cooperative behaviour). This attitude is represented by the members of the works committee. The work committee attains a control function over workers' behaviour and since such knowledge will be transmitted to the corporate level, actions can be taken at fairly low costs.

The right to attain primary control rights within the democratic firm is granted to every member and it should be obtainable by every member on a voluntary level. The choice of participation is to be ensured on the basis of democratic principles but the free choice has to protect the choice of abstention as well. Primary voluntary control rights aim at decisions to be taken on a departmental level.

2.6.3 Performance Related Income and Secondary Control Rights

Secondary control rights are assigned purely on the grounds of performance and managerial knowledge and can be attained on a purely voluntary basis by all employees within the classic firm. These rights are assigned on a compulsory basis to members in management positions within the democratic firm. These rights contain the full bundle of property rights and imply direct control and decision-making rights for corporate policy within the employment firm. The number of rights to be handed out is limited and depends on the overall company asset situation. The value of rights is determined by demand and supply and no restrictions should depreciate this value. Since employees who buy these shares expect positive future income streams, the expected profits become part of their utility function since income effects are to be expected. Overall this causes an increase in productivity of those employees. Once more the fact that the variables of the utility function are substitutionable to a certain degree and that secondary right holders who are willing to give up their wage-income are going to become stockholders should not be overlooked. This certainly depends on the share value, the number of shares and the expected profits. The maximum number of shares to be purchased has to be decided in such a way that a limited substitutionability between wage-income and profit-share persists. This is necessary because inside ownership linked with wage-income increases efficiency. The joint employee-stockholder status improves the information flow and reduces transaction costs.

Secondary rights within the democratic firm are assigned on the basis of performance. Performance is measured by an indicator which the member wants to maximise, since a positive relationship exists between performance related income, i.e. profit-share and utility. The establishment of the indicator should not be costly since the quality of performance which is expected on a managerial level is defined *ex-ante* with the creation of the managerial position. The management function expresses the indicator and since the individual productivity is qualifiable, the costs of measurement ought not to be very high. A membership agreement defines the indicator related income and profit and a limited number of secondary property rights are handed out to members who perform well. Because the number of secondary rights is limited, a high degree of competition is expected at the managerial level. Although this kind of inter-firm competition increases each individual's willingness to perform well, there are costs connected with this behaviour. Members may try to manipulate the indicators, behave selfishly and non-cooperatively and team work might be difficult to realise. Although the costs this behaviour creates are positive and not negligible it can be expected that these costs are internalised in the long run since those employee-members hold ownership rights in the firm. Furthermore control can be taken by holders of primary rights who themselves through their ownership status have defined negative control rights towards the behaviour of other members. Secondary property rights within the democratic firm are control rights which are not capable of sale. They constitute the ownership and participatory right at the corporate level and are attached to a performance related income and profit-share.

2.6.4 The Work Committee, the Representative Board and Wage Negotiations

The work committee and the primary representative board are made up of motivated employees and members respectively and control the workers' performance. These institutions have the right to propose alterations within the work environment and participatory rights towards corporate policy. The decision-making process should not be based on a majority vote and not involve parity representation, as employees (members of the democratic firm respectively) can attain secondary rights and therefore a parity representation of employees and stockholders or secondary rights holders would be jeopardised.

Wages are negotiated between capital representatives and employee representatives within the conventional firm and between the primary and secondary board respectively. The negotiation leads to a band of nominal wage increases. The actual decision following this guide-line has to be taken at the corporate level by negotiations between stockholders or secondary rights holders respectively and holders of primary rights on the one side and the work committee and secondary rights holders on the other side.

A codeterministic structure which is assumed to improve efficiency leads to a reduction in costs and to a higher productivity within this flexible structure as compared to the legally imposed codetermination or joint-investment structure. The proposed control structure within the democratic firm secures the interests of the members, the creditors and the consumers.

2.7 Theoretical Synthesis

This chapter has aimed at identifying a general theoretical basis for the analysis of transforming economic systems. General system theory has been referred to in order to define the economic system in relation to the global societal system and to understand it in relation to partial societal systems. It has been established that the economic system itself is a partial social system, with the individual being the central subject of any such social entity. A behavioural function was defined, which noted that partial social systems interact and are interrelated. The economic system has been found to bring about economic behaviour depending on the institutional framework. Since it has been set out as the aim of the thesis to analyse the transformation of the economic system, the economic system as partial social system had to be classified according to its structures, elements and features to understand the concrete changes.

The institutional framework has been identified as building the basis of economic action and process because a humanistic approach is employed: the human being is perceived as the centre of any framework and action. Various economic systems and frameworks were identified according to different approaches which aim at the classification of economic systems. The DIM-approach has proven useful to describe the organisational framework according to decision-making, information and motivation structures within various systems. These structures can be used to classify economic systems and broadly differentiate, in a dichotomous tradition, centralised and decentralised economies and to lend the property rights structure a classifying nature. The strictly static nature of this approach was noted and the attempt to add dynamic quality to this classification has been made by emphasising evolutionary approaches which originate in various theoretical fields.

Dynamic evolutionary theories were differentiated depending on the approaches being either non-deterministic or deterministic in nature. Deterministic approaches were rejected as the theoretical basis for the analysis of the economic transformation process due to the reasons given in the according sections. Non-deterministic approaches are conceived to be valid and appropriate as analytical base. Similarities and interconnections between these various approaches were found in their emphasis on institutional economics and corresponding behavioural relations. System-theoretical considerations, the institutional understanding as well as organisational theory can be found to coincide with evolutionary non-deterministic approaches. Nevertheless some aspects of deterministic theories such as the concept of moral allegiance in Schumpeter's group dynamics, the open system in Wiles' approach are appreciated and are part of the constitutional economics and the general perception of evolution. Also Galbraith identifies a motivational structure that is purpose-related in Weber's sense which can be broadly defined as the general motivation in the form of self-interest in any classical capitalist system. This motivational feature is then turned to in the theory of constitutional economics and the structure of control inside the firm.

The analytical basis for the study of the East German transformation is a synthesis of normative utilitarian approaches, such as the institutional DIM-approach and ordo-liberal approaches, the property rights theory and liberal and constitutional approaches in their humanistic and rights-based foundations. The latter humanistic views are addressed because they raise fundamental questions regarding the concept of systems and their influence in utilitarian approaches must be appreciated. However, it must here be referred to the methodological principle - laid out in section 1.2- that factual policy implementations and altered institutional patterns should be assessed against the background of the (potentially) defined and desired objectives. It will be shown in the next chapter that the principles of thought of the East German transformation are fundamentally utilitarian in their institutional nature and this justifies the methodological pursuit of neoclassical principles in places within the analysis. Moral thesis is thus not possible to analyse here because of utilitarian principles being the basis of behavioural functions and morale is not constituted as a principle of action. In this respect it was attempted to elaborate on new organisational forms which implement some of these principles. This control and ownership structure will be later identified as potentially having increased motivational efficiency.

2.8 Modelling of a Dynamic Transformation Approach

The selection and appraisal of the relevant theoretical approaches represents - despite the conceptual relevance - the lack of appropriate dynamic transformational approaches in order to explain and analyse sufficiently why systems change and what kind of behavioural relationships exist within this process of change. Although the static nature of the comparative system analysis is apparent, this analytical framework can be used to express the conjunction of a changing normative constraint and the adjustment process of the systems. A theoretical framework will now be established which concentrates on the dynamisation of the behavioural relationship between changing normative constraints and the adjustment of the partial economic system. The interrelation of partial social systems will be expressed in an adjustment model which culminates in the finding that the change of system elements and structures are not to be seen independently but have to be portrayed within the context of the general system. Rigidity can be found to exist potentially if the structural change has not been internalised in the form of complementarity with the social norm - if to be found - and the other partial systems. The adjustment model attempts to create a dynamic system theory and focuses on behavioural social interrelations. A general link between humanistic based motivational implications can be found in their correlation to the adjustment related rigidity factors in the form of accepted societal goals.

2.8.1 Basic Assumptions

The classification of institutional characteristics builds the methodological basis of the analysis. The interactions of participants are based on a set of information and a certain behavioural pattern. Individual behaviour originates in a specified decision rule or an individual utility function. If a utility function is attributed to a participant, his actions are defined by the desire to maximise utility and behaviour is motivated by the elements of this function and the given set of information. Assuming individual action is specified by orders the "participants' decision to comply or not to comply with an order...depends...on his assessment of the loss or inconvenience he would suffer if he were forced to leave the organisation..." (Koopmans & Montias, 1973, p.40).

Besides the common social objectives such as stable employment and income (an aim which might have to be temporarily abandoned in order to achieve growth), aims specific to certain systems can be recognised. Decentralised decision-making linked with private property, contractarian practice and private commercialism within a legal framework is opposed to central decision-making and control over the output mix and the distribution of output. These opposed objectives deliver the traditional dichotomous classification between East and West (until the late 1980s).

The different objectives and norms and their respective weights describe and influence the economic process, performance and outcome. It should be noted that the continued existence of the system with objectives and norms depends on issues of influence and power (Weber, 1947, 1968). The objective inherent in all systems to maintain and widen individual power describes the feasibility of system changes. The perception of changes potentially being opposed by individuals and groups of individuals leads to the notion that an open and liberal society is a necessary condition for evolution and natural selection. System changes tend to be hindered by those individuals or groups of individuals who are the beneficiaries of the present system and who do not want to forego the non-pecuniary - influence and power - and pecuniary gains. Whether those participants can prevent a system change depends on their scope of influence, e.g. the Russian nomenclature until the late 1980s was able to prevent any radical system changes by its strong influence in political affairs.

The nature of a change can be described as either evolutionary or revolutionary. Evolutionary change is spontaneous in its nature and is not initiated by a conscious act, i.e. it does not aim at a particular final state. The origins of an evolutionary change can be found in changing weights of norms and this change is unconsciously initiated by individuals or groups of individuals. The changes take place within the given institutional framework and are essentially dependent on the political structure of the system and the decision-making processes. Liberalism is another prerequisite for evolutionary changes as the concentration of power which limits the scope of action might not allow an unconscious development. The social decision-making process permitting, spontaneous changes not initiated by a conscious act that take place within a given framework can lead to an entire change of the framework and system in the form of the development from a rudimentary to a complete and final state. This can be explained as a step-by-step process which constitutes a gradual change of value and norm weighting. However it has to be recognised that evolutionary changes depend on diversity and competition.

A revolutionary change can be described as a conscious creation or adoption of a new institutional framework. Although revolutionary changes are often connected with forceful changes one can perceive revolutionary changes as a result of weighting amendments to norms which lead to an entire change of the institutional basis.

2.8.2 The Adjustment Model

The institutional framework of the economic system is assumed to determine the economic activity in interrelation to the socio-economic environment and the political system (see equation 2.1 in section 2.2.2.1). The interrelation of the political system with the environment gives scope for the assumption that the components of the systems (i.e. their elements) are determined by a given norm which defines particular principles and methods and thereby sets a particular behavioural rule. The results of the economic activity can be measured as

a) the production of goods and services and
b) the achievement of wider national goals.

The creation and definition of national goals depends on the societal decision-making process and the political structure of the society.

Formalising the above relationship the societal goal function can be written as

$$B = Q + G \qquad (2.6)$$

where B denotes the achievement of societal goals, Q economic output (goods and services) as one particular societal goal and G are the remaining societal goals.

The national production function Q, where A is the standard level of production (state of technology) and includes any ordinary input factors (which will not be pursued further), where S_e is the economic system and S_p the political framework is summarised in equation 2.7. The model is reduced to the economic and the political system and the environment is omitted (a similarity between the political change and the social environment is assumed). A limited substitutability between the economic system and the political framework is assumed since it is conjectured that they influence the economic activity (e.g. democracy and decentral economic planning). A functional relationship exists between the institutional and political framework and the production of goods and services because it defines the scope of action. For simplicity the production function is defined as linear homogeneous and of the Cobb-Douglas type with the partial elasticities x and z[40]. Marginal productivities in the conventional sense have to be substituted by partial marginal products such as dQ / dS_e and dQ / dS_p. The "marginal product" of the economic system can be interpreted as the effect on the economic output by the addition of a structural element to the particular system. An example is the introduction of the element of free prices within a command economy.

$$Q = A \cdot S_e^{x} \cdot S_p^{z} \qquad (2.7)$$

Since the institutional and political framework is determined by a norm parameter, the constraint of the production function can be introduced:

$$C = (n \cdot S_e) + (m \cdot S_p), \qquad (0 < n , m < 1) \qquad (2.8).$$

The parameters n and m denote the adjustment elasticities of the system framework to changes of the norm and thereby describe the rigidity of the framework and C is defined as the norm constraint. A rigid system is expressed by a low value of n or m and a change in the norm has a small impact on the system, the scope ranging from a flexible system to dictatorship, in the latter case the value the elasticity parameter is going towards zero.

The remaining societal goals G are defined by the existing norm and it should be assumed that this norm defines the institutional framework, i.e. the economic and political environment:

$$G = f(N) \qquad (2.9),$$

where N describes the present societal general goals, a and b being present individual norm parameters, which can be written as:

$$N = (a \cdot S_e) + (b \cdot S_p) \qquad (2.10).$$

The outcome of economic activity Q is constrained by the norms which define the system and the political framework, so that (2.7) is to be maximised under the constraint (2.8).

In order to maximise the production output the Lagrange method can be used and the following function (2.11) which is to be maximised can be constructed:

$$L = A \cdot S_e^{x} \cdot S_p^{z} + h\,(C - n \cdot S_e - m \cdot S_p) \qquad (2.11)$$

$$dL / dS_e = A \cdot x \cdot S_e^{(x-1)} \cdot S_p^{z} - h \cdot n = 0 \qquad (2.11a)$$

$$dL / dS_p = A \cdot S_e^{x} \cdot z \cdot S_p^{(z-1)} - h \cdot m = 0 \qquad (2.11b)$$

$$dL / dh = C - n \cdot S_e - m \cdot S_p = 0 \qquad (2.11c).$$

Rearranging the above derivation, formula (2.12) can be derived:

$$(x / z) \cdot (S_p / S_e) = n / m \qquad (2.12).$$

The remaining societal goals G (i.e. the pre-defined objectives) are also to be maximised under the constraint of the economic production process (equation 2.13). No other constraint is conceived since the norm defines the goals. Changing the individual norm parameters a and b, will affect the economic and political environment and thus the norm, which defines the societal objectives, is changed.

$$L = f(S_e, S_p) + h\,(Q - A \cdot S_e^{x} \cdot S_p^{z}) \qquad (2.13)$$

$$dL / dS_e = fi' - h \cdot A \cdot x \cdot S_e^{(x-1)} \cdot S_p^{z} = 0 \qquad (2.13a)$$

$$dL / dS_p = fii' - h \cdot A \cdot S_e^{x} \cdot z \cdot S_p^{(z-1)} = 0 \qquad (2.13b)$$

$$dL / dh = Q - A \cdot S_e^{x} \cdot S_p^{z} = 0 \qquad (2.13c)$$

Rearranging the above derivation the following formula (2.14) can be derived:

$$(x / z) \cdot (S_p / S_e) = fi' / fii' \qquad (2.14).$$

Using (2.12) and (2.14)

$$fi' / fii' = n / m \qquad (2.15).$$

2.8.3 Conclusions from the Adjustment Model

The relative changes of the societal goal function (dB) due to institutional changes (dS_e) and political changes (dS_p) following normative alterations have to be equal to the relative value of the adjustment elasticities (n,m) for the goal function to be maximised. The materialisation of societal goals and the maximisation of the production function depend on the values of the rigidity factors (adjustment elasticities) whilst the achievement of desired societal goals depends to a very high degree on the rigidity of framework adjustment to changes in the norm (a,b, x, z).

If the institutional and political framework are rigid in the face of exogeneous changes in the norm, the achievement of the societal goals which have thereby changed will not be maximised. In the case of cultural indoctrination and a low value of rigidity we can assume a fast adjustment process. The internalisation of norm changes is vital for the adjustment to changes. An attempt to measure rigidity factors could be based on the general political framework. The societal decision-making process can be assumed to define the values of rigidity and the time span of the adjustment process.

The above equations show that economic activity in a dynamic world of changing system elements and the policies adopted represent a constantly adjusting process. The uncertainty about influencing factors rules out any approach to explain economic activity as a self-perpetuating process. The entire relationship has to be exposed in order to draw conclusions about the transformation process. The rigidity factors operationalise the study of changes in the social structure and how these changes are internalised. The second step is to analyse the implications of the structure for economic activity itself and this can be carried out based on an analysis of behavioural relationships to comprehend the implications of institutional changes. The origin of changes in the institutional framework (i.e. elements of the economic system) depends on the societal decision-making process.

The entity of the decision-making structure can be divided into two levels, the societal and the individual scope of decision. Since the interaction of the two levels has been recognised above in terms of the rigidity factors, the degree to which the societal framework determines the economic activity itself depends on the structure of the economic system. The societal structure can be classified in the range from liberty (seen as the possible individual influence in terms of the democratic decision-making process) to a strict authoritarian doctrine. The structure of the economic system can be classified in the same manner depending on the scope of individual influence in decisions concerning economic activity. The decision-making process coordinates economic activity and the scope ranges from individual decision authority to central uniform decision authority. Once the methodology and approach of transforming the East German economic system has been identified and their economic implications have been analysed the adjustment model will be employed (in chapter 6) to draw conclusions on the effectiveness of the chosen approach, its strengths and weaknesses.

Chapter 3 contains an analysis of the method chosen to transform the East German economic system. It will be shown that only rarely, are any of the previously discussed reform suggestions towards a democratic firm taken into consideration. Instead the methodological basis can be identified as the system classification by Eucken: decentralisation and the establishment of private property rights were the main factors of transformation. The institutionalising of the classifying elements was pursued by the means of legal regulations and the specially set up Treuhandanstalt.

Chapter Three
The Institutionalisation of the East German System Transformation

3.1 Introduction

The East German economic transformation initiated in 1989/90 primarily aims at the establishment of system elements which classify a market economy, in the sense of decentralised decision-making authority and the existence of private property. The transformation methodology is thus theoretically based on the previously described classical dichotomous approach of identifying economic systems (chapter 2, sections 2.2 and 2.3). The transformation of a centrally-planned economy with state-ownership into a market economy with private ownership requires political decisions regarding the concrete privatisation approach. It is expected that bureaucratic hierarchies will be substituted by markets which have to be created (Williamson, 1979). In order to create an economic framework predominantly based on the criterion of private property an incentive system which enables the economy to function in an efficient manner has to be established. This focuses on the introduction of well-defined property rights and ideally the property transformation must be carried out quickly so as to minimise potential negative macroeconomic implications of the transition (lack of investment, unemployment etc.).

The creation of property rights can have different forms of which the following three were discussed as part of the German privatisation debate:
a) Previous owners who were expropriated are restituted with their former property.
b) Property rights are newly allocated and assigned on a factual basis or on a voluntary purchasing basis, i.e. vouchers for workers or the selling of vouchers. This particular scheme would however have ignored the rights of previous owners (before expropriation) and would have probably been overturned by the German Constitutional Court (Siebert, 1991).
c) The property right is allocated to the present user. This allocation of property rights to the present user may after all have benefited the former East German nomenclature.

The multitude of possible privatisation approaches and the opportunities to observe the contemporary realisation of some within Eastern Europe, China etc. are staggering. The aim of this chapter is however not to analyse the approaches with regard to their various merits since the economic and political situation of the German transformation differs from the other countries' backgrounds. Instead the particular methods of transferring the former GDR's national and peoples' property into private ownership as well as modifying the enterprise structures are the target of analysis in this chapter. The privatisation approach aims at a fast privatisation mainly due to the specific political circumstances of the unification. The methodology of privatisation applied is twofold and concentrates as such on the new privatisation and the re-privatisation. Formerly expropriated property was to be re-privatised and peoples' property was to be sold. The property transference was accompanied by an institutional change and an alteration of economic forms and norms.

The property transference and the transformation of economic life are to be appreciated against the background of the constitution, specially created institutions of transformation such as the former Treuhandanstalt (established on in March 1990 and ceased to exist in December 1994) and the legion of legal regulations created to enable a smooth adjustment process. Following the tradition of system-theoretical thought, the relevant ideological, socio-economic and institutional foundations of the former East German system will be emphasised in the following sections so as to allow an appreciation of the essential basis and original status-quo of the transformation's inauguration. The institutional transformation of the economic system took place in the form of establishing decentralised corporate structures, decentralising and breaking up large-scale enterprises and privatising them.

3.2 The Former East German Economic Structure of a Socialist Planned Economy

3.2.1 Principles of the East German Political Economy

The former East German economic system was politically and constitutionally committed to a socialist planned economy. This political dedication can be found in the manifesto of the socialist unity party SED (1976, Part II, C) where the state is identified as the main instrument of the (working) people who are guided by the working-class to form the developed socialist society on the way to communism (translated by the author). Constitutionally the GDR was the political organisation led by the working-class and the Marxist-Leninist party (Article 1 Clause 1 DDRV)[41], and the socialist planned economy was one of the "inviolable principles of the socialist social system" (Article 2 Clause 2 DDRV). Economic policy was placed at the centre of global policy by the SED and the party pursued a policy of unity and economy.

The main principles of the socialist economic order were:

1. The means of production were socialised property and the right of disposal (i.e. the entire bundle of the property right) belonged to the leadership and planning committees of the SED and the state. This implies that the people and the

working class itself had no direct right of disposal - only delegated and indirect ones.

2. Production and distribution were centrally planned and directed. The state directed by the party committee held global economic functions concerning production, allocation and distribution and it was assumed that the state represented the economic interests of society.

3. Distribution was supposed to follow the principle "every man according to his abilities and every man according to his performance".

4. Corporations were mainly engaged in carrying out directed orders and decisions and therefore possessed little right of autonomy.

5. Economic policy had to ensure that the principles of social property and central planning and direction continued to function well and that the objective of increasing the standard of living was achieved by economic growth and the modernisation of economic structures.

3.2.2 The Structure of Planned Economic Operation

Centralised planning and management of production and distribution was - next to the specific order of property relations - the essential structural characteristic of this economic system. This principle stipulates that all individual economic dispositions were to be coordinated and managed according to objectives defined in central plans. A central planning institution had to coordinate objectives set by economic policy with the resources and economic capacity of branches and companies, and accordingly set priorities. Besides the organisation of the entire economy the planning institution was subject to the duty of meeting plan requirements - which narrowed enterprises' autonomy - as well as to centrally set prices. The organisation of planning changed seven times since 1948 and the time coverage of the plans varied plentifold. The structure of economic operation and management was described by Rytlewski (1985) in a way depicted in the following diagram (3.1). It reflects the hierarchical and vertical structure of economic planning in the form of party political authorities and state authorities assigning various production units with plans for their economic operation. The flow diagram epitomises the unilateral relation between the aforementioned authorities and the actual production units.

3.2.3 The Organisational Structure of Combines

The fundamental economic basis within the centrally planned economy of the former GDR was the combine. A combine was characterised by the conglomeration of several nationally-owned enterprises and their central

Diagram 3.1: Structure of Planned Economic Operation and Management:

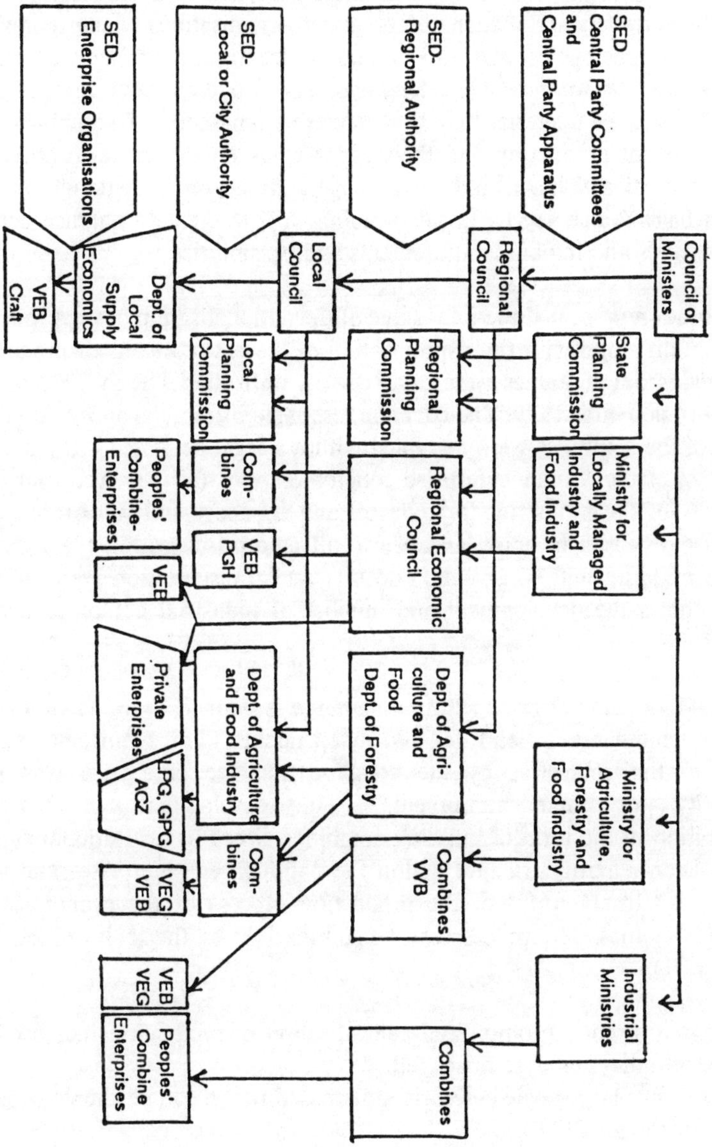

Source: Rytlewski (1985), p. 1501

and unified management. Mainly small and medium-sized enterprises which produced similar goods and services or utilised similar production methods or raw material were combined within these organisations. Combines were horizontally, vertically and diagonally integrated organisations which represented the large-scale businesses and the central concentration of decision-making authority within the former GDR economy. The economic environment of the former GDR was characterised by the industrial landscape of combines, their conglomeration of production and their dependency on exporting to other East European countries. They could be managed either on a regional or on a centralised basis (since 1981). Local combines had to create a balance between sector necessities and regional requirements and possibilities.

Combines represented the final stage of the nationalisation of the production process. It went along with the expropriation of the entire means of production. The first industrial combines were established within the GDR in 1968 and the process continued until 1979. The concrete responsibilities, relevance and general objectives of the combines were regulated within a legal act dated 8th November 1979.[42] Most of the former enterprise conglomerations (VVBs) were put under the authority of the ministries for industry and economy and were replaced by combines (and ceased to exist) and nearly all enterprises within the industrial sector, the building and construction sectors and transportation were affected. Table 3.1 shows the development and number of industrial combines between 1970 and 1988.

The individual enterprise within a combine is defined as an economic unit which was commercially and legally independent. Plan requirements were delegated to the enterprise by the combine and the enterprise was given responsibility for their attainment.[43] The development of enterprise conglomeration in the form of building combines aimed at institutionalising the central decision-making structure within the nationalised enterprises and at the creation of a "closer entity" of the production process of the economic units within the combines. The process can be summarised by the tables (3.2a, 3.2b) and figure (3.1):

1.) The degree of concentration and centralisation of production increased and the number of individual enterprises fell.
2.) The number of large-scale enterprises increased which can be shown using the number of employees (3.2b).

In 1989, 836 800 employees were employed by enterprises employing between 1 000 and 2 500 employees. The highest partial industrial production was achieved by 212 enterprises employing between 2 500 and 5 000 people (figure 3.1).

Table 3.1: Number of Industrial Combines (1970-1988)

Year	centrally-managed combines	regional-managed combines
1970	35	0
1976	45	0
1980	130	0
1981	133	93
1982	133	93
1983	132	93
1984	133	93
1985	129	95
1986	127	95
1987	126	93
1988	126	95

Source: Statistisches Jahrbuch der DDR, 1989

Table 3.2a: Index for Conglomeration of Enterprises in Selected Sectors (1950-1989), 1950=100

Year	Industrial Sector	Building and Construction Sector
1950	100	100
1960	68	80
1970	49	89
1980	19	54
1985	14	49
1986	14	48
1987	13	48
1988	13	48
1989	13	48

Source: Statistisches Jahrbuch der DDR, 1989, own calculations

Table 3.2b: Number of Large-Scale Enterprises (1965, 1980, 1989)

	Industrial Enterprises with >5 000 Employees
1965	48
1980	85
1989	99

Source: Statistisches Jahrbuch der DDR, 1989

Figure 3.1: Number of Enterprises and Employees (1 000s) and Industrial Production (Ostmark bn) - according to the number of employees (100s) employed (1989) -

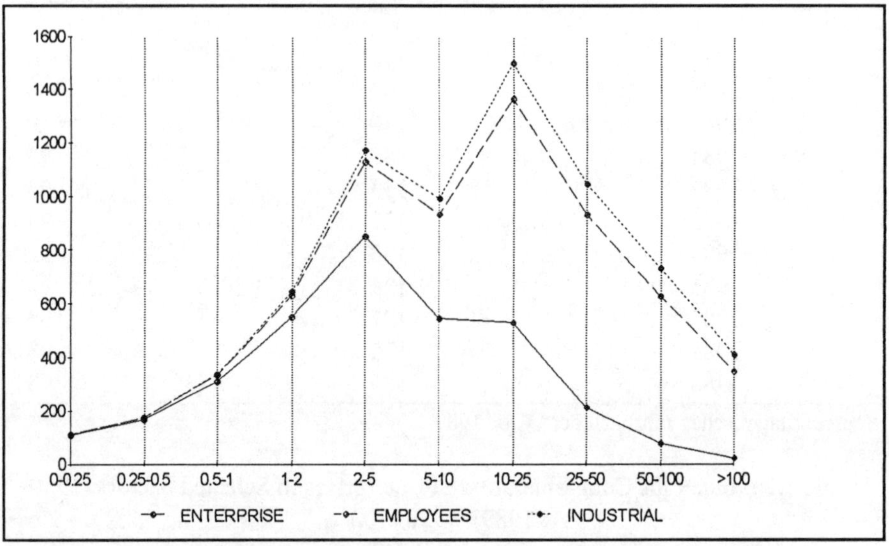

Source: Statistisches Jahrbuch der DDR, 1989

3.) The individual enterprises became increasingly dependent on the combines and their performance was highly influenced by the combines' development.
Tasks and functions concerning the production process were centralised within the combine. This applied in particular to research, development, investment, construction and sales etc. The centralisation of key areas led to high enterprise dependency on the combine's decisions with respect to the production process.

4.) The combine became the basic managing unit of industry, building and construction, transportation and communication. The enterprise conglomeration within the sectors of agriculture and industry is presented in table 3.3.

Table 3.3: Corporations in Agriculture and Industry within the GDR (1970-1989)

	1970	1975	1980	1985	1988	1989
Agricultural Cooperatives	9 009	4 621	3 946	3 905	3 855	3 844
Industry (VEBs, Combines)	11 564	8 477	5 031	3 526	3 408	

Source: Statistisches Bundesamt, 1990

At the tenth party conference of the SED (11.-16.4.1981) the two-staged planning and directing system (ministries and combines) was announced as particularly successful as it implied a fall in production costs (Honecker, 1981)[44].

3.2.4 The Ownership Doctrine of Marxism-Leninism

3.2.4.1 The Three Phases of Expropriation

The creation of the German Democratic Republic on 7th October 1949 was ideologically seen as the transformation of capitalism to socialism and theoretically followed the Marxist Law of Motion. Dictatorship of the proletariat was introduced and the so-called peoples' democracy established, which merely existed as a formal party pluralism but *de facto* consolidated all political organisations under the roof of the "National Front". The National Front was lead by the SED, the single socialist unity party. The social transformation under the impact of the ideology of Marxism-Leninism concentrated - as declared by the Marxist Law of Motion and the Dialectic Materialism - on the socialisation of private property, mainly the means of production. Three main phases of socialisation can be distinguished according to the years the socialisation took place: 1945, 1952 and 1972 (Gesamtdeutsches Institut, 1984; Haase, 1990).

The expropriation of private property (i.e. of large concerns without compensation) was introduced in 1945 under Soviet occupation and followed the orders of the Soviet Military Administration. Part of the affected property was used for the compensation of Soviet claims for reparations and returned from Soviet state property to GDR peoples' property in 1952/53 (Cornelsen, 1981). The agricultural reform in autumn 1945 expropriated all property of land owners whose estate exceeded 100 hectares and all property of active national socialists and war criminals without compensation (reimbursement). The latter type of expropriation followed a referendum in Saxony (June 1946) which was implemented in the other *Laender* by the following August. The 2.1 million hectares of land were used to settle about 200 000 agricultural workers as well as refugees from former Eastern areas (e.g. East Prussia) as self-employed farmers. Farmers who only owned little and low quality land were also assigned additional land in order to increase their agricultural potential. The agricultural reform created the original state corporations in the form of the agricultural nationally-owned production unit (VEG) and the nationally-owned industrial enterprise (VEB). A few years later, in 1948 the creation of the VEB trading organisations put service companies, in particular retail companies under state ownership and organisation. The expropriation of war criminals' concerns had been materialised by August 1946 and the property was transformed into peoples' property. At that time the national production split into 40% which was created by national property, 40% of the production remained in the private sector and the remaining 20% was created by Soviet Stock Companies. In 1948 40% of industrial production was transferred into peoples' property and in 1950 49.2% of the net product was produced by nationally-owned enterprises (Westermann, 1993).

The Soviet Stock Companies were the holders of the former state property and property of the national socialist party (NSDAP) as well as the property of the *Wehrmacht* and were handed over to the GDR. The first phase of expropriation followed the socialist interpretation of history which is identical to the theoretical thesis of Marxism-Leninism and in particular with the necessary evolutionary developments which were predicted in the Marxist Law of Motion. The historic interpretation is characterised by the belief that national socialism and Prussian militarism originate in private property and large-scale land-holding (*Junkerdom*) and the ownership of industrial concerns.

The second phase of expropriation was initiated by the Second Party Conference in 1952 which proclaimed the creation of socialism and followed the first five-year-plan (1951-1955).[45] The collectivisation of the agricultural sector started with the creation of agricultural production cooperatives (LPGs) and covered more than 85% (1961) of the land. In 1960 nearly all private agricultural enterprises were combined into agricultural cooperatives. This development followed the 5th party conference in 1958 during which mass collectivisation was decided upon. More than 83% of the industrial production was produced by VEBs by 1955 and the collectivised sector of craft trade had grown to 28% in 1960 (trade collectives were introduced in 1953). In 1956 state participation was introduced for private industrial companies and the corporate form of semi-state companies in the form of a limited partnership was created. The owner of the enterprise was liable to the extent of his entire wealth whereas the state's partnership was limited. This form of private property was abolished in 1972 with the final expropriation of semi-state partnerships. This phenomenon was due to the increased difficulties private companies had to face (e.g. supply of material and labour, tax burden) and the central ambition of the state to gain influence in the operation of companies whose success was mainly due to private engagement and ambition.

Between 1961 and 1971[46] may be called the period of the establishment of the developed socialist society (Weber, 1991). Ludz and Ludz (1984) on the other hand divide East German history into two main phases: The first phase (which combines the aforementioned two phases) up to the establishment of the Berlin Wall (1961) represents the period of securing power after which (at the latest at the 6th party conference in 1963) the establishment of an economic and societal system that functioned well became the main objective. The last (and here third) phase of socialisation (1972) is part of this era of effectivisation and is characterised by the creation of 11 000 new VEBs out of the decomposition of industrial production cooperatives in the trade sector, corporations with limited state partnership and private enterprises in the industrial and construction sector.

In contrast to preceding socialisations the third phase was characterised by compensation paid to those who lost their private properties.[47] The third phase represents the main constitutional differences between social and cooperative property and the conversion of cooperative property into social and thus state property.

3.2.4.2 Constitutional and De Facto Significance of Socialist Property

Socialist property was constitutionally divided into three categories according to Articles 9-13 DDRV: peoples' property, cooperative property and social organisations' property. Peoples' property included (amongst others) natural resources, water, mines, banks, VEGs and industrial VEBs. Cooperative property was represented by agricultural productive cooperations, production cooperatives in the trade and fishery sector, consumption cooperatives etc. Social organisations' property included all property held by organisations such as the FDJ (*Die Freie Deutsche Jugend*, youth organisation), FDGB (*Der Freie Deutsche Gewerkschaftsbund*, head union organisation) and the SED.

Personal property was allowed according to Art. 11 DDRV in the form of savings, furniture, personal belongings, estates to be used for recouperation and property claims due to proprietary rights. Private property existed in the form of small craft and trade enterprises and within the agricultural sector and in the form of blocks of flats as a subsidiary source of income (Art. 14 DDRV).

Socialist peoples' property was *de facto* as well as constitutionally state property and included all means of production. The peoples' property rights were executed indirectly through the state and the state party (SED). Rights of disposal and utilisation were administered within this political framework by central and local economic committees and the appointed heads of VEBs, VEGs, combines etc.[48]

The form of cooperative property (typically represented by agricultural production cooperatives, LPGs) technically identified the individual peasants and farmers who contributed land to the cooperatives as the owners of their respective land, i.e. in accordance with law. The agricultural productive cooperation for example was characterised by the restraint of disposal for the (technical) owners by the fact that they did not have the right to sell the property. The right of disposal and the earnings of the cooperation were owned by the cooperation itself, but the income of the employees constituted itself twofold, partly depending on the cooperative's earnings and partly on the individual's performance and the respective share the peasants and farmers had originally brought into the cooperation.[49] The socialisation of 1972 transformed a great part of cooperative property into peoples' property and thereby widened the state's scope of action.

Socialist property separated the property right of utilisation from the right of disposal and assigned these two rights to two groups of economic subjects. The differentiation is closely linked to the necessities of meeting the requirements of the economic plan and the earning of bonuses. Employees of state corporations were paid a basic wage plus additional wages for the meeting of plan data or even exceeding the required data (Weidenfeld & Zimmermann, 1989). The property right of utilisation (*Nutzungsrecht*) was concentrated in the state organs of economic committees, such as the Council of Ministers, Planning Commission, Technical Ministry and Industrial Ministry. The right of disposal (*Verfuegungsrecht*) on the other hand was held by the economic units, i.e. corporations, managerial and executive organs. The right and the duty of disposal was delegated by industrial ministries to individual economic units which were not allowed to appropriate the returns and earnings of the unit itself. The economic unit's right of disposal, whose scope of action was limited due to one-year and five-year-plans,[50] mainly focused on initiating plans and putting them into concrete forms. The low variability of the holders of the right of disposal had again led to the failure to implement any inventions and the lack of international competitiveness of the East German economy (Bentley, 1992).

The overall property structure and the main socialist property structure manifests itself in the shares of this property form of the net product which is exemplified in the following table (3.4).

Table 3.4: Socialist Property Form and Share (%) of Produced Net Product* (1950-1989)

Year	nationally-owned and cooperative enterprises (%)	private enterprises (%)
1950	55.3	44.7
1960	83.2	16.8
1970	85.0	15.0
1980	96.0	4.0
1985	95.9	4.1
1988	95.7	4.3
1989	95.7	4.3

Source: Statistisches Jahrbuch der DDR, 1989, *net product is defined as the newly created national income, i.e. the gross national product minus production costs (depreciation, expenses for utilisation, consumption of produced goods and services)

3.2.5 Insufficient Reform Efforts (NES, ESS)

The East German reform period of the New Economic System (NES) introduced by Ulbricht between 1963 and 1970 concentrated on the idea of linking central state planning with indirect control of enterprises using monetary means of direction, the so-called "economic leverages" (Apel & Mittag, 1964). The implementation of the economic reform was necessary because of the ascertained weaknesses of the planning methods which were evaluated as too detailed. They concentrated too much on gross production and national reference numbers and offered scope for manipulation by the enterprises themselves through the suggestion of soft plans (Roesler, 1990). The system of economic leverages was designed to increase the production of high quality goods, the utilisation of modern technology and the rational employment of production funds. This was surmised to be achieved with the definition of profits as the means of measure for the grade of utility for economy and society, and required a revision of competences, duties and rights of economic corporations and the institutions planning the economy.[51] Yet the centrally planned organisational structure of industry as well as the structure of ownership rights remained untouched. Nevertheless the economic leverage was assumed to come into place if the economic rights of VEBs were extended and managerial principles introduced. The introduction of conglomerations of VEBs in 1958 (VVBs) and their increased relevance transferred administrative work from the VEBs and thus made it possible for them to take on the responsibility for their financial funds and to follow the principle of generating the necessary means themselves. This axiom became apparent in the regulation from the 25th September 1964 which decided that any investment plan had to be self-financed instead of being financed through state budget (Apel & Mittag, 1965).[52]

The Economic System of Socialism (ESS) which was introduced in its basic form at the 7th party conference in 1967 (Ulbricht,1969)[53] concentrated on the specification and introduction of indirect managerial methods and the replacement of state management. The ESS took the NES further and was mainly characterised by the introduction of dynamic prices and the granting of bonuses depending on net profits. According to Roesler (1990) the introduction of concrete structural planning was the most important regulation of the ESS and qualifies as being along the lines of the NES concerning its content but he doubts whether the methodology was appropriate to allow corporations the designated relative financial freedom. Concrete structural planning concentrated on a rather small part of the economy and the aim was to enforce the development of this economic part so as to increase the potential to compete and overtake Western industrial nations.

Although the economic reforms produced a short-term upswing, growth problems arose due to the promotion of particular economic areas and this disrupted economic life which eventually led to the return to centralisation in the early 1970s (Cornelsen, 1981). The post-reform policy during the period under Honecker concentrated on raising the standard of living and implementing a policy which concentrated on the consumption side of the economy.

The process of economic transformation intended to change the pattern of the East German economic structure described above. An institutionalist approach was adopted in attempting to achieve this transformation. The institutional basis was the temporal establishment of the institution Treuhandanstalt (also known as Treuhand, THA) and the implementation and enforcement of newly passed legal regulations as well as the adaptation of existing West German law. The method of institutional transformation will be elaborated within the remaining parts of this chapter. Its inadequacy and the introduction of further rather pragmatic transformational policies will be referred to following the analysis of the initial institutionalist approach.

The transfer of property from national to private ownership and the introduction of decentralised planning employed a twofold transformation in three steps which did not necessarily follow a temporal sequence. The first step was the conversion of national wealth into wealth held by the trust agency and local authorities. The second step was the decentralisation of company structures and finally private property rights had to be established through a structural privatisation policy. The legal regulations for the deconcentration and separation of economic units were passed after the transference of wealth to the Treuhand and after some enterprises had already been sold. This can be interpreted as a lack of political knowledge and general ambiguity towards the exact privatisation strategy. The concrete methods of the institutionalisation of the economic transformation are illustrated in the following sections and will not necessarily correspond to the above sequence, instead they are structured according to the system patterns identified above.

3.3 Transformation of the Centralised Structure of Organisation and Decision-Making

Prior to German unification the reform government of Hans Modrow[54] assigned preliminary property rights to the trust agency Treuhandanstalt and the corporatisation of former nationally-owned enterprises was initiated. At this time of transformation the East German government still held the central decision-making authority for economic affairs and thus also for all enterprises.

The first step of institutional transformation concentrated on the establishment of decentralised structures of organisation. Formerly centrally planned and directed enterprises were converted into companies with decentralised decision-making and information structures. This approach follows closely the DIM-approach (Neuberger, Duffy, 1976) since it is believed that organisations which are characterised by decentralised structures are more likely to survive the competition within a market economy. The central aim was to create efficient structures and it is surmised that motivation within decentralised and less hierarchical organisations is higher than within strictly hierarchical orders (Weber, 1947). The second pillar of the organisational transformation is the trust institution Treuhandanstalt whose structure also followed decentralised principles.

3.3.1 Corporatisation of Nationally-Owned Enterprises

The Treuhandanstalt (formerly known as *Anstalt zur treuhaenderischen Verwaltung des Volkseigentums*) was officially established on 1st March 1990 and the original decree of foundation determined the institution's objectives of denationalising the economy, transforming company structures as well as safeguarding and protecting the peoples' property.[55] The trust agency was to exist until a new constitution was accepted. It was subordinated to the government and had to report to the Peoples' Chamber. The East German Council of Ministers passed an administrative act - also on 1st March 1990 - to transform nationally-owned combines, enterprises and organisations into company structures which were suitable for a market economy, i.e. stock companies. Corporations which were listed in the East German Registry of the Peoples' Economy (*Register der volkseigenen Wirtschaft*) were transferred into joint stock companies (KGs). Included in the Registry were mainly nationally-owned economic units (VEBs), combines, nationally-owned organisations and other legally independent economic units. The decree of March 1990 assigned national property which was listed in the above mentioned register to the trust-holding institution. The total number of state-owned enterprises and plants within this registry surmounted to 8 000 enterprises comprising 45 000 plants (Treuhandanstalt(a), 1994). At this stage of corporatisation no decisions were taken regarding the re-assignment of ownership and all property remained in the ownership of the people. Nevertheless the Modrow-government discussed - predominantly in February 1990 - several options of joint-ventures in the form of sales of shares (50%) of public stock companies to Western European countries. (The decree on joint ventures was passed in January 1990 and opened up the possibility of international co-operation and selling shares to foreigners.) Most of these projects also considered the allocation of shares to employees of the respective enterprises (Luft, 1992).

The Treuhandanstalt held these companies' shares by trust and was not assigned property rights prior to the passing of the *Treuhandgesetz* (THG), the law prescribing the objectives and actions of the Treuhandanstalt. The institution was supposed to restructure enterprises that were still peoples' property. The enterprises were transformed into corporate bodies and the corporate rights were carried out by the Treuhandanstalt. Although the possibility of the

Treuhandanstalt selling corporate shares existed, the privatisation requested a special legal act which had to be accepted by parliament. With the passing of the Treuhand-law (THG) on 17th June 1990 the original purpose of the Treuhandanstalt (to administer peoples' property in the interests of the general public) was remodelled to the purpose of evaluating, privatising and using the property. By law all East German registered state-owned enterprises were transformed into public stock companies and companies with limited liability which became the property of the Treuhandanstalt by making the institution the rightful owner of the shares and assigning the economic power of disposal to this institution.

Corporations which had not been transferred into stock companies by the 1st July 1990 were transformed by law into stock companies (Paragr. 11 THG). In particular the law specifies that combines were to be transferred into public stock companies (AGs) and nationally-owned enterprises (VEBs) and similar economic units into companies with limited liability (GmbHs).

3.3.2 The Assignment of Limited Private Property Rights to the Treuhandanstalt and TH-Corporations

Property which was formerly held on behalf of the corporate enterprises either by the trust agency or other subjects of rights and duties by German law (*Rechtstraegerschaften*, predominantly holding real estate property) was accordingly assigned to the stock companies. Although Paragraph 11 of the THG transferred peoples' property into the ownership of corporations, the enterprises were not the holders of full property rights because companies' shares were owned by the Treuhand and the TH-enterprises. Nevertheless the new law established private property rights through the general creation of stock companies and the shares of the entity of transformed companies were assigned as property to the respective TH-stock companies (the division of the TH-stock companies was industry-based).[56] In total the ownership of some 8 000 former state-owned enterprises and 44 000 plants was re-assigned.

According to Paragraph 1 Clause 4 THG, the trust institution Treuhandanstalt became the owner of the stock companies which were created by the transformation of former national economic units. The THA served the privatisation of national property employing principles of a social market economy by law. Property of the newly organised enterprises was transferred to companies owned by the TH-AGs and the structures were those of stock-companies which pursue objectives set by themselves.

3.3.3 The Decentralised Structure of the Treuhand

The THA qualified as an institution under public law (*Anstalt des oeffentlichen Rechts,* Paragr. 2 THG) and was characterised by the combination of the assignment of administrative wealth and administrative employees in order to pursue specific public objectives which were outside the normal scope of state and public administration. The main features of this institution were that it did not have any members (in contrast to conventional corporate bodies) and that its creation required a decree in the form of a federal law (Article 87 III Basic Law). This respective decree was passed in form of the Treuhand-law.

The decentral organisational structure of the Treuhand is laid down in Paragraph 5 of the TH-statutes dated 18th July 1990 (*Satzung der Treuhandanstalt*) and the THG also stipulates that the THA was allowed to fulfil its objectives within this decentralised form by using TH-corporations (Paragr. 9 THG). Corporate enterprises which were created out of the former nationally-owned enterprises, combines etc. were transferred to the Treuhand corporations and were to be monitored by the Treuhand head office and the regional Treuhand subsidiaries. The THA carried out its tasks by using the TH-stock companies which had to secure the privatisation and utilisation of national property according to commercial business principles. According to Paragraph 7 of the THG, TH-stock companies had to be created by the founders supplying the entire equity capital and their shares initially were not tradeable. The TH-stock companies immediately became owners of shares of stock-companies and companies with limited liability which were held by the THA. The TH-council of administration allocated the shares to different stock companies according to suitability (e.g. on grounds of regional issues). The structure of action was decentralised by assigning enterprises with less than 1500 employees to 15 TH-subsidiaries which had been operating fairly autonomously. Industrial divisions of the TH-head office in Berlin dealt with the larger enterprises. Treuhand-AGs were established in the following economic sectors: heavy industry, investment goods industry, consumer goods industry and service industry.[57]

The decentralised structure of the Treuhand can also be exemplified by different TH-organisations having been designed and made responsible for the realisation of individual areas of economic transformation. The TLG (*Treuhand-Liegenschaften-Gesellschaft*) was designed as the organisation to manage real estate property which was considered essential for the operation of commercial enterprises. A separate TH-organisation was responsible for the management of real agricultural and forestry property: the BVVG (*Bodenverwertungs- und -verwaltungsgesellschaft mbH*) was created in 1992 for this purpose. Most of the agricultural and forestry property has been subject to new privatisations because expropriations in this area were carried out as part of the extensive agricultural reform before 1949 and are irreversible.

The THA was controlled by the Federal Government and the Finance Ministry with the act of unification. The federal government had to appoint an administrative or supervisory board to the THA. The THA supervisory board of the THA consisted of 20 members, five of whom were representatives of the new *Laender* and the remainder (as well as the chairperson) were appointed by the federal government.[58] The supervisory board appointed the president and the four members of the board of governors (*Vorstand*) and the board of governors itself appointed the members who represented the THA within the supervisory board of the TH-corporations. However the intended factual benefit of this decentralised structure on the corporate level can seen ambiguously if one considers the origin of the relevant members of the THA and its respective bodies. The board has been identified as containing representatives of main interest groups of the German economy (Carlin 1993): "The Ministries of Finance and Economics were represented, a number of large German companies, foreign business, the trade unions, the East German federal states and the Bundesbank." The HWWA Institute for Economic Research in Hamburg doubted that Western management and Western members of supervisory boards were interested in creating productivity and competitiveness in the East German market because of their desire not to establish potential competitors for their own branches. It was also suggested that in some cases the closure of an enterprise was preferred to the privatisation or selling of the enterprise to a third party (Haertel, *et al*, 1992).

The area of responsibility of the THA was extensive and, despite the institution's control by the Federation (*Bund*), this structure of decentralisation has not always implied benefits. Doubts can be expressed regarding the ability of civil servants to take decisions with respect to corporate situations and the fates of enterprises. Despite these concerns, the composition of the THA's boards seems to have reflected some factual competence. Moreover the fact that the agency qualifies as an independent organisation despite the Federation's control might have ensured that decisions were taken on economic rather than political grounds. Despite the specific political-economic interests of the East German region the Treuhand's activities legally fell into the Federation's area of responsibility and not into that of the new federal states (Westermann, 1993). Although structural and regional policy are generally allocated to the federal states they could only take part in the decision-making process via their representation in the administrative board of the THA (Article 25 Clause 2 Sentence 2 UT).

3.3.4 The Organisational Structure of Newly-Corporated Enterprises

The decentralised organisational structure of the THA in the form of TH-AGs was supported by the legal necessity of newly created public capital stock companies forming supervisory boards according to German corporate law (Paragaphs 95-116 AktG). German corporate law regulates companies with limited liability less strictly in that they can appoint a supervisory board if any such institution is established in the articles and memorandum of association (*Gesellschaftsvertrag*). Supervisory boards have the general functions of supervising corporate governance and inspecting yearly accounts and company reports. Supervisory boards of TH-corporations have had the particular functions of debating reform proposals with the - mainly East German - management and to monitor the creation and implementation of restructuring plans. The companies' supervisory boards were characterised by majority representation of Western, mainly German companies, according to Carlin and Mayer (1992). This phenomenon might be explained with the above mentioned constitution of the boards themselves, i.e. the mainly West German members of the THA supervisory board announce the members of the board of governors which itself appoints some members of the TH-corporations' supervisory boards.

Employee representation within supervisory boards had been suspended until April 1991 and the employees' right of suggestion was temporarily transferred to the unions represented in the supervisory board (see Chapter 2, section 2.4.2.2.1 for legislation on codetermination). The former Modrow-government passed a law concerning participatory rights of employees in the decision-making process of restructuring enterprise. This law was accordingly suspended after the general elections on 18th March 1990.

The institutional process has substantiated the decentralisation policy and transferred major corporate decision-making authority to the private sector. The decision-making and information structures have been decentralised and corporate policy is executed within the newly corporatised corporations by East German management and employees. The question occurs whether the East German employees and managers were capable of successfully materialising these functions of autonomous decision-making which had been transferred to them within a very short period of time. An attempt to import Western managerial and technological knowledge via the Treuhand, its subsidiaries and the supervisory boards of the Treuhand-corporation was made, but the low propensity to migrate to the East by West German employees still creates a severe problem for the diffusion of knowledge and in particular of managerial responsibility and decision-making willingness.

3.4 Deconcentration of Combines as Basis for Competitive Market Structures

The time sequence which has been followed *de facto* can be described as the transference of wealth and the right of disposal to the Treuhand as the initial step followed by legal regulations regarding the privatisation policy. The fact that strategies to deconcentrate large-scale enterprises and regulations were introduced at a time where the process of privatisation had already started, represents a weakness of transformation policy.

3.4.1 Competition Law and Policy: Principles and Assumptions

The transfer of national property and wealth has been regulated by the THG which expresses the principle decision in favour of the economic order of a market economy and implies, besides the necessary establishment of private property rights, the creation of structural assumptions in order to achieve workable competition between companies. The structure of concentrated combines was not compatible with this principle since no workable competition could develop within the given structure of production. (Competition is defined here as stipulating a sufficient number of enterprises which decide independently and produce and supply economically and efficiently.) Thus deconcentration was inevitable in many cases, i.e. combines had to be broken down and split into several production units in order to create the necessary foundation for a competitive market economy.[59]

German legislation does not provide a particular explicit economic constitution. However different individual legal regulations and individual laws qualify as quasi competition law. These regulations focus on the establishment of conditions which allow the creation of competitive market structures and the promotion of small and medium-sized companies. To achieve an efficient policy of deconcentration the establishment of a deconcentration committee was suggested (Cox, 1990) but not put into practice. Instead a legal solution was chosen and the deconcentration issue was transferred to the Treuhand for execution.

Deconcentration policies which focus on the most relevant forms of horizontal and vertical combines can thus be claimed successful if they create competitive enterprises (in the sense of conventional economic theory). The policy therefore had to follow the principle of establishing the minimum economic size of the business required to be nationally and internationally competitive. The deconcentration of enterprises as well as the separation of economic parts had to ensure that minimum economic sizes did not conflict with the realisation of economies of scale. The determination of a minimum economic size had to consider that such size essentially had to allow technical and scientific progress and innovations. Furthermore care had to be taken that important advantages of economies of scope, which were created by vertical conglomeration and which might have strengthened the chances of the survival of enterprises, were not lost. Positive and negative effects of vertical integration thus had to be evaluated individually in each case. It has however been generally assumed that the size-argument is a precondition for the successful implementation of a market economy based on competition. The main objective of competition policy according to particular German competition laws (*Kartellgesetz, Gesetz ueber marktbeherrschende Stellung*) has been interpreted - with respect to East German company structures - as the deconcentration of vertically integrated businesses in order to create workable competition and to decrease the inflexibility which was associated with the combine structure. The law specifies that market situations which are legally considered as not competitive (e.g. in the sense of market shares) are only allowed to exist or to be created by merger if a general public interest exists and this would require ministerial permission.

Not all economic areas were to be deconcentrated (e.g. water, electricity) and a pragmatic approach was followed in these cases. Any deconcentration policy was dependent upon the definition of the relevant market and this was to be considered as the entire German or European market. The deconcentration of any combine had to be evaluated on a case by case basis and any cost-efficiency analysis was assessed individually.

With respect to horizontally integrated combines, the transformation aimed at deconcentrated enterprises employing resources at their normal capacity. This required individual analysis of different economic areas due to sector-specific circumstances. The objective here was also to create enterprises which produce at minimum costs and generate an economic rent. Deconcentration *per se* in any case would not have been sensible and production techniques in particular economic areas had to be given individual consideration. Individual analysis ensured that the newly created small and medium-sized companies were able to produce efficiently. The aspect of "miniaturisation" of production, i.e. efficient production of small quantities within small and medium-sized companies can be made out as having been pursued as the main concept of the deconcentration process. It must be pointed out here that these policies utilise pre-defined conceptions of economic structures and economic actions. The emphasis on utilising these definitions in the sense of German ordo-liberal principles goes beyond the economic policy of creating and safeguarding structures which ensure economic functioning in the Hayekian sense, because the market share and company size approach can be interpreted as aiming at particular final states of interaction between economic agents. The Hayekian institutionalist approach would proclaim the creation of a framework in which economic situations can evolve according to economic forces rather than according to structures which were pre-defined and then implemented.

3.4.2 Pragmatic Deconcentration Sanctioned by the Separation Law - *Spaltungsgesetz* -

With the validation of the THG on 1st July 1990 all nationally-owned property transferred to the THA under the East German reform government of Hans Modrow was to be privatised. During the first few months after the passing of the Treuhand-law the THA met the demand for some small and medium-sized companies which were then sold, but it soon became obvious that an active supply-side policy of deconcentration was necessary in light of the bulk of large-scale units whose capital stock continuously deteriorated due to restructuring policies not yet initiated. On 5th April 1991 the separation law (*Spaltungsgesetz*, SpG)[60] was passed and the THA was authorised to deconcentrate the structures of combines and enterprises in order to meet its objective of privatisation by sale. Paragraph 1 of the SpG sanctions the following two ways of deconcentration:

1.) Stock companies' wealth is split up and the entity of its divided property is thereby transferred to the newly-created stock companies. The transferring enterprise is wound up without liquidation.
2.) Parts of the stock company's property are separated and the entity of the property part or parts is transferred to one or more newly created stock companies. The transferring company continues to exist.

Shares or stakes in the newly formed companies were assigned to the Treuhand or in the case of indirect constructive possession of the original company to the TH-stock company. The representative body of the transferring company, i.e. the board of governors of a public stock company or the managing director of a company with limited liability (and the respective bodies of companies in foundation) had to formulate a plan of division[61] which had to contain specifics regarding the division which was to be legalised by a lawyer. The board of governors was elected by the supervisory board of the respective company according to corporate law (AktG). Although German participatory law determines parity representation of employees within the supervisory board of public stock companies (and it should be expected that the employees were East Germans), supervisory boards have often been chaired by and consisted of at least some West German members (Carlin, 1994). According to Paragraph 2 Clause 4 SpG the division plan had to be forwarded to the works council, which did not have any decision-making authority with regard to the formulation or implementation of any deconcentration policy and neither had employees - apart from their representation within the supervisory board. The plan was eventually decided upon through the acceptance of the corporate members (*Geschaeftsfuehrer*, GmbH) or the shareholders (*Aktionaere*, AGs) of the transferring company, i.e. either the Treuhand or the TH-corporations. The pattern of decision-making regarding the execution of deconcentration can be thus described as the company's representing board having had the right of suggestion and the Treuhand-institutions having had the final right of decision-making concerning the acceptance of the plan.

The segregation and separation of enterprise parts along with their new combination thus became legally possible in order to meet the demands of potential purchasers. The original number of 8 500 enterprises which were held by the THA (THA-portfolio in 1990) increased to 20 121 enterprises and enterprise parts (Treuhand(a), 9/94). The introduction of the separation law in April 1991 induced an increase in privatisation and a monthly total of 544 privatised enterprises and enterprise parts was achieved in May 1991 (Treuhand(a) 9/91). This monthly record was clearly above the average 370 privatisations per month until September 1991 and further monthly figures remained above the previous monthly average. These figures unambiguously reflect the positive impact that the new separation law and deconcentration strategies had.

The timing of the passing of the separation law has been severely criticised and it has been argued that the timing represented the incompetence and helplessness of the government concerning the economic restructuring in East Germany (Luft,1992). Although the separation policy was initially motivated by the structural objective of the promotion of medium-sized enterprises it has been evaluated as a pragmatic approach of selling viable parts of the combines first, and mainly to Western investors. The late introduction of the separation policy and the temporal immobilisation of East German large-scale businesses may well have been a political decision not to create competitors for West German suppliers (Luft, 1992).

It should also be noted that the predominant structures within market economies are not small and medium-sized companies and that imperfectly competitive structures are dominant in the West German economy and also internationally. It is conjectured that the option of creating business groups with similar production profiles which were then to be made viable and which could have created synergy effects was not discussed. Synergy effect considerations were, and still are, interpreted as deemed to be linked with COMECON trade in a fairly blatant manner (Carlin, 1994). It seems that the political decision was mainly to draw Western and foreign investment into the East German region and it has become evident that the main capital is actually held by Westerners (see chapter 6, section 6.3.4). Despite these criticisms with regard to the deconcentration policies, the pragmatic approach in the form of the separation law sanctioning the breaking up of existing structures to meet factual demand can be theoretically justified as amending the initial strictly institutionalist approach of creating pre-defined structures. The passing of this regulation proves the inability of one institution - here the Treuhand - realising market demand and shaping economic structures in the form of its intended aims and objectives.

3.5 Establishment of Unambiguous Property Rights

3.5.1 German Political Unification and its Constitutional Property Rights Implications

It can be suggested that debates on the issue of privatisation were decided by the East German general elections on 18th March 1990 and the victory of the Christian Democrats (40.82%) over the Social Democrats (28.88%). The latter suggested publicly prior to the elections that shares in investment corporations should be allocated to East German citizens.[62] The outcome of the elections formed the future of the transformation process and the time to prevent "the final expropriation of East German citizens" (*Buergerbewegungen, Buendnis 90*, Green Party) had passed. It was surmised by the former East German Minister of Economics, Christa Luft (1992) that the citizens at this stage of change were more interested in the actual currency conversion than in issues on property and ownership, i.e. the previous vehement public engagement ceased to exist. The reform concept of the Modrow government concentrated on the establishment of competition, a slow privatisation of corporate shares and creation of private ownership, the restructuring of companies prior to privatisation, deconcentration of the combine structure as well as the liberalisation of international trade and the freedom of economic activity. The outcome of the elections in March 1990 and the establishment of the Christian Democratic government might be interpreted as a change from economic reform programmes within an East German state to political unification. The trust agency's prerogative of safeguarding peoples' property with respect to interests of the general public was changed with the new legislation shortly before unification under the de-Maziere government (CDU, *Demokratischer Aufbruch, Deutsche Soziale Union*).

Prior to German unification a change in the constitution of the GDR on 17th June 1990 established the right of private property for real estate and means of production (Article 2, *Gesetz zur Aenderung und Ergaenzung der Verfassung der Deutschen Demokratischen Republik vom 17. 6.1990*).[63] The GDR joined the Federal Republic under Article 23 of the German Basic Law[64] on 3rd October 1990 which made the basic law applicable to the new *Laender*. Accordingly the guarantee of private property, its duties and the principle of property serving the public welfare (Article 14 Basic Law) became applicable. The initial constitutional change of 17th June lay down the necessity for further concrete regulations concerning East German property. The process of privatisation and transforming nationally-owned property into private property was correspondingly regulated by the amendment regarding the obligations of the trust agency and the passing of the Treuhand-law on the same day. Paragraph 1 THG formulates the order to privatise national property. The objects of the creation of property rights were a) privatisation of corporations, b) re-privatisation (to former owners), c) reinstating of real estate to their former owners, d) restitution of wealth to local authorities and e) privatisation of dwellings.

The Treuhand, besides becoming the owner of all stock companies which evolved from all former national enterprises also dealt with publicly owned land (formerly part of the VEGs) in the agricultural sector (28% of the agricultural land and 66% of forestry at the time of transference). The Treuhand-law determined that the Treuhandanstalt was to take care of the economic, ecological, structural and ownership specific peculiarities of this sector regarding its privatisation and restructuring. The agricultural and forestry sector's privatisation had thus not been clearly specified within the law. Clearer regulations were laid down in the third bylaw to the Treuhand-law dated 29th August 1990.[65] This bylaw assigned the wealth of the nationally-owned agricultural enterprises (VEGs), national forestry enterprises and organisations, national fishing enterprises and nationally owned farms to the Treuhand as a trust holding institution. Corporations which were formerly managed by local authorities became federal property of the Treuhand and local authorities could apply for the restitution (of for example transport companies). Publicly owned real estates were assigned as property to the regional administrative body. The *Bundesbahn* and *Post* became owners of the relevant institutions and the ownership of public dwellings was assigned to local authorities.

Despite the main aim of privatising national property, property according to Paragraph 1 THG *could* - as long as specified in legal regulations - be transferred to local authorities (*Gemeinde, Staedte, Kreise, Laender*) as well as into public ownership. National property which used to be employed for local purposes and services *was* to be transferred to local authorities, *Staedte* and *Gemeinden*. Excluded from the transformation was national property which was subordinated to the legal entity of the state, the *Deutsche Post*, *Deutsche Reichsbahn*, waterway-administration, administration of public road-infrastructure, corporations and institutions under local authority and economic units which applied for liquidation etc.

The economic system order intended (namely that of an efficient market economy) required the establishment of private property of the means of production as the prevailing type of property right. These private property rights were designed to be created in a two-way approach: re-privatisation and new-privatisation. As will be noted in section 4.2, re-privatisation is to be understood as the restitution of property to former owners prior to nationalisation and collectivisation, and new-privatisation is to be defined as the sale of property objects to new purchasers. The initial priority lay with the re-privatisation according to the Unification Treaty. The promulgations of additional laws and regulations (*Gesetzeserlaesse*) since the UT has been passed have nevertheless re-designed the process of re-privatisation, including changing its weight and degree of importance. The precedence of investment over restitution has changed the initial concept of privatisation and established the superiority of new and third privatisation.

In order to draw conclusions about the merits of this chosen path of privatisation it is necessary to establish facts regarding the legal framework. The appraisal might touch the area of constitutional economics but it does not attempt to touch on matters of the constitutional right.

3.5.2 Re-Privatisation of Peoples' and State Administered Property

Private ownership of the means of production is a constitutional element of a market economy. Although most real economies are mixed economies - some areas are dealt with by the public economy - public involvement in economic affairs mainly needs specific reasoning and investigation. Against this background of principles it had to be investigated which combines and nationally-owned enterprises were to be privatised and which areas were to remain within the public sector.

The extensive debate regarding the methodology of establishing private property rights has emphasised - besides the investment priorities - the discussion concerning compensation, formal or real restitution of the property. The general advocation of repressing property restitution and concentrating instead on new privatisation (Siebert, 1991, Sinn, 1992) was constitutionally suppressed. The debate focused subsequently on the precedence of compensation before restitution. This notion was rejected by Willgerodt (1993) who points to the fact that the cost and time of administration associated with the assessment of the eligibility for compensation are identical to - not higher than - those associated with factual restitution. This notion can be supported as the value (amount) of compensation had to depend on the sales value if the property has been made subject to new privatisation through sales. The apparent difficulties regarding those properties which are impossible to sell (i.e. according to the rule of law and the principle of legal un-ambiguity), are accompanied by more basic and mundane facts, such as the creation of another constitutional problem.

Administrative work, steps to ensure the eligibility of the potential former owner and the inspection of his guarantee to continue the commercial business involved in restitution are merely substituted by negotiations with potential buyers. The fiscal budget might also be considered as another aspect for preferring factual restitution over compensation. A preference for compensation can only be substantiated if the sales value of the property (i.e. the purchasing price the THA is paid) is higher than the compensation value, which is rendered impossible as the sales value is the only value which could qualify as a compensatory measure. Compensatory payments could be surmised under these circumstances to be guided by Paragraph 16 Clause 1 InVorG (Investment Precedence Law) which manifests the payment of the sales value to the former owner in the case of the precedence of investment before restitution. With regard to the debate about new-privatisation or re-privatisation, Willgerodt (1993) suspects the costs of new privatisations to be generally higher than those of re-privatisations. The frequent reductions in the sales price, employment subsidies and other financial support which were to be observed and noticed with respect to the TH sales operations as opposed to the denial of dis-emcumbrance of loans from the past (*Altkredite*) can be interpreted as circumstantial evidence for his impression.

3.5.2.1 Restitution: Benchmark Figures

Re-privatisation - generally stipulated in the unification treaty - and its different issues have to be investigated with regard to its factual application and interpreted in the purview of the THG, the property law and thus its several amendments.[66] This section describes the principles under which property has been restituted to its former owner.

Prior to German unification a joint declaration between the two German states[67] expressed the necessity to deal with issues of unclear property rights. A clarification of property rights was deemed indispensable due to the migration from the East to the West and the contrasting legal regulations in the two states. Legal and socio-economic circumstances were considered to have created uncertainty regarding citizens' ownership rights and, in order to re-establish stability, the arrangement of property issues was to be pursued in a way that was reckoned socially acceptable for different interest groups. The constitutional principles of legal un-ambiguity and protection governed the bi-lateral agreement to establish legal harmony via the clarification of pre-eminent property issues. Accordingly benchmark figures regarding the reinforcement of restitutional private ownership were agreed:

1.) Neither right of restitution nor compensation exists for property expropriated under the statute of occupation by the Soviet Union (1945-1949).

2.) Control over real estate property, corporate property and other forms of wealth by a trust agency and other similar means of control which restrict the right of disposal are to be eliminated. The right of disposal over property is therewith to be restituted to those citizens whose property was held in state trust because of their refuge from the GDR or whose property was confiscated on similar grounds.

3.) Real estate property which was expropriated between 1933 and 1945 and after 1949 is to be restituted to its former owners or their heirs. In cases where restitution of real estate property is impossible (i.e. the property's purpose and utilisation have been changed during its utilisation as national property) the former owners will be compensated. Compensation or allocation of similar property will also apply in circumstances in which property has been legally purchased by third citizens of the former GDR. Compensation will be granted instead of restitution where restitutive rights exist.

4.) Enterprises and enterprise participations expropriated between 1949 and 1972 are to be restituted to their former owners under the precondition that the business continues. The former owner is to be restituted with the enterprise or the shares of the enterprise created by its corporatisation. Instead of restitution the former owner can claim for compensation.

5.) Former owners or heirs of enterprises expropriated in 1972 have the right to re-purchase their former property.

6.) The German Democratic Republic is obliged not to sell any property for which ownership issues are not settled. A certain period of time is granted for citizens to apply for their claims.

7.) According to the implementation of the Joint Declaration in the Unification Treaty, Article 41 UT states that the regulations concerning open property issues are not to hinder economic development in East Germany. Conflicts between any individual interests of restitution and the public interest of investment are to be decided in favour of investment plans. Both German governments agreed that the legal and administrative framework regarding property rights have to be arranged as to avoid investment impediments. This includes regulations which enable investment in cases where property issues have not yet been solved.

3.5.2.2 The Principle of Injustice of National Separation: Restitution and Return of Property to the Previous Owners

As the Joint Declaration of June 1990 preceded unification and merely expressed benchmark principles, further legal regulations became necessary to operationalise the above norm. On 23rd September 1990 the first version of the Law for the Regulation of Open Property Issues (VermG) was passed. It was further amended in July 1992 and regulates restitution and compensation of former owners of expropriated property.

Three categories of the VermG's purview can be differentiated: expropriation, state administration and national socialism.

The first purview of expropriation covers the last two phases of expropriation, i.e. the first phase carried out under the statute of Soviet occupancy between 1945 and 1949 is excluded.

The law regulates (along with other issues) property rights regarding property which was:
a) expropriated without compensation and transferred into peoples' property,
b) expropriated with compensation less than the citizens of the GDR were entitled to at that time,
c) sold to a third party by either state administration or the holder of the right of disposal after its conversion into peoples' property, or
d) transferred into peoples' property according to the Committee of the Council of Ministers' decree of 9th February 1972.

The second categoric purview concentrates on the totalitarian and administrative appropriation of property which belonged to people outside the GDR or to those who fled. The law regulates the elimination of :
a) state administration of those peoples' property who left the GDR without the necessary authorisation,
b) preliminary administration of West German citizens' and juridical West German persons' property titles by state institutions of the GDR and
c) administration of foreign property assigned to the GDR.
The elimination of these property holdings and the respective claims of owners are dealt with accordingly.

The third category focuses on victims of national socialism and applies regulations issued by the Allies in July 1949 regarding the presumption of property bereavement due to persecution (Anordnung BK/O (49) 180 der Alliierten Kommandantur Berlin vom 26. Juli 1949, VOBL fuer Grossberlin I S. 221). The law is to be applied correspondingly regarding claims by citizens and organisations who were persecuted during 1933 and 1945 on racial, religious or political grounds and whose property was therefore confiscated.

As the Joint Declaration by the Federal Republic of Germany and the German Democratic Republic regarding the Regulation of Open Property Issues from the 15th June 1990[68] was integrated in the Unification Treaty it thus qualifies as binding for the German government and parliament. With unification any property owned by the people of the GDR was transferred to the Treuhand and accordingly the joint declaration from June 1990 specifies those who are eligible for either restitution or compensation. In accordance with the joint declaration, the property regulation (VermG) excludes any expropriations carried out during the Soviet occupation between 1945 and 1949 which affected citizens of the former GDR and West Germany, and foreigners (Paragraph 1, Clause 8a, VermG). This regulation implies that the entire first phase of expropriations in East Germany and thus the extensive agricultural reform carried out in autumn 1945 was omitted and no property claims could thus be realised. Of major importance during this period of expropriation was the nationalisation of large industrial enterprises which was also omitted. This regulation caused several constitutional appeals which were rejected in the decision by the Federal Constitutional Court on 23rd April 1991. Nevertheless the Constitutional Court committed the German legislative to establish regulations regarding compensations and a wide scope of action was granted. The respective legal regulations were combined in the passing of the compensation law EAGL (Gesetz ueber die Entschaedigung...)[69]. Furthermore no restitution was possible for expropriated property which was dealt with under international law and any international treaties concerning these property issues were accepted therewith (Paragr. 1, Clause 8b VermG).

Two different kinds of expropriation during the existence of the German Democratic Republic can thus be differentiated according to the VermG. Expropriations or similar actions are:

1.) Actions which have their origin in the foundation and basis of the socialist economic system and its definition and classification of property within the socialist society.
2.) Discriminating action (e.g. expropriations) affecting those individuals whose residence was outside the GDR and refugees, i.e. those who fled the socialist regime.

Regarding the restitution of property the property law (VermG) in principle only takes account of those expropriations which qualify under the second category and these expropriations are often referred to as having been caused by the "injustice of national separation". The philosophy behind the property law is that expropriations in the former GDR which were compensated for according to GDR regulations do not cause any restitutive claims. Citizens of the former GDR, West Germany, or foreigners could have been affected in the same way. Neither did compensations which might be evaluated as too low according to current Western standards cause any claims of revaluation according to the property law.

These restitutive principles can be explained with reference to the practical impossibility of reassessing all expropriations and property transformations carried out during the time of the GDR's existence. The regulations concentrated on those property issues which were caused by the "injustice of the national division". It was therefore decided to include only those property matters which were caused by the national division. The cause of national division is defined as measures carried out by the former GDR which have affected German citizens or foreigners because they had their residence outside the GDR or left the area without authorisation from the respective authorities. Included are thus those expropriations and state property administrations which were caused by the above circumstances.

Nevertheless the principle of restitution on the basis of injustice of national separation was extended by the decision to define a purview of exceptions. This purview includes four conditional cases which are not characterised by any immediate reference to the national division. Instead they were circumstantially caused by the development of the GDR. The area of inconsistencies includes the following circumstances:

1.) property transferred into peoples' property according the decree by the Committee of the Council of Ministers of 9th February 1972 (Paragr. 1d VermG),

2.) real estate letting property which has been transferred into peoples' property because the rent income did not cover costs and thus caused indebtedness (Paragr. 1 Clause 2 VermG),

3.) property rights attained by a third party, purchaser or the state due to unreasonable circumstances, i.e. corruption, abuse of power, coercion or deception (Paragr. 1 Clause 3 VermG) and

4.) property deprivation due to constitutionally illegal decisions (Paragr. 1 Clause 7 VermG).

It was argued by Westermann (1993, p. 93) that the above circumstances have been additionally included, because of the rather small number of relevant collectivisation and state administration with no compensation.

Property which was characterised by its transference into peoples' property according to any of the above cases and the three purview categories (i.e. expropriation, state administration, persecution and inner state development) was to be restituted to its original owner according to Paragraph 3 Clause 1 VermG. Property held by state administration was to be returned to its owner and the trust holding was to be eliminated (Paragr. 11 Clause 1 VermG). Restitution and return of property required a formal application by the eligible person and the period of time in which a claim could be made was limited.

3.5.2.3 Restitution to Local Authorities and Corporations under Public Law

According to the Unification Treaty (Article 21 UT) the entire state assets of the GDR which had directly been employed for administrative duties were transferred to and became part of German federal assets. Former nationally-owned property (here real estate buildings etc.) was allocated to public corporations depending on which corporate body had carried out certain administrative duties on 1st October 1989. Public assets, such as real property, financial forestry and land property which was not directly employed in administrative duties was assigned to the trust administration by the federation. This regulation also included taking care of the so-called *Altschulden*, created during GDR-times and transferred to local authorities which are currently unable of paying back these debts to the Federation (Busse,1995).

3.5.2.4 Enterprise Restitution: Some Empirical Results

The THA managed a total of 11 937 enterprises[70] during the time of its existence (Treuhandanstalt(b), 30.12.1994) of which 1 588 were re-privatised (which constitute a share of 13.3%). The ratio between total privatisation (new-privatisation and re-privatisation) and re-privatisation can be established by subtracting those enterprises which have been restituted to local authorities, liquidated etc. (4 028) from the total number of managed enterprises so that the ratio is 7 909 by 1 588 which is 5 to 1. Out of the privatised enterprises 20.1% were re-privatised by the end of 1994. The development of re-privatisation over time is represented in table 3.5.

The THA was in a position to take decisions with regard to re-privatisation according to Paragraph 30 Clause 1 Sentence 2 VermG if the return of the property could be agreed upon between the former owner and the holder of the right of disposal, i.e. often the THA. The process of re-privatisation dealing with the restitution and compensation of the former owners of the corporations (these corporations had to be separated from the new privatisation) by the Treuhand, dealt with 15 000 applications for re-privatisation. By December 1994, 9 038 cases were finished, of which 6 048 applications for restitution were accepted and 884 were compensated for, 890 were rejected and 1 216 were subject to investment precedence decisions (Treuhandanstalt(a), 12/94).

Table 3.5: Managed and Re-Privatised Enterprises - over time by the THA -

Year	Managed	Re-privatised Enterprises	% of total Enterprises	% of privatised
01/92	4 719	633	13.4	18.2
03/92	5 607	755	13.4	18.5
06/92	6 730	862	12.8	17.7
12/92	8 678	1 188	13.7	19.4
03/93	9 328	1 274	13.7	19.7
09/93	10 550	1 511	14.3	21.1
12/93	10 948	1 573	14.3	21.2
03/94	11 209	1 578	14.1	20.7
06/94	11 618	1 585	13.6	20.5
12/94	11 937	1 588	13.3	20.1

Source: Treuhandanstalt(a), various issues

The application for property restitution generally had to be submitted to the property offices and the Federal Office for Open Property Issues (BAROV) dealt with 151 183 applications with regard to enterprises (12/94) of which a total of 79 362 (52.49%) were dealt with by the end of 1994, representing an increase of 15.31% to the year before.

The completed cases of 79 362 divide in the following way:
a) certification of justified application (19.2%),
b) certified compensation with regard to value alterations (3.6%, of which 99% originated in Mecklenburg-Western Pommerania),
c) temporary vesting order (1.5%),
d) enterprise separation (1%),
e) agreement between former owner and holder of the right of disposal (4.6%, these include the above cases of restitution by the THA, figures do not include any figures for Berlin),
f) re-instatement (return) of a similar property according to Paragraph 6 Clause 1 VermG (22.6%),
g) abolition of state administration (0.7%),
h) re-examination of previous certifications (2.8%),) compensation certificates (8.8%).
j) rejections (27.7%) of which 23.3% were based on Paragraph 1 Clause 8a VermG (Soviet occupancy) and,
k) withdrawal of application (5.8%).

In nearly 30% of filed applications a positive verdict was issued with regard to the return of the property to its former owner (a-e). The re-instatement of a similar property takes up a considerable share of more than 20% reflecting the difficulty of returning the property in its original condition. The numbers of negative decisions amount to 21 250, more than half of those filed in Mecklenburg-Western Pommerania. This also coincides with the high number of certified property value alterations (2 481) which make up 86.2% of the total number of altered values. Aggregated values of decisions taken by the BAROV regarding real estate property are represented in figure 3.2.

The total value of peoples' property which was to be restituted to its former owner was estimated by Cornelsen (1991) to cover 30% of the total peoples' property. The calculation was derived from the fact that enterprises expropriated under Soviet occupancy accounted for 70% of the production capacity of 1948 and these properties were excluded from restitutional claims. The data represents that the method of re-privatisation must not be neglected because of its empirical significance. Although exact property values for the respective privatisation methods - apart from estimations - are not available, the numbers of affected enterprises emphasise that a complete sale of former nationally-owned property was not exercised. Restitution can be identified as a major form of the establishment of private property rights.

Figure 3.2: Final Decisions Regarding Real-Estate Property by the BAROV

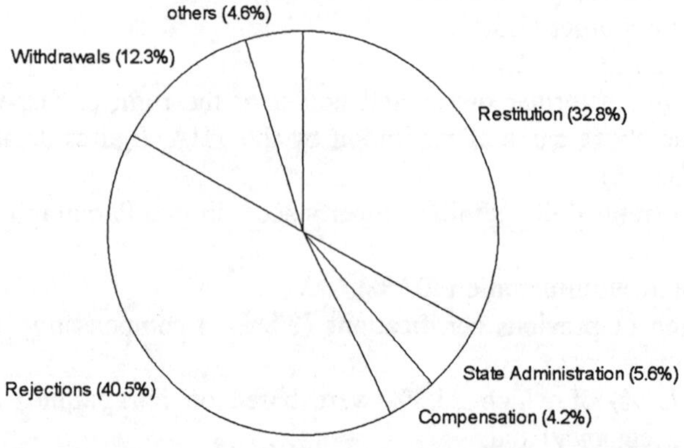

Source: Bundesanstalt zur Regelung offener Vermoegensfragen, Pressemitteilung, 31.12.1994, no figures available for Berlin

3.5.2.5 Synopsis and Economic Implications

The procedure of transforming the organisational and decision-making structure, the transfer of property into the trusteeship of a newly created institution and the corporatisation and separation of enterprises was less time consuming by far than the process of re-privatising nationally-owned property. Various legal regulations had to be approved on a constitutional court basis, political implications were not to be neglected and the process of identifying the rightful owners itself proved to be highly administrative and bureaucratic. Particular issues associated with the process of restitution hindered the economic transformation at least in the short-term.

Major problems occurred from the decision to return property and restitute property expropriated during 1933 and 1945 and after 1949 to its original owners. The assignment of property rights to a person assumed that it is possible to nominate the person, corporate body or other to which the right was to belong. In the case of recreating and restructuring private property rights systematic problems developed with the differentiation between real estates and corporations (companies). The owner of the real estate might not have been identical to the owner or owners of a corporation who might have used the particular estate. This problem of designation of differing and competing property claims could occur.

As long as the process of restitution has not been completed, the economic development of a corporation or land is insecure because only the owner of the particular property right is entitled to decide which development concept and path is to be taken. This created a major initial problem of operation for the Treuhand which could only invest if the future concept of the corporation was decided upon and the plans of the new owner were known. Furthermore it could be expected that the new owner was not prepared to invest as long as his property and ownership rights were not specified and the ownership had been included in the land registry.

The vital necessity for investment in the East German region was temporarily hindered by the unclear assignment of ownership rights. The process of restituting socialist property to former owners proved very time-consuming and the respective properties could not be used. In order to further the process of investment particular legal regulations were created to provide investment opportunities and incentives. New ownership laws were introduced in March 1991 in addition to the Treuhand-law in order to alleviate the restraint of disposal (by the Treuhand) which was relevant until all property titles were fully allocated. The decision of the Constitutional Court aimed at easing the negative implications of ownership uncertainty. Unsolved property claims were a major impediment for investment. Specific regulations were formed in order to enable investment to proceed. These regulations concentrated on real estate and corporations which were affected by claims of restitution (VermG) and generally provided precedence of compensation to restitution according to the Investment Precedence Law in order to speed up the privatisation process.
Before the influence of investment precedence regulations is analysed the method of privatisation by sale of corporate shares will be dealt with.

3.5.3 New-Privatisation Through the Sale of Corporate Shares

3.5.3.1 Market Simulation by the Treuhand

The Treuhandanstalt as the owner of most of the GDR's property on behalf of the Federation (*Bund*) operated as simulating the supply side of the market in the sale of property during the transitional period. Although the THA and its successor (*Bundesanstalt fuer vereinigungsbedingte Sonderaufgaben*, BVS) have been under the control and jurisdiction of the Federal Minister of Finance according to Article 25 Clause 1 of the Unification Treaty they have acted formally independently with regard to new-privatisation.

The preamble of the Treuhand-law specifies the institution's purposes as to minimise the economic involvement of the state as much and as soon as possible through privatisation, to increase the competitiveness of as many companies as possible, to ensure employment, create new jobs and to provide land estate for commercial purposes. Furthermore it was intended to use the national property to guarantee savers' shares after the property's utilisation for structural adjustments and rehabilitation of the budget. Besides these structural objectives the THA was also appointed to complete and carry out GDR borrowing and debt issues (Articles 23, 27 Clause 7, UT).

The main tasks handed to the THA with the trusteeship were the trust administration of property which belonged to political parties, mass organisations, agricultural and forestry cooperations, the restitution and sale of property, the re-establishment of regional property etc. The different areas of the new-privatisation objectives of the THA were specified in the Treuhand-law and were:

a) to privatise and administer national property following the principles of a social market economy (Paragr. 2 Clause 1 THG),
b) to support the structural adjustment of the economy meeting the necessities of the market by influencing the development of companies which can be rehabilitated, sustaining their competitiveness and privatisation (Paragr. 2 Clause 6 THG),
c) to create efficient economic structures and promote companies by decentralising and deconcentrating their structures so that they can survive within the market (Paragr. 2 Clause 6 THG) and
d) to privatise and reorganise national property within the agricultural and forestry sector (Paragr. 1 Clause 6 THG).

The duties and objectives of the trust agency had to be carried out in accordance with and by reference to the decentral organisational structure of TH-corporations (sections 3.3.3 and 3.3.4). The TH-stock companies had to guarantee the achievement of their task with the help and employment of the relevant consultant organisations and the TH-corporations' tasks were (according to Paragr. 8 Clause 1 and Paragr. 9 THG):

a) privatisation through the sale of corporation-shares or property shares,
b) securing efficiency and competitiveness of the companies,
c) closure and utilisation of property which belongs to companies or company parts which were not to be rehabilitated,
d) creation of structures within the companies in accordance with requirements of the market and particular objectives of the social market economy and
e) the promotion of companies' self-financing ability by employing monetary and capital markets.

Within the above framework the Treuhand took over the role of the market with regard to the decision of whether an enterprise was going to continue its existence. The Treuhand decided about the company's future and decided between the three options of a) liquidation, b) making the company viable and c) selling it. The trust agency analysed the corporate business situation with regard to the company's safeguarding of jobs, investment plans, sales value and to a minor extent certainly lobbied interest groups' interests. The subsequent section is predominantly concerned with the TH's role of privatising property in the form of sale.

3.5.3.2 Methods of Privatisation

3.5.3.2.1 Evaluation of Peoples' Property

Prior to any sale of enterprises or enterprise shares the Treuhand had to provide an opening balance sheet of the portfolio of its enterprises. According to the *D-Markbilanzgesetz*[71] enterprises whose registered office was located in the GDR on 1st July 1990 were to prepare opening balance sheets in DM. As all nationally-owned enterprises were transferred into the ownership of the Treuhandanstalt on 1st July 1990 the THG accordingly requested (Paragr. 20 THG) that the enterprises were to hand over their balance-sheets to the Treuhand by 31st October 1990. Taking the inventory of the GDR's property proved very complex and difficult.

Two main possible methods of property evaluation can be differentiated according to German corporate and accounting law: evaluation on the basis of the capitalised earning capacity value on the one hand and evaluation on the basis of the net asset value on the other. The method of *capitalised earning capacity value* is based on the calculation of the future revenue to be yielded by the enterprises. The capitalisation of future income streams, normally calculated on the basis of profit-and-loss-accounts, is here estimated as the asset's value in the present derived from realised revenue. Due to the loss of Eastern European markets and concern about the enterprises' chance of surviving within a competitive market economy, the profit-and-loss-accounts of GDR-enterprises were handled with extreme care. Furthermore even if methodologically new methods of accounting and balancing had been utilised these criteria were applicable to a very limited scope as they referred to data which could not be extrapolated into the present or future.

The *net asset value* on the other hand is defined as the debt value subtracted from the aggregated value of the enterprise's material assets. As this evaluation is principally based on enterprises' balance sheets this method also proved difficult due to the lack of data availability. As no efficient markets for capital and real estate existed in the former GDR because of the lack of tradeability, the data obtained from balance sheets was assessed as not reflecting real values. Furthermore prices for plants, production equipment etc. were centrally controlled and fixed, periods of utilisation were comparatively long and capital was generally assigned with low levels of depreciation. As these methods of evaluation did not correspond to the standards applied in Western industrial countries the existing values proved very ambiguous.

As both methods were attached with serious problems the Treuhandanstalt mainly combined the two methods. The term net asset value was re-defined and the basis of calculation was amended by changing the way that enterprises' assets were evaluated on the basis of their sale value. The value of enterprises' net asset capital can thus be surmised to have been principally calculated on the basic sale values of enterprises' real property, capital and inventories. The sale value was to be accounted on the principle that asset's price had to be recuperated by future revenue within five or ten years and this practice represents the influence of the methodology of the capitalised earnings capacity value. The aggregated value of individual property assets represents its capitalised earning capacity value.

Considering that the method of evaluation was unclear and not straightforward the former peoples' property's values calculated and published often diverged by considerable amounts. With time, a trend of a decreasing value of peoples' property nevertheless became obvious and was unanimous. The initial calculation of the financial implications of privatising peoples' property can be interpreted as optimistic as it was assumed - with passing the TH-law in 1990 - that revenue derived from the sale of enterprises would exceed its expenditures. The incoming revenue of the THA was primarily to be used for structural adjustment of corporations - horizontal financial budget balancing (*Finanzausgleich*) - and secondly for budget-purposes and coverage of THA-expenditure according to Paragraph 5 Clause 1 THG. TH-expenditures were assumed to cover the cost of interest payment for existing enterprises' debts and programs to make enterprises viable. This positive assessment was not substantiated as the following figures prove. (The figures include enterprise as well as agricultural property.)

The Treuhand assessed the capitalised earnings capacity value of peoples' property in autumn 1990 as DM 600 bn.[72] At roughly the same time Wolfram Krause, former financial head of the Treuhand estimated the net asset value based on past balance sheet data between DM 180 bn and DM 250 bn (Christ & Neubauer, 1991). The Federal Ministry of Justice calculated the sale value of peoples' property to be restituted or returned to their former owners in spring 1991 as DM 120 bn. Calculations by Luft (1992) which were based on this figure valued peoples' property in terms of their sale values as DM 280 bn. In 1991 the Treuhand was still considered to dispose over a gross asset value of DM 200 bn which was suggested to be lowered due to the lack of profitability of many enterprises and thus small enterprise sale values (Bundeskabinett, 1991). The vast divergence became strikingly obvious by the Treuhand's publication in 1992 which showed the value of peoples' property to be retrospectively assessed in the

D-Mark Opening Balance Sheet at a net asset value based on sale values of DM 81 bn for 1st July 1990. The listing of these figures depicts the lack of knowledge and awareness of the respective institutions with regard to property's values. During the transitional period of privatising formerly nationally-owned property the initial optimistic illustration of structures and values grew increasingly invalid and this represents the limits of one institution assessing an entire economy and simulating a market.

3.5.3.2.2 The Principle of Mass Privatisation

On the basis of this last value and the assumption that 30% of peoples' property was to be returned or restituted, a calculated DM 57 bn of property was transferred to the Treuhandanstalt to privatise, restructure or liquidate. The initial portfolio of the Treuhandanstalt was classified on a six-point scale according to each enterprise's potential viability in the market economy. The evaluation of whether an enterprise was viable depended on the abilities of its management, its product and service, and whether demand and potential partners existed in the West. Furthermore the evaluation was based on the assumption that wages were going to converge and thus labour opportunity costs were included. The evaluation concluded that 70% of the initial portfolio was potentially viable.

The sudden increase in the supply of real assets, properties and inventories must be interpreted as a shock to the real asset market which resulted in a fall in prices for these properties. This situation was underlined by the fact that potential purchasers in the GDR did not have the necessary equity capital at their disposal. The major share of the necessary capital had to be borrowed from financial markets and this increase in capital demand implied an immense increase in short-term interest rates (the discount-base rate set by the Deutsche Bundesbank in July 1992 was 8.75%, the highest post Second World War rate). The high interest rates automatically induced a deterioration of real property values. The discrepancy between low expected future income streams from real asset utilisation and high capital interest payments worsened the purchasing and investing propensities. Furthermore the number of properties with expected capitalised earning capacity values such that they could have recouperated the sales price and the high interest rates was thus decreasing rapidly. This led to the fact that the enterprises and enterprise parts sold were those with high earnings capacity, whereas a large number of inefficient enterprises - in terms of the high interest rates - were left unsold or liquidated.

According to Sinn and Sinn (1992) this sales policy proved to be an economic maze which did not consider microeconomic implications because marginal privatisation strategies which might otherwise have proved successful were applied to privatise an entire economy. The aim of a rapid privatisation and the budget constraints gave the three options (i.e. privatising, restructuring or liquidating) different weights. The immense public cost of restructuring along with keeping enterprises which proved difficult to sell might be argued to have enhanced the propensity of the Treuhand to liquidate. The time-objective of privatisation might have also extrapolated the uncertainty of potential investors and buyers as to whether the properties had any future earnings potential at all. Commitments regarding job and investment guarantees also had negative implications for real asset prices and potential buyers' willingness to sign the contract-requirements. This was often associated with reducing the initial price as well as creating financial reserves so as to meet penalty payments for guarantees which had not been held. This will be analysed further in detail below.

The privatisation process was supposed to have been completed by the end of 1993 at which time the Treuhandanstalt was to cease existence but the institution continued its operation until the end of 1994. The objective of rapid mass privatisation had been met by the Treuhand (section 3.5.4). It must nevertheless be admitted that sales revenues certainly did not meet initial expectations - of several hundred billion DM - due to the aforementioned circumstances. The sales revenue of the mass privatisation by the Treuhandanstalt was DM 64.9 bn (July 1994) and had been realised by the two concrete methods of new privatisation: outsider privatisation and insider privatisation.

3.5.3.2.2.1 Outsider Privatisation

The sales strategy of the Treuhandanstalt aimed at finding purchasers who were willing to undertake substantial investment in the enterprises and could offer management skills suitable for the respective businesses. The objective of the privatisation process of selling to purchasers whose management matches the prevailing enterprises' assets, in turn places emphasis on a sound financial background. These qualitative requirements were mainly fulfilled by Western (capitalist) investors. The privatisation strategy which aimed at the financial and managerial transformation of enterprises in order for them to survive in a competitive market economy, was thus directed toward potential purchasers who could instigate the process of enterprise adjustment. The basic strategy of outsider privatisation was mainly a two-way approach, selling corporatised enterprises on the one hand, and selling separated or newly-aggregated enterprise parts on the other hand.

The main activity of the Treuhand (according to Paragr. 2, Clause 6 THG) aimed to influence the transformation of potentially viable enterprises in the form of making them competitive and then privatise them. The enterprise structures were to be decentralised *suitably* so as to form viable enterprises and an efficient economic structure. This terminology chosen in the Treuhand-law represents the institution's considerable and wide scope of action and the pragmatic nature of action. As the enterprise structures were mainly characterised by centralism and large sizes, the Treuhandanstalt pursued a pragmatic single case approach to particular sales agreements. *Suitable* enterprise structures were to be established by the trust agency by splitting up enterprises according to the purchaser's profile which became possible with the introduction of the separation law. This legal authorisation enabled the THA to meet the purchaser's structural specifications within the institutional approach.

The above mentioned two-way approach of actual privatisation had thus been followed: the corporatisation of enterprises prior to privatisation and a pragmatic reorganisation of enterprises still to be sold. The initial strategy of corporatisation which was successfully fulfilled by 1st July 1990 aimed at selling entire businesses to purchasers who themselves could fulfil the qualitative financial and managerial requirements. This initial scheme with its belief in the self-curing powers of private markets, emphasised the potential of the investor to carry out the remaining restructuring tasks in order to establish viable competitive and efficient enterprise structures. The scheme was later extended towards more pragmatic economic policies (see chapter 5, section 5.3).

The transformation of viable enterprises into efficient and privately owned units aimed also at to preserve the core activities of the businesses (Carlin, 1994), in order to secure employment (preamble THG) and realise a socially acceptable process of transformation (preamble UT). This aim of preservation was surmised to be met strategically by the requirements placed on potential purchasers. The purchaser did not only have to justify his financial and managerial profile, he also had to prove that the enterprise had prospectives for the future in terms of the existence of a substantial market for its output as well as research and development plans.

Apart from the conventional form of basic outsider privatisation (outside the respective enterprise) in the form of selling to established companies, the Treuhandanstalt started a programme in 1992 for those enterprises which had been declared potentially viable but were not expected to attract sale interests in the short-term, those which required a large amount of restructuring and employed at least 250 employees (Treuhandanstalt(b), March 1993). The model was aimed at privatising part of the Treuhand's task of privatisation through the establishment of so-called *Management GmbH & Co. KGs* (*Kommanditgesellschaft*), a special corporate form of limited partnership. Partners of these organisations are the THA and a *Management GmbH*. The capital shares of this limited partnership were entirely held by the THA whereas a *Management GmbH* - without any capital participation - was responsible for executive management (Frisch, 1993). A *Management GmbH* consisted of two to three managers and a minority participation of the THA. The *Management KG's* portfolio comprised a limited number of potentially viable enterprises as the

THA's contribution in real assets. This model has aimed at the transference of restructuring subjects and privatisation to experienced managers. This corporate form enabled the THA to remain the owner of potentially viable enterprises and at the same time separate these companies' managements. Participating managers have faced income prospects in the form of bonuses in the case of successful privatisation. In order to achieve a rapid privatisation the bonus payments were designed regressively (successively decreasing after a certain sum).

The THA provided the finance - for at least three years - for restructuring the enterprises of the KG and for making them viable. Frisch (1993) argued that enterprises of the KG in contrast to those held by the THA were primarily interested in making them viable. In January 1994 five *Management KGs* existed which comprised 71 formerly state-owned enterprises (Treuhandanstalt(b), January 1994). *Management KGs* have the advantages of bringing managerial experience and performance incentives into the process of restructuring prior to privatisation in contrast to a sometimes bureaucratic process carried out by TH-subsidiaries. It might though nevertheless be surmised that *Management KGs* were set up in order to improve the Treuhand's record of privatisation achievements. Furthermore this corporate form increased the probability of attracting investment into these enterprises and being under the name of *Management KG* rather than THA raised the chance of privatisation, since the remaining companies within the TH-portfolio were less likely to be sold due to the lack of confidence in the remaining enterprises. Since 1992 external privatisation capacities such as special investment banks and fund holding companies had experienced increasing importance. Fund holding companies such as the *Deutsche Industrie Holding* and *Sachsenfonds* which are characterised by their financial and corporate independence from the THA proved to successfully privatise enterprises via participating enterprises (*Beteiligungsgesellschaften*) and private capital.

At roughly the same time as the introduction of *Management KGs* the form of Management-Buy-Ins (MBIs) was designed to be another alternative method of outsider privatisation which aimed mainly at enterprises with a maximum of 250 employees (Treuhand(b), 6.11992). MBIs were characterised by the THA selling enterprises or enterprise parts to managers outside the former GDR and the model placed emphasis on sale to foreign investors and bridging the management shortage. The sale requirements for this method were similar to those of MBOs (see below) and potential purchasers had to have a substantial record of industrial and managerial experience. Suitable enterprises were publicly advertised according to industrial specifications and this operation attempted to moderate the flow of information by engaging international consultant agencies and investment banks. Potential MBI candidates were put in contact by the THA with a capital partner, either a participating or holding organisation. The model of MBIs was desired also to involve the existing East German management in order to combine know-how regarding small and medium-sized enterprises. Alongside the form of MBIs a general advertising campaign which began in January 1992 endeavoured to speed up the sale of small and medium-sized enterprises (Treuhand(b), 7.2.1992). All remaining small and medium-sized TH-enterprises were advertised in well-known newspapers and magazines.

It can be concluded that enterprises sold to outsiders have undergone either the basic process of restructuring in the way of corporatisation, labour shedding and decentralisation or basic restructuring and pragmatic formation of new entities (deconcentration) through the separation of enterprise parts. The first method was basically carried out prior to privatisation whereas the second method worked alongside the sale itself. Nevertheless both methods classify as top-down methods of privatisation, i.e. the sale to competent outsiders who are able to meet the necessary sale requirements. Outsider privatisation is characterised by the belief that the purchasers have the ability and knowledge of the industry required to make the enterprises consistently viable. The enterprises' viability is assumed to be secured if the purchaser has access to financial capital and is likely to establish effective corporate governance. Although it has been possible for potential East German investors generally to gain access to financial capital as financial markets were existent after unification, managerial and technological knowledge which could substantiate the enterprise's survival in Western competitive markets could predominantly be offered by West German investors and those from foreign industrial market economies.

The structure of sales to outsiders has been designed to encourage established West German and foreign firms to invest into large enterprises whereas management involvements were designed to focus on small and medium-sized enterprises (MBIs, *Management KGs*). The establishment of a considerable base of medium-sized enterprises was explicitly targeted in the Treuhand-law as well as in the Unification Treaty. The THA attempted to meet this target through the lightening of the privatisation process for investors in and purchasers of medium-sized enterprises as to form MBIs.

3.5.3.2.2.2 Insider Privatisation in the Form of MBOs

Insider privatisation (i.e. the sale of enterprises or enterprise parts to the enterprise's existing East German management) was not initially a strongly pursued option by the privatisation agency. East Germans had been mainly excluded from purchasing enterprises due to the aforementioned sale requirements. Nevertheless, and not at least through the introduction of the separation law, it became possible to separate enterprise parts which could then be sold to existing management. MBOs are the most frequent form of insider-privatisation where the initiative of privatisation comes from the management itself. As with outsider privatisation the management has to establish a future concept for the enterprise and prove personal ability and managerial know-how regarding corporate governance. The Treuhandanstalt explicitly emphasised the option of separating individual enterprise departments and privatising them - besides small and medium-sized enterprises - in the way of MBOs (Treuhandanstalt, 1992).

The Treuhandanstalt generally considered enterprises as suitable for MBOs which a) offered products which were based on competitive advantages, b) sold to stable and mainly regional markets and were not subject to revenue fluctuations and c) held sufficient capital as security. MBOs were advised to consult commercial banks with regard to debt financing. In cases where different potential purchasers applied for the enterprise the Treuhand committed itself to decide in favour of the MBO and generally advised MBIs to be joined with MBOs. Although the Treuhand was unwilling to lower sale prices it offered financial support for MBOs in terms of extended pledges (*Buergschaften*) for up to two years. It negotiated credit options and offered the possibility to the MBO of purchasing the enterprise or enterprise part excluding real property which then could be rented out and a respective pre-emption right (*Vorzugsrecht*) would be established.

This form of privatisation from below created mainly small and medium-sized enterprises and the total number of enterprises and part-enterprises sold amounted to 2 667 MBOs, 18.7% of the THA's privatisation activities (Treuhandanstalt(a), 6/94). The majority of MBOs (77.2%) were created under the supervision of TH-regional subsidiaries (2 060). As small and medium-sized enterprises were organisationally assigned to subsidiaries, one can deduce the rather small size of enterprises created through MBOs.

Although employee participation was generally possible as every person could potentially be an investor, participation was mainly linked with MBOs as employees could purchase enterprise shares or stocks, could become silent members or be part of a participating organisation. No specific supportive regulations and options existed for employee participation as this form of privatisation had hardly been an option pursued in the process. Instead the Treuhand pointed out that employee participation merely qualifies as a particular form of capital investment and thus does not qualify as a separate privatisation method (Treuhandanstalt, 1992).

3.5.3.3 Incorporation of a Selected Behaviour Function

The method of new-privatisation emphasised the utilisation of a selected behaviour function defining some of the restructuring actions of the new private owners. Although the entire privatisation process by the Treuhand was predominantly institutionally based and the curing forces of markets were assumed economic transformation was prescribed as to ensure a socially acceptable enterprise and property transformation. The process of restructuring was to be carried out by the enterprises' owners and thus it was unknown what concrete action would be chosen with regard to the enterprise's future. Once the property was transferred the Treuhand's transforming action was ended: economic actions and decisions were to be taken independently on the basis of decentralised economic planning. The subjection of the institution's activity to the aim of a socially acceptable transformation required the definition of the latter and the identification of certain acceptable social and economic situations. This subjection and the belief in the market forces led to the definition of acceptable situations in the form of the respective investment prospects and the employment situation.

Any form of new privatisation - inside or outside - required investment and employment guarantees, and the purchasers of former state-owned enterprises were given subsidy payments. These subsidies depended on the sales value, i.e. a subsidy was mainly granted in the case of a negative present value of the enterprise. The aggregated sales packages are represented in table 3.6.

Table 3.6: Aggregated Sales Packages

until	Sales Revenue	Job Guarantees	Investment Guarantees
09/91	DM 13.62 bn	722 000	DM 46.88 bn
12/91	DM 19.50 bn	930 262	DM 84.00 bn
01/92	DM 20.30 bn	967 270	DM 86.70 bn
03/92	DM 26.80 bn	1 078 295	DM 98.50 bn
06/92	DM 30.70 bn	1 223 709	DM 114.00 bn
12/92	DM 40.10 bn	1 400 677	DM 139.50 bn
03/93	DM 41.60 bn	1 438 447	DM 146.70 bn
09/93	DM 44.70 bn	1 492 813	DM 152.40 bn
12/93	DM 48.10 bn	1 486 875	DM 186.60 bn
03/94	DM 49.10 bn	1 502 109	DM 190.20 bn
06/94	DM 52.70 bn	1 460 883	DM 198.20 bn

Source: Treuhandanstalt(a), current issues

A discount on the sale price was negotiated according to the number of jobs guaranteed and investment projects planned. These investment and employment contracts covered a certain period of time and the maintenance of these contracts has been monitored by the THA and the BVS. The assignment of the property to a new private owner was thereby not entirely dependent on the price of the property and did not follow the principle of the highest bidding party. Instead the price of the property was substituted by the property's "value". This value of the property consisted of its price and the negotiated guarantees the new owner had to agree to in the form of a binding contract. The employment and investment guarantees are defined here as truncated property rights, i.e. the new owner was not assigned with the full right of disposal rather he was obliged to design his corporate policy according to the contract. The contract was temporarily limited and would normally expire after 5-10 years. (It will be shown further down how these contracts affect the actual value of the property right and how it affects the property rights theory as being falsifiable.) It has therefore been necessary to know which period of time is covered by the contracts and whether their expiry would initiate substantial job shedding and a freezing of investment. It has been argued by Willgerodt (1993) that job and investment guarantees by the purchaser were entirely unnecessary as long as they were in the latter's interest (as he would have fulfilled them anyhow). In circumstances where they went beyond the voluntary warranty they were often supported by TH-subsidies in the form of the writing off of loans, the lowering of the sales price etc. Subsidies of this form can be interpreted as having distorted the market result - simulated by the THA - and monitoring the fulfilment of the contracts has involved high costs. Job guarantees were enforced by contract and committed the guarantor to pay a penalty of about DM 40 000 per job guarantee which was not realised. (Despite the job and investment guarantees demanded by the Treuhand potentially lowering the enterprises' revenue-earning potential these contracts can be interpreted as having the effect of internalising social costs of transformation, which will be discussed and analysed in the next chapters.)

The imposition of the employment and investment guarantees was supposed to increase the economy's production potential and ensure a socially acceptable economic change, for example by reducing labour shedding during the transitional period. In particular the investment guarantees aim at influencing the marginal capital coefficient. Net investment increasing economic capacity is expected and this is supposed to ease the transformational pressures created by the severe capital depreciation shock. It can therefore be concluded that the emphasis in the new privatisation policy has been on reducing the transitional adjustment deficiencies created by the capital and wage shocks (see chapter 5, sections 5.2.2, 5.2.4 and 5.3.3). The privatisation by the Treuhand and the sales agreements have produced investment guarantees worth DM 130.4 bn in total of which DM 54.2 bn (51.6%) materialised by the end of 1995 (table 3.7).

It was agreed that a total of DM 81.4 bn would be invested into the production industry of which the manufacturing sector has a share of 62%. The bulk of the investment guarantees (DM 44.2 bn) will materialise during the years 1995 and 1996 which still leaves DM 53.2 bn to be realised thereafter. The utilisation of these contracts - in particular as them being part of the sales agreement and their point be noted that the knowledge of one institution simulating the entire supply side of the property market is limited and this process involved high information and monitoring costs.

Table 3.7: Investment Guarantees (DM bn) According to Time of Materialisation and Economic Sectors

Economic Sectors	'91	'92	'93	'94	'95	'96	'97	'98	'99	> 2000	total*
A	0.0	0.0	0.1	0.3	1.3	0.4	0.9	0.2	0.1	0.5	3.7
B											
C	0.0	0.6	8.7	0.1	0.1	3.6	0.2	0.0	10	0.7	24
D	0.0	0.0	0.1	0.1	0.0	0.0	0.7	0.0	0.0	1.0	1.9
E	0.1	0.7	3.7	7.9	11.5	10.9	5.2	2.4	1.2	7.5	50.9
F	0.0	0.2	0.4	0.9	0.9	0.6	0.8	0.3	0.3	0.2	4.6
G	0.1	0.2	0.5	1.2	1.1	1.1	1.3	0.3	3.2	0.7	9.7
H	0.0	0.1	0.4	1.5	2.3	1.8	2.5	1.1	0.5	4.0	14.2
J	0.0	0.5	0.9	3.9	3.9	4.6	2.0	2.0	0.9	2.7	21.4
total*	0.2	2.2	14.8	15.8	21.2	23	13.5	6.3	16.2	17.2	130.4

Source: Deutsches Institut fuer Wirtschaftsforschung (1991-1995), own calculations; A=Agriculture and Forstry, B=Producing Industry, C=Energy and Water, D=Mining, E=Manufacturing Industry, F=Building, G=Trade and Traffic, H=Services, J=others; *mistake in sum total is due to rounding

3.5.4 Record of the Privatisation by the Treuhand

The sale of enterprises held by the Treuhand could take two different forms: a) the sale of an enterprise as an independent and entire economic unit or b) the sale of part of an enterprise (asset deal; Carlin, 1994). The Treuhand's portfolio pictures the development of enterprise and enterprise parts, their privatisation, liquidation and re-privatisation and is shown in table 3.8. The Treuhandanstalt finished its operation at the end of 1994 and its operative tasks were transferred to its succeeding institution BVS and the Federal Ministry of Finance (BMF). Projects of privatisation and associated tasks which were not concluded by the THA were to be completed by the MBGB (enterprises) and the TLG (real estate property) which were directly subordinated to the BMF (MBGB = Management-Beteiligungs-gesellschaft Berlin GmbH, TLG = Liegenschafts-gesellschaft der Treuhandanstalt). The BVS has predominantly been responsible for the management of sales contracts and the finalisation of the liquidation. The enterprise transference to local authorities has mainly been in the realm of public transport and utilities.

Table 3.8: Treuhand's Portfolio of Enterprise Transformation

Treuhand's original portfolio: 1.7.1990	
Enterprises	8 500
Plants	44 000
Treuhand's pre-final portfolio: 1.9.1994	
Privatisation (entirely, partly)	
privatised enterprises (100%)	6 139
privatised enterprises (50%)	274
parts of enterprises	7 374
Enterprise-reprivatisation to former owners	1 585
Enterprise-transference to local authorities	268
Enterprise-liquidation	3 578
Remaining Enterprises	450
Treuhand's final portfolio: 31.12.94	
Privatisation (entirely, partly)	
privatised enterprises (100%)	6 321
privatised enterprises (50%)	225
parts of enterprises	7 374
Enterprise-reprivatisation to former owners	1 588
Enterprise-transference to local authorities	265
Enterprise-liquidation*	3 561
Remaining companies transferred to the MBGB & TLG	475

Sources: Treuhandanstalt 1990, 1994; Treuhandanstalt(a) 9/94; Treuhandanstalt(b), 21.12.1994. *The published number of liquidated enterprises in 12/94 is smaller than the one in 9/94 because liquidating enterprises has been a continuing process. The given figures represent the number of enterprises which are classified for liquidation, so that variations can occur (e.g. caused by the sale of enterprises which have been classified as to be liquidated). The number of enterprises transferred to local authorities (9/94 and 12/94) fell for the same reason, i.e. their sale.

Table 3.9 represents the time profile of the monthly numbers of sales by the Treuhand and shows that the number of enterprises and enterprise parts sold peaked in the first half of 1992 with a halving of sales by the first half of 1993.

Table 3.9: Enterprises and Enterprise Parts Sold by the TH - aggregated per six months -

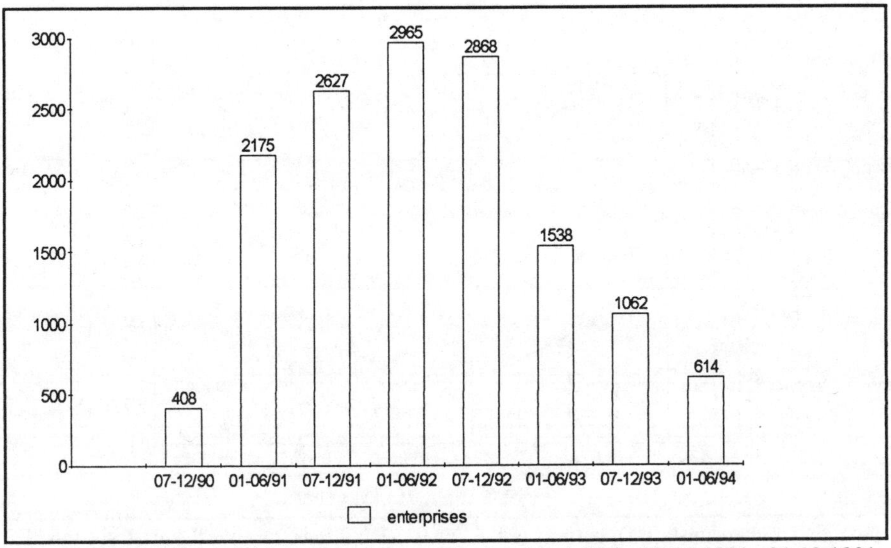

Source: Treuhandanstalt(a) current issues; Treuhandanstalt(c), 30.09.1991, 31.12.1991, own calculations

Although the privatisation performance of the Treuhand indicates a successful development in respect of the numbers of sales of enterprises and enterprise parts, the utilisation of this data is very unsatisfactory as it does not provide any indicators of the quality of the respective items. It seems thus appropriate to refer to the implied consequences for employment, investment and the actual receipts from sale (table 3.10). The total number of employment and investment guarantees increased over time - disregarding the negative number of job guarantees in the first six months of 1994 - but there has been a steady decline in the increase in job guarantees.

As can be seen from table 3.11 the number of employment guarantees per firm has considerably decreased over time, which may be explained by the fact that large-scale enterprises were sold first and small and medium-sized enterprises were sold last. The number of employment guarantees per firm fell from over 170 up to the end 1991 to less than 20 for the last six months of 1993. During the first half of 1994 the figure was negative which reflects that jobs, previously agreed to be kept were shed. This development has however been accompanied by an increase in both revenue and investment guarantees per firm.

Throughout the THA's activity of privatisation sale receipts per job guaranteed increased which reflects the fall in jobs guaranteed per sale (Carlin 1994).

Table 3.10: Investment (DM bn) and Employment Guarantees (1 000s)
- aggregated per six months -

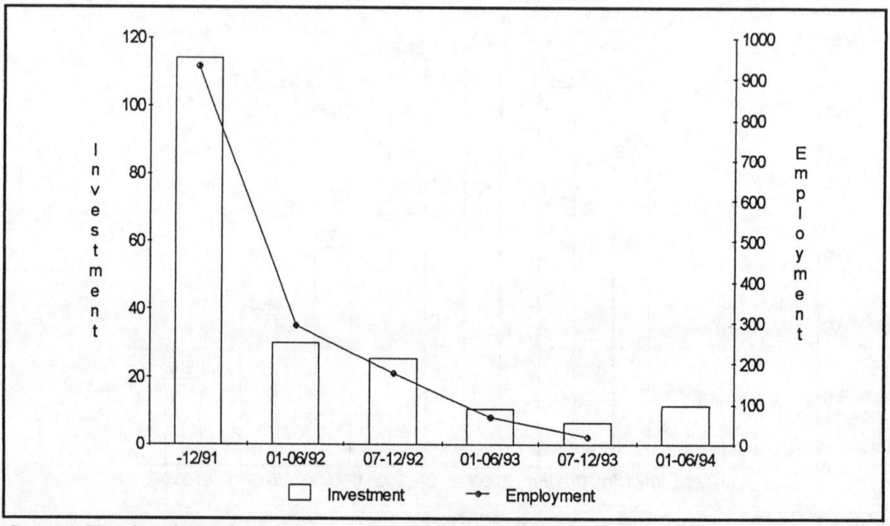

Source: Treuhandanstalt(a), current issues, own calculations. During the first six months of 1994 the published number of employment guarantees was negative (-25 992) because data adjustment made the elimination of some sales contracts with employment guarantees necessary as they were duplicated.

Table 3.11: Revenue, Investment and Jobs per Privatised Firm - aggregated per six months -

	Revenue (DM m) per firm	Investment (DM m) per firm	Jobs per firm
-12/91	3.74	21.88	178.55
01-06/92	3.78	10.12	98.97
07-12/92	3.28	8.89	61.70
01-06/93	2.21	6.89	43.90
07-12/93	4.33	6.12	17.59
01-06/94	7.49	18.89	

Source: Treuhandanstalt(a), current issues, own calculations

The net equity capital of enterprises held by the Treuhand was estimated at DM 81 bn in the Opening Balance Sheet of the Treuhand and the revenue through privatisation was published as DM 73 bn (Treuhandanstalt(b), *Abschlussbericht*, 31.12.1994). It was estimated however that DM 264 bn had to be raised from the capital market in order to enable the THA to fulfil its tasks. These figures reflect the negative aggregated value of enterprises. A large part of these costs was split in the following way:

-discharge of old debts (DM 101 bn (DM 75 bn disencumbering enterprises' old debt, DM 26 bn interest charges)),
-ecological restoration (DM 44 bn),
-costs of privatisation, restructuring and closing-down (DM 145 bn) and
-miscellaneous expenditures (DM 38 bn).

3.6 Concluding Remarks: Institutionalised System Change and Room for Transitional Economic Policy

This chapter identified the underlying socialist economic structures in the former GDR and the approach chosen to transform these structures. Institutional transformation policy aimed at the creation of the intended new structure utilising the main policies of commercialisation, corporatisation and privatisation. It was shown that the transformation was legally and institutionally applied and that economic transformation policy aimed at a smooth adaptation and integration of the new framework. In that sense economic policy was initially designed in the institutional economic sense of creating the economic structure of a decentralised market economy with private property rights and easing the transformation process. The enterprise transformation can thus be classified as the Treuhandanstalt setting the institutional and basic structural framework. This framework follows the classic description of capitalist economies in the form of decentralised corporate decision-making and private property rights.

Institutional economic approaches identified in the preceding chapter can be found to have been utilised as the basic change of the East German economic system. Various aspects of the non-deterministic evolutionary theories made their way into the actual system transformation. The ordo-liberal school of thought manifests itself in the creation of an appropriate institutional framework in the creation of decentralised economic planning as well as - alongside the property rights theory - aiming at the establishment of well-defined private property rights. The privatisation of former state-owned enterprises by the Treuhandanstalt is institutionally characterised by the fact that the institution itself - apart from pragmatic deconcentration - did not carry out any strategic industrial intervention prior to the enterprise's transference into the private sector. The Treuhandanstalt has carried out the special function of competitive restructuring and privatisation and its engagement was limited in time. The THA was assigned the role of a special agency carrying out public activities in the new federal states. The agency's operation did not aim at any corporate governance of enterprises, rather its objective has been described as "privatisation as soon as possible".

As German economic policy constitutionally follows the ordo-liberal school of thought, federal institutions (including the trust agency) have to ensure that the market economy functions well and secure socially acceptable conditions. These preconditions are assumed to have been established through legal regulations and the framework-setting activity by the trust agency and other federal institutions, e.g. *Bundeskartellamt*, federal economic ministry etc.

It can however be debated whether the concrete institutionalising itself can be evaluated as evolutionary as an intended structure was created and this creation was exercised by mainly one institution and legal regulations some of which were already existent prior to unification. Therefore a strict East German economic transformation in the sense of an evolutionary change can not yet at this stage be found. The matters of change clearly contradict liberal economics because they go beyond safeguarding decentralised economic action, their means aimed at a particular structural order. The question whether the chosen order is correct is subject to matters of normative economics and the approach is positivist in nature because of its assumption of Weber's instrumental-rational theory. It is assumed that economic agents act rationally and aim to achieve individual pre-defined objectives. The institutionalisation makes use of these assumptions in the notion that the chosen structure will enable such individual behaviour. These institutional aspects coincide with the DIM-approach with regard to their assumed behavioural functions. Economic evolution has been institutionalised and in this sense contradicts the Schumpeterian evolution theory in the evolutionary definition.

It has been argued by Siebert (1991) and Heimpold *et al* (1991) that the transformation in East Germany followed the Schumpeterian development process and this interpretation fails to acknowledge major facts concerning the theory itself and its interpretation regarding the actual transformation process. Transformation might be interpreted as being initiated endogenously, but the transformation itself is institutional in nature and dependent on defining the system's exogeneously constructed boundaries. Schumpeter's differentiation of market evolution and system development is to be maintained. Market and product development in the East German case is not characterised by evolutionary destruction as markets must be surmised as having been destroyed by external factors such as this integration into a contrasting and incompatible structure. Had the system continued to exist the markets might have been able to develop and change but the destruction of the system implied the destruction of existing markets.

Any market development has had to be subsequent to the re-institutionalising of the framework and thereby has become compulsory (rather than evolutionary). Nevertheless the markets are free to develop further once the institutional framework has been established by federal institutions such as the Treuhandanstalt and the process of conscious institutionalising is finished. Only the continuous economic development succeeding the institutional transformation qualifies as evolutionary. This notion clearly represents the boundaries of any further central economic intervention in the sense of strategic economic policies by federal authorities, as free economic development is targeted after the establishment of the institutional framework.

Nevertheless it has to be acknowledged that the scope of action available to central political authorities and to the Treuhand itself has been designed as being open to interpretation (such as chosen wordings like "suitable means" in legal references) and as such left open areas of non-defined policies and means of action. Although the strategic restructuring of enterprises in the way of establishing new markets, new products and major capital investment as part of the transformation process has been left predominantly to the private sector (i.e. those companies privatised or transferred to the private investors) it will be shown later that transitional policies were introduced in a pragmatic way. The exclusive institutional approach presented in this chapter proved to be insufficient in its temporal aspect and the adjustment of economic action was characterised by deficiencies which made further pragmatic intervention into the factual development necessary. Employment subsidies for example followed structural principles and the general aims of German regional policy as the granting of subsidies depended on regional and structural circumstances (see next chapter). Conflicts between short-term economic-political objectives and the theoretical foundation of the transformation approach in institutional economics led to the implementation of transitional economic policies. The entity of political means of economic policy aimed at, and was justified with, the establishment of a socially-acceptable framework for a market economy. Despite the advocation of competition and as little intervention as possible by the state these ordo-liberal principles - which were followed during the establishment of the West German post-war economy - were not the dominant parameters to be applied during the transitional period. Beise (1995) refers to the comparatively higher utilisation of these principles in East European reform states. No help was received in Eastern Europe like the former East Germany has had and this went along with a larger reliance on competitive forces.

Chapter Four
Transitional Privatisation Policy: Objectives, Instruments and Theoretical Implications

4.1 Introduction

This chapter intends to analyse the concrete means of privatisation as part of the institutional change. The economic policy of the East German transformation has combined the institutional change - detailed within the previous chapter - with particular economic objectives. It will be established that the approach went beyond the basic creation of private property rights and applied, by employing a selection function certain economic beliefs and principles about the assumed behaviour of individual economic agents. The employment of the ordo-liberal approach based on Eucken as the theoretical institutional framework for the East German economic transformation has focused on the creation of definite private property rights. The combination of this approach with the beliefs of the Property Rights School emphasised the individual as being motivated by self-interest and therefore creating his own utility function. The individual decision-maker desires to maximise his utility rather than the firm's profits. It is assumed that the utilisation of resources will improve due to the change from a public property structure to a private one. The approach aimed at identifying the "best" private owners, leading individual economic action in the direction of particular behaviour with various macroeconomic aims such as investment and employment and the aim of reducing and internalising transformation costs.

Economic growth was one aim of the transition. It was believed that directing economic behaviour towards capital investment and safeguarding employment would prevent the East German economy from being sustained by the financial transfers it has been receiving from the West since unification. The establishment of private property rights has been made subject to this aim, in particular the increase in net investment to produce a capacity effect. Social costs of economic transformation can be identified as costs created by the alteration of the economic system and the period of economic adjustment. Such costs can be recognised in the necessity to support the unemployed - those made redundant as part of the actual transformation process -, the creation of a new economic infrastructure, the provision of housing etc. These social costs of transformation were addressed and it was aimed to internalise them by the chosen privatisation policy. In particular political means were found to assign to a third investor property which was classified as to be re-privatised and for which the former owner was to be compensated. The methodology of new privatisation also aimed at the reduction of costs to society by defining a selected behaviour function (section 3.5.3.3) and thereby incorporated objectives of economic policy into the institutional establishment of private property rights (section 2.3.1.2). This privatisation policy will be analysed on the basis of the transaction cost approach as part of the property rights approach introduced in the theoretical part of the thesis. This analysis will form the basis for identifying and modelling the THA privatisation approach in the later chapter 6 with regard to welfare implications and the evaluation of the concrete transformation policy, its weaknesses and strengths as well as enabling a revision of the approaches identified as being valid to be applied in transformation economics. The next section explains the "follow-up" approach ensuing the institutional set-up of the structural transformation. This follow-up approach and the approach of new privatisation will then be analysed regarding its implications on social transformation costs. It will be argued that these have been partially internalised based on the assumption of negligible costs of transaction. The overall method employed for the privatisation within the category of open property issues (i.e. those properties whose identity of owners has not yet been decided) coincides with the definition of a selected behavioural function identified as part of the procedure of new privatisation.

4.2 Open Property Issues: Institutionalised Support of Capital Investment

4.2.1 The Principle of Restitution and the Restraint of Disposal

The institutional transformation identified in the preceding chapter initially followed ordo-liberal principles and this implied that central authorities were merely concerned with the establishment of a framework for a market economy that functions well. This also suggests that the Treuhandanstalt should not engage in any strategic restructuring and only carry out the basic restructuring of enterprises such as corporatisation and separation. Institutional restructuring as part of the privatisation carried out by the Treuhand aimed at establishing the socially-acceptable conditions of a market economy. These principal constitutional guide-lines prevented federal institutions such as the Treuhand from carrying out any strategic investment. This is evidenced by the fact that the record of investment in TH-companies is smaller than that in already privatised enterprises. However it was recognised that property which was still held by the Treuhand made private investment virtually impossible due to insecure property issues. The process of a successful transformation with the objective to achieve similar standards of living in the two German regions depended on rapid and substantial investment. The main precondition for investment was a functioning market within which property could be supplied and bought. Since this did not exist it represented a major drawback. Even private land or real estate ownership was characterised by uncertainties about property values, possible growth rates of value and potential property claims by former owners or their heirs. This inevitably led to a decrease in supply and severe price fluctuations. Measures had to be found to incorporate desired economic behaviour into the privatisation methodology. These measures were created by passing legal regulations in particular enabling investment by the private sector into enterprises which were not yet privatised, i.e. still to be sold or restituted.

The support of capital investment in the new federal states has been linked in particular to regulations regarding the restitution of property to its former owners. Initially a Law for Special Investment (BInvG=InvG) was enacted on 23rd September 1990 (BGBL II, S. 885, 1157), amended by the Law to Eliminate Hindrances of Privatisation (*Hemmnisbeseitigungsgesetz*, BGBL I, S. 774) dated 22nd March 1991 and it became effective as the "Law for the Precedence of Investment in case of Restitutional Claims under the Property Law" (*Investititonsvorranggesetz*, InVorG) as part of the Second Amendment of the Property Law (14.7.1992).

The first phase of legally administering the implementation of private property rights and enforcing re-privatisation was initiated by the joint declaration and in particular by the enactment of the property law (VermG). The following principle was formulated: In circumstances where expropriations are to be reversed, the property has to be restituted to its rightful owner (Paragr. 2, 3 VermG). This excludes - as has already been pointed out in section 3.5.2.1 - property which was expropriated under Soviet occupation, namely expropriations undertaken throughout the land reform (*Bodenreform*) and the expropriation and nationalisation of large industrial enterprises. The restitution of corporations has been regulated in Paragraphs 6-6b VermG and in many cases of state-owned real properties restitution claims could be enforced (see Willgerodt, 1993).[73]

The legal regulations generally differentiated between the restitution of real estate and the restitution of enterprises. According to Paragraphs 3 and 8 VermG the former owner of land property could choose compensation instead of real restitution. Restitutive claims had been made transferable with the preeminence of the *Hemmnisbeseitigungsgesetz* so as to alleviate the investment by potential third parties. The restitution of enterprises proved more difficult because the initial entity at the time of expropriation might have ceased to exist. The arising difficulty of identifying the owner and the potential economic necessity of separating enterprises were pin-pointed as the major critical points regarding the principle of restitution rather than compensation *per se* (Westermann, 1993). A further major problem accrued from the rule to pay or deduct a compensatory sum in the case of restituting an enterprise which had experienced appreciations or depreciations in value since its transfer from peoples' property to the holder of the right of disposal, mainly the THA. It was often argued when the progress of privatisation was slow that restitutive claims were responsible for the lack of investment. Doubts as to whether certain real estates on which enterprises that were to be sold were situated might have had to be restituted often hindered potential buyers (Siebert, 1991). The negative attestation (i.e. the confirmation of the non-existence of claims of re-privatisation) proved a rather time-consuming and bureaucratic act. At the end of 1994 the BAROV received a total of 3 324 510 inquiries with regard to applications for restitution of which 92% were testified as negative (Bundesanstalt zur Regelung offener Vermoegensfragen, Pressemitteilung 31.12.1994).

Restitutional claims were dealt with administratively[74] and until any final decree and decision regarding the ownership of the property had been taken a restraint of disposal under Paragraphs 3, Clause 3 VermG was put into force. The general effect of Clause 3 was that the person, or institution, which held the right of disposal of a real estate was denied the transaction of legal acts without the approval of the potentially rightful owner if the latter had filed a restitutional claim. This regulation represented another hindrance of the tradeability of real estates, such as buildings and land, which were essential for further investment. The complexity of the process of property restitution and the restraint of disposal according to Paragraph 3 Clause 3 VermG initiated regulations to alleviate investment.

Although a general priority of investment over restitution had been defined within the Unification Treaty (Article 41, Clause 2) it did not prove successful as the declaration was too vague (Watrin, 1991). The creation of further legal regulations thus became inevitable. The initial regulation laid down the possibility not to restitute property rights if the respective property (real estate) was urgently needed for special investment plans (which had to be further specified), in particular for the establishment of commercial businesses and if the investment proved to have positive implications for the economic development and the employment situation. These general regulations were put into more concrete legal forms (laws) with the passing of the property law (VermG) and the investment law (InvG). Since these initial regulations too did not prove to be sufficient given the prevailing economic difficulties in East Germany to secure the desired investment a further extension of the framework of cases for the precedence of investment occurred.

4.2.2 Initial Regulations: Property Transactions in the Case of Restitutional Claims

The property law provided a general exclusion clause (Paragr. 5 VermG) which excluded the restitution of real property (land, buildings) in the following cases:
- the property's purpose of utilisation had been changed with considerable costs and this utilisation is in the public interest;
- the property had been designated to common usage;
- the property had been employed in the building of dwellings and housing estates; or

- the property had been employed in commercial usage or had become part of an enterprise and for which it cannot be separated without considerably impairing the business.

The usual interpretation of this exclusion clause emphasised that the utilisation of this property within the commercial unit had to have been initiated by the property's expropriation and thus did not include the *status quo* utilisation of real property within commercial businesses (Westermann, 1993). The noticeably narrow purview of this exclusion clause necessitated regulations for the precedence of transactions. The legal wording distinguishes between "simple" and "super" regulations for economic transactions despite restitutive claims.

4.2.2.1 Simple Regulations for Transactions

Simple regulations of the InvG and VermG extended the regulation of Article 41 Clause 2 Unification Treaty. The unification treaty only considered the restitution of real estates which should not occur, if the property was needed for urgent investment purposes. These however were not clearly defined. Investment purposes were merely described widely as the establishment of business premises and the notion that the promotion of investment would be economically desirable, creating or securing employment. The unification treaty thus did not provide any regulations regarding investment support within enterprises. These regulations were accommodated within the investment and property laws, which both came into force on 29th September 1990 and were two of the last laws issued by the GDR. The two laws defined the following forms of property transactions despite claims of restitution (InvG, Paragr. 3-8 VermG, excluding Paragr. 3a VermG):

a) real property: sale, hereditary building lease, dwelling ownership, partial ownership, letting, leasing, limited material rights (servitude), investment by the right of disposal's holder (the actual user) himself; and
b) corporations: sale, leasing, investment by the right of disposal's holder himself.

The original investment priorities applied only to real estates and corporations which were burdened with a claim for restitution and excluded any property held under state authoritarian trust (Fieberg & Reichenbach, 1994). The regulations of the two laws enabled the holder of the right of disposal in the case of particular investment purposes to dispose over the property despite the restraint of disposal of Paragraph 3 Clause 3 VermG in the case of an application for restitution. The InvG was designed to allow the realisation of urgent and special investment purposes for real estates and buildings and Paragraph 3 Clause 3 VermG (1990 version) regulated the property transactions only if they were inevitably necessary. These original regulations were extended and therewith included cases for the precedence of investment over restitution for enterprises in the 1991 version of the VermG. The legal alterations signify a deviation from the original principle of restitution. They differentiate between real estate property and corporations and will be described in more detail below.

Real Estate Property

The discrepancy of interest between the individual claim for restitution and the national interest of the implementation of investment had been the basis of the legal provisions of the Law for Special Investment, which has since been abolished (InvG, *Gesetz ueber besondere Investitionen*). Paragraph 1 of the InvG allowed property transactions (disposition, letting, leasing) for the current holder of the right of disposal for real properties originally in national ownership if special investment objectives were given even though a claim for restitution might have been filed. The regulation only qualified those real properties which had been expropriated and transferred into national ownership, i.e. those properties which were included in the registry "Property of the People". As any national property ceased to exist with the ratification of the unification treaty the right to dispose of the property was accordingly held by:

-restructured national corporations (GmbHs) and combines (KGs), or
-local authorities under public law, or
-the Treuhand.

These holders of the right of disposal were assigned with a full right of disposal if a particular investment objective existed in spite of restitution claims. The validity of Paragraph 3 Clause 3 VermG was thus suspended if any of the three cases listed in Paragraph 1 Clause 2 InvG was given. Specified special objectives were:

a) job preservation or job creation, in particular through the establishment of commercial business premises or a service company,
b) provision for required dwellings for the population,
c) necessary infrastructure creation

and the utilisation of the real property for these types of investment was expressed as *necessary*. The classification of the qualified property excluded those expropriated properties which had been under compulsory (controlled) administration[75].

The InvG distinguished between two different forms of investment:

1.) The holder of the right of disposal disposes of, leases or lets the property to a third investor (Paragraph 1, Clause 1 InvG). The leasing or letting contract could be up to twelve years (Paragraph 1a InvG).

2.) The holder of the right of disposal undertakes the investment himself (Paragr. 1c InvG).

The investment projects were given prescribed periods of time in which they had to be realised and this period could only be extended if the investor was not deemed responsible for the delay. Had the investment objective however not successfully been achieved within this period of time due to the investor's fault, the property was to be restituted to the rightful owner (Paragr. 1 Clause 3 or Paragr. 1c in conjunction with Paragr. 1d InvG). Had the project been successfully carried out after all, the rightful owner could claim compensation for the value of the realised price from the disposition of the property before the investment. In the case of a small difference between the sale value and the market value the owner could choose between the two (Paragr. 3 InvG, abolished). Had the investment project been carried out by the holder of the right of disposal the rightful owner could claim compensation for the property's market value at the time before the investment (Parag. 3 Clause 1a InvG). In both cases 1) and 2) the restitution of the real property to the rightful owner could only be enforced if the investment objectives had not been met within the prescribed period of time through the investor's fault.

Corporations

Similar regulations existed for the disposition or lease of corporations since 1991 according to Paragraph 3 Clauses 6 to 8 VermG (a new version of the property law has also abolished these regulations). Here the appropriate right of disposal was partly held by the Treuhand (TH-corporations) and as long as the claim for restitution had not been affirmed, disposition or leasing was allowed if the transaction created or secured employment, enabled investment which would increase competitiveness, or if the rightful owner could not guarantee that he would keep the corporation in existence or undertake any reconstruction.

Applications for these transactions were to be filed by the end of 1993 and the purchaser or leasor had to prove that the corporation was to continue in its particular existing form and it would be reconstructed. The rightful owner had to be informed. In cases where the promised measures were not achieved during the first two years after the transaction, the rightful owner attained the right of restitution. Had the investment measures successfully achieved the objectives, the rightful owner could demand compensation for the corporation's market value at the time the claim for restitution became void. According to Clause 7 (abolished) of Paragraph 3 VermG (old version) the holder of the right of disposal himself could undertake measures to achieve the employment and competitive objectives if he made the necessary equity capital available. The equity capital was to be appropriated to capital reserves and was only allowed to be used for the adjustment of annual debts.

4.2.2.2 Super Regulations for Transactions

In contrast to the initial simple regulations, "super regulations" covered a considerably smaller field of investment forms: sale, letting and leasing but comprised both real estate and enterprise property. All other forms of investment were subject to the simple regulations and, depending on who held the right of disposal, these transactions were either subject to the investment law (real property) or Paragraph 3 Clause 7 property law (corporations).

In cases where the right of disposal was assigned to institutions and local authorities under public law such as the Federation, states, counties, communes and cities or to the trust agency Treuhand, the validity of Paragraph 3 Clause 3 VermG could be suspended under Paragraph 3a VermG (old version). Paragraph 3a VermG was introduced by the enactment of the "Law in order to eliminate hindrances to privatisation" and was designed to be valid until the end of 1992. At that time it was planned that Paragraph 3a should be substituted with a less extensive regulation which would be an amendment of the investment law until the end of 1993. The objectives which had to be met by an investment project in order to allow the disposition, letting and leasing of real property or corporations were the same as under the simple regulations.

The main difference to the simple regulations was the formal procedure which was simpler and quicker in the purview of Paragraph 3a VermG (old version). The holder of the right of disposal had to inform the administrative body about the desired transaction and the potential rightful owner had a mere right of opinion. The decision concerning the precedence of investment over restitution was then taken by the holder of the right of disposal who only had to take into consideration whether the rightful owner himself expressed similar intentions concerning investment.

Paragraph 3a VermG (old version) generally represented the legal right of transactions to be taken by the Treuhand. In the case of the priority of investment over restitution, compensation would be granted for the amount of the sale value plus the relevant earnings accruing from leasing or letting respectively. This provision allowed contracts to be valid as long as the suggested investment objectives were achieved in general. Clause 9 of Paragraph 3a (abolished) declared the precedence of this regulation over the simple regulations of the InvG.

The scope of authorisation was limited to institutions under public law (in light of the wide scope of the regulation) so as to provide decision-making without despotism and with consideration of the rightful owner's interests. Furthermore this scheme was envisaged to hasten the economic adjustment process because most of the former nationally owned property was held by institutions under public law, e.g. *Laender* and communes and this property was made subject to accelerated investment programmes. Super regulations were thus only applicable to institutions under public law and the Treuhand - excluding single Treuhand-corporations - and were limited to the investment forms of sale, letting and leasing.

4.2.3 Final Regulations: The Precedence of Capital Investment over Restitution

The initial slow East German economic inauguration and the weak record of capital investment initiated an extension of the purview of investment priorities in the form of passing an additional law in 1991 (*Gesetz zur Beseitigung von Hemmnissen bei der Privatisierung von Unternehmen und zur Forderung von Investitionen*), establishing the precedence of investment as part of the amendment of the property law in 1992 (*Gesetz zur Aenderung des Vermoegensgesetzes und anderer Vorschriften*).[76] The Investment Precedence Law (InVorG)[77] was announced as Article 6 of the Second Amendment of the Property Law on 14th July 1992.

Paragraph 1 InVorG allowed real estate and corporations - which were or might have been inflicted with restitutional claims according to the property law - to be used (entirely or partly) for special investment purposes and the property's owners were paid compensation.

4.2.3.1 Forms of Capital Investment and Investment Purposes

Paragraph 2 InVorG Clause 1 regulated those circumstances under which the constraints of Paragraph 3 Clause 3-5 VermG were not to be applied. The following forms of capital investment deferred restitution claims and transferred them into compensatory payments provided a certificate of investment precedence was awarded.

<u>Real Estate</u>

a) Forms of Investment

- The holder of the right of disposal sells, lets or grants a lease on the property.
- The property has been assigned with a building lease or servitude and this may be expanded to other land properties as well.
- Partial or house ownership regarding the real estate is created.
- A building or construction is created, expanded or rebuild.

b) Investment Purpose

i) Protection or creation of employment opportunities

One of the three investment purposes is the protection or creation of employment opportunities through the establishment of a commercial corporation or a service company. The legal regulations did not prescribe a minimum number of jobs to be protected or created in order to ease the regulations for small and medium-sized companies. The regulations did not include any rules or instructions concerning how jobs were to be secured or created.

ii) Supply of housing

The original regulation in the form of Paragraph 3a VermG (old version) supported an investment plan which could serve the supply of housing in that it should satisfy a *considerable* amount of housing needs. *Considerable* housing needs were characterised by the demand of fundamental parts of the population which were not expected to be met within a suitable period of time by either the existing housing stock or the new creation of housing without additional building land. Because of the serious housing shortage in the East a considerable need for housing could generally be expected.

This legal regulation did not explicitly define the number of people considered to have considerable housing needs and this terminology was dropped within the Investment Precedence Law (Paragr. 3 InVorG). Within the final regulation it suffices to create new housing or to recreate housing in areas which are uninhabited or impossible to live in. It also provides for the possibility of building or restoring houses for one or two families as long as this is in accordance with urban development.

iii) Necessary further infrastructure investment

Infrastructure measures are development and construction works of all kind such as roads, public utility and disposal equipment (electricity, water, sewage, gas), facilities and equipment for the development of commercial and industrial areas. Within the former regulation of Paragraph 3a VermG these measures had to be necessary for investment measures to secure or create employment or to satisfy considerable housing needs. The new InVorG stipulates infrastructure measures which are necessary for any kind of investment or have been initiated by investment. The purview of infrastructure measures has thus been widened.

<u>Corporations</u>

a.) Forms of Investment

- The holder of the right of disposal sells or grants a lease with regard to the corporate shares or the corporate assets.
- The holder of the right of disposal carries out the investment himself.

b.) Investment Purposes

i) Protection or creation of employment opportunities, or to enable investment which will improve the competitiveness

The same investment purpose had been expressed in Paragraph 3a VermG and had been adopted within the new InVorG in 1992. This investment purpose can certainly be seen as a frequent form of investment in corporations particularly as no quantification of employment creation or securing is given.

ii) No guarantee of further existence of corporation

The former owner did not guarantee to keep the corporation as an on-going business, neither did he guarantee to make the enterprise viable. This investment purpose was directly adopted from the VermG without any modification. The prospect of the owner not undertaking investment himself might have led to a closure of the enterprise by the holder of the right of disposal or the closure after restitution. The costs which would have been necessary to keep the enterprise until the final closure by the owner might not have been negligible. It has to be noted on the other hand that it might have been difficult for the former owner to express the required guarantee, especially if he himself had not been attached to or been engaged within the particular business for some time. The same applies to persons who inherited a corporation. This notion represents the somewhat negative expectation of performance regarding restitution to former owners. It seems that the sale to an outsider (i.e. a new privatisation) was expected to prove more successful than the restitution of corporations to former owners.

iii) Liquidation or insolvency could not otherwise be prevented in the long run

The possibility of preventing the liquidation or insolvency due to otherwise unavoidable payment difficulties or indebtedness qualified as another newly introduced investment purpose.

4.2.3.2 Formal Procedure and Interpretation[78]

Any investment plan had to be investigated to see whether it met one of the three special investment purposes (Paragr. 4 InVorG). The THA chose the "best" of the investment plans, however the interpretation of the "best" was not predetermined. The THA had thus a factual possibility of selecting directly on the basis of its own views. The certification of investment precedence to a particular investor was identical to the selection procedure of choosing a purchaser in the case of new privatisation. The investment plan had to be attested by the certificate of investment precedence (*Investitionsvorrangbescheid*). This certificate was generally issued by the holder of the right of disposal himself. The Treuhand was however not allowed to issue the certificate as long as it held the right of disposal itself - apart from the exemption clause of Paragraph 25 Clause 2 InVorG which enabled the THA to certify the investment precedence in cases in which properties of TH-corporations were involved.[79] The property law (VermG) arranged the procedure of issuing the investment certificate informally and no application had to be submitted since no proceedings for the assignment of the investment certificate existed. Potential investors simply had to address the holder of the right of disposal, i.e. local authorities under public law (*Bund, Laender, Kommunen*) or the Treuhandanstalt. The decision-making power with respect to the acceptance of an investment plan lay thus in the hands of the holders of the right of disposal who had to make sure that the relevant legal provisions and requirements were met. The local property office was to be informed about the planned transactions and, if any restitution claims were known, the rightful owner was to be notified as well (Paragr. 3a Clause 3 VermG). Both regulations for the termination of the restraint of disposal (simple, super) assigned the rightful owner the right of comment, i.e. he had to be given time to study the relevant files and the opportunity to give his individual opinion about the investment plan. In the case where the rightful owner himself was interested in undertaking investment, it was still the holder of the right of disposal who made the final decision which of the alternative investment plans should be implemented. The legal investment aid alleviated the restitution claim of the rightful owner only to the degree necessary for further investment. The ideal case was thus the restitution of the property and successive investment undertaken by the owner himself. The rightful owner nevertheless had to demonstrate that his investment plan was equivalent or similar to the plans of third investors. The right of comment which was assigned to the rightful owner characterised and gave effect to this principle in that the latter could make his alternative investment plans explicit and the restitution would not be restrained if the plan proved to be useful.

The procedure of assigning a certificate of investment precedence has been extensive and time consuming. Once the investment certificate had been issued the proceedings for the restitution were frozen and the former owner who filed for restitution was informed that his property was needed for investment purposes. Although he had a right of comment, the decision taken by the holder of the right of disposal qualified as an administrative act as long as the owner did not himself suggest a similar investment plan within the following six weeks (Paragr. 5 Clause 3 InVorG). However the second amendment of the Property Law committed the holder of the right of disposal in Paragraph 21 InVorG to assign the investment certificate to the former owner if he offered a similar investment plan and was able to guarantee personally and economically the implementation of the investment plan. If Paragraph 21 was not employed, Paragraph 19 InVorG, which regulates the public bidding process could be used. This public bidding process was often exercised by the TLG. The process was characterised by publicly asking for investment plans and the acceptance of a bid immediately qualified as a certificate of investment precedence. The former owner had no right of comment and was only assigned with the certificate himself if his investment proposal was similar to the best of the other proposals. The latter regulation can be interpreted as a legal possibility of a likely exclusion of the former owner from his property and compensatory payment being the only option because of the reduction in his chances of being approved as the investor. Although the bidding process simulated a market situation on the demand side, the Treuhand was still in the position of a monopolistic supplier. It could determine whose investment proposal qualified as the best and the legal regulations gave no indication as to how the "best" plan should be interpreted. The procedures regarding the establishment of investment precedence made use of elements employed in the sale to outsiders (Willgerodt, 1993; see section 3.5.3.2.2.1).

The initial lack of a compensation law has been suggested as a possible reason for the inefficient procedure of restitution and the speculative restraint (Willgerodt, 1993). Former owners tended to file their claims for restitution but as no law existed until the end of 1994 regarding the respective compensation they would only be paid in the case of a renunciation (*Verzicht*) and would instead aim for compensation and postpone the factual restitution of the property. Factual restitution and compensation in the case of investment precedence (Paragr. 16 InVorG) was more lucrative for many former owners.

Under the investment law (Paragr. 2 InvG) the holder of the right of disposal (actual user) had to apply to the head of administration of the *Landkreis* or the mayor for the assignment of the investment certificate. This meant that neither the investor nor the rightful owner held the right of application. The holder of the right of disposal was in the position to choose between different investment plans and make a pre-selection.[80] The rightful owner and the constituency (*Gemeinde*) had the right of comment and the local authority of the *Landkreis* made the final decision whether or not to issue the investment certificate. The investment certificate did not represent the final decision. Only the contract with the investor was the final decision which qualified as an administrative act (in contrast to the super regulation where no certificate was necessary and issued and the holder of the right of disposal made the decision keeping in mind the relevant requirements). Some empirical results with regard to numbers of applications are presented in table 4.1.

The figures represent that the number of re-privatised enterprises and enterprise parts has stagnated more or less since 09/93 representing the impact the regulations for the precedence of capital investment over restitution have had. Restitutions by the THA have to be valued against the background of 3 000 completed cases of restitution by 29.9.1990.

Table 4.1: Applications for Enterprise Restitution, Forms of Enterprise and Enterprise Part Re-Privatisation (over time, aggregated values)

Year	Completed Applications for Enterprise Restitution	Re-privatised THA-Enterprises	Re-privatised Enterprise Parts
01/92	3 680	735	2 599
03/92	3 906	764	2 602
06/92	4 701	857	2 837
12/92	4 008	1 188	2 820
03/93	7 579	1 274	2 910
06/93	7 976	1 360	2 712
09/93	8 420	1 511	2 703
12/93	9 038	1 573	2 696
03/94	9 809	1 578	2 741
06/94	10 158	1 585	2 714

Year	Re-privatised Enterprise Assets Paragr. 6 (6a) VermG	Enterprise Sales Agreed by Former Owner	Sales & Inv.Prec.
01/92	442	84	
03/92	451	89	
06/92	817	190	
12/92	1 210	415	
03/93	1 406	447	
06/93	1 534	*690*	
09/93	1 641	495	
12/93	1 779		1 216
03/94	1 956		1 464
06/94	2 064		1 509

Year	Investment Precedence	Compensation	Rejections by LAROV & Withdrawals
12/92	447	387	377
03/93	598	498	446
06/93	*491*	621	568
09/93	608	759	703
12/93		884	890
03/94		993	1 077
06/94		1 072	1 216

Source: Treuhandanstalt(a), current issues. Data for the number of re-privatised enterprise assets according to Paragr. 6 (6a) VermG from 06/93 onwards include property restitutions based on law of 7.3.1990. Data written in italic represent deviations as the results of database restructuring.

The enterprises and enterprise parts were restituted according to Paragraphs 17-19 of the Law Regarding the Creation and Operation of Private Enterprises and Enterprise Participations. According to the above figures and information supplied by the BVS[81] about half of all enterprise sales were accompanied by investment precedence decisions (merely 10% of real estate sales).

The vast number of legal regulations with regard to investment precedence cases has *de facto* moved away from restitution and focused on the privatising to third investors. If no third investor made any acceptable investment proposal restitution was nevertheless exercised and the former owner was only financially compensated if he could not suggest a superior investment plan. These investment plans targeted social areas such as infrastructure, housing, creation of jobs etc. The investment plans can thus potentially internalise social costs. This internalisation of social costs is assumed because transformation costs as defined above would have had to be paid in the form of government expenditure and would have been partially re-allocated to the tax-payer. These investment projects are characterised by their social spill-over effects and like the new privatisation guarantees aim at increasing the nation's production potential. The selection of a private owner followed the Treuhand's selection function and incorporated the selection element "external benefit" in form of the spill-over effect of the private investment plan which was sought to be maximised.

4.3 Property Rights-Theoretical Implications

4.3.1 Transaction Costs as Public Costs

The creation of the East German private property rights structure was institutionalised through the creation of the state institution Treuhandanstalt. The economic, monetary and political unification of the two German states necessitated the rapid establishment of the framework guaranteeing that the new economic system would function well. This form of societal transformation has predefined the rapid identification of private owners as the objective of privatisation. The constitutional right of private property prevented the neglect of previous owners of expropriated or nationalised properties and had to consider *de facto* restitution or compensatory payment to the former owners. The option of selling the entire property to new owners and compensating old ones would have involved high administrative costs as well as the compensatory payments. Compensation could have been paid by the new owners, but the selection function (i.e. the emphasis on investment and employment guarantees, see section 4.4) already narrowed down the property rights. The option of new privatisation and restitution reduced the comparative transaction costs and was chosen as the two privatisation methods. The general decision in favour of the principle of *de facto* restitution can only be supported from an economic stand-point. Had new privatisation (i.e. the sale of the entire East German national property) been decided as the only method of establishing private property rights, a considerable amount of compensatory payments would have been allocated to West Germans which would have implied a monetary withdrawal from the East. Compensation paid to East Germans on the other hand without any economic pre-determination of usage (in contrast to real compensation in production factors) would have been mainly used for consumption purposes as can be deduced from consumers' behaviour in East Germany immediately after the economic unification. Both methods of privatisation (sale privatisation and restitution) are characterised by transaction costs which are positive and not negligible. These transaction costs have been made the burden of a third party within the privatisation method and neither the purchasing owner nor the former owner had to provide for them. Although the TH could have - in the case of no real restitution - carried out the function of an indirect clearing agency between the former owner and the new purchaser, the insecure nature of the sale classifies compensation as a monetary transference from the fiscal budget to mainly private households in the West and in the East. Payment of compensation on a commissions basis would have been impossible to maintain given budget-considerations, e.g. the case of an unsuccessful sale would have impounded considerable administrative costs on the privatising institution. Against the background of the constitutional necessity of returning or restituting property to former owners, the principle of restitution in real property was certainly preferable to the case of extending the privatisation agency's responsibility for selling property with regard to budgetary implications. The opportunity costs involved with the restitution are certainly smaller than the ones associated with new-privatisation. If one disregards the possibility of an entire denial of the existence of any former ownership rights in the GDR (which were curtailed and later abandoned during Marxism-Leninism) and the option of the sheer sale of all property without any compensation payments (which would have been constitutionally impossible), the payment of compensation rather than restituting property would not have implied any major advantages to the chosen principle of restitution. According to Coase and Demsetz (1972, 1973) it is generally acknowledged that private property rights internalise externalities if transaction costs are zero or negligible. In the case of the economic transformation in East Germany, the establishment of private property rights does not follow the evolutionary process from communal to private rights (chapter 3, section 3.5) unless the institutionalising of the transfer from communal to private rights is interpreted as evolutionary itself. The assignment of private property rights (new privatisation and re-privatisation) via the institution of the THA, local authorities and organisations under public law involves costs which account for a considerable sum of government expenditures. As the costs involved regarding the restitution of property to former owners and the assessment and/or finding of alternative investors are mainly of an administrative nature (the administrative procedure has been indicated above) the sum total of transaction costs in either case can be considered not to differ considerably.

However, it is not necessarily argued that the potential new owners face no transaction costs at all attaining the private right. Information costs are present but are negligible because of the Treuhand's method of publicising the respective properties to be sold. The formulation of the relevant employment and investment guarantees in the case of sale privatisation involves research as well as administrative costs. These costs too do not prevent an optimal reallocation of resources because if the proposal is successful the guarantees become contractual agreements and reflect in the value of the property (which will be referred to and analysed below). The case of investment precedence over restitution also implies costs of formulating investment plans and the same applies here with regard to the individual evaluation of the respective property. These positive transaction costs do not classify as having sub-optimal allocative effects because no divergence exists between the price and the value of the right exchanged, i.e. such divergence is rejected by the new formulation of the value of the property right determining its allocation. Therefore it is assumed that the transaction costs of attaining the private right are negligible for the potential new owner. It can however be argued that only those individuals and organisations with the necessary wealth endowment are able to participate in the privatisation process and this classifies as a general prerequisite for every reallocation of resources and any change within a ownership structure.

4.3.2 Re-Definition of Some Property Rights-Theoretical Assumptions

According to the Property Rights School private property rights under the assumption of negligible transaction costs will be socially preferable to any other form of ownership because of the internalisation of social costs. Therefore only the private rights structure is perceived as stable because of this responsiveness to external changes which again will be internalised.

As has previously been argued the transaction costs of changing the East German ownership structure were negligible for the potential new owners because these transaction costs qualifying as public costs were created and paid for by the Treuhandanstalt. This presumption would suggest according to Coase (1960) that any private owner is as good as the next one as long as they price the property the same. This suggestion will be proved as only being applicable under certain restrictions. Within the East German privatisation process any exchange of property rights was made subject to the value of the property right because it represented an element of the individual's utility function. As will be argued later government restrictions with regard to the use of the property truncate the property rights which is supposed - according to Coase - to lower its value. It will be shown that this reduction in the property's value will have positive income effects. Not only will the distribution of the resources change but also the distribution of income. The change in the structure of the East German property rights has affected the way people behave and through this effect on the economic behaviour, the identity of the owner and the content of the property right has affected the allocation of resources, the composition of output and the distribution of income. The property rights approach must be re-defined if applied to the East German privatisation model.

4.3.2.1 Value of the Property Right as Allocative Force

The privatisation model of the East German economy designates a variation from the concept of the price determining the identity of owners. The price is conceived as a secondary factor indicating the property's value and the utility it can generate for the owner. The German model can be argued to go beyond utility generation for the potential owner: it introduces the utility the new owner can generate for the society by owning the property right. Here the potential utility which can be generated by the respective owner is operationalised by the value of the property right. The value the potential owner places on a particular property is indicated by the willingness to agree contractually to various forms of guarantees and plans which form part of the "price" to be paid to attain a property. This perception forms a fundamental amendment to the conventional conception of resource allocation within the property rights theory. The conventional idea of the price of a resource is extended by the concept of the resource's value. The value is variable, whereas the price itself, though being negotiable, is unqualifiable. The variability of the value is expressed in the difference in individual sale proposals which imply various utilitisations of the resource. This amendment implies that despite a given price of the resource the allocation of the resource can be influenced via the concept of value which qualifies the utilisation to which the respective owner contractually agrees. The function that described the process of selecting the new owner thereby set a definite assumption: Any exchange of property rights is subject to the value of the property right and this value represents substantially the individual's utility function. The best use of the property by a potential owner was operationalised by the value potential owners placed on the property. The allocation of resources, the distribution of income and the composition of output can only be expected to remain unchanged in the case of a transaction of a private property right if two holders of a right place the same value on it, have identical and homogeneous utility and production functions, behave according to the principles of the *homo oeconomicus* and are solemnly driven by self interest. Although it can be expected that private property rights will enforce the utilisation of a resource with regard to the individual's self interest, a Pareto-efficient situation can only be expected if the individual who values the right the most is assigned with it. The highest value is not necessarily the highest monetary price, but can be the commitment to certain governmental rules. This privatisation policy placed the emphasis on the selection of owners and is based on the knowledge regarding their future economic behaviour and aimed at the achievement of an overall economic capacity effect. The aspect of employing a selection function for the identification of the owner will be further elaborated in section 4.3.3.

4.3.2.2 Positive Transaction Costs and the Creation of Private Property Rights

The notion of the property rights school, which maintains that the magnitude of transaction costs determines the identity of owners and the economic outcome, is not applicable in the German privatisation model. The transaction costs of changing the structure of ownership from a public to a private one and creating contracts are not negligible. However these transaction costs of identifying a new owner have not been assigned to the new owner, instead they were regarded as social costs of transforming the property rights structure and were carried by the Treuhandanstalt. Positive non-negligible transaction costs did not have to be paid by the new or the old owner and therefore did not qualify as a factor determining the particular ownership structure and the eventual economic outcome. The suggested internalisation of external effects only applies to intra-firm external effects according to the conventional property rights approach. The incongruity between private and social effects follows insufficiently defined property rights only in the case of intra-firm externalities. Here the establishment of private property rights itself has created external (social) costs in the form of the transaction costs of the Treuhandanstalt. It can not therefore be deduced that insufficient structures are the result of positive transaction costs. Transaction costs were positive and not negligible but a private property rights structure has nevertheless been established.

4.4 Interpretation: Integration of a Selection Function

4.4.1 Definition of Political Objectives and the "Best" Private Owner

The promulgation of legal regulations to alleviate investment can be interpreted as *ad hoc* laws which qualify as auxiliary functions for achieving the general economic objectives of the transformation, unification and the institution Treuhandanstalt. The Treuhand can be seen to have originally been designed as a clearing office between new investors, new buyers, owners with restitutional claims and the respective properties. The unsatisfactory investment and privatisation process during the first few years of the institution's existence forced the legislature to add further legal regulations. These have certainly restrained claims for restitution to some extent and have alleviated the possibility of decrees in favour of new investors. It became possible to make the decision to sell a property, which has been filed for restitution to outsiders and this smoothed the path of new privatisation even though restitutive claims might have existed.

The restitution of enterprises, enterprise parts and real estate property has been designed ultimately to serve the function of an efficient market economy with private property rights and markets for goods and service as well as markets for production factors. Re-privatising enterprises has aimed at the creation of markets that function well within a competitive market structure and which efficiently produce and allocate goods and services. Furthermore the establishment of private enterprises has been considered the basis of employment. The number of enterprises to be restituted to former owners was considerably smaller than the number of enterprises to be newly privatised, i.e. sold. Large-scale industrial enterprises were mainly expropriated between 1945 and 1949 under Soviet occupation and these cases were excluded from restitution and legally expressed as irreversible. The THA directly privatised these enterprises via the sale of shares and former owners were compensated according to the compensation law.

Enterprises which were to be restituted to their former owners were thus often not *de facto* restituted, but instead the option of compensating the former owner for the usage of his property by the holder of the right of disposal has been taken. The property right of a former owner has only legally been respected if no other person or institution offered a better usage of the property than the potential owner himself. This exclusion of any investment precedence or previous transactions has factually been necessary for assigning the property right by restitution to the former owner. The claimant himself has had no right of determining the kind of property transactions until it has been legally enforced through an administrative act that the property should be returned to himself.

Legal regulations (after reunification) regarding the establishment of private businesses by restitution as a method of privatisation have concentrated on the prospects for investment by the potentially restituted former owner and any other potential investor. The investment plan has been the de facto decisive factor for the assignment of the property right, which in fact is similar to the new privatisation, as the criteria of employment safeguarding and investment guarantees determine who will be the eventual purchaser. The enterprise has been returned to the former owner if no investment precedence certificate existed or if the former owner has not himself chosen compensation instead. Although this seems to contradict constitutionally Article 14 Basic Law, the private property right was not legally created by unification - it has been enforced by an administrative act of formal restitution. Although the former owner has not been assigned the full bundle of property rights straight away (with the passing of the respective laws) he could act according to Paragraph 3 VermG and transfer or mortgage his claim or have his restitutive claim impounded.

Although enterprises were generally to be restituted to their former owners, the countless cases of legal exemption cause the restitution to be the exception from general compensation in the case of special investment purposes. The former owner could generally choose compensation in monetary terms instead of the factual restitution (Paragr. 8 VermG). Apart from this voluntary right of choice the owner was also compensated for those cases in which his property could not have been restituted. Restitution was considered impossible if the business no longer existed and if the reinstating of the business was commercially unlikely. Furthermore the property was not to be restituted if the enterprise was sold - mainly by the THA - in conformity with existing legal rules, or if the property is attached with particular rights of usage which were legally purchased before 18th October 1989 by individuals, religious organisations or charities (Paragr. 4 Clauses 1 and 2 VermG).

But certainly the most controversial case is the vast number of investment precedence cases and the compensation procedure for the former owners. In contrast to the former owner's option to choose a type of compensation in a third property - if his land property has been legally purchased by a third person - (Paragr. 9 Clause 2 VermG) no reimbursement in real production factors has politically been designed. In cases where third parties have expressed interest in the property and were able to suggest a credible investment plan, a selection depending on the investment purpose has decided about the assignment of the property right. Formerly existing property rights were thus mainly restituted to those owners who were willing to undertake investment and were willing to guarantee the further existence of the enterprise and the utilisation of the production factors. This can be exemplified with regard to special procedures of investment precedence.

Paragraph 18 InVorG comprises a particular procedure for investment projects which are classified as part of special development plans. These development plans have constituted part of particular construction laws and the investment proposals did not require the acceptance through an investment precedence certificate. The former owner who filed a restitutive claim has had no right of comment and even if he proposed a similar investment plan, this plan has not been accorded any preference. The public bidding procedure of Paragraph 19 InVorG has allowed local authorities as well as the THA to ask publicly for offers of investment plans. The acceptance of any of the offered plans has had the legal effect of an investment precedence certificate. The former owner has had the right to submit a proposal as well and his plan was given precedence as long as it was similar to the best other plan. A similar regulation regarding the former owner's situation was designed in the procedure of Paragraph 20 InVorG. Investment plans which included several pieces of land property could be accepted by a general decree. This decree constitutes the precedence of investment before the entity of the restitutive claims filed with regard to the respective properties. The former owner has been granted preference before any other potential investor if his plan is similar and comparable to the general plan which covers several land properties.

The gist of these procedures is expressed in Paragraph 21 InVorG: the former owner is generally to be preferred as an investor, but even this regulation grants a possibility of assigning the certificate to a third investor within three months of the former owner filing his investment plan. The former owner on the other hand has been assigned merely two weeks within which he has to file his plan in the case of a previous investment proposal by another potential investor. The possibility of the former owner who filed a claim for restitution having his property factually restituted in the case of competing investment proposals has been considerably narrowed by the InVorG. If his investment plan is not approved, he will be paid financial compensation. Compensation in the form of a different real property was not designed as an option particularly in the case of another investor being given precedence over the property. The only case where real compensation has been granted is the case of the impossible restitution because a third person has legally purchased the property (Paragr. 9 Clause 2 VermG). This regulation only applies to land property. No such rule exists for any case of investment precedence, i.e. whenever a former owner is unwilling or unable to propose the relevant investment plan he is paid financial compensation rather than real compensation in assets. This notion represents the weight that has been placed on investment with regard to privatisation via rcassigning properties to former owners.

These regulations however seem to oppose the hypothesis of the property rights school with regard to the thesis that private property rights will contribute *per se* to the best possible utilisation of factors. The theoretical approval of this thesis would imply the immediate restitution to former owners no matter which investment inclination the individual holder of the private property right had. It supports this author's critique of Coase's theorem in the second chapter (section 2.3.1.2.3, a change in the allocation of private property rights will not change the output mix in the case of negligible transaction costs). Furthermore the legal restitutive regulations suggest that one institution is able to decide, on the basis of suggested investment projects, who will make the best use of the property right whereas the former owner himself is unable make this decision. The interpretation of the TH's and local authorities' and *Amt fuer offene Vermoegensfragen's* presumption of knowledge in Hayek's sense is often dismissed with regard to the lack of market experience of East Germans. This is further substantiated with the expectation of a rather low business profile of East German property holders by West German policy makers and economic scientists which has been criticised by East German writers (Luft, 1992).

4.4.2 Truncation of Property Rights and Internalisation of Social Costs

The assignment of property rights according to the above regulations follows the thesis of private property rights internalising social costs in the following way: The change of the East German economic system which has been brought about by the general change of Eastern European economies and the economic and political unification of the two German states can be interpreted as a societal change. This social change produces situations which might be interpreted as externalities. The closure of enterprises for example produces social costs which indirectly result from the collapse of production in several industries due to the downfall of the Eastern European market area as well as the lack of competitiveness and of technological and managerial know-how. The social costs are generally caused by structural deficiencies, in particular obsolete means of production and imperfections of factor markets and markets for goods and services, and result in high unemployment. Not only to establish private property rights as a constitutional element of a market economy besides decentral decision-making authority, but also to internalise these social costs has been considered as an important motive to establish private property rights.

The theory of property rights suggests that the assignment of the private property right will follow the individual's concept of self interest. The individual's concept of self interest determines his incentives and thus his behaviour. With regard to the principle of restitution and its repudiation, the individual's utility function, which expresses his self interest, is considered to be derived from investment plans *ceteris paribus*. The value of the property right to the potential owner depends on the utility function the individual assigns to it. This utility function and subsequently the value of the property right is made operational by the investment plan and proposal which symbolises the individual's expected utility, i.e. investment return. The investment plan is thus considered by the assigning institution to be able to internalise the social costs, such as the need of housing, infrastructure etc. Social costs have been created by evolutionary change, i.e. by the widening of the economic scope of action and the opening of the system. In particular the collapse of production in specific sectors, the lack of competitiveness as well as technological and managerial know-how create an economic adjustment process which requires public expenditure which is here defined as social costs of transformation. These transformation costs focus on the areas of unemployment, infrastructure, sectoral and regional deficiencies.

Although it is acknowledged that the general change of the system of property relations (common ownership beforehand, now creation of private ownership rights) will affect the allocation of resources and the distribution of income, the property rights school would not expect differences in the economic outcome (and the best internalisation of social costs) with regard to who (new purchaser, former owner or investor) will be assigned with the private right under the above perfect market situations and circumstances. But here it should be expected that the use of a property and it's property right depend on the *value* the user places on the property. The privatising institutions have applied a methodology to operationalise the potential investor's and former owner's utility of the property. The differences in the investment plans and in the determination to guarantee the relevant investment or employment guarantees symbolise the values (of the privatising institution) attached to the property right. The highest-valuing (and bidding) person or organisation is eventually assigned with the right to use the property. It is therefore assumed that the value of the private property right determines its utilisation and as long as the value of the property right is identical to the market value of the property right, the allocation of the resource or the enterprise can be expected to be Pareto-efficient. The legal regulations employed regarding re-privatisation take care of these circumstances. As long as the privatising institution sufficiently takes over the role of a market for these property rights - that had been possible to create if all former owners would have been immediately restituted[82] - it can be assumed that the usage of the property is allocated to the owner or investor who values the disposal of the property the highest.

The property right assigned to a new owner or a third investor is truncated by the investment and employment guarantees and investment plans (i.e. the property is not assigned to the respective owner's full disposal) he has committed himself to a particular utilisation of the property and he will be financially penalised or will be deprived of the property unless he abides by the contract. In contrast the former owner who has filed for restitution and has not been confronted with any alternative investor's interest or public bidding procedure will be assigned with the full bundle of property rights, i.e. the property is at his full disposal. The traditional property rights school according to Coase *et al* manifests that the value of a property right decreases with the truncation of the property right. Thus the value of the property right assigned to, for example, a third investor (investment plan + sale price = value) should *ex definitione* be lower than the alternative value had the full property rights bundle been assigned to the former owner. The limits of this approach can be identified in the assumption of the objective of a certain institution to equalise the value of the property right with its market value as a prerequisite for the optimal assignment to a new owner because the outcome of individual economic plans can not be foreseen and is not quantifiable.

4.4.3 Income and Distribution Effects

The transaction costs of attaining a respective property have been found as being positive but negligible (sections 4.3.1 and 4.3.2). Thus only the value placed on the property decides upon the assignment of the property right. The party placing the highest value is assumed to make the best usage of the property. It can thereby be suggested that - in the case of potential restitution - the assignment of the property right to either the former owner or the third investor (in the case of a sale by the THA) will result in different production mixes and distributions of income. The assumption of similar and negligible transaction costs according to the property rights theory denies the existence of such effects if property is transferred from one private owner to another. The other investor's investment sum can be interpreted as the price of the property's usage which is then similar to the standard procedure of a sale as transaction of the property right between former owner and purchaser. With the assumption of negligible transaction costs to the potential property right holders and the THA or any other institution simulating a sale-like transaction, the question remains whether the assignment to either of them (new purchaser or third investor) will result in different end-situations. The transaction cost approach as part of the property rights theory (Coase, 1960) hypothesizes that under these circumstances and the existence of homogeneous production functions and perfect market situations, the economic outcomes of either case are identical with regard to the output mix and the distribution of income. The assumption is that the transaction of property rights under these circumstances will not have any income or substitution effects.

According to the existent theory the assignment of the private property right to either the former owner or the investor will *de facto* affect the allocation of the resources, the production output and the distribution of income. The reason for this is the difference in the property right's value. The bundle of property rights eventually assigned to either the investor or the former owner varies according to the above legal regulations, i.e. the former owner is assigned with the full bundle of property rights and the investor's rights are contractually truncated.

Two potential situations for the previous owner have to be distinguished under the InvG in the case of a third party having applied for the attainment of the property. If the previous owner's property is restituted no investment plan is formulated. If the property is not restituted and instead the former owner compensated a contract is formulated between the actual user and the investor. In both cases apart from administrative costs no extra wealth is created or eliminated within the period of the existing unified Germany. In the case of compensation the sale value is transferred from the investor to the actual user (THA) and then to the previous owner.

It is generally assumed that the assignment of a property to alternative users who place different values on the property alters the distribution of income as well as the output mix. This shows that despite negligible transaction costs the alternative potential owners would create diverse economic outcomes. However it is here suggested that even if the two owners attach the same value to the property a variation of the output mix and the distribution of income can be caused. This variation is due to the emphasis that is at this point placed on the *constitution of the property's value* which can change the economic outcome. A high sales price represents a different motive and utility than a lower sales price combined with high employment and investment guarantees and thus represent different use of resources. Diverse economic outcomes and distribution of income must be expected. This also surmises that two identical values placed on one property equal to the market value of the product surmises a Pareto-efficient allocation of the resource. Despite this neoclassically assumed Pareto-efficent situation, the case of two potential owners with heterogeneous utility functions but nevertheless identical property values can be conceived as potentially creating a differentiation in the allocation of income and the output mix.

Distributive effects of changes of property right assignments can be expected if authorities or institutions assign the rights centrally and they are not allocated by the market. The allocation of property rights according to the privatisation methods employed in the East German case identifies private owners of property and thereby the owners of factors of production. The allocation creates private wealth and the distribution of wealth is characterised by a change that does not only differ from the previous situation with regard to the consistence of wealth but is signified by e.g. an increase in capital supply. This will alter the income or profit of the economic unit that has been newly assigned with the wealth-resembling factor of production. The transference of a factor of production or resource from national property to private property therefore has income effects. The distribution of the newly created wealth is pre-defined by the concept of the property's value and it is thus expected that only those who are already endowed with wealth are potentially assigned with the property - neglecting the case of restitution. This discriminatory selection function has led to the current ownership structure with intercorporate West German owners predominating (see chapter 6, section 6.3.4). An increase in the unequal distribution of wealth was predetermined and people without original wealth despite intellectual or managerial knowledge were excluded as potential participators. The initial endowment and the centralised definition of the selection function and the property value assumptions by the Treuhand have influenced the distribution of wealth, the output mix and the distribution of income. It is not the subject of this thesis to analyse concrete distributive effects of the chosen privatisation method and their ethical justification but it shall nevertheless be pointed to Rawl's concept of a just societal change which is defined as having been created as long as the worst off member of society has been made better off despite any variation in the actual distribution of wealth (Rawls, 1973).

4.4.4 First-Best and Second-Best Solutions

The axiomatic principle of the privatisation methodology can be expressed as follows: As long as the benefit of creating private property rights (and the internalisation of social costs) is greater than the costs of creating these private property rights (transaction costs as social costs) a welfare improvement has been achieved because of the internalisation of externalities. Externalities shall be internalised by private owners and the identification of the new owner follows this cost and benefit analysis. Externalities are here defined as the transformation costs which have been created by the changes of structures and elements within the institutional framework and have thereby affected the economic environment. Externalities qualify thus as evolutionary changes, e.g. the structural changes within the economy produce external costs. These externalities change the production function and cause alterations in the cost-benefit structure - for the enterprises as well as for the privatising institution in the form of public budget considerations. The East German property right structures have not evolved freely, instead they were consciously created due to the design of a selection function and the application of a cost-benefit analysis. Furthermore these conscious considerations were not undertaken by independent economic actors but by one central institution, the Treuhand. The conversion from a public ownership structure towards a private property one is thereby denied any evolutionary character in the form of unconscious design and decentralised coordination of economic plans. This particular privatisation policy has tried to operationalise the purchaser's or investor's utility function by defining the elements which constitute the property's value *ex-ante*, i.e. guarantees and specific investment plans. It is then assumed that the highest valuing party who will be assigned with the property right will ensure a Pareto-efficient allocation. It is however obvious that the *ex-ante* determination of utility elements is problematic in the sense of unforeseeable economic results. The individual utility function predescribes the individual's economic behaviour which is assumed to be known. Another major problem is the accountability of guarantees and investment plans as part of the property's value.

The Treuhand's maxim for the identification of the respective owner has been defined as follows: The one who places the highest value on the property will make the best use of it and the best use is defined as to further the functioning of an efficient market economy. Rather than assuming that the first private owner is just as good as the second one, discriminating assumptions are made with regard to the potential owners. The former owner is only identified as the new one in the case of a negative test, i.e. no better party to use the property can be found. A legal act is necessary to enforce the ownership of the former owner, until then the claimant has no property right apart from being considered as a second-best potential property right holder.

The following ranking of possible property assignments are the result of the costs-benefit analysis:

1. New Privatisation with Employment and Investment Guarantees

2. Third Investor with Investment Plan and Compensation to former Owner

3. Restitution with Investment Plan

4. Restitution

The assignment of the property to a new owner truncates the property right due to the contractual agreement to employment and investment guarantees which forms part of the property's value function together with the sales price. The assignment to a third investor alongside the investment plan and compensation of the owner also truncates the property rights bundle. The investor is committed to a particular utilisation of the property and the investment plan is either supposed to create social benefits or internalise social costs. The restitution of the property to its former owner in the case of him filing an investment plan "just as good as the third one" has the advantage of not necessitating any compensating payments but it must be assumed to create smaller benefits because any better third investor would have been preferred. The least preferred case is the restitution of the property to its former owner because it demands the transfer of the full property rights bundle and can not be accompanied by any further benefit-creating contracts. In the first three cases a single government organisation takes over the role of the market and selects the most favourable private owners. The selection method emphasises the factors of employment, investment and internalisation of social transformation costs (e.g. infrastructure costs). It was assumed that the transfer of the economic restructuring responsibilities to private owners and their internalisation enforces the process of economic adjustment.

The transfer of the property to a new owner or investor with truncated property rights is assumed to be the first-best solution as it represents the Pareto-superior situation during the period of transition. Despite the assignment of the full bundle of the property rights, the case of restitution is only the second-best solution because the utilisation of the property is not pre-defined. The assignment of the property right to an investor who is more willing to invest in the property, enterprise or land than the former owner will result in a more efficient allocation of resources and internalise some social costs which were created by the property (e.g. *Altlasten*). The first-best solution defines the property's utilisation as part of the national production function and in that respect takes care of the non-comparibility of private utility functions.

The political decision for the first-best solution rather than the market solution of restitution expects a Pareto-superior situation in the case of a truncation of the property right during the period of transition. A first-best situation of legal regulations is expected to be Pareto-superior to a full assignment of the private property rights bundle during the transitional period because the utilisation of the property at the time of the re-privatisation is not pre-defined. The utility functions of the alternative users are non-comparable because the utilisation might be private or commercial and the usage of the property as a factor of production in a commercial way is assumed to be superior. The assignment of the truncated property right however defines the property as a factor of production. In contrast the full assignment to a private former owner with a restitutive claim might withdraw the property (e.g. land, building) from the production process. These considerations might nevertheless only be considered as valid during the transitional period until markets which function well have been established and market deficiencies have been eliminated. This can nevertheless only be expected as long as the privatising institutions realistically simulate an effective market for private property rights and in particular the transparency of the quasi-market has been created. This can be expected if Paragraph 19 InVorG is employed and the civil servants are equipped with economic and commercial expertise.

The property rights theory lacks universal validity because utility functions can not be compared, and as Buchanan and Stubbleline (1962) have pointed out, Coase's analysis is only applicable to inter-firm externality relationships. Following Hayekian thought it can however never be the case that one organisation has the entire knowledge to simulate a market and take decisions which would have been made under market circumstances. However the transitional period is characterised by market imperfections and the correctness of the allocation of a property right by the institution can only be judged and commented upon by the markets, once they have been fully established.

4.5 Conclusions

The political decision to give precedence to investment is economically desirable particularly in the short and medium term and enforces the process of transformation and economic adjustment. Nevertheless it must be noted that this decision interprets the former owner's property right as the duty to attempt to make the best usage of the property or enterprise. The assignment of the property right to the former owner depends on his economic determination and on the availability of options by third parties. The legal situation of the former owner might be constitutionally criticised. His position depends on the circumstances: if third investors file investment plans then he will be discriminated - with regard to his own choice - against other former owners if his property holds investment value. The former owner has a right to be assigned with the property right but this right is not assigned automatically, the process of restituting the property is nevertheless simpler and quicker if the property does not hold any investment value. If investment value in the form of special investment purposes is attached to the property the former owner has to engage in the same procedure as any other investor and his right of restitution becomes a mere right of comment - and sometimes not even that, as the procedure following Paragraph 18 InVorG indicates. Although the process of re-privatising enterprises and factors of production according to the previously described regulations can be time-consuming, the focus on the structural adjustment of the property is theoretically approved of with regard to the desired economic transformation toward a market economy. The factual implications of the institutionalised transformation of the East German economy for the economic process, the economic adjustment and the implemented pragmatic economic policies will be described and discussed in the next chapter. This will form the empirical basis for the synopsis of the validity of the chosen transformation approach, its limitations and the value of alternative approaches previously presented (chapter 2) in Chapters 7 and 8.

Chapter Five
Economic Implications and Post-Institutionalisation Policy

5.1 Introduction

The previous two chapters identified and analysed the transformational approaches which were employed in the East German case as a mixture of non-deterministic evolutionary approaches with the dominance of ordo-liberal thoughts and principles of the property rights school. At this point it becomes necessary to investigate the real adjustment of the economic process to form the basis for an evaluation of these chosen approaches and to point to their limitations. It will be found that the transitional period is characterised by adjustment deficiencies. Deficiencies were identified by authorities initiating economic policy. These policies will be presented and it will be shown that they have predominantly focused on macroeconomic aggregates and neglect some of the behavioural deficiencies which were created by the chosen institutional approach. These findings present room to refer to some approaches presented in Chapter 2 which will be further analysed in the next chapter. A methodological justification of the referral to the empirical analysis is given with the fundamental assumption by the author that it is important to evaluate employed political means and instruments with regard to their intended effects if one wishes to assess the effectiveness of the economic policies and approaches chosen. To remind the reader, the fundamental objectives of the economic transformation were identified as creating a market economy with decentralised decision-making authority. This market economy was supposed to function efficiently, have created private markets for goods, services and production factors, raise the East German pre-unification living standards to the level of the West German state and limit economic policy and interference to the safeguarding the functioning of the system - keeping in mind the aspect of the social market economy. It will be established that not only some of the aspects of the institutional approach are debatable on principles of liberal economics, but that post-privatisation policy is characterised by interventionist tendencies. The justification of these policies can be found in the constitutional commitment to a social acceptability. Again the reader is here referred to the next chapter where, in particular, approaches of constitutional economics will be reiterated and it will be argued that some of the later introduced economic political measures might not have been necessary if alternative transformational approaches had been integrated into the institutional transformation model.

5.2 The Initial Economic Reorganisation Shocks

5.2.1 Fundamental System Modifications Restated

The economic transformational period can be classified as a period during which the economy adjusted to the shocks which were created by the alteration of the economic system. The institutional change, the opening of the economic system, the exposure to international competition, the introduction of a new monetary system, behavioural adjustment pressures as well as the adaptation of new principles brought about by the societal change produce situations which are sub-optimal because of the time-lag associated with the realisation of changes and the eventually intended adjustment.

The creation of an institutional infrastructure included the establishment of an incentive structure which enables private individuals to act independently and according to their own wishes. The order comprises a legal system including commercial law, a separation of the private and the public market, clear conditions of fiscal policy and the institutional framework for the functioning of factor markets, i.e. the markets for labour, land and capital as well as the money market. Behavioural functions and relationships for these macroeconomic aggregates as well as for the individual economic actor were modified. Economic planning has been established as being exercised on a decentralised basis and the coordination of these plans was supposed to function according to market mechanisms. The banking system and the institution of the central bank had to be re-established. The objective of monetary stabilisation implied the creation of money which tends to have a stable value as well as the creation of a monetary order which conveys certainty and trust to individuals. This monetary stability is - following post-war West German monetary policy - believed to be created by the institution of an independent central bank, the state being prohibited by statute from supporting itself through the printing of money, a two-stage banking system and a capital market. A new constitutional regulation of the property structure was introduced and a clear and unambiguous legal framework was enacted to create a successful institutional transformation.

Despite the consistency and conformity of these institutional changes with the altering norm and the change of the remaining partial social systems (see section 6.2.2.4) the transformational period has been characterised by shocks which necessitated fast economic adjustment. The real adjustment of the economy has aimed at macroeconomic aggregates such as production, investment and employment, which has implied the creation of new enterprises and the transformation of existing ones by deregulation, restructuring, liquidation and privatisation. Both new and old enterprises have had to adjust to the new circumstances. Having classified the main transformational elements, it must be noted that the German case of economic transformation has been unique because some of the transformational objectives had already been attained under the act of political unification and the adaptation of the West German economic order and the monetary system. The West German institutional framework was adopted under Art. 23 of the Basic Law and its monetary system was implemented by the creation of the Monetary Union.

The initial lack of speed of the economic adjustment can be explained by the shocks which were created by the system modification and the transformation shock can be split into the following three partial shocks:

1.) Capital Depreciation Shock,
2.) Currency Appreciation Shock and
3.) Wage Shock.

The transformation made the obsolete structure of capital assets obvious and initiated a severe depreciation of capital. The high living standards within the former GDR as compared to other socialist economies were financed out of the capital which prevented any capital modernisation (Deutsches Institut fuer Wirtschaftsforschung *et al*, *zwoelfter Bericht*, 1995). The transition to a market economy created a supply shock which suddenly made a substantial share of the production potential unusable. The currency appreciation emphasised the slump in production because East German products became un-competitive in the international market due to the increase in prices coupled with the considerably low quality of product by international standards. The wage shock initiated by the wage negotiations and the decision to raise wages above labour productivity has had a severe effect on costs of production. These partial shocks are further detailed below.

5.2.2 Capital Depreciation Shock

Soon after unification it became obvious that East German enterprises were hardly able to survive the international competition due to high costs of production and low product quality. Production within the GDR was also characterised by the depth of production stages and the large size of the businesses. Product prices hardly represented relative scarcities because of state subsidies, deficient international division of labour and the monopolistic position of most of the combines. Often one combine constituted the entire industry and was protected from international competition by the state's policies of separation and the GDR's involvement in the international coordination within Comecon. Furthermore no prices were available for any input factors and the low level of innovation and the lack of technological knowledge made production inefficient. Productive capital was hardly renewed and the production equipment was obsolete. At the time of the economic unification the enterprises were faced with a severe devaluation of capital and a comparative fall in capital productivity due to the obsolescence of production means. The slump in production is closely linked to the collapse of the export sector due to the lack of international competitiveness of the East German products. Monetary union has had the effect of a currency appreciation and made export products to Eastern European trading partners very expensive as goods were now traded in convertible Deutschmarks. Exports from East Germany declined from 1990 to 1991 to a third of their original levels. Imports from Eastern European countries - the former Comecon area - decreased despite the currency appreciation and this can be explained by the increased imports from West Germany. The East German surplus of imports over exports has been increasing since the unification and was estimated by the Sachverstaendigenrat (1994) for 1995 as DM 220.5 bn (in 1991 prices) representing an increase of 3.5% compared to the previous year.

As a result of the capital and production deficiencies, industrial production in East Germany decreased to a third of its level prior to unification in 1991 and just regained its 1990 output level in 1995. In 1991 productivity in East Germany was less than a third of that in Western Germany. Eastern Germany produced 7% (1991) of the German gross national product (BIP) whereas it could have arithmetically achieved 25% according to its share of population. Prior to unification it was expected (predominantly by politicians of the CDU) that the East German economic region would in 1993 have achieved self-sufficient growth. "Self-sufficient growth" is defined as a national growth rate which makes transitional transfer payments from the West unnecessary as the economy recreates and renews the economic infrastructure by itself. It was suggested that East German production would follow a development in the type of the J-curve adjustment (Siebert, 1992). Following the reduced production of those enterprises which survived the economic changes and the closure of many companies, the entire production volume would fall into a slump after which it would eventually stabilise. Subsequent to this stabilisation a gradual upswing in production would start. At the end of this adjustment process the level of production was expected to be higher than the initial one. In 1995 this prognosis seemed to have been validated as industrial production did not only achieve the initial output level of 1990 but was also expected to grow further. This growth can be substantiated by the increase in orders within the manufacturing industry. The next table (5.1) represents the index of net industrial production and its development between 1989 and 1995. It shows that the East German production volume decreased during the time period from 1989 until 1991 to a third of the initial volume which represents the slump in terms of the J-curve development. The GDP of East Germany declined by 50% as compared to autumn 1989. Production started stabilising in 1992 when the upswing is thought to have come into existence.

A sectoral differentiation of the J-curve development can be ascertained which will be further elaborated below. A severe slump could be manifested in the production of capital investment goods.

Table 5.1: Index of Net Industrial Production in East Germany 1989-1995, II/1990=100

time	index
I /1989	202.0
II/1989	200.0
I /1990	187.0
II/1990	100.0
I /1991	76.3
II/1991	77.4
I /1992	79.1
II/1992	83.1
I /1993	87.4
II/1993	93.9
I /1994	98.4
II/1994	108.0
I /1995	174.4

Source: Statistisches Bundesamt, Fachserie 4, Reihe 2.1, current issues, own calculations calendar monthly

If the third quarter of 1990 is set equal to 100 the index of the production in 1995 is 50% of the third quarter of 1990. The production of the primary and the production goods sectors declined to 70% of the third quarter of 1990. In contrast no decline can be found in the food industry. A positive development has already started in the area of services and building. One reason for this development is that these services are not tradeable and are not exposed to international competition. Additionally the demand for building services has been stimulated by the financial transfers from the West.

The transitional phase has been characterised by a capital shortage and an excess supply of labour. According to Johannes Ludewig, State Secretary of the Federal Ministry for Economics and Special Emissary for the New States, the capital shortage and in particular the weak equity structure can still potentially jeopardise the industrial recovery in East Germany (Handelsblatt, 4.4.95). He also points out that the lack of (own) equity capital hinders the small and medium sized companies - particularly those that were privatised as MBOs - which rely on their own financial strength to finance their growth. Economic policy with respect to subsidy regulations had to adjust to the transitional economic deficiencies. The general fall in East German output had been accompanied by a demand shock in the West German economy.

5.2.3 Currency Appreciation Shock

The monetary union reversed the conventional process of integration. It is academically suggested (Balassa, 1962) that the integration of real markets, goods, capital and labour must be completed before an integration of the monetary area can be realised. On 1st July 1990 - as part of the German Economic, Monetary and Social Union[83] - the Deutschemark (DM) became the sole monetary unit in the GDR and the Deutsche Bundesbank was simultaneously adopted as the monetary authority replacing the State Bank. A market-based banking system was introduced with the monetary union implying free movement of financial capital and individual access to capital and interest rates which are not centrally set. The currency revaluation of one East German Mark into one Deutschemark applied to wages, salaries, rents and other recurrent payments. The currency reform allowed East German residents to convert private savings at parity rate up to a certain amount depending on age. Those under 14 years were allowed to exchange DM 2 000, residents between 14 and 58 were allowed DM 4 000 and those above 58 were allowed to convert DM 6 000. Other existing financial assets and liabilities were converted at a rate of Ostmark 2 to DM 1. Persons who were not resident in the GDR as well as institutions were allowed to convert their assets acquired before 31st December1989 at a rate of Ostmark 2 to DM 1 and those assets acquired after this date could be changed at a rate of 3 to 1. The average conversion rate was Ostmark 1.8 to DM 1 and this was surmised as effective by Lipschitz (1990) due to the potentially deflationary impact of the depreciation. This view has frequently been rejected and as will be seen subsequently with regard to the real effects of the monetary and economic union the conversion rate had severe effects on the competitiveness of East German industry. It seems more accurate to describe the currency reform as having had an appreciation effect and therefore increasing the slump in production.

The Deutsche Bundesbank has traditionally used a flexible money supply target - rather than the alternative of interest rate or exchange rate targeting - as a guidepost for monetary policy, i.e. the target range allows variations within a certain limit. Until 1988 the German central bank used central bank money (CBM) as its target which was then substituted by M3 in order to reduce the influence currency substitution has on the monetary target.[84] The money supply growth as an intermediate target is academically acknowledged to be efficient if the central bank is able to control money supply and to predict monetary demand with a satisfactory degree of accuracy. The forecasting of the money demand has been increasingly problematic after unification as the impact of the monetary union can be described as a shock. Here economic theory recommends interest rate targeting in order to prevent the real effects of a monetary demand shock. This notion has however been rejected by the New Classical Macroeconomists as interest rate targeting can lead to inflation in the case of rational expectations. Money demand is interest rate inelastic according to empirical studies carried out by Friedman and Schwarz (1982) which leads to the development of the new quantity theory of money and thus the support of money supply targeting. The money demand shock caused by the German monetary union was accompanied by a real demand shock (predominantly for West German products) which had a singularised effect of increasing interest rates in the case of given money supply. In the case of the real demand shock being stronger than the money demand shock, money supply targeting has been surmised as being superior (Mayer, 1992).

In 1994 the target for the monetary aggregate M3 reached its original 1990 growth level of 4%-6% (and continued to remain being set at this level throughout 1995). It was reduced to 3%-5% during 1991 and was slightly higher in 1992 (3.4%-5.5%). Since unification the Deutsche Bundesbank has pursued an expansionary monetary policy and in 1994 the money supply exceeded the level designed by the nation's production capacity. The monetary target was exceeded during the years 1992 and 1993 and the Bundesbank set the monetary target for 1994 (until the third quarter) at 5%. Despite the expansion of the monetary target the target was again exceeded in 1994, i.e. the third succeeding year. In 1995 the monetary aggregate M3 grew over the period from 03/95 until 9/95 by 2.5%, i.e. it did not reach its set target.

Inflationary tendencies are defined as an increase in money supply exceeding the growth of production capacity (potential). Until 1990 the inflationary tendencies of the late 1980s were brought down to a yearly average growth of M3 at 4.6% in 1990 which was within the lower range of the growth target. Until the middle of 1991 the growth of money supply slowed down due to the increased monetary capital formation in East Germany. Since the middle of 1991 monetary growth has accelerated (average yearly M3 growth rates: 1992: 8.1%, 1993: 7.8%, 1994: 8.9%) and a policy of gradual interest rate adjustment was carried out. The Bundesbank acknowledged the excess money supply. It made use of a rather pragmatic policy and increased interest rates such that the short-term interest rates were higher than the long-term ones and this characterises a restrictive policy counterbalancing the expansion of money supply.

During the first years of economic and monetary union the Bundesbank carried out a flexible approach of adjusting interest rates subject to certain conditions of money supply growth. Since then the Bundesbank has gradually increased its discount and lombard rates[85] to its highest post-war rates of 8.75% and 9.75% respectively until on 15th September 1992 it started reducing them. The last reduction happened on 15th December 1995 at which date the discount rate was lowered to 2.5%. At the same time the lombard rate was reduced to 4.5%. The bank statistics published by the Deutsche Bundesbank show that money supply M3 rose by 20% during the middle of 1990 to the middle of 1991.

Table 5.2. shows the development of the money aggregate M3 in quarterly values since 1990.

Table 5.2: Monetary Development since 1990, M3

time	DM bn
1990	1503.0
1991	1597.7
1992	1718.7
1993	1906.7
1994	1937.0
1995	2007.4
1996*	2003.5

Source: Deutsche Bundesbank, current issues, own calculations, *until May 1996 incl.

It can be concluded that the monetary integration of the East German area has been successful in that it did not create severe inflationary tendencies and the monetary growth had been sustained by a restrictive monetary policy. However the monetary conversion from the former East German currency into the West German Deutschemark has had the effect of a currency appreciation which has increased the difficulties the East German production has faced since the economic integration.

5.2.4 Wage Shock

The demise of enterprises which were unable to survive implied a severe collapse within the labour market. The employment level had been inflated due to the principle of employment within the socialist economy. Now as labour demand is a derived demand employment had to follow developments in the goods markets. The influence the collapse in production had on the labour market was accentuated by the increase in average monthly wages per employee following integration. The average monthly wage increased from Ostmark 1 170 in the final quarter of 1989 to DM 2 060 in the final quarter of 1991 which is a rise of 76%. The East German national productivity was only 30% of the West German level during the years 1990 and 1991. The wedge between productivity and wages implied a low incentive for enterprises to demand new labour and difficulties of keeping the existing labour force. Severe labour shedding was necessary for enterprises to survive. Siebert (1992) has polemically painted the picture of the East German wages reaching the US level in 1992 alongside a national productivity equal to Mexico's.

There was a substantial loss of jobs during the immediate aftermath of unification and this required a basic transformation of behavioural attitudes.

Flexibility, mobility, responsibility and the ability to take decisions had to be substituted for risk-adversity and an acceptance of decisions taken by others. Nevertheless in 1993 19.4% of the German population resided in the new states and the East German yearly average share of the labour force (i.e. those in employment plus the unemployed) was only marginally lower (18.9%). However the share of the East German labour force accounted for 33.6% of the total German unemployment and only 17.4% of German employment.

The number of people in employment in the former GDR fell by nearly 3 million from 1990 to 6.35 million in August 1996. In July 1996 a yearly average of 1.147 million people (15.4%) were registered unemployed of which 59.4% were female. The corresponding rates for West Germany were 9% as rate of unemployment and 43.4% for women in July 1996. Table 5.3 summarises some of the developments in the labour market.

Table 5.3: The East German Employment Sector 1989 - 1996 (in millions)

	1989	1990	1991	1992	1993	1994	1995	1996
-labour force	9.86	9.1	8.13	7.51	7.28	7.41	7.54	7.44
-number of unemployed	0	0.24	0.91	1.17	1.15	1.14	1.16	1.09
-people in occupation	9.86	8.86	7.22	6.34	6.13	6.27	6.38	6.35
-number of employed	9.68	8.54	6.86	5.93	4.68	5.79	5.49	5.43
-number of self-employed	0.18	0.32	0.36	0.41	0.45	0.48	0.89	0.92
-unemployment rate (%)*	0	2.6	10.3	16.1	15.8	16	14.7	15.7

Source: Sachverstaendigenrat zur Begutachtung der gesamtwirtschaftlichen Lage (1991a), Tabelle 23; Deutsches Institut fuer Wirtschaftsforschung *et al*, various issues; Bundesanstalt fuer Arbeit (1996) and previous issues; Bundesanstalt fuer Arbeit (1994, 1995). Figures for 1995 and 1996 are based on monthly data for October respectively, *unemployment rate defined as those unemployed as a proportion of those in paid employment. Workers in short-time employment are also included in this numbers of employed.

The effects of the economic transformation on the development of the employment sector can be described as a U-form. Since 1990 the fall in employment has decreased and the valley of the U can be interpreted as having been reached. The fall in the number of employed people 1991/90 was 18.5%, in

1992/91 it was 12.1%, in 1993/92 it was 3.3%, in 1994/93 the number of people in employment rose by 2.3% and in 1995/94 by 0.2%. The preliminary figures for 1996 however indicate a worsening of this development, showing a fall in the number of employed people (Bundesanstalt fuer Arbeit, 1996 and previous issues). Moreover, the yearly total of unemployed registered in East Germany has fallen by 0.6% from 1993 to 1994, however there was an increase in 1995 (table 5.3).

At the same time the development of the labour supply (i.e. the employed plus the unemployed) shows a similar movement. The labour force decreased from about 9.1 million in 1990 to about 7.4 million in July 1996. The fall in supply of labour has slowed down from about 0.9 million in 1991/90 to 0.2 million in 1993/92, the years 1994 and 1995 showing an increase which might again be offset by the current development (table 5.3). The initial fall in labour supply was due to the migration which today can be suggested to be compensated for by migration from the West.

The Bundesanstalt fuer Arbeit (1994) has also suggested that demographic changes and particular instruments of labour market policy account for the loss in the labour force (until 1994). Labour policies regarding arrangements for premature retirement and those for occupational training and education have created a situation where the loss of older employees is not made up for by recruitment of younger people. Premature retirement in the form of the "*Altersuebergangsgeld*" has had a significant impact on the supply of labour. This scheme allows men and women older than 57 who have been unemployed since unification to take premature retirement and the programme was designed to expire by the end of 1992. Nevertheless applications for this scheme were still being accepted during the first months of 1993 and a yearly average of 639 000 people were subject to this *Altersuebergangsgeld*. Further means of occupational training and education have been utilised in order to achieve an adjustment of the human capital to market requirements and in particular to accelerate the learning process with regard to new technologies and managerial techniques and skills. In October 1992 the number of people undergoing these retraining methods peaked at more than 500 000 and decreased to a yearly average of about 380 000 in 1993 (206 751 in August 1996). Besides these labour market policies the so-called "quiet reserve" of people who are not officially registered as unemployed but are looking for employment has increased. The yearly average (1994) of 150 000 people in this category consists of a high proportion of women. As a result of the combination of a fall in female employment, a low chance of re-employment and increased costs of child care etc. there has been a withdrawal of women from the labour market or a movement into the quiet reserve (Bundesanstalt fuer Arbeit, 1994). The quiet reserve continued to increase in 1994 by 90 000 to a total of 210 000 people (Bundesanstalt fuer Arbeit, 1995).

The on-going fall in labour demand has been caused by the structural change the East German economy has been undergoing. Despite the growth of production and output the creation of new employment opportunities is slow because of cost and rationalisation pressures in the private sector. However certain economic sectors such as the construction sector are showing increases in employment whereas the expansion within the service sectors has been experiencing a fall in its growth. The manufacturing industry as well as agriculture are still suffering severe labour shedding. The impact of the economic transformation on the labour market has been attempted to be alleviated by the Treuhand-policy of a moderate form of enterprise liquidation.
Nevertheless the forecast increase in employment after the dramatic fall in employment will not reach the initial former GDR's employment level due to the generally assumed hyper-employment which existed in socialist economies. The effects on employment did not merely happen due to over-employment and the deficiencies of human capital, they were also created by wage adjustments due to monetary union. The adjustment of East German wages and their alignment to West German levels is expected to have been materialised by the end of 1997. The increase in real wages has affected the cost structure of private enterprises which has had a deteriorating effect on the employment situation. The wage shock has created severe economic adjustment problems. The process of adjustment of the employment sector is not continuous and is also influenced by the effects of production with time-lags.

5.3 Mediation of the Process of Forming New Economic Structures

5.3.1 The Ordo-Liberal Concept and the Scope of Central Action

The economic transformation in East Germany has had effects on the general macro-economic level because of its creation of high unemployment as well as the original slump in production and severe recession due to the above described shocks caused by economic reorganisation. The economic transformation had been institutionalised - as was pointed out before - and sectoral as well as regional structures have been highly influenced by the actions of these institutions. The institutional transformation had been shaped by actions of the Treuhand and the creation of the legal framework of a market economy (e.g. private property rights, contractual freedom and contractual protection (*Vertragsschutz*)). The Treuhand pursued a policy of rapid privatisation, restructuring of industrial cores and liquidation of enterprises which were not viable. It must thereby be analysed to which degree the Treuhandanstalt *de facto* influenced the process of economic adjustment and whether particular economic end-situations were defined *ex-ante*. This part of the analysis is essential because the non-deterministic evolutionary approach of ordo-liberal economics and its connotation with property rights-theoretical principles was identified as here being the principal justification for the chosen institutional approach. The re-definition of property rights-theoretical assumptions and the political adaptation of the amended interpretation was already concluded in the preceding chapter and it must now be analysed which concrete policies were carried out and which factual effects they have had so as to allow an evaluation of the adopted approach.

As has been described in chapters 3 and 4 the institutional policy has concentrated on the establishment of a decentralised decision-making structure and a private ownership structure. The policy of restructuring enterprises focused on the decentralisation of enterprises and separated property has legally been transferred to a new or old owner. By employing the privatisation policy of an integrated selection function the identity of owners was qualitatively pre-defined and certain assumptions about their economic actions were made. The sales price depended on the property's future earnings potential as well as the guarantees and in the case of a third purchaser on the investment plan. It has been assumed in accordance with the ordo-liberal principles that the restructuring of the East German economy will be more efficient the swifter this installation of new private owners. This privatisation methodology is based on the assumption that the enterprises are provided with capital, management skills and production and technological know-how via the privatisation. The economic-political motive of this particular method of privatisation once again follows ordo-liberal principles. In particular no central and direct restructuring of enterprises and industrial sectors was allowed to be exercised because a central institution such as the Treuhandanstalt is assumed to be incapable of anticipating the end result of economic activity. It has therefore been assumed that fast privatisation will lead to any necessary restructuring. The dispersed property holding has privatised the actual internal restructuring process of enterprises and the Treuhand partly supplemented this internalisation of restructuring by investment and employment guarantees[86] the new owners had to give. To which degree the Treuhand factually determined the building of aggregated economic structures will be pointed out in the next sections.

5.3.2 Implications of the Policy of Institutional Transformation

5.3.2.1 Concentration of Sectoral Adjustment Deficiencies

Table 5.4 represents the Treuhand's role and influence with regard to restructuring the economy. The Treuhand indirectly affected the emerging structure of the East German economy through its decisions with regard to the fate of enterprises, i.e. whether they should be privatised, restructured before selling or liquidated. It can be derived from these figures that the Treuhand has speeded up the process of structural change by deciding which enterprises were to continue operating and which were to be liquidated. Liquidation ratios of companies exceeding 40% were realised in the economic sectors of agriculture

(65%), paper and printing (62%), leather, textiles and clothing (50%) and electrical engineering (40%). The rate of liquidations within the steel industry, light metallurgy and railway carriages was lower. This is due to the large sizes of these enterprises which have proved difficult to separate and sell (e.g. *Eko Stahl, Deutsche Waggonbau*). These enterprises also employed a large proportion of the working population which made liquidation socially unacceptable. At the end of 1994 only 3.7% of liquidations had been achieved which reflects the high level of temporary structural preservation policy carried out by the German government.

Table 5.4: TH-Portfolio According to Economic Sectors (number of enterprises)

	A	B	C	D	E	F
Agriculture and Forestry	570	97	9	4	37	372
Energy and Water	247	198	2	23	0	16
Mining	31	20	3	0	0	5
Chemical Industry	261	135	37	0	0	79
Plastic products	180	76	40	0	0	63
Stone & Earths	486	306	73	3	0	96
Iron & Steel	461	230	83	0	1	107
Mech. Engineering	1 114	621	128	1	1	316
Vehicles	371	232	43	0	2	90
Electrical Engineering	488	218	59	1	0	197
Precision Engineering	86	35	21	0	0	29
Metal Products	328	121	78	0	2	125
Wood & Wood Products	498	189	136	1	0	167
Paper & Printing	249	132	42	0	0	74
Leather & Leather Goods	165	36	26	0	0	102
Textiles & Clothing	532	129	123	0	2	263
Food, Drink & Tobacco	869	463	128	9	1	246
Construction Industry	1 020	694	191	15	1	113
Finishing Trade*	211	120	68	4	0	19
Trade	1 377	779	90	4	2	468
Traffic & Transport	417	221	17	63	0	113
Insurance & Finances	18	11	0	0	0	1
Services	2 169	1 283	107	133	1	555
others	215	118	67	2	0	27
Total	12 363	6 236	1 571	263	50	3 661

Source: Treuhandanstalt (1994);A=total, B=privatised, C=reprivatised, D=returned to local authorities, E=vesting orders, F=liquidated, *includes building

The analysis of the relationship between liquidation and labour shedding in individual economic sectors depicts the severity with which particular areas have been confronted as part of the structural change. Table 5.5 reflects these ratios which should be interpreted in the following way: If the ratio is below 1, the sector suffered a higher percentage loss of jobs than the percentage fall in enterprises due to their liquidation. The data identifies the mining sector, the manufacturing industry and the agricultural sector as the sectors affected the most. The service and state sector as well as the construction industry are characterised by the relative fall in employment being smaller than the rate of liquidation.

Table 5.5: Ratio between Sectoral Enterprise Liquidations (aggregated until 9/94) and Fall in Sectoral Employment (6/89 - 6/94)

Economic Sectors	Sectoral Ratio between Liquidation and Fall in Employment
Agriculture and Forestry	0.82 : 1
Energy and Mining	0.13 : 1
Manufacturing Industry	0.46 : 1
Construction Industry	2.06 : 1
Trade and Traffic	1.11: 1
Services, State & others*	3.58: 1

Source: Statistisches Bundesamt (Statistisches Jahrbuch der Bundesrepublik Deutschland), current issues; Treuhandanstalt(a), various issues; Treuhandanstalt (1994), own calculations, *The fall in employment within the service sector does not contradict previous figures because the state neutralises the increase in employment. Aggregated values for the fall in sectoral employment can be used as there was no unemployment during GDR times.

Besides these tendencies enforced by the actions of the Treuhand the opening of the economy as part of the institutional transformation in East Germany has had significant implications for its sectoral and regional economic structures. The abolition of the inner German border has changed the relative economic significance of geographical regions and economic sectors within the new *Laender*. Former peripheral areas along the German border as well as Berlin have experienced increasing economic importance whereas formerly eastern regions have often lost their significance following the disarrangement of the COMECON. The former - almost exclusive - orientation of foreign trade (apart from minor trade relations with West Germany) towards COMECON related countries has impeded the adjustment of industry which was related to those foreign trade partners. The structure of the East German economy in comparison to the West German one prior to unification (table 5.6) was characterised by a relative predominance of sectors which have lost some of their economic importance during the last few decades, such as the agricultural, the primary and the heavy industry sectors. The trade and general service sectors on the other hand were under-represented within the East. The economic structure of East

Germany can generally be described as having been dominated by producing for the investment goods market rather than for general consumption (Mueller, 1993). The structural change in Western industrial economies during the post-war period towards service-oriented sectors has not taken place in the East as such. This structural obsolescence of the East German economy has slowed down the process of transformation, in particular of privatisation and real economic adjustment. Privatisation was affected because of the outdated enterprises' production equipment in sectors which have already been identified as areas with a high structural adjustment requirement, e.g. the iron and steel industry.

Judging by the number of employees in different economic sectors the agricultural sector had been assigned higher significance in the former GDR than in the FRG. The same holds for the economic sectors of mining and heavy industry, such as mechanical engineering (table 5.6). This data has been inflated by the obsolescence of industrial equipment, the repair of which later entered the services category.

Table 5.6: Sectoral Employment in East and West Germany

	GDR (1989)	FRG (1990)	GDR %	FRG %
Agriculture, Forestry, Fishing	**923 500**	**961 000**	**10.8**	**3.4**
Energy and Mining, incl. Water	**255 031**	**466 000**	**3.0**	**1.6**
Manufacturing Industry	**2 956 323**	**8 941 000**	**34.5**	**31.4**
Chemical Industry	331 848	644 000	3.7	2.3
Metallurgy	136 383	687 000	1.6	2.4
Mech. Eng./Vehicles	961 797	2 364 000	11.2	8.3
Electrical Engineering	459 128	1 247 000	5.4	4.4
Textiles and Clothing	387 878	468 000	4.5	1.6
Foods	275 157	743 000	3.2	2.6
others	404 132	2 788 000	4.7	9.8
Construction Industry	**559 900**	**1 914 000**	**6.5**	**6.7**
Trade	**876 800**	**3 728 000**	**10.2**	**13.1**
Traffic and Communications	**639 100**	**1 588 000**	**7.5**	**5.6**
Services and others*	**2 361 100**	**10 835 000**	**27.5**	**38.8**
Total	***8 571 754***	***28 433 000***	***100***	***99.9***

Sources: Mueller (1993); Statistisches Jahrbuch der DDR 1989 (1990); Statistisches Bundesamt (Statistisches Jahrbuch der Bundesrepublik Deutschland, 1989). The number of employees for the GDR does not include any apprentices; the classification of other manufacturing industry includes light industry and building material for the GDR. *The classification of other services includes 266 000 employed in the sector producing crafts and 251 200 employed in other producing sectors.

The overall sectoral divergence between the two German nations points to the structural deficiencies in the East. These structural deficiencies can be evaluated as a major hindrance of a speedy economic integration of the former planned economy into the market of internationally competitive industrial economies.

The transition period of East Germany's economic conversion into a market economy is characterised by continuing changes in individual sectors' economic importance. In particular the manufacturing sector and the agricultural sector are identified as the economic sectors which have suffered the most severe economic collapse. Total employment has fallen since the beginning of 1990 by nearly 40% until the first half of 1994, employment within the manufacturing industry fell by 66% and that in the agricultural sector decreased to just over 20% (table 5.7). More than a third of all enterprises within the manufacturing industry transferred to the Treuhand were and will be liquidated . Simultaneously a third of the labour force employed in this sector by the end of 1989 was made redundant by the end of 1991. The agricultural sector, the primary and manufacturing industry have experienced employment losses throughout the time of transformation whereas the development in sectors such as the construction industry and services is represented by a fall in employment until mid or end 1992 which has from then on been replaced by an increase in employment. The service sector however is the only aggregated sector which experienced a net increase in employment (13.3%) throughout the last five years and this positive development has been acknowledged by the DIW (Deutsches Institut fuer Wirtschaftsforschung *et al*, *Zehnter Bericht*, 1994) as long-term.

Table 5.7: Sectoral Change in East Germany 1989-1994 (in 1 000s)

A.Sectoral Employment (1 000s)

Economic Sectors	I/89	II/90	I/91	II/91	I/92	II/92	I/93	II/93	I/94
A	985	656	468	361	290	251	229	218	204
E	306	271	243	222	212	197	178	157	147
M	3265	2653	2364	1839	1404	1342	1206	1153	1100
C	846	660	569	570	706	749	757	791	800
T	1652	1320	1292	1218	1162	1158	1154	1189	1205
G	962	670	870	966	992	996	1036	1065	1090
S	1750	1705	1458	1454	1436	1427	1412	1380	1403
TE	9932	8035	7369	6767	6354	6276	3135	6116	6113

B. Sectoral Gross Value Product (%), II/1990 - II/1992, not deflated (at yearly prices)

Economic Sectors	II/90	I/91	II/91	I/92	II/92
Agriculture and Forestry	4.2	-2.2	4.1	-0.4	2.9
Producing Industry	41.2	40.0	32.7	36.4	33.7
Trade and Traffic	17.5	16.9	14.0	13.0	12.0
Services	16.3	23.3	24.0	29.0	25.7
State, priv. hhs etc.	20.8	22.0	25.2	22.0	25.7
Total Gross Value Product	100	100	100	100	100

Source: Treuhandanstalt (1994); Deutsches Institut fuer Wirtschaftsforschung (1994), A=Agriculture and Forestry, E=Energy and Mining, M=Manufacturing Industry, C=Construction Industry, T=Trade and Traffic, G=Services, S=State, TE=Total Employment, priv. hhs = private households

The relevance and importance of individual economic sectors has altered and this structural change has brought about a fundamental alteration of the constellation of production and employment. The negative development in the manufacturing industry in the East has been accompanied by a recessional development in the West. The main manufacturing sectors have however experienced an increase in orders since the second quarter of 1993 which has also had a positive impact on employment with a time lag of one year (Table 5.7). Despite the increase in economic growth the situation in the labour market remains critical with a total number of nearly 1.2 million (16%, unemployed as share of the workforce) having been unemployed in East Germany in April 1996. Another 600 000 persons were employed in the second labour market and are engaged in job-creating measures, vocational training or re-education. In 1989 the GDR's gross national product was Ostmark 286 bn, after the economic merger it fell to DM 195 bn in 1992 and amounted to DM 301 bn in 1994 (in current prices).

Despite the high rate of TH-liquidations in the manufacturing industry the fall of employment in this sector has stagnated and the number of incoming orders has been increasing since the beginning of 1993. The drastic fall in employment and production had been caused by the primary shock of opening the economic system. The sectoral structural change can be described as the effect of a drastic fall in production and employment which can be evaluated as having overcome its nadir, whereas the structural adjustment of economic sectors must be seen as on-going. The fall in production and employment has partly been due to the shock of the economic and monetary union which led to sudden competition from the West, a sharp increase in labour costs unaccompanied by any increase in labour productivity, a fall in traditional exports and rationalisation within enterprises. The slump in production was also accompanied by a change in demand from products produced in the GDR to those made by Western companies. Economic sectors hit the hardest can be identified as mining, agriculture and industry. These are economic areas which have been undergoing substantial structural change in Western industrialised countries during the last decade or were highly dependent on the COMECON market, such as the ship-building industry. A comparison of distributional insolvencies in Germany - East and West -, by the Treuhand, in the UK and the US was carried out by Mayer and Carlin (1994). East Germany has a relatively low proportion of insolvencies in the service sector which is represented by this sector's increasing share of GDP. The rate of Treuhand liquidations however in the manufacturing industry considerably exceeded the post 1986 share in West Germany, in the US and the UK. This has been interpreted as a particular deliberate Treuhand-policy so as to lower the rate of bankruptcies as opposed to liquidations. The control over a liquidated company remains with the Treuhand whereas that of a company declared bankrupt has been transferred to the courts and here mainly creditors' interests are pursued.

5.3.2.2 Concentration of Regional Adjustment Deficiencies

The disparity of regional structures adds importance to the need for regional policy in East Germany alongside sectoral structural policy, which chiefly aims at the temporary preservation of particular economic areas to make the process of economic transformation socially acceptable. The two pillars of structural policy - sectoral policy and regional policy - are highly linked as will be reflected and which will give an indication of initial regional structures as well as the process of structural change within these regions. For the sake of simplicity in attaining statistical material East German federal states will be defined as economic regions. Due to this definition it will soon become obvious that the structural change gives a rather similar picture throughout the states. Table (5.8) reflects the sectoral structures - based on employment numbers - of the federal states prior to unification.

The particular feature of the Treuhand's contract management of individual privatisation deals has been the negotiation of investment and employment guarantees. The distribution of guarantees by federal states reflects essential regional differences. By September 1994 a total of 1 487 281 jobs and investment of DM 206.5 bn were guaranteed through sales which gained a total of DM 64.9 bn. The following table reflects the regional quantitative divergences in sales revenues, investment and employment guarantees. The figures describe a uniform pattern regarding the individual states and they can be summarised in a quantitative listing of Treuhand achievements (table 5.9).

Table 5.8: Regional Sectoral Structures (November 1989)

Brandenburg (excluding Berlin)

Manual and White Collar Staff:

Manufacturing Industry	331 500	(48.3%)
Trade	81 300	(11.8%)
Building Trade	57 500	(8.4%)
Housing and Local Authority Services	25 500	(3.7%)
Transport	17 800	(2.6%)
Science, Education, Culture, Sport, Health, Welfare and Recreation	170 200	(24.8%)
Total	686 500	

Saxony

Manufacturing Industry	817 800	(46.1%)
Trade	157 900	(8.9%)
Building Trade	92 800	(5.2%)
Housing and Local Authority Services	45 500	(2.6%)
Transport	36 600	(2.1%)
Science, Education, Culture, Sport, Health, Welfare and Recreation	322 400	(18.2%)
Total	1 773 000	

Saxony-Anhalt

Manufacturing Industry	483 900	(54.6%)
Trade	96 400	(10.9%)
Building Trade	63 400	(7.2%)
Housing and Local Authority Services	30 700	(3.5%)
Transport	19 100	(2.2%)
Science, Education, Culture, Sport, Health, Welfare and Recreation	192 900	(21.8%)
Total	886 400	

Thuringia		
Manufacturing Industry	445 300	(61.3%)
Trade	76 400	(10.5%)
Building Trade	48 000	(6.6%)
Housing and Local Authority Services	22 300	(3.1%)
Transport	17 900	(2.5%)
Science, Education, Culture, Sport, Health, Welfare and Recreation	117 000	(16.1%)
Total	726 900	
Mecklenburg-Western Pommerania		
Manufacturing Industry	166 300	(34.1%)
Trade	71 800	(9.5%)
Building Trade	46 700	(9.6%)
Housing and Local Authority Services	33 200	(6.8%)
Transport	20 400	(4.2%)
Science, Education, Culture, Sport, Health, Welfare and Recreation	149 700	(30.7%)
Total	488 100	

Source: Federal Office of Foreign Trade (1991)

Table 5.9: Regional Shares of Sales Revenue and Investment and Employment Guarantees

Federal States	Sales Revenues in %	Investment Guarantees in %	Employment Guarantees in %
Berlin & Brandenburg	49	46	35
Saxony	24	24	29
Saxony-Anhalt	12	14	13
Thuringia	9	8	14
Mecklenburg-Western Pommerania	6	8	9
	100	100	100

Source: Treuhandanstalt(a), 30.9.1994, own calculations.

Klemmer (1993) analysed regional aspects of the privatisation on a much smaller regional basis and split the data for federal states (available from the THA) into data for districts. This data was regionally based on the postal code system and represented the stock of enterprises held by the Treuhand on 10.3.1991 and 26.1.1993. He weighted the regional structure according to the following factors: infrastructure, structure of settlement, availability of factors of production, supply of land (*Flaechenangebot*), economic climate and provision of service companies which can attend to the enterprises. He identified the infrastructure of traffic (road, air, rail) and telecommunications as being particularly important. Regional development tendencies were identified as being increasingly dependent on geographical location because of the increasing importance of logistics. The evaluation criterion regarding regional development was defined as the degree of privatisation. This grade depended on the privatisation achievements of the Treuhand, i.e. the fall in the number of enterprises held by the Treuhand as well as the fall in the number of jobs linked to these enterprises. Klemmer was able to identify positive developments (according to "privatised" jobs) in particular in the cities of Erfurt, Weimar, Jena and around Berlin as well as along the former East-West German border. He also identified a large decrease in the number of enterprises to be privatised in the southern half of the former GDR comparing the stock of enterprises in 1993 with the stock in 1991. He generally identified a positive relationship between successful Treuhand-privatisations and regional development potential. About 10% of successful privatisations can be explained by regional characteristics. Furthermore an increased density of population has favoured privatisation whereas a small number of inhabitants has had an opposite effect. Regional problem areas have been identified as: Muehlhausen, Apolda, Suhl, Riesa, Goerlitz and Bitterfeld. Some of these have been identified with sectoral problems of privatisation, partly due to the dominance of large-size enterprises. His findings correspond to the regional quantitative privatisation-ranking in table 5.9 and the federal states of Saxony-Anhalt and Mecklenburg-Western Pommerania can be identified as being characterised by weak economic structures.

The overall structure of the economy in East Germany has been characterised by deficiencies in the infrastructure (such as energy supply, telecommunications, transport and traffic), ecological burdens and damage, institutional temporal adjustment delays originating from re-privatisation, legal and administrative regulations. The overall structural development within the years 1990-1994 has been described by Naegele (1994) as pointing to the past. Regional structures have traditionally been characterised by the creation of industrial sites in northern regions during GDR times whose sectors - predominantly coal and steel - have been undergoing decreasing demand in the Western world. As the significance of these economic sectors is far less in traditional industrial areas such as Saxony, Saxony-Anhalt and Thuringia, the southern regions provide a higher development potential than the ones in the north. This structure has been linked with the Italian scenario of Mezziogornio (in the Italian south) which may find its German equivalent in Mecklenburg-Western Pommerania (Siebert, 1991; Wegner, 1991).

Statistical publications of the Treuhand suggest hardly any regional differences regarding its record of enterprise handling, i.e. privatisation, liquidation etc. If federal states are defined as regions, table 5.10 reflects a generally similar pattern throughout the states. Federal states' ratios of enterprise privatisation lay between 47% and 61% whereas liquidation was inevitably between 29% to 31% of all cases. As this is roughly the original prognosis given by the Treuhand with regard to enterprises' futures it seems that only sectoral changes were not anticipated by the privatisation agency. However, the distribution of sectoral structural deficiencies reflects the same concentration in particular regions as above which seems to contradict official statistics.

Table 5.10: TH-Portfolio According to Federal States

	A	B	C	D	T
Federal States:					
Berlin & Brandenburg	1 586	159	43	810	2 589
Saxony	1 893	769	89	1 242	3 993
Saxony-Halt	1 035	281	26	573	1 915
Thuringia	1 063	222	53	604	1 942
Mecklenburg-Western Pommerania	746	140	52	386	1 324
total	6 323	1 571	263	3 615	11 773

Source: Treuhandanstalt(a) 9/94, A=privatisaed, B=reprivatised, C=returned to local authorities, D=liquidated, T=total. The total number of enterprises and enterprise parts varies from those in this table because the net portfolio, i.e. those still to be handled with and vesting orders were disregarded.

The prime objective of economic policy has been the creation of a "*Mittelstand*" and the location of future industries within the regions identified as structurally weak (Beyer, 1995). High rates of unemployment, as well as in some cases employment on the secondary labour market of 20% of those people employed, continue to represent problems which are unlikely to be resolved in the near future. Furthermore privatised companies which have so far been given financial support or have to repay their loans are likely to suffer substantial losses in particular against the background of their weak equity structure. Although increasing economic growth rates as well as drastic improvement of the infrastructure network can be expected it has been surmised by East German politicians that the process of structural change will take at least another decade. Instruments of post-privatisation policies aiming at the alleviation of the adjustment of economic structures will be analysed below.

5.3.3 Post-Institutionalisation Policy

Economic policy has addressed the imperfections created by the reorganisation shocks which have manifested themselves in sectoral and regional adjustment deficiencies and macroeconomic aggregates of investment and employment. Political instruments which have aimed to influence these aggregates were introduced after the alteration of the system framework and employed the approach of influencing variables linked with these economic aggregates by a behavioural relationship.

5.3.3.1 Transitional Investment Policy

Private investment has been essential for economic adjustment in the new states. Capital investment depends on market conditions and a prerequisite is the economic actor's knowledge of respective conditions and the ability to interpret them. The economic reorganisation in East Germany has been confronted with internal conditions which have not allowed an intrinsic rapid and market-based adjustment, i.e. the market forces have not been strong enough to guarantee a sufficient progress and process of economic adjustment due to adjustment deficiencies. Investment policy is highly related to the target of eliminating sectoral and regional deficiencies and creating a *Mittelstand*-market structure. Investment subsidisation has been financed by institutions such as the European Union, the *Bund*, the *Laender*, banks, the Treuhand etc. Investment support programmes have focussed on investment allowances, special depreciation allowances, investment grants and loan programmes (Federal Ministry of Economics, 1994a, 1994b, 1994c) and have highly influenced market behaviour. The Deutsches Institut fuer Wirtschaftsforschung *et al* (*Zwoelfter Bericht*, 1995) observed that virtually all investors have made use of investment allowances and the majority have additionally employed either the investment grant or the loan programmes. The most dominant forms of transitional investment policy will be detailed below.

5.3.3.1.1 Tax-Based Programmes

Tax-based programmes such as investment allowances and special depreciation allowances have aimed at increasing net investment and have had the effect of creating an incentive structure for the private owner to implement the derived net investment according to his individual investment function. These programmes qualify as transitional economic policy because they are temporarily limited and in the given form only apply to the new states. Both forms of allowances are tax benefits for which a legal right exists.[87] Those eligible for the two tax-based investment support programmes are people and shareholders who pay income tax or corporate income tax except companies such as banks, insurance companies, electricity and gas companies and trading companies.

The first pillar, the investment allowance, has been granted for the purchase and production of new, depreciable and movable assets, except for low value assets, cars and aircraft. It has been essential that these assets were used within the company for at least 3 years. Investment projects (which began after 30.6.94 and will be finished before 1.1.97) are currently granted an allowance of 5%.[88] The sectoral orientation of the investment policy is characterised by the existence of an allowance of 20% allocated to companies which invested until 1.1.1995 in the manufacturing and craft sector and where the basis of valuation did not exceed DM 1 m. The allowance expires at the end of 1996. An investment allowance of 10% aims in particular at medium sized companies within the manufacturing and craft sectors and this option will expire in 1998. These investment allowances aim at influencing the urgency of investment, at supporting companies within sectors which have been identified as suffering from structural change (in particular the manufacturing industry) and at strengthening the market position of small and medium sized enterprises. By the end of 1994 a total of DM 14.5 bn had been granted in investment allowances. [89]

The second pillar of the tax-based investment support scheme, the special depreciation allowances, allows assets to be subject to a depreciation allowance of up to 50% - as long as they were purchased, produced or advance payments were made towards their purchase or production after 31.12.90 and before 1.1.97. In addition to the conventional method of depreciation the allowance of a maximum of 50% is deducted from the tax in the year of purchase or production and in the following four years. Currently no statistics of the total loss in tax revenue exist and statistics for 1992 are expected to be published in 1997 (Federal Ministry of Economics BMWi, 1995).

Johannes Ludewig, State Secretary to the Ministry of Economics and expert in the East German economy, has suggested a limitation of the applicability of the investment allowance of 5% to identified industrial problem areas. The scope and payment of this allowance however will be extended until the end of 1998 (Handelsblatt, 6.3.95).[90] It has also been suggested by Ludewig as well as by Saxony's Economic Minister Schommer that special depreciation allowances should only be applicable to the manufacturing industry as of 1997 and be reduced well below 50% (Handelsblatt, 6.3.95).

5.3.3.1.2 Investment Support under Regional Development Schemes

Investment grants were designed as part of the framework of the Joint Federal Government/*Laender* Scheme "Improving the Regional Economic Structure" (*Gemeinschaftsaufgabe "Verbesserung der regionalen Wirtschaftsstruktur"* GA)[91]. Investment projects have been supported by this scheme if the project has been considered appropriate to increase directly the total income within the particular economic region through the creation of additional sources of income as a primary effect. This regional development scheme has concentrated on two forms of support: investment grants for commercial companies and investment grants for commerce-related infrastructure.[92]

No legal right exists for the investment grant. The award of the grant in itself and the amount are discretionary and decided upon by the economic ministers of the individual *Laender*. Investment projects of commercial companies are assessed according their economic importance. This prerequisite is assumed to exist if the commercial company applying for support manufactures products and supplies services which are predominantly (at least 50%) designed for supra-regional sale. A particular "positive list" defines products and services, and goods produced by the crafts sector, which are assumed to meet the supra-regional sale requirement. Supra-regional sale is defined as outside a radius of 30 kilometres of the local community in which the business is located. Commercial companies[93] engaged in this form of supra-regional sale can be granted financial support of up to 23% of the investment costs. The investment project must aim at the start up, the expansion, conversion or basic rationalisation of a company as well as the acquisition of a liquidated company or one on the verge of being liquidated. The concrete amount of investment support depends on the supported region and the particular investment project, and varies between 12% and 23%. The highest level can be granted for business start ups in the region defined with the highest support requirement. Commercial investment with GA-investment grants has saved 1 million jobs and the creation of new employment opportunities has meant that more jobs have been created than existing jobs have been saved in the specified regional areas (Deutsches Institut fuer Wirtschaftsforschung *et al, Zwoelfter Bericht*, 1995).

Higher investment grants than the one for commercial companies - above 23% - are allowed for investment projects which aim at improving the commerce-related infrastructure. These grants can vary from 50% to 90% depending on the regional area of support. The European Commission has however set a general maximum for public support of 35% of the investment costs.[94] Commerce-related infrastructure is defined as the investment necessary for the improvement of the commercial-economic infrastructure. This definition is further specified and emphasises a) the development of industrial and commercial sites, which also includes any re-utilisation of industrial and commercial sites currently lying fallow, b) the creation or expansion of the transport and traffic system, the energy and water supply and distribution channels and the creation of installations for the disposal and clearing of sewage and waste, c) the creation or expansion of commercial and technological centres which support the starting up of new businesses, the technological transfer or the development and production of new products and d) the creation or expansion of training and education centres, further education facilities and re-educating amenities.

The final investment grant can exceed the maximum support and amount to nearly the full payment of the investment cost if the two areas for GA-investment grants are joined together (in some cases this is a prerequisite anyway). Besides the major investment areas for commerce-related infrastructure, investment grants can also be allocated to projects aiming at the development of land for tourism and public amenities which can be used for tourism, as well as the development of research and development facilities and centres.

GA-investment grants (1994: DM 11.9 bn were budgeted for investment grants) have been jointly funded by the government (50%) and the new states (50%), and additional resources have been supplied by the regional fund of the European Union[95] (EFRE, for example 1994: DM 1.9 bn). Until 1995 a total investment of DM 137 bn was supported by GA-investment grants of which DM 119 bn accounted for investment in commercial companies and DM 18 bn in commerce-related infrastructure. However infrastructure investment - weighted with the total investment volume - was supported more intensely than commercial investment. Recent allegations of resource-mislocation particularly in relation to infrastructure support focusing on commercial sites have been rejected by the Federal Ministry for Economics (1995) on the grounds that commercial sites which have been supported out of the GA-funds have been utilised by 70%-80%.

The individual states in East Germany are - according to the allocation of competences and the principle of subsidiarity based on the basic law - responsible for the implementation of the GA-support, in particular for the decisions with regard to the actual support taker. The states are thus obliged to ensue that the investor abides by the support rules and the federal government ensures that the states act according to the *GA-Rahmenplan*. This control is executed by the Federal Ministry of Economy who reviews every support acceptance with regard to its compatibility with the support framework.

The support under regional-development schemes has chiefly benefited small and medium sized enterprises. During 1992 and 1993, 93% of all investment grants were allocated to companies with less than 500 employees and these companies also account for 94% of the total investment volume supported by this scheme (Federal Ministry for Economics BMWi - cited in Deutsches Institut fuer Wirtschaftsforschung *et al*, *Zwoelfter Bericht* 1995). Furthermore the share of investment projects (85%) and the share of jobs created or secured (60%) reflect that smaller companies have been dominant within the investment under the regional-development scheme. It has to be noted that the federal government allocated loans of DM 15 bn (1990 - 1992) to local authorities within the new states. These loans were granted according to Article 28 UT where the government committed itself to take part in a local loan programme (*Kommunalkreditprogramm*) to enable the new states to carry out infrastructure investment. The majority of the loan has been allocated to environmental infrastructure (Federal Ministry for Economics BMWi, 1995).

The majority of projects which have been supported by the GA fulfil the criteria of support on a supra-regional sale. Between 1991 and the third quarter of 1994 nearly 14 000 applications were approved for financial support within the manufacturing sector and the total of planned investment in these projects amounted to DM 117 bn. This involved a financial allocation of DM 22 bn of which the federal government bestowed DM 10.8 bn (Federal Ministry for Economics BMWi, 1995). The average sum of investment per application was DM 8 m in 1991 and this subsequently decreased to DM 3.9 m during the first three quarters of 1994.

Table 5.11 represents investment projects which were planned and carried out within the manufacturing sector and for which investment grants were allocated according to the GA. The data reflects the dominance of large-size investment projects.

Table 5.11: Investment within the Manufacturing Industry Supported by the GA - according to the year of approval and the size of investment 1992 until 1994 -

Investment Level	1992	1993	1994
< DM 0.5 m	1.0	1.1	2.5
DM 0.5 m - DM 1 m	1.4	1.9	3.9
DM 1 m - DM 2.5m	4.6	5.5	10.2
DM 2.5 m - DM 5 m	5.8	7.4	10.7
DM 5 m - DM 10 m	10.1	10.1	13.6
DM 10 m - DM 100 m	44.4	36.9	41.2
>DM 100 m	32.7	37.3	18.0
total	100	100	100

Source: Deutsches Institut fuer Wirtschaftsforschung *et al*, *Zwoelfter Bericht* (1995)

The focus of these projects has changed over the years. Whilst projects involving the purchase of an enterprise or the new creation of one increasingly decline follow-up investment (i.e. the extension of existing capacities, modernisation of existing capital and change of location) increase (Deutsches Institut fuer Wirtschaftsforschung *et al*, *Zwoelfter Bericht*, 1995).

5.3.3.1.3 Loan Programmes for "SMEs"

The emphasis of support for small and medium-sized enterprises (SMEs)[96] has been focused on the start-up phase. Within this spectrum, the equity capital assistance (business start-up programme and guarantee programme for freelance professions) totalled DM 28.5 bn between 1990 and 1993 as support loans, an annual average of more than DM 8 bn. These programmes supported the set up of 150 000 new businesses (160 000 by mid 1994) which either secured or created about 1.3 million new jobs and carried out investment of DM 58 bn (Deutsches Institut fuer Wirtschaftsforschung *et al*, *Zwoelfter Bericht*, 1995). The manufacturing industry accounted for about 50%, the service sector and freelance professions (doctors, journalists etc.) for one fifth each and the trade sector for one sixth of all support loans to the *Mittelstand*. The majority of loans were allocated to federal states which are dominated by small and medium-sized enterprises, i.e. Saxony and Thuringia. The loan programmes have initiated rises in employment, turnover and investment. The equity capital structure remains a central concern as the equity capital shares in East and West still diverge according to the Kreditanstalt fuer Wiederaufbau, KfW (Handelsblatt, 12./13.5.1995).[97] The loans programmes for medium-sized companies are dominated by the EKP (Equity Capital Assistance) programme, the ERP (European Recovery Programme) business start-up programme and the KfW programme for SMEs.

The EKP programme is a loan programme which has aimed at building up equity capital within newly-established companies as well as creating additional investment in newly-acquired small and medium-sized companies. Companies with inadequate equity which can prove to follow a sustained company and management concept are eligible. The company must be classified as a small or medium-sized enterprise and must be economically independent (this excludes majority participations greater than 50% by another company). The programmes follow the principle of close subsidiarity, i.e. loans are only granted in those cases where no capital can be obtained on a private basis. Equity capital assistance supplementing a company's capital by up to 40% of the investment sum or the acquisition costs can be allocated up to a maximum loan of DM 700 000. A loan of up to DM 2 m can be granted in the case of a promising privatisation to a new owner or alternatively reversion to the former owner. The investor has to contribute with his own assets which should not exceed 15% of the investment volume. The loan is given for up to 20 years and is interest-free for the first three years. Between the fourth and sixth year the interest rate is fixed (2%, 3%, 5%) and thereafter the market rate is to be paid. Another variant of this loan programme targets small and medium-sized companies wishing to fund a viable business plan, a major part of which consists of investment together with a partner. The scheme aims at East German entrepreneurs who wish to make use of external management competence and partners who are willing to supply management know-how and risk capital to small and medium-sized companies in the new states. The partner's contributions have to improve the economic potential and competitiveness of the company and the partnership capital is designed as a loan to finance the company's concept which is predominantly investment based. This equity capital assistance is limited up to a maximum of DM 5 m. Until the end of 1994 this programme approved payments of DM 12.4 bn of which DM 11.9 bn had been paid (Federal Ministry for Economics BMWi, 1995).

Another means of supporting investment in small and medium sized companies are the ERP-programmes. The ERP-Fund was originally set up after the Second World War and was aimed at the economic reconstruction of Germany. It has since addressed regional and sectoral areas of the German economy in need of support and has also been employed to support SMEs in East Germany since March 1990, i.e. whilst the GDR was still in existence. The ERP-Fund allocates loans with low interest rates to individuals, members of freelance professions and small and medium-sized companies for financing business start-ups and investment in the new states. Until 1994 a total loan volume of DM 40 bn had been allocated to the new states of which DM 33 bn was paid out (Federal Ministry for Economics BMWi, 1995). Two fundamental schemes can be distinguished: a) ERP business start-up programme (*Existenzgruendungs-programm*) and b) ERP company reinforcement programme. The business start-up programme aims at the establishment or acquisition of companies including follow-up investment within the three years of the start of the company, take-over of shares in a management capacity and financing the first inventory of goods. The company reinforcement programme can grant loans if companies or people in freelance professions (except healing professions) invest in the start-up or take-over, the expansion or conversion, or the fundamental rationalisation of companies. The maximum loan is here DM 2 m and the interest rate is fixed for the term of the loan. This programme has financed up to 50% of the eligible costs and the ERP business start up programme has financed up to 85% of the eligible costs in the new states (Weber, 1995).

The KfW has the general objective to hand out loans (medium and long-term) for projects which serve the reconstruction and development of the German economy. Companies in industry and commerce as well as individuals in freelance professions with a maximum annual turnover of DM 1 bn aiming to carry out such projects are eligible for maximum loans of up to DM 10 m. The investment project has to aim at the essential start-up investment, to secure or expand companies. For the new states the term of loan is 10 years. Two particular loan programmes which are supported by the KfW have been in existence which concentrate on investment support for SMEs: a) the KfW / Treuhand Industry Loan Programme and b) public loan guarantees. The KfW / Treuhand Industry Loan Programme has targeted manufacturing and industrial service companies owned by the Treuhand. Companies have been eligible for financial support if they carry out investment which helps the company to adjust to the market and to remove remaining obstacles to privatisation. The project aims at the promotion of reconstructing investment (*Sanierungsinvestititonen*) and product modernisation. Companies with assets of less than 300 000 ECU and less than 500 employees were mainly addressed which reflects the concentration of investment support on SMEs.[98] This programme has not specified a maximum loan and has financed up to 50% of the investment costs and the loan term has been 10 years with a grace period of up to 2 years. Public loan guarantees are guarantees by banks which agree to stand surety for loans granted by loan institutes, building societies and insurance companies to investors setting up new businesses and expanding existing businesses (BMWi, 1994d). (Loans which are granted for the restructuring of enterprises are not covered.) Usually the loan is guaranteed up to 80% and the maximum amount to be guaranteed is DM 1 m per business. The federal government as well as the states support the guarantee banks with 70% of guarantees from their side and these guarantees are supported by a particular ERP guarantee. Furthermore the Deutsche Ausgleichsbank offers a guarantee programme for private and commercial SMEs. This scheme grants guarantees for long-term investment loans which are used in the take-over of an enterprise or investment in East Germany which has proved worthwhile supporting. An investment is generally considered worthwhile subsidising if it creates, expands, restructures or modernises a business. The guarantee covers 80% of the capital (DM 1 m - DM 20 m), interest, commission and costs and the federal government and the states underwrite 85% of the guarantee. The guarantee programme offered by the federal government has aimed at companies which have not been held by the Treuhand and has covered investment loans normally involving large sums, at least DM 25 m. Investment projects which serve a national economic interest are also covered and the guarantee is split between government and states (60 : 40).

5.3.3.1.4 Effectiveness of Investment Policy

The combination of public investment by the Treuhandanstalt during the initial transformation period, investment guarantees as part of the privatisation policy and the substantial investment support for the East German economy has initiated a considerable capital influx into the economy. In 1991 a total of nearly DM 10.9 bn was invested by Treuhand corporations which was about one fifth of the total investment by companies. This amount gradually decreased because of the fall in the THA's portfolio of enterprises and it was estimated that the 1994 investment of DM 1.4 bn represented only about 1% of companies' investment (Deutsches Institut fuer Wirtschaftsforschung *et al*, *Zwoelfter Bericht*, 1995). According to the sectoral structure of Treuhand enterprises the majority was invested into the mining and energy sector and manufacturing industry of which the chemical industry, steel, metal and the construction industry were the main beneficiaries. Despite the fall in total investment, investment per employee has increased since 1992. The investment carried out by the Treuhand has been aimed predominantly at sectors with particular structural problems whereas investment support was aimed at the creation of a particular market structure, the restructuring of the economy and enterprises as well as the modernisation of production techniques. The latter forms of investment, although being subsidised, were left to the private market.

Due to the extensive investment support obsolete production processes have been largely replaced. The industrial base however is still weak and according to Ruediger Pohl the phase of re-investment will only start for many investors after the commencement of the initial investment phase (Handelsblatt, 7.3.95). Investment support remains necessary for those companies in which re-investment might be hindered by weak profits. The government is still required to supply risk capital because companies have so far not been able to build up the necessary financial reserves. Investment support has to focus on the selection of weakly managed enterprises and concentrate on the support of those which are viable in the long run. Public support has initiated a successful economic start which however has not yet achieved its end. Nevertheless the external financial requirements of the new states will decrease but no elimination of the means of support can yet be forecast. The successful GA and SME projects have made the *Mittelstand* the engine of the recovery.

Pohl (1995) suggests that investment support has become less important now that it has become essential to improve the competitiveness of East German companies. The capital structure has been successfully updated and it is becoming essential to relocate public resources to objects of economic policy which sustain lasting improvements in economic growth and competitiveness. Despite the large sum of public net transfers to East Germany (until December 1995: DM 680 bn) the process of transformation has not yet been fully effected and public support is still essential. Investment support should thus be reduced on a gradual basis. Investment support has assisted a total investment volume of DM 700 bn (1991 - 1995) and investment per capita in 1994 in East Germany (DM 11 400) was above the amount in West Germany (DM 8 600). Investment support has been imperative because the replacement of the old capital stock would have otherwise been hindered by market forces, not least because of the weak infrastructure. East German companies still suffer from their lack of experience and this is particularly apparent in trading markets, marketing and distribution. Poor competitiveness implies a high investment risk and weak sales figures. Re-investment is nevertheless essential to the long-term adjustment and integration into the competitive market economy and investment support is still essential to bridge this "disadvantage".

5.3.3.2 Instruments of Transitional Labour Market Policy

Transitional labour market policy has aimed to alleviate the adjustment of the labour market to structures of a social market economy by trying to build a buffer for the collapse in employment and absorb the labour market shock. The objective is to support the establishment of a self-sufficient employment system which is based on an internationally competitive market economy. The main means of achieving a stable employment situation has been private investment which creates long-term employment opportunities. But as long as the private initiative can not sufficiently create this environment the principles of the social market economy require an absorption mechanism through labour market policy.

The instrument of short time employment has addressed the employment shock and aimed at reducing the social impact of the unemployment situation. The relevance of short time employment is however deteriorating which is illustrated by the yearly figures. The yearly average of people in short time work in October 1996 was 48 746 as compared to 370 000 in 1992 and 1.62 million in 1991. The Bundesanstalt fuer Arbeit (1994) endeavoured to reflect the positive impact of short time work on the overall employment situation and weighted the number of short time jobs with a yearly loss of 46% of working hours (October 1996: reported as 51.6%) and calculated that short-time employment has temporarily saved the equivalent of 83 000 jobs in full time employment (25 152 in October 1996). Short time work does not qualify as increasing the quality of the labour force, rather it targets the social acceptability of the economic transformation.

A secondary labour market has however been created as a temporary instrument in order to reduce the high unemployment originating from the economic transformation. It also seeks to help the adjustment of the labour force to the changed framework. This secondary market has created particular organisations (*Beschaeftigungsgesellschaften*) which use job-creating measures and re-educate employees.[99] There is an emphasis on environmental measures as well as those of restructuring infrastructure and plant. Secondary labour market policy reduced the number of unemployed by 1.2 million in 1994 (1.5 million in 1993, 1.8 million in 1992).

The principal instruments of labour market policy have been:
a) Vocational Training
b) Further Professional Education
c) Vocational Rehabilitation
d) Support of Paid Employment and Self-Employment
e) Job-Creating Measures
f)Wage Subsidies for the Long-Term Unemployed
g) Seasonal Financial Support of the Building Sector and

h) Premature Retirement.

In 1994 a total of DM 18.7 bn was spent on instruments of labour market policy which is a 20% reduction compared to 1993. Seventy percent of this reduction was caused by lower expenditures for further professional education (DM 7 bn in 1994 compared to DM 10.4 bn in 1993). Expenditure however for job-creating measures decreased by a much smaller degree (DM 1.8 bn) to DM 8.7 bn. Due to the rise in supply of professional education the expenditure for vocational rehabilitation increased by DM 75 m to DM 602 m in 1994. In total, expenditure for active labour market policy as part of the total expenditure of the Federal Office for Labour decreased from 39% (in 1993) to 34% in 1994.

One particularly important instrument of job-creating measures was introduced with the framework of Paragraph 249h AFG (*Arbeitsfoerderungsgesetz*).[100] Paragraph 249h AFG was introduced at the beginning of 1993 and is limited in time until the end of 1997. This instrument concentrates on the support of employment in particular fields such as environment, social services and youth work. Employers who take on previously unemployed people[101] according to this legal regulation receive a wage subsidy of DM 1 779 per month (in 1995;in 1994: DM 1 585; in 1993: DM 1 260) for up to three years. This is about the same sum the labour office and administration spends on average for an unemployed person in the new federal states (Handelsblatt, 7.2.1995). The policy aims at "financing work rather than unemployment" (Institut fuer Arbeit- und Berufsforschung der Bundesanstalt fuer Arbeit IAB, 1995). According to the IAB study 70% of those employees who have been supported by this programme were employed on projects linked with investment. In particular a share of 44% were employed in projects which aimed to improve the infrastructure, especially in those areas essential for the economic recovery. Projects supporting the field of infrastructure are directed at the acquisition of business estates by the redevelopment of land and buildings which was previously used by industry, agriculture or the military forces. The IAB's research has also identified that the sectoral utilisation of Paragraph 249h reflects the initial regional and sectoral structures of the East German states. Infrastructure projects were very significant in Saxony-Anhalt (62%) which has traditionally been an industrial area whereas projects within the area of science and services as well as residential and urban improvement were dominant in East-Berlin. In February 1995, 99 843 people were employed in jobs which were financially supported according to Paragraph 249h AFG.

A joint programme between the KfW and the EU addresses small and medium-sized companies which carry out investment and offer long term employment opportunities. According to regulations set up by the European Investment Bank, only projects within economic areas such as the production and manufacturing industry, tourism and business-related services (as opposed to those supplying directly to the end consumer) can be considered for this support programme. The scheme supports any investment in Germany (thus it is not concentrated on the new states) which helps long-term employment and requires a long-run allocation of financial resources. As a supplement to the low-interest loan (7%, 4/95) the European Union can pay a lump-sum allowance per newly-created job.[102]

The switch in emphasis of transformational economic policy from the alleviation of the post-unification shocks towards the establishment of a self-sufficient economy can be identified from the quantitative data with regard to labour market political instruments. The number of people in job-creating measures fell from its maximum of 404 900 in May 1992 to 206 700 in October 1996.

5.3.3.3 Research Policy and Technological Progress

The obsolescence of production techniques as well as the poor quality of products has been identified as a concern adversely affecting economic adjustment and enterprises' competitiveness. Technological progress which aims to improve these factors of the East German production function has been addressed by research policy which can be identified as another essential instrument of economic policy aiming at the establishment of a self-sufficient East German economy.

The former centrally organised research infrastructure was privatised as part of the fundamental institutional change. The restructuring of industrial research has been supported by institutions of the federal government and the state governments. The federal government granted a total of DM 930 m for the restructuring of industrial research between 1990 and 1993. In 1994 the government allocated another DM 720 m for research and development within the industrial sector. Until the end of 1994 a total of DM 2.4 bn had been dedicated to restructuring R&D capacities to increase the technological competitiveness of East German companies, to enforce the innovative strength of SMEs, to promote the establishment of businesses on technological grounds and to create an infrastructure which supports R&D (Federal Ministry for Economics BMWi, 1995).

The dominant instruments of the public research policy have been the following:

a) KfW Innovation Programme
b) TOU - Setting Up Technology-Oriented Companies
c) Research Participation and Cooperation
d) R&D Personnel Promotion
e) Research Promotion in Manufacturing Industry and

f) Promotion of Segmented R&D Areas

The KfW innovation programme focuses on product innovation and concentrates on the technological areas of information and communication technology, material technology, biological and genetic technology. It supports the R&D phase as well as the phase of introducing the innovation to the market with a loan which has a period of grace attached to it.

The TOU is a project by the Federal Ministry for Research and Technology (BMFT) which aims at promoting the setting up of innovative companies and at supporting existing companies which operate in advanced technologies and can be assumed to improve the innovative climate in the new states. The scheme supports the phases of i) preparation and formation of documents to appraise the planned innovative projects and show their technological and economical feasibility, ii) innovative projects until market maturity of the product, process or service, and iii) market introduction. The three phases are supported with allowances, grants and loans. The product, process or service to be developed has to indicate clear competitive advantages and market opportunities due to the technical innovation involved, the project has to be technically and economically feasible, the implementation has to involve high development costs with a high but estimated risk. In addition the applicant must show that his assets are not sufficient to fund the innovation.

The BMFT has developed a programme for research participation and cooperation to increase private engagement in research and development. The Ministry identified weak equity structure and high risk as the major hindrances to the realisation of research, in particular for small and medium sized companies. The weak equity structure in particular of young technological companies has been addressed by i) the Technology Participation Programme for Young Technological Companies and ii) Participation Capital for Young Technological Companies. The first programme aims at commercial companies which are allocated loans if they are engaged in research with young technology companies. The eligible companies have to be equipped with the financial capital and the human capital to supervise and monitor the planned innovation project. The second programme (a combined scheme between the BMFT and the Technologie-Beteiligungsgesellschaft mbH (technology-participation, TBG)) focuses on young technological companies which can apply for participation by the TBG as long as these companies can find a third participant who is willing to participate at the same level (*Beteiligungssumme*) as the TBG and agrees to supervise the participation on the basis of a cooperation contract. Both schemes effectively increase the equity capital of young technological companies. Linking the financial support to the innovation projects increases the probability of these projects being successful and effectively improving these companies' competitiveness. Furthermore the technological know-how of the participating company has spill-over effects with regard to the technological human capital of the young technological company. The technical risk has been addressed by the Arbeitsgemeinschaft Industrieller Forschungsvereinigungen e.V. (AIF, Otto von Guericke) which supports research cooperation between SMEs in the new states. The AIF supports research cooperation - further defined as transnational and national cooperation - between companies and research establishments where R&D projects involve considerable technical risks. The programme supports technological transfer and cooperation, aiming to improve the companies' innovation potential and thereby increasing the competitiveness of SMEs in the new states (the AIF finances up to 50% of the eligible expenditure). Contract Research and Development East (AFO) as well as Contract Research and Development West-East (AWO) aim at the full utilisation of existing R&D facilities. In joint cooperation with the BMFT these programmes also aim at the full utilisation of companies' research facilities as well as the research capacity of institutes and universities, award grants or finance part of the eligible costs.

The BMFT (in cooperation with AIF) offers a promotional programme to boost R&D personnel and addresses SMEs with less than 1000 employees in industry, crafts, building, agriculture and forestry, transport and traffic who can carry out research and development using their own personnel. An increase in the R&D capacity of these companies is assumed if they take on additional qualified R&D personnel with degrees from specialist institutions or higher education institutions. The support is carried out in the form of a personnel allowance. A similar programme (*Personalfoerderung Ost*, AIF) supports the costs of R&D personnel employed by SMEs which carry out research and development.

Small and medium-sized companies within the manufacturing industry which aim at the development of new products and processes could apply for grants from the VDI/VDE-Technologiezentrum Informationstechnik until the end of 1995. The promotion of research and development within manufacturing industry focuses on two dominant weak points of the East German economy: obsolescence of production techniques and products.

The BMFT offers two more support programmes for R&D projects within particular technological areas. The Support Programme Biotechnology 2000 supports SMEs located in Germany which undertake projects which aim at the development of new bio-technological products, processes and methods, including genetics. A high potential for innovation has been identified in the area of biotechnology and the positive impact this could have on the East German economy is acknowledged by this support programme. SMEs which are already engaged in biotechnology research or plan to do so in the future and which need basic equipment to carry out this research are eligible for the BMFT support. A more general programme is the Support of Research Projects by the BMFT which aims at achieving an internationally acknowledged high level of R&D efficiency.

Its set up is similar to the Biotechnology 2000-scheme but it places emphasis on a wider field of technological areas, some of which are: energy, information technology, electronics, material research, laser technology, aeronautics, physical and chemical technologies and transport and traffic systems. It can be concluded that research policy which has been especially designed for the transitional period focuses on the establishment of a market structure with room for small and medium sized companies. It identifies the weak equity capital structure as potentially hindering technological progress which is considered a prerequisite for the formation of internationally competitive enterprises.

5.4 Growth Perspectives

The transformation from the socialist economic system to a market economy can be understood as the phase of adjustment succeeding the major shock of the implementation of the new economic system. The transformation from the centrally planned economy to a market economy is a process of creating anew following a fundamental change of the economic conditions. It is necessary to consider the differences in stock and flow variables. National production, savings and consumption as flow variables recreate themselves in a different guise every period. In contrast stock variables such as the stock of capital, human capital and infrastructure, only change gradually and those are the main values which have to be worked on in order to achieve successfully the restructuring of a planned economy. The transition is thus a dynamic process and the adjustment to a shock needs time. Any transformational economic policy has therefore to concentrate on the adjustment of stock variables, i.e. human capital, investment and enterprises. This approach was supported by the Sachverstaendigenrat zur Begutachtung der gesamtwirtschaftlichen Entwicklung and recommended to the German government as the appropriate measure to create growth in the new German *Laender* (1991a, 1991b). Incentives for private infrastructure investment were expected to create growth and the extension of the capital stock was classified as necessary to increase labour demand. Various growth-theoretical considerations with relevance to the chosen transitional economic policies are discussed.

5.4.1 Capital Accumulation and Capacity Effect

The amount of capital accumulation in East Germany required eventually to create a capital stock proportionally similar to the West German one has been estimated by Siebert (1992). The private sector capital stock in West Germany amounted in 1992 to DM 4 800 bn. Taking into consideration a respective population of 25% in the East German *Laender*, the East German capital stock requirement amounts to DM 1 200 bn. This figure should have been achieved at the end of the adjustment process in order to create similar productivity ratios for input factors as well as similar growth rates in both German regions. It has been assumed by Siebert (1992) that 30% of the finally necessary capital stock has already been available in the former GDR. Based on this evaluation the East German economy requires a total investment of DM 840 bn. The same arithmetic methodology can be applied to infrastructure capital where the Western capital totals DM 2 200 bn and at the final stage of adjustment that of the East should be DM 547 bn. If the 30% scheme is applied once again the target of net investment of DM 400 bn must be achieved. Net investment into the capital stock of the former GDR totals at DM 1 240 bn excluding investment for capital depreciation, building and housing and the disposal of ecological waste. Within these calculations the basis of the West German capital stock was assumed to stay constant although in practice a growth rate in the capital stock of 3-4 percentage points could be expected. In the East the dramatic closure of enterprises and the obsolescence of production capital caused a negative capital accumulation of the "old" capital. In 1994 the average value of capital assets within the private sector originating from former GDR times was estimated as DM 200 bn in 1991 prices which represents two-fifths of the 1991 volume (Deutsches Institut fuer Wirtschaftsforschung *et al*, *Zwoelfter Bericht*, 1995). This segregation of inefficient capital as well as the accumulation of new capital are determinants of the marginal capital coefficient.

Historical data regarding countries' capital stock structures and their economies' growth rates have been interpreted to identify a significant correlation between capital accumulation rates and economic growth (Siebert, 1992). These empirical findings are to be interpreted in relation to the principle of acceleration within the investment hypotheses (Harrod, 1939). A high accumulation of capital is necessary to create high national growth rates. Germany on the one hand had to recreate and accumulate most of its capital stock in the post war period and the economy at this time was characterised by considerably higher growth rates (7.5% average during the 1950s). This relationship has also been acknowledged by Baumgart *et al* (1960) who identified a falling average capital coefficient for Germany during the fifties. In contrast Great Britain in that period was equipped with a good capital stock and achieved average growth rates of merely 2.5%. It represented a mature economy following the principle of the business cycle.

The above mentioned examples of the relation between growth rates and capital accumulation allow us to refer to Domar's (1946) marginal capital coefficient. The marginal capital coefficient (v) is defined as the ratio between net investment (I) and the change in production capacity (P) and is summarised in the following equation (5.1).

$$v = I / dP = I_t / (P_{t+1} - P_t) = (K_{t+1} - K_t) / (P_{t+1} - P_t) \qquad (5.1)$$

The marginal capital coefficient (further specified as the ratio between the growth in capital (K) and the growth in production potential according to equation 5.1 is the reciprocal value of the marginal capital productivity. A capacity lag is assumed because the investment in period t generates an increase in production capacity in period t+1. It is here surmised that the smaller the marginal capital coefficient the larger effect on the economy's capacity. The size of the subsequent marginal capital coefficient for East Germany after economic and political change must however be interpreted against the background of the initial capital depreciation. The obsolescence of production capital alongside the closure and liquidation of enterprises must be acknowledged as a reduction in the capital stock which made the modernisation and renewal of capital stock even more inevitable. This development is interpreted as having been initiated by technological progress in other countries necessitating immense capital modernisation and renewal to bring about a net expansion of the capital stock. Net expansion of capital implied qualitative capital expansion which was necessary and resulted from the initial capital depreciation. The high quality of net investment can be assumed to generate a rather small capital coefficient. Quantitative data should not be isolated from qualitative issues in an attempt to derive growth prospectives. Table 5.12 reflects values for net investment. This accumulation of capital in the form of net investment increases the economy's production potential.

The values for net investment in East Germany over the four years given show an expansion which increases the national production potential composed of the potential production volume of enterprises, government and private households. The high growth in production potential assuming a given growth in capital would give the marginal capital coefficient (defined as the change of the capital divided by the change in production potential) a rather small magnitude suggesting high national growth rates *ceteris paribus*. The increase in capacity is however - disregarding the rigid assumptions of the theory of diminishing returns - generally not exclusively dependent on net investment. Rather one should consider alterations to human capital capacity and other resources such as technological know-how. It is thereby investigated to what degree the change in capacity has been caused by investment and to what extent it has been influenced by other factors, i.e. human capital and resources. It can however be assumed that the technology embodied in the capital has been updated. This has been referred to above and can be defined as co-determining the quality of investment.

The introduction of economic and political unification had the effect of producing various exogeneous influxes. The capital expansion, the expansion (qualitative and regional) of international trade and the incentives of the market economy represented a major chance for investment and innovation. These effects have been interpreted as shocks because it is assumed that political unification was not instantly internalised into economic life. In particular the economic policy of privatisation has acknowledged the necessity of an increase in net investment to raise production capacity and has implemented particular privatisation instruments which aim at the management of these adjustment shocks.

Table 5.12: Net Capital Investment in the New *Laender* (DM bn, 1991-1994)

Economic Sectors	1991	1992	1993	1994
Agriculture and Forestry	1.2	1.3	1.1	1.1
Producing Industry	29.8	39.3	47.5	49.9
of which				
-Energy and Mining	9.1	14.0	18.2	19.2
-Manufacturing In.	17.3	21.0	24.2	25.5
-Construction In.	3.4	4.3	5.1	5.2
Distribution	4.4	5.3	5.7	6.0
Transportation and Communication	16.9	23.0	24.8	26.8
Services (excl. housing)	7.3	11.0	17.0	22.0
Total (private enterprises)	59.6	79.9	96.1	105.8
Public Sector, Non-Profit Organisations	15.4	24.0	25.2	29.0
Privatised Enterprises	0.2	2.2	14.7	15.8
Treuhand-Enterprises	10.9	6.8	2.3	1.4
West German and Foreign Enterprises	26.0	42.0	49.0	54.0

Source: Statistisches Bundesamt, current issues; Sachverstaendigenrat zur Begutachtung der gesamtwirtschaftlichen Lage (1994); net investment expressed in current prices

The assignment of ownership to a property depended not only on the price of the property but on the value of the property right which could - in the case of shock management - have either been determined by the imposition of employment and investment guarantees or the imposition of binding investment plans. The expansion of capital investment - supported by transitional investment policies - following the major adjustment shocks is assumed to have initiated an endogeneous growth process which has been described as the accelerator-multiplier relationship.

5.4.2 Endogeneous Business Cycles Expressed as Accelerator

Post-privatisation economic investment policy addresses the growth perspectives of the endogeneous business cycle. The net investment is accelerated by growth of national production and the private investor is supposed to form a capital investment function which depends in particular on the desired capital stock and the actual capital stock. The implementation of the derived net investment depends on the urgency factor. This urgency factor has been addressed by investment policy by amending the incentive structure. An attempt has been made to create a motivational impulse to convert the urgency factor towards unity so that the divergence between the desired and actual capital stock will be eliminated within the following period of time by net investment.

The initial necessity of net investment is supplemented by the requirement to form an investment function in the form of the principle of acceleration (Harrod, 1939). Within the previous accumulation-capacity model net investment was defined as independent of the growth in national income. The implementation of the national growth rate makes the model more dynamic and describes an endogeneous generation of net investment.

A combination of the two dynamic approaches by Domar (1946) and Harrod (1939) can be employed to give the conditions for steady state growth and can be utilised to demonstrate and explain the endogeneous business cycle if the accelerator-multiplier relationship is adopted. Net investment (I) is defined as a function of the growth of income and thus the growth of production over time according to the investment coefficient (v* accelerator). This relationship is expressed in the following equation:

$$I = v^* \, (dY/dt) \qquad (5.2).$$

The condition for equilibrium growth (5.3) is the identity between savings and investment and since savings are determined by income (S = sY) the growth rate of national income is determined by the marginal and average savings ratio and the accelerator (v*) (Harrod, 1939, 1948):

$$(dY/dt)\, 1/Y = s/v^* \qquad (5.3).$$

The interpretation of the above acceleration hypothesis depends on the assumptions regarding temporal delays in the case of a discontinuous interpretation. If it is assumed that investment decisions depend on future expectations which are derived from past experiences, investment in period t can be expressed as the difference between the planned increase in production and the current production (5.4).

$I_t = v^* (Y_{t+1} - Y_t)$ (5.4)

On the basis of equation 5.4. and

$S_t = sY_t$ (5.5)

as well as the equilibrium condition of $S_t = I_t$, the warranted rate of growth (w_{Yb}) is defined as

$w_{Yb} = (Y_{t+1} - Y_t) / Y_t = s / v^*$ (5.6)

The warranted rate of growth s/v* can also be derived assuming an investment function with a different periodisation. Equation 5.7 shows the way in which investment in period t can be expressed as a function of the difference between the desired capital stock (K^*_t) and the actual capital stock (K_t) in a certain time period, where g denotes the coefficient which measures the proportion of this discrepancy which will be changed within the period.

$I_t = g (K^*_t - K_t)$ (5.7)

Only the assumption of the discrepancy factor g being equal to unity suffices the accelerator-multiplier relationship. A discrepancy or urgency factor g smaller than unity can be assumed as reacting to investment incentives and moving towards unity. These incentives can be created by economic policy aiming at the reduction of the discrepancy factor. The transitional investment policy did not aim at influencing the variable "desired capital stock" as this would have qualified as active economic (process) policy. On the contrary the instruments of transitional economic policy have concentrated on creating an incentive structure which generated an increase in investment by addressing the urgency factor.

Using the relationship between capital investment (K) - as the difference between desired and actual capital stock - and output (Y) where v* denotes the number of units of capital which are required to produce one unit of output and g shall be assumed to be equal to unity in equation 5.8, the accelerator-multiplier formula (5.9.) can be derived:

$K = v^* \cdot Y$ (5.8)

$I_t = v^* (Y_t - Y_{t-1})$ (5.9).

Investment policy succeeds in creating accelerated investment on the basis of influencing the national discrepancy factor. A discrepancy factor equal to unity has generated the following relationship between net investment and economic growth. A fall in the rate of growth will lead to an absolute fall in investment just as a rise in the growth of output will lead to an increase in net investment. If national output consists of consumption and investment and the consumption function is expressed in terms of the marginal propensity to save the rate of growth can be expressed in terms of v*, the capital output ratio (accelerator) and the savings ratio s:

$$Y = (1 / 1 - b)\, I \text{ or } Y = I / s \text{ and } dY / Y = s / v^* \qquad (5.10).$$

This principle implies that a growth rate of output above zero will accelerate the growth of investment. If an equilibrium situation below full employment is assumed this process will continue until full employment is achieved. At this point the economy can not grow any more, the output growth rate will be zero and this causes a fall in investment. The new equilibrium situation will be achieved once gross investment is zero and the negative net investment is equal to the rate of depreciation. Transitional investment policy has employed instruments which have aimed at the urgency factor which is defined in the accelerator-model. This factor has been addressed in the form of the chosen instruments influencing private investment-decisions by using the incentives of financial support after the private decision has been taken. This form of transitional economic policy can theoretically be supported with its creation of an endogenous business cycle and forming the necessary assumption for existing positive growth rates to accelerate capital investment.

Two different scenarios with regard to economic growth on the basis of the capital stock and the capital productivity exist. The optimistic one assumes that the current level of real investment will continue until the end of 1997. The capital stock would increase by 3% and the production potential would rise by 50%. This scenario suggests growth in production of 10%. This does not eliminate necessarily the differences in productivity between East and West but the two regions will start converging by the year 2000 (Goerzig *et al*, 1994). A more pessimistic scenario assumes a less dynamic development of investment and the increase in efficiency and productivity will have a lower impact. This suggests that regional differences will remain. Such a scenario might also be explained by a growth theory which places respectively higher emphasis on the development of human capital. The necessity of qualitative improvement of the human factor of the national production function and its implications for national growth will be analysed in the next section.

The accelerator-model assumes a constant savings behaviour, a given growth of the labour force and fixed technical coefficients of production. The capacity model as well as the endogeneous business cycle model are thus limited in their applicability to the East German case of transformation. In particular, the dynamic nature of the factors of human capital and technological know-how and the essential requirement for the quality of human labour to adjust will imply an alteration of the technical production coefficient, i.e. to which extent the new technological input can be utilised. These issues will be addressed in the following section on the new theory of growth.

5.4.3 The New Theory of Growth and Human Capital

The capacity effect caused by the increase in net investment in the East German case can be assumed to have been smaller than the marginal capital coefficient might suggest. The lack of managerial experience, technological know-how and the temporal deficiencies of human capital to adjust behaviourally to the conditions of the market economy can be identified as major transformational impediments. It will however be argued that the increase in net investment is linked to the introduction of modern technology so that an exogeneous introduction of technological change might be suspected. Whether the growth of the production potential will be transferred into the growth of real production depends at the same time on the growth of human capital quality. Human capital quality can be described as the productivity of the factor labour. This production factor is in the position to convert the increase in capacity into real economic growth. Behavioural imperfections can be assumed as regard to managerial and technological experience and the availability and conversion of a learning curve. The investment acceleration theory is therefore insufficient to explain the grade of capital utilisation by human capital.

The adjustment of human capital - e.g. to technological change - can be defined as being more rigid than the adaptation of modern capital (further detailed in chapter 6, sections 6.3 and 6.4). The size of the marginal capital coefficient must therefore be amended and the capacity effect must be expected to be smaller than derived from the expansion of the production potential. Exogeneously and endogenously caused capacity effects will therefore be distinguished and accordingly the capacity effect is the greater the less rigid the adaptation of resources is, in particular human capital. The magnitude can (with reference to adjustment model, see chapter 2, section 2.8) be defined as smaller in the case of an endogeneous change than it would be in the case of an exogeneous influence. Whether the growth of production potential will be transferred into the growth of real production depends not only on the growth rate of real income and - assuming constant prices - on the demand for money, i.e. the grade of capacity utilisation. The growth of human capital quality defines the scope of capacity materialisation.

Investment has been acknowledged as one of the main factors essential for the economic adjustment of East Germany. The creation of new employment opportunities depends to a great extent on the realisation of investment. This was ascertained by German transitional economic policy and the public subsidisation of capital investment. The inefficiency of East German companies is not based exclusively on the obsolete state of the production equipment. New products with which new markets can be opened have to be found by the enterprises themselves and this requires - other than the immediate acquisition of production technology - time and the investment alone is still not enough.

As has been shown above growth theory concentrating on capital accumulation and the marginal capital coefficient cannot sufficiently explain economic growth within societies which have fundamentally changed. The fundamental societal change has been accompanied by norm changes and the individual scope of action has been widened. The development of post-socialist economies depends to a high degree on the internalisation of deficiencies of the behavioural patterns. The modern growth theory appears to be relevant in interpreting adjustments in East Germany. Romer (1986) includes in particular the availability of qualified human capital, the existence and attraction of technological know-how as well as the realisation effects of the learning curve. The new growth theory thus extends the definition of factors determining economic growth. Besides the traditional factor of capital accumulation the equipment with human capital is included.

The human capital structure within the former GDR was characterised by the close association of qualified labour with political identity. The so-called "intelligensia" were assigned privileges and socialist life confined qualified labour to the ultimate socialist aim of "scientific-technological revolution" in order to establish and secure the socialist state. It has been demonstrated (Bentley, 1992) that the graduate labour force was educated in a more specialised way than for example West German students. However the labour force was highly trained with regard to post-school qualifications. University education concentrated on traditional subjects such as engineering rather than modern ones like information technology, which can be shown from the fact that there were only 164 graduates in information technology in the former GDR compared with a total of over 2800 in West Germany in 1988. Research and development was severely impaired due to the lack of integration into the international scientific world. Visits to conferences or "joint ventures" of academic work were generally not permitted. All these factors point to the necessity of bringing the labour force up to date with research and technology and modern know-how. With regard to the less skilled work force the vertical flow of information within centralised organisational structures did not offer any form of intrinsic involvement due the response function being mono-directed (see chapter 2, section 2.2.3.3). The training of non-graduate employees was predominantly exercised in coordination with education facilities within the enterprises which employed them (combines, LPGs, VEBs etc.). The training also included professional and political-ideological education which once again points to the conjunction of labour and political identification (Vogt, 1984).

The inadequacy of the labour force can be expected to be eliminated in time if one accepts Kaldor's (1957, 1962) technical progress function as well as Arrow's (1962) theory of technical progress which concentrates on the learning by doing principle. The learning-model focuses on the consideration that past investment induces a learning process due to the experience gained. These learning effects increase the state of knowledge as well as the potential productivity, i.e. the quality of human capital. Technological progress increases the efficiency of labour and capital. Technological progress takes mainly two forms: product innovation and process innovation. Product innovation involves the qualitative improvement of products. Process innovation results in an improved production process which moves the isoquant inwards, i.e. the same output can be produced with a smaller amount of input factors. Both forms of technological progress are essential for the long-term adjustment of the East German economy. Technological process often necessitates the generation of new capital and is thus linked to investment. This accumulation of new capital leads to a capital stock which is increasingly heterogeneous (vintage-approach, i.e. newer capital is associated with higher capital productivity) and has differentiated capital productivities. The impact of technological progress on human capital is characterised by the association of the technical progress function with the learning by doing principle.

Transitional economic policy has concentrated beside the above advocated influence of the capital divergence factor on increasing the propensity to technological progress by stimulating research and development. However the limitations of economic transformational policy soon become obvious because changes in human behaviour and the materialisation of learning curve effects are time-consuming. Human behavioural adjustment is here considered to be effected by more fundamental issues such as the notion of whether the chosen approach of transformation (i.e. the institutionalist approach) has made an internalisation and adaptation on a human behavioural level possible. This notion and the apparent relevance of theoretical approaches introduced in Chapter 2 will be discussed in the next chapter.

5.5 Conclusions

The economic system change in East Germany has created adjustment shocks which led to particular regional and sectoral problem areas within the East Germany. Adjustment deficiencies were addressed by economic policy which has concentrated on macroeconomic aggregates like investment, employment, technology and research. An attempt has been made to construct a theoretical framework which identifies potential growth-inducing variables which will eventually reduce economic insufficiencies. Net investment has been identified as inducing a capacity effect. This capacity effect, if transformed into a growing production, will generate further net investment via the accelerator-multiplier. These effects however need to be supplemented by an increase in the quality of labour, implementation of modern technology as well as the generation of technological process. The economic and political unification, social implications and political pressures - maximisation of votes - has necessitated the speed up of the process of transformation by implementing certain economic-political instruments. Economic policy based on ordo-liberal principles is not allowed to be designed as economic process policy which would imply knowledge of the final state of the economy and an according intervention into economic life. Economic policy has therefore been aimed at creating a framework which produces incentives to let the economic actors act according to their own functions but alleviate some of the burdens of economic adjustment. In particular instruments have been employed to accelerate the process of capital accumulation to create self-sufficient growth.

The identified necessity of net investment in order to create a capacity effect has been addressed by the privatisation policy. The assignment of enterprise shares - in particular - to the bidder who places the highest value on the property in the form of employment and investment guarantees is interpreted here as shock management. The privatisation policy has allocated the handling of the employment and the capital depreciation shocks to the new owners. Employment and investment guarantees were compulsory and have in particular created net investment which generated an increase in the national production potential. The endogeneous business cycle and the acceleration of net investment has been addressed by the transitional economic policy. In particular instruments have been applied which aim at influencing the capital discrepancy factor and thereby have implemented an incentive structure to generate increased net investment by financially supporting specified areas of the economy.

The improvement of the quality of the labour force can not be addressed in a direct way but it is assumed that learning effects and technological and managerial spill-over effects will be created by the previously mentioned transitional economic policy as well as the creation of an incentive structure which leads enterprises into carrying out further research and development and thereby reduces the insufficiency of the East German production function. Quality of labour force considerations suggest the analysis of the behavioural adjustment as part of transformational economics which can be realised by referring to the adjustment model and alternative system-analytical approaches presented in Chapter 2. The succeeding analysis allows an evaluation of the institutionalist approach with transitional economic policy instruments as transformational approach based on the East German case study.

Chapter Six
Application of the Adjustment Model to the East German Transformation

6.1 Introduction

Post-privatisation policy has aimed at influencing the decision-making pattern. The chosen approach of mediation did not focus primarily on behavioural adjustment, but on the adjustment of macroeconomic aggregates. The forthcoming sections thereby look at two levels of the transformation: Firstly the transformation of the institutional framework will be analysed employing the dynamic adjustment model (section 2.8), and secondly the same model will be used to look at the adjustment of individual behaviour following these institutional changes. Section 6.2 is based on these adjustment-theoretical considerations (see chapter 2, section 2.8) as well as system-theoretical (see chapter 2, section 2.2) and analyses the institutional transformation with regard to the reaction flexibility of the former East German system and how norm changes affected partial economic systems and their interactions. The notion of compatibility of norm changes with the system changes will be looked at and the grade of the new economic system's order considered. Section 6.3 establishes that behavioural adjustment deficiencies exist and analyses potential causes of these deficiencies. They imply a time lag of the economic adjustment process and the analysis shows that the internalisation of structural change is incomplete.

6.2 System Change and Rigidity Analysis

6.2.1 Low Reaction Flexibility Defined Un-Sustainability of Previous System

The East German transformation classifies as a system transformation because of the alteration of system elements and their characteristics (see chapter 3, sections 3.3, 3.4 and 3.5). The structures of information, motivation and coordination have been addressed, and their transformation has been established. It has been system-theoretically assumed throughout the thesis that elements are factors which serve to achieve partial objectives. These partial objectives are not to be interpreted separately from a social goal function which constitutes a general norm which has been assumed to be historically defined (see section 2.2.2.2).

The principles of dialectic materialism as the theoretical basis of Marxism-Leninism necessitated the congruency between political and socio-economic system elements in the form of the basis-superstructure theorem (section 2.3.2.2.2). The high correlation of partial system elements and their identification with the social goal function in the form of the structure of the economic system (i.e. the ownership of the means of production) was factually restricting the entire societal structure. This determining interrelation prevented the alteration of elements of the economic system because of its effect of negating dynamic system principles. The restrictive definition of system elements resulted in a high grade of the system's order.

The former East German system of Marxism-Leninism is thus characterised by a low reaction flexibility to external influential factors. Open protestations in favour of political and economic changes which signify the dynamic pattern and evolutionary character of social systems could not be integrated into the existent system. Dynamic pressures could not be provided for within the given system which thus proved incapable of being sustained. A strict mechanical interpretation of system in the form of organised complexity does thus not render as appropriate because human action generally defines any system as changeable (Leipold, 1985; North, 1985). Referring to Koopmanns and Montias (1973) the economic system is not a closed partial system. It is exposed to interactions with other partial social systems and the environment and the grade of the system's order defines its reaction flexibility with regard to external influences.

The low reaction flexibility and the rigid definition of system elements within the East German system caused the eradication of the system itself and necessitated the adoption of a new system framework. If one merely considers the environmental factor of political pressure in the form of demonstrations protesting for more liberal and individual action, it becomes obvious that the restrictive definition of the given system did not allow any evolutionary change since the system was incapable of being amended to integrate freedom of action. The system was rigid in the form of the ownership of the means of production determining the superstructure, freedom of action being defined within the system as part of the superstructure, i.e. factors which could not change due to the unchanged ownership structure. The congruence of political and socio-economic factors as a principle of dialectic materialism rejects an evolutionary system development within the framework of the given system. Instead fundamental transformation was required.

6.2.2 Rigidity-Analysis of System Transformation

6.2.2.1 Some Principles Restated

The fundamental transformation of the East German societal system requires an analysis of the internalisation of norm changes within the newly established system (a norm has been defined in section 2.2.1 as a prevailing feature of a set environment of a particular historical stage which is a behavioural rule of interdiction). This notion of the internalisation of norm changes (i.e. the degree to which a new system has developed according to norm changes) can be looked at by referring to the institutional structure of the new system. The alteration of particular elements and features of the system were considered as part of the structures of information, motivation and decision-making (see chapter 3). These structures and their layout describe a behavioural pattern according to system-theoretical considerations

It has been assumed that individual behaviour is defined by utility functions. Two of Weber's classifications of individual behaviour (section 2.2.3.4) will be followed which reflect the changes in the behaviour functions as a result of the transformation. Motivation is thus here to be generally considered to either be value- or purpose-rational and their relevance will be discussed in the next section. The existence of a norm has been assumed and this norm defines specific principles, methods and behavioural rules (section 2.2). It has been outlined in Chapter 2 that an internalisation of changes depends on rigidity factors and the adjustment model (section 2.8) has suggested in particular that the achievement of desired societal goals depends on the rigidity of framework adjustment to changes in the norm.

6.2.2.2 Norm Changes and Interactions of Economic System Participants

A norm change is here assumed to be indicated by the public protestations and demonstrations for more individual liberty and freedom of action. (Throughout the existence of the GDR no change with regard to the acceptibility of freedom of speech can be established. It can thus be assumed that any potential previous norm change can be negated as there has not been any similar public movement prior to the one discussed here. Of course the assumption of social norm change is vague as there is no consistent way of establishing that the change is approved of by all individuals. Here, it can only be assumed that the outcome of the first democratic general elections in 1991 reflected a change in the prevailing norm features. The electoral approval of the political, social and economic unification with West Germany proves evidence of this fundamental adaptation of new societal beliefs.) These actions have preceded the East German system transformation. The former societal system of the German Democratic Republic restricted individual action unless it was consistent with values which were defined by socialist principles (see section 3.2.1). This form of individual action (sanctioned if compatible with given socialist values) suggests that individual behaviour in former East Germany had been value-rational in attempting to create a socialist state. (The term "value-rational" is not euphemistic because a socialist norm existed and the system had been supported by East German citizens which was reflected in the membership in party-political organisations, i.e. individual values were in line with social ones. Furthermore the mechanism that sanctioned particular behaviour implies that behaviour which was not value-rational was oppressed.) The alteration of the norm has implied alterations of the structure of the economic system. These changes circumscribe the alteration of the institutional framework which is supposed to act as the frame defining the limitations of individual action and in particular economic behaviour.

The economic system has been described as interactions between participants, orders, rules, organisations and the legal framework of the economy (chapter 2, section 2.2.2.1). The change of the structure of interactions manifests an alteration in the structure of information, motivation and decision-making (chapter 3). The private individual and the private enterprise are now principally the dominant economic actors in their roles as economic units for consumption and production. The order of interaction has changed from mono-directed flows of information towards decentralised and multi-lateral purpose-related information channels (see section 2.2.3.3). These channels are utilised according to principles of hierarchical orders within organisations and this structure is closely related to the functions individuals and sets of individuals are assigned with. For example the function of an employee within a private enterprise is designed by his job description within his employment contract and corporate decision-making authority is either held by the owners or contractually-assigned individuals within the enterprise - disregarding rudimentary participatory employee rights. However, the private economic actor (outside his pre-defined role of the contractual employment agreement) acts on a more general level independently in the form of saving, consumption etc. The individual utility function has become the principle incentive and motivation structure, so that the individual no longer acts according the value-rationale but the purpose-rationale (Weber, 1947). This coincides with behaviour determined by self interest.

6.2.2.3 Adaptation of a New Societal Goal Function

The elements of the former GDR's societal goal function were derived from dialectic materialism and based on Marxism-Leninism (see chapter 2, section 2.3.2.2). The entity of social goals were defined by the structure of the economic system and in particular by the relation between production forces and production methods, i.e. the ownership of production means. The partial social systems were derived from the economic system, i.e. the organisation of the production and the production means were supposed to have determined social life. Thus the basis of the economic system determined societal life as the superstructure. The institutional framework of the former East German economic system as the basis of society was described by particular elements of the system. The production means were nationalised and *de facto* only committees and organs of the party or the state had any right of disposal. Production, distribution, coordination of the economic plans, finance and social policy as well as the design of economic incentives were centrally planned and exercised.

The change of the East German economic system (chapter 3) can be described as part of the change of the societal system, if social systems are assumed to be divided into the dichotomous categories of capitalism and socialism. The adaptation of the West German constitution classifies the change from the communist system with the axiom of a planned economy and public ownership to democratic capitalism, the change of the economic system being part of the global societal change. The economic system is thus defined as a partial social system and the fundamental structural elements of this system have been altered alongside the remaining systems such as the legal and political framework. Factors which have been identified as classifying the economic system have changed, such as the property right structure, the control and organisational structures. It has since changed towards private ownership and only selected economic areas are kept under public ownership and control. The entire decision-making process has been decentralised. Enterprises and households which had limited autonomy and a limited scope of action were given full autonomy - with the exception of some public enterprises. The legal and political systems were adopted from the former West Germany and are based on the principles of the personal right of legal unambiguity and parliamentary democracy with social responsibility.

The social goal function (chapter 2, section 2.2.2) was defined as constituting a form of national choice of economic objectives and a form of ultimate objectives of society[103]. It can thus be described as having changed from concentrating on the creation of a classless society with rewards attributed according to the principle of need and the maxim of economic growth increasing living standards. Instead it has become a society whose goals focus on democracy with rewards attributed according to the principle of proficiency, social responsibility and the personal right to legal unambiguity. In the next section the analysis will consider whether the changes of partial societal systems have been compatible with these norm changes.

6.2.2.4 Compatibility of Norm Changes and Partial Societal System Changes

The Marxist-Leninist norm specified and constrained economic and political systems. The transformation has erased system elements (e.g. five year plans, see chapter 3, section 3.2) and replaced them with new ones (e.g. individual plans, sections 3.3, 3.4, and 3.5). The change of the economic system as well as the re-shaping of the legal and political framework were coherent with the change in the norm (see above). The norm change towards more liberal individual action and definition of individual utility and behavioural functions can be described as synonymous with, for example, the establishment of decentralised decision-making and individual private property with regard to the economic system. With regard to the political system, democratic principles and the division of power coincide with some degree of participatory political right by individuals. The adjustment elasticities of the system framework to changes in the norm are positive.

The compatibility of the partial social systems reflects the internalisation of norm changes within the partial systems and thus describes a fast adjustment process with regard to the institutional set up. The change of these structural features within a considerably short period of time (6 years) represent a high degree of framework adjustment to norm changes. It can also be argued that this was caused by the un-sustainability of the previous East German societal system (section 6.2.1) and the resulting need to create or adopt an entirely new system. Structural frameworks have altered congruently and internalised changes in the norm. Referring to the adjustment model (section 2.8), the adjustment elasticities of the former East German system framework to norm changes can be surmised to have been zero which necessitated the adaptation of an entirely new system. This applies to both adjustment elasticities n (economic system) and m (political system, see section 2.8.2), because neither the economic nor the political system could continue their existence (e.g. no continuation of the Peoples' Chamber). This can be classified as a revolutionary change as defined in section 2.8.1 because of the conscious creation or adaptation of a new framework as the result of weighting amendments to the given norm. The introduction of the new institutional framework with regard to the economic system can be classified as exogeneous (details of the institutionalised transformation in chapter 3) and economic variables have been expected to adjust according to their behavioural relationships (adjustment and its deficiencies of economic aggregates were described in chapter 5, sections 5.3 and 5.4). The institutionalising of the transformation has been successfully achieved because no disparity existed between the parameters describing adjustment elasticities of systems to norm changes, i.e. between the degree by which the norm changes were transformed into changes of individual partial societal systems. (If for example a norm change causes a structural change of an economic system in the creation of private property rights whilst at the same time no amendment of this society's legal system in protecting private property was caused, the institutional framework of the economic system could not have been put into place successfully.)

The implementation of the ordo-liberal concept of economic policy has herewith proved to be successful. It aimed, according to Eucken (1950, 1952), at the establishment of a suitable institutional framework which defines the scope of economic action but which does not forecast or design any economic outcome. The economic plans are accordingly designed individually and are to be coordinated through the market mechanism. This consciously-constructed framework is compatible and consistent with norm changes and with the other partial social systems. The framework of private ownership and decentralised economic planning is for example consistent with the creation of personal liberty, the personal right to legal unambiguity (to mention only a few of the amended maxims of the legal and political partial systems).

6.2.3 Grade of the New Economic System's Order

The institutionalised change has modified the economic environment and exposed the economic system and life to external influences. The implementation of a newly structured East German economic system classifies as a transformation and this process has been analysed according to the interaction of the economic system with remaining partial social systems, the environment and the social goal function. The reaction flexibility can thereby also be assumed to define the grade of dynamism.

It has been assumed that structural elements of the economic system influence economic behaviour and that these structures thereby predefine the economic process (see ordo-liberal theory of economic systems, section 2.3.1.1). The economic behaviour and the economic process are subject to the scope of action that is characterised by the structural elements and features. The scope of individual economic action is circumscribed by the structure of information, motivation and decision-making. The structural transformation has created a dispersion of information between various economic agents who are principally assumed to decide independently whether they need to attain particular information and are also self-responsible for such information gathering. It was previously established that the structures of information, motivation and decision-making are highly correlated (DIM-approach, section 2.2.3). Once the economic agent has attained a given set of choices through the process of information gathering he is generally assumed to be in the position to decide upon his own action according to his interpretation of the available information and in accordance with an individually defined utility function. This utility function is here assumed to be purpose-rational in its motivational structure. These decentralised structures and the forming of individual economic plans which are coordinated on a market basis imply a high scope of action within the institutionally defined limitations. The decision-making process has principally been decentralised with every enterprise and household now having individual authority. Individual economic action is principally confined to the boundaries of legal sanctioning, for example the exercising of a private property right is not merely defined by the right of action but limited by the duty not to obstruct third persons. The coordination of private plans by the market which is characterised by dynamic developments (products, prices etc.) imposes uncertainty on future events which therefore can not be anticipated. It can thus be concluded that the structural elements of the economic system allow a high scope of individual economic action which implies a low grade of order. This low grade of the economic system's order is associated with the effect of dynamising the economic system as it now provides the flexibility to react to changes. This dynamisation prescribes the influx of various external and environmental influences. This open system is supposed to survive in the long-run if it allows the adjustment of the system to these environmental factors. It is here necessary to return to Hayek's definition of ordered behaviour (section 2.3.1.2.3). He defined (1963) any behaviour according to rules as reducing the scope of action and such behaviour is then called "ordered". Since it has been established that the new East German economic system has been institutionalised it was suggested that norms and rules specifying economic behaviour exist. Certainly it must be noted that, for example, the rule of not obstructing a third person whilst exercising a private property right reduces the scope of action. But a negation of any rules within social systems would jeopardise the existence of such systems because chaotic complexity contradicts the fundamental definition of systems as an entity of elements and their characteristics.

In this section it has been shown - referring to the adjustment model - that the institutional change has been successfully implemented and that structural changes of the economic system were compatible with norm changes as well as being compatible with those changes of different partial societal systems.

6.3 Adjustment Deficiencies of Economic Behaviour

The partial elasticity x which has been defined as the partial marginal product of the economic system (dQ/dS_e) in section 2.8.2 (i.e. the degree by which the changes of the economic system have changed national economic output) suggests that behavioural adjustment deficiencies can exist. Individual behaviour has to adjust to the norm changes which created structural changes. As has been shown in chapter 5 transitional economic policies were necessary to mediate the process of economic transformation. It was theoretically suggested in the adjustment model (in chapter 2, section 2.8.3) that relative changes of the societal goal function alongside institutional and political changes following normative alterations have to be equal to the relative value of the partial adjustment elasticities. This will be further elaborated upon in this section.

6.3.1 "Marginal Product of System Change" as Adjustment Elasticity

Reaction flexibility of the system to environmental changes is not synonymous with reaction elasticity of the economic product (as the outcome of the economic process) to changes in the institutional structure. The general assumption of the structures determining economic behaviour and thereby influencing economic process does not give any indication of the value of marginal productivities, i.e. the partial marginal product of the system amendment. The individual's behavioural adjustment is thus not directly expressed by the institutional adjustment of the system to norm changes. Whether the change in the individual decision-making structure has been internalised by the economic agents, for example, is a question of the adjustment elasticity, i.e. the degree by which the economic behaviour changes, caused by a change in the structure.

It shall be suggested here based on the previously described necessity of post-institutionalisation policy (chapter 5, section 5.3.3) that the adjustment elasticity has been too low and that this elasticity is subject to some specific forms of the system's order which will be explained in the remaining sections of this chapter. The adjustment model helps to identify two levels of the transformation: Firstly, it helps to analyse the factors which influence a successful implementation of a new institutional framework (section 6.2). Secondly, it goes beyond the institutional level and helps to understand the adjustment of individual behaviour (section 6.3). Here, the system-theoretical assumption of the institutional framework determining economic behaviour proves to be insufficient. The system change has been shown to have been successfully achieved. But still there are adjustment deficiencies remaining which have so far prolonged the process of economic adjustment and economic integration. It will be suggested - despite the change of the institutional framework being synonymous with norm changes - that the chosen structures have been insufficient to achieve the desired economic behavioural adjustment.

Thus the successful implementation of the institutional change does not allow us to overlook the deficiencies in the adjustment of the real economy and the obstacles of economic integration. The national production function within the adjustment model was defined as being dependent on the state of technology and the partial economic and social systems (equation 2.7 in section 2.8.2). A correlation between the state of technology and the amendment of the economic system can be assumed because the dynamic nature of the economic system due to the high reaction flexibility also dynamises the factor technology. It shall here therewith be assumed that the adjustment of the real economy is caused by two factors: the partial marginal product of the system change and its effect on the state of technology. The system change has demanded, for example, an adjustment of the standard level of production and an adjustment of the production input factors. Real economic adjustment deficiencies were identified in the previous chapter and have been addressed by transitional economic policies in the form of moderating the adjustment process. This fact points to the process of internalising institutional changes. The adjustment of the production input factors, in particular capital, technology and labour, have been identified as changing rather slowly. The low productivity of labour (sections 5.2.4 and 5.3.3.2) can be argued to be caused by deficiencies within the organisational structure and the slow adjustment of behavioural patterns. Since the institutional transformation was imposed according a top-down approach the real economy has had to adjust to economic forces which were formerly excluded from the system.

Some specific forms of the economic system's order will be suggested to have influenced the specific marginal productivity of the structural change which will be hypothesised to be responsible for some adjustment deficiencies of the real economy. This notion leads to various suggestions why the institutional transformation was established before the phase of economic behavioural adjustment had been finished. On the other hand it leads to the suggestion that the chosen structures were incomplete, that the process of norm changes had not been completed by the time of the implementation of the new institutional framework or that there is merely a time-lag of behavioural adjustment. It will be concluded that all these factors are relevant.

6.3.2 Time-Lag of Behavioural Adjustment

Despite the successful implementation of the institutional change the real economy has not responded straight away. Rather a time-lag of behavioural adjustment can be identified. Economic variables have responded slowly to altered system elements and the individual economic unit requires time to adapt to the widened scope of economic (and social) action. Individual behavioural functions have changed with the societal change, despite the norm change having initiated the system's new features. Behavioural relationships have changed because the variables determining the economic action were replaced. Time is required to learn how to act independently and not merely follow directives and orders which were centrally issued. No experience existed as to how to act economically efficient and as to which parameters to adjust if a determining variable changed. Behavioural adaptation has been attempted by intra-firm training and using skilled West German managers.

The time difference between the completion of the institutional change (i.e. the implementation of the a new system framework and the adjustment of behavioural patterns) is due to the need for individual economic units to acquire experience within the changed system. The external influx of managerial and technological know-how and skills - as has been targeted *inter alia* by the privatisation method - is not sufficient because for the East German economy to function without any external support the economic units need to gain this knowledge themselves. Spill-over effects from the temporal assignment of West German managers to East German firms are not denied, however it should be acknowledged that self-experience is essential and is time consuming. The learning process is a process of interaction which is based on feedback between the system and its environment. Behavioural patterns are altered via the experience which is fed back to the economic unit. Within the previously closed socialist system there was no need for managers to alter behaviour or decision-making patterns due to the mainly vertical and centralised flow of information. People have to learn how to handle the changed and continuously altering environment. The implementation of the institutional change can therefore not be expected to have instantaneously produced a well-equipped and skilled production force or to have altered production functions and introduced all necessary behavioural changes. An adjustment of human capital quality is essential to convert an increase in production capacity (e.g. by capital investment) into economic growth. The scope of capital utilisation is thus defined by the growth in human capital quality. It is expected that the inadequacy of the labour force will be eliminated over time (Kaldor, 1957, 1962; Arrow, 1962). The time sequence of adjustment is conditioned by the degree to which the chosen transformation approach allows an internalisation and adaptation of the changes on a human behavioural level. It was established in the previous chapter that transitional economic policy has not addressed the quality of labour force as such. Rather economic aggregates were addressed which are supposed to create a capacity effect. Neither the specific form of institutional transformation nor the transitional economic policies aimed at and succeeded in the elimination of behavioural deficiencies. It is thereby expected that the quality of human capital will be increased over time due to the realisation of the learning curve.

6.3.3 X-Inefficient Decentralisation of Organisational Structures

The introduction of a decentralised decision-making structure as part of the altered corporate structure is generally assumed to increase economic efficiency. The organisational structure has been decentralised in the form of enterprises designing individual plans of supply and independently forming production functions and functions for the demand of input factors. The flow of information in the form of the response function has changed. This function which describes the flow of information depends within a decentralised organisation on the preceding messages and knowledge is supposed to be dispersed. Within the formerly centralised structure the response function was characterised by the central gathering of information. The organisational structure influences the behaviour of economic agents and within the organisation three aggregates of agents can be identified according to the nature of interaction: the owners, the employees and managers with corporate decision-making authority.

It is relevant to analyse the employee's role and function within organisations, because the comparatively low East German labour productivity suggests a particular behavioural adjustment deficiency within the labour market. Actions of employees within the work environment are defined in a contractual employment agreement and are purpose-related. Employees' awareness of and identification with the work environment can be assumed to have increased with the corporatisation of enterprises because of the changed information structure. The economic coordination has changed from informational centralisation towards informational decentralisation and this dispersion of information is surmised to increase economic efficiency (section 2.2.3.3). Despite a movement towards a more horizontal transmission of information the distribution of decision-making authority follows the classic employment firm (see section 2.5.1) and is associated with more or less hierarchical structures of organisations. The degree to which economic actions are exercised depends to a large degree on the homogeneity of economic agents' objectives and whether they are mutually tolerable or exclusive. The degree of hierarchy within the newly formed corporations can be deduced from the particular organisational form of a company with limited liability (GmbH) or a public stock company (AG). Also the adoption of the conventional employment firm suggests limited distribution of decision-making authority.

The classification of enterprises according to their legal corporate forms suggests a considerably high centralisation of control and decision-making authority. The legal form of the GmbH which a capital company with an equity share capital of at least DM 50 000 (*GmbH-Gesetz*) has been identified as more significant in East Germany than the legal form of the AG. An AG is characterised by a minimum capital stock of DM 100 000 (*Akt-Gesetz*) and this corporate form was identified as less dominant in 1993 than it was in 1991 (Carlin, Mayer, 1994). The ratio between the number of GmbHs and AGs increased by two thirds between 1991 and 1993 which indicates the greater significance of the legal form of GmbH. This implies that a large share of managerial control is held by the enterprises' owners. The enterprise form of the AG is characterised by a less centralised structure of control and less influence of the owner on corporate policy. This is partly due to the frequent form of outside-ownership within public stock companies. The structure of the GmbH is more centralised than that of the AG with the distinguishing form of a supervisory board as well as the board of directors (management board). The board of directors consists of managers and they are the central institution which govern and manage the enterprise. This structure together with the significant number of GmbHs point towards a high degree of managerial dependence from the owner. If the approaches by Leibenstein (1966) and Ellermann (1990, 1992) are accepted, X-inefficiency can thus be expected to be present within the newly corporated enterprises because of the particular hierarchical structure and structure of decision-making (see section 2.2.3.4 and 2.5).

Furthermore the structural change of organisations has applied conventional corporate forms and not endeavoured to apply any of the ethical and constitutional principles with regard to relationship between the structure of control inside the form and organisational efficiency (Chapter 2, sections 2.4 and 2.5). Economic efficiency can thereby be assumed not to have been maximised. The increase in organisational efficiency due to the implementation of the decentralised decision-making structure can be suggested to be less than optimal. A comparison of motivational incentives and behaviour between socialist and capitalist enterprises is difficult because X-inefficiency depends on the motivational structure and it was observed that a change from value-rational behaviour towards purpose-rational behaviour has taken place. Some form of work alienation which is suggested to have been found in the former centralised socialist firm can thereby also be argued to exist within the newly-created corporate forms due to the lack of worker participation (see Furubotn, 1985). Despite the adoption of the post-war structure of mandatary participation by large industrial enterprises - which has so far proven more controversial than helpful with regard to wage negotiations - some degree of work alienation can still be expected. The employment contract confines the employee's parameters of action and defines restricted variables of his utility function. The employment contract reduces the employee's objectives to the variables salary and performance, but generally excludes corporate parameters (e.g. take-overs).

Here, two factors can thus be suggested to have prevented a swift behavioural adjustment: Firstly, the adjustment of the employee's utility function which expresses objectives within his work environment is time consuming. Secondly, as long as the objectives of the economic agents within the organisation are not mutually tolerable the coordination of economic action is not efficient (Weber, 1947, 1968). The corporate and managerial structures lead to the suggestion that some objectives are exclusive. The mere aim of an employee to secure his employment position might contradict the owner's aim of maximising profits. Motivational factors - though having been implemented - leave the factual relationship between production input factors and production output unqualified (Ellermann, 1992; see section 2.5.1.5). The adoption of the classic employment contract within the firm rather than seeking to introduce more complete labour contracts in the form of factual responsibility leads to the identification of the current motivation and incentive structure as a source of inefficiency. That an increase in utility compatibility would lead to a rise in the proficiency of the organisation's participants has been established by Hurwicz (1969). X-efficiency and thereby the economic efficiency of the enterprise, could have been increased by the introduction of democratic principles of industrial democracy. This implementation would lead to a movement from inside the production frontier towards the frontier (Leibenstein, 1966; Ellermann, 1990).

This inefficient decentralisation, namely, the corporate form basically identifying control with ownership alongside the weak motivational structure of the conventional employment firm has had the effect of qualifying one aspect of the weak partial adjustment elasticity. The lack of internalisation of these decentralised system structures implies that the structural changes were not successfully converted into the national production function as shown by the low labour productivity. The marginal product of the implementation of new corporate and employment forms can be surmised to have been smaller than it might have been if alternative structures in the form of participatory elements had been introduced. However, it must be noted that a comparison of East German with West German productivity ratios can not be pursued to prove the suggestions made above because of identical corporate forms. Nevertheless it shall be maintained that a link exists between the structure inside the firm and the economic efficiency.

6.3.4 Concentration of Ownership and Intercorporate Control

Franks and Mayer (1994a, 1994b) analysed ownership and control patterns in different countries (Germany, France, UK, USA) and ascertained a multiplicity of structures. The analysis focused on large companies quoted on the stock markets. In the UK the majority of shares were found to be held indirectly by institutions (pension funds, life assurance firms and mutual funds) in contrast to the system in the USA where individuals directly hold shares. In France and in Germany a considerably lower degree of corporate activity than in the USA and UK was found. In particular the authors identified that in West German (as well as in French) firms the corporate sector is the largest group of shareholders. In West Germany a high proportion of companies are owned by West German families and firms whereas the large stakes in East German firms are mainly owned by West German companies. The allegedly high influence of banks could not be supported since only 5.8% of the sampled companies had banks holding share stakes in excess of 25% but this was explained by banks being holders of bearer shares and exercising proxy votes. Furthermore German firms are characterised by more concentrated ownership in comparison to companies in the USA and UK. In nearly 85% of all German companies (a sample was used) one shareholder owns at least 25% of the shares. In cases of concentrated ownership direct control is exercised via boards (Franks, Mayer, 1994b) and markets for corporate control are not well established.[104]

A recent analysis of a similar kind which includes the East German asset market has been carried out by Carlin and Mayer (1995). The paper ascertains that the concentration in East Germany is even higher than in large West German firms. The transfer of ownership and corporate control to West Germany has been deemed necessary by the aforementioned authors to complete the process of restructuring. The paper reflects on this development considering that the Treuhand and the economy's sale to a domestic "foreign" market has been the majority factor making the East German transformation superior to other post-socialist countries in Eastern Europe. The following table (6.1) represents the findings by Franks and Mayer (1994a) and Carlin and Mayer (1995) reflecting the concentration of ownership (which is here defined as the largest share held by one shareholder).

The concentration of ownership goes along with a concentration of control. Shares of enterprises were mainly sold as voting-shares. The requirement of the East German companies for managerial knowledge and skills held by West Germans and foreigners initiated the transfer of control to those with this knowledge and experience. As Carlin and Mayer (1995) have pointed out the "transfer of control has been integral to the acquisition of outside finance, markets and managers". This control has been described as following the German model of "inside control", corporations are intercorporately holding shares.

Table: 6.1: Concentration of Ownership in East German Privatised Firms, Large West German and UK Companies

	Firms Sold by THA until 9/94 in %	Large West German Companies in %	Large UK Companies in %
Major Shareholder < 25%	5.5	15	87
Major Shareholder > 25%	94.5	85	13
total	100	100	100
Major Shareholder > 50%	72.5	57	6

Source: Carlin, Mayer (1995), table 3 - mainly based on Franks, Mayer (1994a)

"Insider systems are ones in which the corporate sector has controlling interests in itself and an outsider investor, whilst able to participate in equity returns through the stock market, are not able to exert much control." (Franks, Mayer 1994b). This is opposed to the system of outsiders where individuals and institutions are shareholders, which has been described as typical for the UK and the USA.

This insider system (Frank, Mayer, 1994b) is different to the total acquisition of companies and it has been suggested that this type of control once it has been fully evolved in the East will reduce the concentrated West German control and ownership in East German firms. Such a development is suggested because the establishment of private markets and private ownership of company shares enables the transfer of control and ownership. This might eventually diffuse the concentration enabling East German companies to attain a higher degree of control. It must be noted that inside control is defined as intercorporate control - opposed to inside ownership in Ellerman's (1990) sense as the ownership by those working inside the firm.

The phenomenon of intercorporate control has been further substantiated by Franks and Mayer (1994a) who identified that within enterprises with a large major shareholder (holding more than 50% of the shares) this shareholder was often West German (corporate, family, government and other). This concentration of ownership and control in West Germany is accompanied by enterprises with a single major shareholder being found rather in large than in small enterprises. Carlin and Mayer (1995) identified nearly 90% of large-scale privatised former Treuhand-enterprises - which employed more than 500 employees - as being owned by a single majority shareholder (>50%). More than 50% of these enterprises with major shareholdings are held in the form of company ownership in West Germany and this supports the general assumption of large-scale acquisition of East German companies by West German enterprises. Enterprises with dispersed shareholdings have been identified as having been privatised by the methods of either MBIs or MBOs (chapter 3, section 3.5.3.2.2.2). 25% of smaller enterprises had no majority shareholding and a total of 18.5% of all enterprises sold by the Treuhand were cases of MBOs. This correlation can be further substantiated by the general finding that ownership concentration increases with the size of the firm and those enterprises with less concentrated ownership holdings are owned by East Germans.

As has been pointed out by Carlin and Mayer (1995), the East German property owned by East Germans is dominated by families as owners and this points to the cases of restituted or returned property. Families in East Germany own 11.2% of all firms which employ less than 500 employees as opposed to only 2% of those firms employing more than 500 employees. Table 6.2 is based on the Carlin and Mayer findings which identify West German companies and West German families as the dominant owners of enterprises sold by the Treuhand. They are followed by East German families and East German companies.

The structural dominance of corporate ownership can be interpreted as having been more likely to carry out financial and capital investments in the East as families or dispersed individual owners might not have been able to transfer such large capital sums. The structure of intersectoral corporate ownership and control which has evolved might have positively influenced the transfer of human capital, particularly management. This concentration of ownership in the West German (or foreign) corporate sector has been targeted by the Treuhand-privatisation policy in the form of requiring investment and employment guarantees and the case of investment precedence over restitution.

The dominance of West German owners has been necessary for East Germany to gain access to finance, managerial knowledge and skill. Finance has been primarily provided by Western companies or by public subsidies rather than by banks. Intercorporate ownership as the major form of ownership worsens the problems for particular economic sectors. Sectors which are characterised by excess capacity such as the steel and mining industry can be expected to be highly unlikely to invest in enterprises within these sectors. Thus the privatisation of problem sectors has created a rapid but also a dramatic and sometimes socially unacceptable transformation and restructuring of the economy. This is reflected in the sectoral aggregation of the remaining enterprises still to be sold by the BVS. In these areas structural policy has had to be applied. It had been discussed (Luft, 1992) that those enterprises within these sectors should be kept in state ownership to stretch the time period of privatisation.

The concentration of (predominantly outside) ownership in the Western part of Germany as well as the intercorporate control, despite implementing

Table 6.2: Ownership Dominance by West German Companies and Families

Ownership	Firms Sold by the THA from mid 1990 until 10/94	Frms Sold by the THA from 01/92 until 09/94, with less than 500 Employees	Firms Sold by the THA from 01/92 until 09/94, with more than 500 Employees
	Share of Firms	Share of Firms with Single Major Shareholder	Share of Firms with Single Major Shareholder
Company in WG	25.9	26.9	55.7
Company in EG	10.9	12.7	12.1
Foreign Company	2.6	2.7	6.8
Co. not known	1.4	1.6	1.8
Family in WG	12.8	15.3	7.1
Family in EG	12.2	11.3	2.0
Govt & other	6.2	7.6	3.0
Total No. of Firms with Single Major Shareholder	8 351	*3 959*	*355*

Source: Various tables from Carlin and Mayer (1995), own calculations, numbers in italic: between 01/92 and 09/94, 5 217 enterprises were sold with less than 500 employees of which 75.9 % had a single major shareholder (= 3 959), between 01/92 and 09/94, 397 enterprises were sold with more than 500 employees of which 89.4% has a single major shareholder (= 355), EG = East Germany, WG = West Germany, Co. = company

managerial and technological know-how, can be suggested to have created non-identical objectives between the managerial workforce and the agents executing certain functions within a firm during the transitional period. Due to the intercorporate control the firm's behaviour can be assumed often to be tacitly cooperative - rather than competitive - which has negative implications on the motivational structure inside the firm.

6.3.5 Company and Market Restructuring: Decision-Externalisation

It can be further argued that corporate organisational structures and the intercorporate concentration of ownership and control in West Germany has not achieved behavioural adjustment in the form of the enterprises' restructuring. The institutional change has been implemented as a transformation of enterprise and market structures by the policy of corporatisation and privatisation by the

Treuhandanstalt. This first stage of transformation has been described in chapter 3 as the corporatisation of enterprises and the breaking up of large-scale enterprises and combines. This step was dominated by the Treuhand's decision as to which enterprises should be restructured, privatised or liquidated. This judgment was given even further structural influence when the Treuhand had to adjudicate on the fate of industrial sectors. Closure, restructuring or even the settling of new enterprises within sectors have influenced the present and future market structure. Because the Treuhand's policy has affected the production capacity of economic sectors it might here be argued that the Treuhand *de facto* exercised a conscious design of economic structures. This might be criticised from the point of view as to whether this single institution has had the knowledge and information to take such decisions. However, the principle sanctioning such action has been the Treuhand-law as the legal base. The Treuhand has exercised its duty of creating an effective market structure which would be efficient and allow enterprises to survive competition. The horizontal, vertical and regional separation of combines and large-scale enterprises by the Treuhand has influenced the structures of these companies. The restructuring of companies was realised on a decentralised basis with the involvement of the advisory and supervisory boards of these companies regarding membership of these boards (see section 3.3.3). The diverse forms of privatisation have had direct effects on the economic structures, whereas the greatest of such consequences has been produced by the decisions with regard to liquidations. Market exit, in the form of liquidation enforced by the Treuhand, can be interpreted as creating an efficient economic structure and lies thereby within its responsibility. The most relevant and frequent form of this first stage of structural change of the market structure has been horizontal merger, i.e. the sale of enterprises or enterprise parts by the Treuhand to companies which were already established within the market. Data provided by the Federal Mergers Commission (Bundeskartellamt)[105] shows that during the time period 1990 until 1992 horizontal mergers dominated accounting for more than 90% (Mueller, 1993a) and with 85.6% in 1993 (Bundeskartellamt, 1994). This has been supported by the findings of Carlin and Mayer (1995) which showed that West German purchasers of West and East German firms came predominantly from the same sector and that the proportion of horizontal mergers was higher in East Germany than in West Germany. This has been interpreted as indicating a possibly greater need for restructuring after acquisition in East Germany than in West Germany. Vertical mergers involving the sale of an enterprise of a preceding or succeeding production phase have also taken place but have been less significant (2.9% of all mergers). A similar tendency has been identified for conglomerate mergers (5.4% in 1992). The policy carried out by the Treuhand created considerable merger activity, in particular more than generally found in West Germany (Frisch, 1993).

This initial stage of corporatisation, separation and privatisation has had to be succeeded by further internal restructuring of enterprises as well as the development of market structures able to survive. Internal restructuring has partly already been decided upon in the form of employment and investment guarantees. As it has been established in the previous section that most of the privatised enterprises are owned by West German companies, it must be surmised that decisions regarding the restructuring of enterprises have predominantly been taken by economic agents outside the East German economic region. Market structures will be surmised to depend usually on existing market forms, market entry and exit, the internal growth of companies, and mergers of enterprises. This stage also includes insolvencies and bankruptcies of enterprises enforced by the market. According to Mueller (1993a) mergers are the most significant factor involved in the creation of the prevailing market structure. Elements such as market entry and exit as well as internal growth can be neglected. Cases of market entry and exit (according to the traditional definition of new firms entering or leaving the market) have only recently been identified as the degree of market-knowledge as well as the degree of risk-friendliness in East Germany can be assumed to have been low. Internal growth can be neglected at least for the first two to three years of transformation as few private companies existed during GDR times. Internal restructuring in companies has not yet been finished and might even only start once the investment and employment guarantees have expired. The enforcement of a system of a market economy via the installation of certain institutions as well as the transference of ownership into private hands allow for the private and market economic way of restructuring. Due to the structure of corporate control and the shape of the two stages enterprise restructuring has mainly been decided upon by the Treuhand, West German and foreign owners. This particular concentration of decisions regarding internal restructuring has not only had the effect of introducing managerial know-how. The adjustment of behavioural patterns, the gaining of knowledge and acquiring experience must follow the process of restructuring. The process of decision-making has basically been regionally externalised by the method of outsider privatisation as one form of mass privatisation (Chapter 3, section 3.5.3.2.2). This approach focused on the purchaser's function of restructuring. The selection of potential MBO-privatisations depended predominantly on the particular product range, sales function and capital structure. The small number of insider privatisations in comparison to outsider privatisations (18.7%) suggests a low evaluation of East German managerial abilities by the Treuhand. This notion suggests that adjustment of managerial know-how has been essential and necessary and that the behavioural adjustment of individual economic actors has been slower and more time consuming than the establishment of the new institutional framework. A gradual transformation in contrast to the top-down approach can be hypothesised to have achieved a more contemporaneous transformation of structures and behavioural patterns.

6.4 Conclusions

This chapter aimed firstly at establishing the relationship between norm changes, their transfer to the level of new structures of the system, and the compatibility of changes of the structures of partial social systems. Secondly, it aimed to look at the relationship between the structural change of the economic system and its effect in changing the national economic outcome. This marginal product of system change has made the notion of adjustment elasticity worthwhile considering, i.e. the degree to which the structural change is internalised and transferred on to the behavioural level, thus increasing economic efficiency.

It was found that the institutional change of the economic system was inherently coherent with the change of other partial social systems as well as with the norm changes. Thus no disparities within the fundamental process of institutionalising the new economic structures existed. An institutional framework was created which allows the individual economic unit to plan independently, coordinate these plans via the market mechanism and established the fundamental right to private property. System-theoretical and ordo-liberal considerations suggest an according adjustment of economic behaviour. However it was noted that the change of the institutional infrastructure brought about deficiencies in the economic behavioural adjustment. It was established that the adjustment of the economic behaviour of individual units - enterprises and households - was more time consuming than institutionalising the structural change of the system.

The assumption that the introduced structures create fundamentally different economic action must be amended. The behavioural adjustment of the economy has been concluded to partly have been the result of a time-lag of behavioural adjustment, i.e. the fact that experience needs to be acquired and that knowledge needs to be gained. Furthermore the adjustment has been impeded by deficiencies which were created by the particular institutional framework. The predominant organisational structure of the GmbH and its effect on the structures of decision-making, information and motivation, the concentration of ownership of East German enterprises in West Germany and the dominance of intercorporate control, the adaptation of the classic capitalist firm in the form of absentee ownership and the employment contract are aspects that need to be reviewed in order to increase X-efficiency and implement effective incentive and motivation structures. It has been argued that these particular structures effected the marginal product of system change, i.e. the degree by which economic efficiency has been increased. If different structures and a different process of establishing these structures had been established, the marginal product of system change might have been increased *ceteris paribus*. An increased involvement of East German economic participants in the process of structural change might have increased the adjustment elasticity. Thus it can also be assumed that the marginal product of system amendment is higher the more economic actors are assigned with authority defined by the new structures.

However, the internal requirement of amending enterprise structures, as well as the notion that the current structure of West German managerial dominance can be expected to create spill-over effects to the East German labour force and induce the learning process. This points to the reduction of the behavioural adjustment deficiencies over time.

Chapter Seven
The Welfare Concept of the East German Transformation

7.1 Introduction

It will be argued in this chapter that - according to the findings in previous chapters (in particular chapters 3 and 4) - a specific welfare concept has been employed in the process of East German transformation. Any analysis of welfare implications of structural transformation is linked with several conceptional problems. However, such modelling is relevant because it can be argued that a particular social welfare function was pursued within the East German process of transformation. The model which will be presented is a very static and neoclassical approach. The approach is deliberately designed in this form (because the previous findings suggest that the transformation approach was designed in this way) and can be justified because it portrays the particular short-term concept of East German transformation, and in particular the short-term effects the privatisation policy has aimed to achieve. This East German transformation model is very limited and its limitations will be exposed in the concluding chapter (section 8.4). This model helps to identify the major weaknesses of the chosen approach of transformation which supplement particular weaknesses of the transformation which have been pointed out in the previous chapter. Specific assumptions are set to allow a modelling of the approach and allow a comparison of different points in time. It is suggested that this is achieved by limiting the model to comparisons of situations post-liberalisation. Nevertheless the model itself leaves remaining problems, in particular a) a measurement problem (due to information) and b) a time problem, i.e. a policy can pay off in different time periods and the appropriate form of transformation will score differently if one measures the outcome at different future points in times.

7.2 Non-Comparatibility of Interpersonal Utilities, and Social Welfare Concept

Conceptional problems become particularly obvious if the objective of maximising social welfare is set. It requires interpersonal comparisons of utility and the aggregation of individual utilities to a social and collective welfare. A further major problem is the change of individuals' values which goes along with the societal change. This enhances the non-comparability of pre- and post-liberalisation indifference curves because of the change in utility conceptions. As one has to expect variations in preferences accompanying the transformation of a planned economy into a market economy (norm changes, see section 6.2.2.2) the location of the map of indifference curves is surmised to have altered. The alteration of the economic system has effected the scope of action, this changes the scope of possibilities and the entity of potential elements of individual utility functions.

The change in preferences is here given by the societal norm change towards more liberal action which was indicated to have been initiated by the East German people themselves and was thus defined as endogeneous (section 6.2). The adjustment of the partial economic system to norm changes reflects the system's internalisation of the norm changes and thus a fast transformation of the structural change. It thus qualifies as positive economics to draw some newly evolved indifference curves for individuals which represent some value concept post-liberalisation. Not only is the location of the indifference curve map considered to have changed in comparison to pre-liberalisation, the determinants of utility, such as the quality of products or the entire re-definition of a product bundle, set new behavioural relations. As a full absorption of structural change into individuals' utility concepts and behaviour (section 6.3) has been argued not to have been realised, positive rigidity values of adjustment are assumed. The distribution of authority derived from the new structural elements is limited with regard to the identity of economic agents (next to the time-lag of behavioural adjustment in the lack of acquired experience) and this has lead to the conclusion that behavioural adjustment deficiencies exist (section 6.4).

The difficulty of comparing interpersonal utilities among social actors (Harrod 1938; Robbins, 1938; Kaldor 1939) are here reduced by using producers' and consumers' surplus as aggregated utility concepts. On the basis of these partial aggregates a social welfare function can be constructed. Its sum is to be maximised in order to attain allocative efficiency in the sense of the best use of resources. "In all cases...where a certain policy leads to an increase in physical productivity, and thus of aggregate income, the economist's case for such policy is quite unaffected of the comparability of individual satisfactions; since in all such cases it is possible to make everybody better off than before, or at any rate to make some people better off without making anybody worse off....In order to establish this case, it is quite sufficient for him to show that even if all those who suffer as a result are fully compensated for their loss, the rest of the community will still be better off than before."(Kaldor, 1939). The Kaldor-criterion suggests the increase in the sum total of wealth is a sufficient condition to substantiate an increase in social welfare as long as re-distributive policies are employed. It is not part of this thesis to investigate which pattern of income distribution maximises social welfare as this is a rather political and philosophical matter. Neither was it considered part of this thesis to investigate any superiority of the GDR system of total equality in comparison to a system of unequal income distribution given the same sum total of wealth. It shall here however be questioned how the chosen method of East German transformation effects the social welfare (which has been conceptionally found to exist as part of the East German transformation approach) and which can be defined by a social welfare function.

The problem of preference alteration is subdued by employing a comparative-static approach comparing possible welfare situations at the time of post-liberalisation, here first-best and second-best solutions of privatisation (see chapter 4, section 4.4.4). Eggertson's (1990) suggestion of the impossibility of assessing welfare implications of changes in property right allocations shall thereby be ignored. His consideration of a re-location of indifference curves and thereby new measurements of efficiency due to changes in property right allocations does not apply due to the definition of the comparative-static comparison post-liberalisation. In particular the assumption of 1) the endogeneous character of social change (section 6.2.2), 2) the comparison of system-coherent situations (i.e. a given set of a system's structure) within the time concept after liberalisation and 3) the definition of a remaining rigidity factor of adjustment (section 6.3) presents consistency of the utility concept. Thus the most efficient form of privatisation shall then be defined (according to the chosen approach of East German economic transformation) as the one which creates the greatest social welfare according to the relevant definition of the social welfare function. This definition results from the legal research (chapter 4) which has led to the conclusion that a selected behavioural function was employed and that first- and second-best solutions were defined as results of particular privatisation methods.

7.3 Definition of the Welfare Feasibility Frontier and the Social Welfare Function

The institutional change in East Germany has been defined as a change which has aimed at improving social welfare as the basic principle of transformation. As the economic change is the transformation of the socialist system of the GDR command economy into a democratic system of market economy, the social welfare function shall depict the change in efficiency (i.e. the best utilisation of resources) which is theoretically acknowledged to be achieved as a Pareto-optimum in a decentralised market situation of perfect competition, without externalities, and private property rights. Again, the static neoclassical perspective of this concept represents a major limitation of this concept.

As welfare is generally analysed within the concept of marginal utility (Pigou, 1920) a utility possibility frontier can be constructed which represents Pareto-optimal distributions of (individual) welfare between two individuals. The utility possibility frontier is constrained by technological knowledge, availability of resources, etc. A movement along the curve starting at any situation is Pareto-inefficient because it makes one individual better off whilst making the other one worse off. Any point on the welfare frontier is thus Pareto-optimal. It is not part of positive economics to place any ethical interpersonal welfare judgement on the superiority of any of the optimal points (to others) on this utility possibility frontier. The difference of individuals' utility functions is represented by the curve not being strictly concave to the origin (figure 7.1).

Figure 7.1: Utility Possibility Frontier for Individuals A and B (U_a=Utility A, U_b=Utility B)

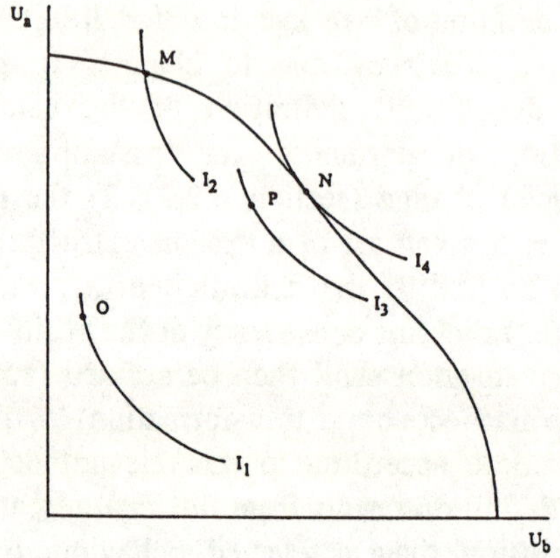

Any point on the utility possibility frontier (figure 7.1) maximises the welfare of one individual given the welfare of the other. A movement from a point O to M increases social welfare (higher indifference curve) as well as producing a Pareto-improvement (movement from inside the frontier on to the frontier). This kind of change is "just" in Rawl's (1973) sense as the change makes even the worse off better off. The movement on the other hand from point P to point M implies a fall in social welfare but is efficient in that it could create a Pareto-improvement by redistributing from point M to point N via regulation. This movement suffices the Kaldor-Hicks criterion for a welfare improvement under the assumption that no interpersonal comparisons are possible, i.e. position M is better than position P if the gainers are in a position to compensate the losers in a way that still produces a net gain. This criterion was criticised by Scitovsky (1942) as it might also apply to a movement back to the original situation. He has thereby introduced the so-called Scitovsky criterion of the New Welfare Economics which only qualifies a movement as a welfare improvement if a movement back to the original situation does not suffice the Kaldor-Hicks-criterion. The utilitarian view of a maximisation of social welfare being represented by a maximisation of the sum of utilities can not be applied as a definition of a Pareto-optimum because the individuals' marginal utilities are not the same for everyone. The above case of regulative redistribution for example in the form of employment subsidies, forces the interpretation of the utility possibility frontier as the utility feasibility frontier due to the arising transaction and opportunity costs (DeMeza, Osborne, 1980).

Any of these costs decrease economic efficiency and move the economy away from the utility frontier.

Changes in welfare induced by alterations in production and general market conditions can be expressed as alterations in the distribution of welfare between consumers' and producers' surplus and their magnitude. Instead of defining two individuals' utility functions the welfare function is defined as taking into account aggregated consumers' and producers' preferences in the form of realised market demand and supply curves. This definition satisfies the criterion of objectivity. In contrast a definition of individuals' utility functions does not. Rather a change in production would have changed the bundle of goods and thus the shape and place of the utility possibility frontier, representing a transformation curve for a particular welfare bundle (Samuelson, 1962). The relevant welfare utility frontier represents the highest possible magnitude of consumers' surplus for given producers' surplus for different levels of total social welfare. The welfare possibility frontier thus represents different possible economic situations. It takes care of a *social* transformation curve in terms of a number of social welfare combinations

The welfare possibility frontier represents points of economic efficiency as the sum of consumers' and producers' surplus is maximised, i.e. the frontier represents a situation of a perfectly competitive market situation in a static neoclassical way. All points along the welfare possibility frontier are characterised by the Pareto-condition of "top-level-optimum" that the social marginal rate of substitution is equal to the social marginal rate of transformation. This model represents the particular transformation approach which aimed at the creation of a decentralised market economy, private property rights, competitive market structures and an efficient market process. Any achieved market situation chosen by random can be represented by this concept. It can represent whether set objectives have been achieved and what the implications are for social welfare.

7.4 Axioms of the Social Welfare Function and Definition of Social Welfare Improvements

In accordance to Vickers and Yarrow (1989) the social welfare function can be written as

$$W = S + Pi \qquad (7.1)$$

where S denotes aggregated consumers' surplus and Pi the aggregated producers' surplus. Some distributional-political parameters a and b are introduced below in order to make the function take account of the social responsibility of the German model of the social market economy. The distributional parameters only locate the set of welfare functions. They do not give any verdict with regard to "just" or politically-correct distributions.

The construction of the social welfare function W = W(S, Pi) has to follow the following Hicks-Allen (1934) axioms:

1. Ordinal comparability of aggregated surplus combinations is possible as long as political or governmental organisations set specific rules with regard to distributive goals. (It shall here be assumed that political objectives do not vary mid-term and that policies remain consistent throughout the term of government.)
2. Completeness of preference order is given as it shall be assumed that it is possible to compare all combinations.
3. The comparison of combinations has to follow the principle of transitivity and consistency, i.e. if welfare level W1 > W2 and W2 > W3, then W1 > W3.
4. If W1 is characterised by a higher producer's surplus Pi than W2 but both combinations have the same consumer's surplus S, then W1 > W2. This axiom of the positive marginal utility of producer's surplus (or other) assumes no political discrimination with regard to the origin of welfare. This axiom would certainly not hold for the former GDR or any other socialist country and taxation policy can be surmised to differentiate between the welfare origins - this point shall for reasons of simplicity be neglected and has been excluded as the model concentrates on possible post-liberalisation options.
5. The principle of diminishing returns is to be applied.

The objective of the East German economic transformation is defined in the above sense as an increase in welfare - a rightward shift of the social welfare function -, the condition being an improvement in Pareto-efficiency. A social welfare function which takes care of the above axioms can be drawn.

Figure 7.2: Definition of Social Welfare Improvement

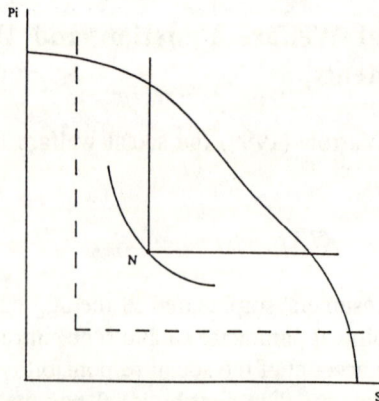

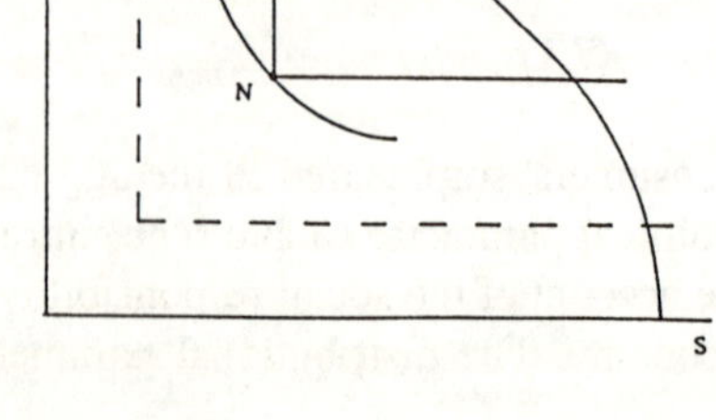

Figure 7.2 takes account of the above axiomisation and facilitates the interpretation of any movement to the northeast from a given point N as an improvement in social welfare conditioned by a Pareto-improvement. This effect has been the political objective of the East German economic transformation.

7.5 Mathematical-Theoretical Formulation of the Social Welfare Function, its Shape and Distributional Parameters, and its Growth Function

The graphic depiction of the welfare function shall be supplemented by its mathematical formulation in order to derive and establish certain characteristics of the welfare concept. These shall later be used to analyse welfare implications of the above described transformation and privatisation concept. The function W = W (Pi, S) shall be converted into a linear-homogeneous welfare function. A substitutional parameter p is introduced and since the grade of substitutability is expressed by the curvature of the welfare function, parameter p (being dependent on the elasticity of substitution) determines the measure of bending. These substitutional considerations were represented in Figure 7.2 by the dashed lines parallel to the axes and the asymptotic approximation of the welfare function to these lines. The substitutional elasticity is therefore positive and below unity and shall be assumed to be constant. The substitutional parameter p is determined by the elasticity of substitution g ($0<g<1$),

$$p = 1/g - 1 \qquad (7.2)$$

and determines the grade of curvature of the welfare function.

Distributional parameters (a, b) are also introduced because the government sets some distributional objectives as part of the welfare function. These parameters co-determine the distribution of social welfare. The distributional assumption can be substantiated by various forms of transitional economic policies and the commitment to a socially acceptable transformation and basic principles of finance policy. The distributional parameters represent the relative surplus shares of the attained welfare. The distributional parameters a and b determine the tilt of the function and are assumed to be constant during the process of transformation, i.e. as long as the distributional policy of one parliamentary term does not change, the placing of the function within the welfare possibility frontier does not change. The welfare function takes the following form[106]:

$$W = [bPi^{-p} + aS^{-p}]^{-1/p} \qquad (7.3)$$

with its partial derivations

$dW/dPi = b\ (W/Pi)^{1+p}$, and (7.4a)
$dW/dS = a\ (W/S)^{1+p}$ (7.4b).[107]

On the basis of the above social welfare function and by multiplying the partial derivations with the ratios between the welfare and consumers' and producers' surplus, the growth of welfare (GW) can be described as:

$$GW = cWPi + dWS, \qquad (7.5)$$

where $c = dW/dPi \cdot Pi/W$ with $dW/dPi = b\ (W/Pi)^{1+p}$, so that $c = b\ (W/Pi)p$ and accordingly $d = a\ (W/S)p$.

The parameters c and d are defined as the partial welfare elasticities: d of a change in the consumers' surplus and c of a change of producers' surplus. Changes in producers' and consumers' surplus shall be assumed to be caused by a movement towards a market economy and the adjustment of production methods, i.e. an increase in competition lowers the prices and increases consumers' surplus and producers' surplus increases due to a lowering in production costs other things being equal. It follows from 7.5 that the welfare growth rate is determined by the growth rates of consumers' and producers' surplus which are weighted by the partial welfare elasticities. These are in turn determined by the welfare-surplus ratios, the substitutional parameter p and the distributional parameters a and b, so that

$$GW = b\ (W/Pi)^p\ GPi + a\ (W/S)^p\ GS \qquad (7.6).$$

The distributional parameters a and b are here considered to have been constant since the time of unification, so that a welfare increase can be drawn as a shift of the welfare function to the northeast without changing the position (because it has been assumed that objectives and policies do not change mid-term). This only holds as long as the political decision making authority does not change its policy of distribution. The latter assumption holds for the case of Germany since there has not been a federal parliamentary change since the start of transformation.

7.6 Social Welfare and Behavioural Selection Function

As the establishment of the desired structural framework implies the institutionalising of private property rights, implications of the alternative methods of privatisation can be analysed according to the value of the property right and the content of the respective property rights bundle. The privatisation method chosen employed a selection function which identified potential owners in accordance with the particular objective of internalising public and social transformation costs. Public costs of transformation are here defined as public expenditure arising from the structural change (e.g. costs of the Treuhandanstalt, unemployment benefits etc.) and social transformation costs are defined as opportunity costs in the form of behavioural rigidity. These transformational rigidity factors were described as economic behavioural deficiencies (chapter 6, section 6.3).

These public and social costs of transformation result from transformational adjustment costs and the social nature of transaction costs arise from the institutionalised establishment of the property rights structure as opposed to private transaction costs (chapter 4, section 4.3.2.2). Public transformation costs thus also account for these social transaction costs. The chosen privatisation methodology identified a ranking of privatisation methods as first-best and second-best solutions on the basis of a cost-benefit analysis (Chapter 4, section 4.4.4). A first-best solution was defined as the newly-assigned property right being truncated, thereby internalising public and social costs of transformation and fastening up the process of adjustment. Clear limitations of this approach have been pointed out before. These first-best and second-best solutions can be implemented into the above welfare function, the function has to be amended by adding the public and social costs of transformation T. These transformation costs are assumed to reduce social welfare as they affect the opportunity set of consumers and producers. A particular economic-political aim of the privatisation has been (besides the creation of a decentralised market-based economy which is supposed to increase consumers' and producers' surplus) to reduce these social costs in the pursuit of first-best rather than second-best solutions. Public as well as social costs of transformation can be interpreted to impose opportunity costs to the economic participants. Public transformation costs for example in the form of unemployment benefits could be spend in a different way if the adjustment of human capital had been less rigid. Social transformation costs could have been lower if the adjustment of economic behaviour had been swifter which then would have increased economic efficiency, and producers' and consumers' surplus. The total costs of transformation (T) are thus dependent on market deficiencies and (via their effect on aggregated consumers' and producers' surplus) are assumed to reduce social welfare according to a distortion factor hT, so that:

$$Pi = f(hT, n) \text{ and } S = f(hT, m) \qquad \text{with } 0<h<1 \qquad (7.8).$$

The distortion factor h is introduced because some costs of transformation are welfare function neutral. These costs of transformation have already been incorporated into the welfare utility frontier. Transformation costs for example arose partly because the privatisation had been institutionalised and the trust agency Treuhandanstalt used up resources. These opportunity costs defined the welfare possibility frontier as a welfare feasibility frontier. Those social transformation costs which are incorporated into the welfare function result from market deficiencies, i.e. the economic adjustment to the new economic system. Thus they are determined by the grade of adjustment rigidity. The requirement, for example, for infrastructure investment classifies as a cost of transformation because the changed economic structure and the opening of the economic system to international competition requires such investment if the system is survive. These costs are essential for the transformation and their internalisation can be assumed to increase consumers' and producers' surplus due to the impact efficient production has on aggregated demand and supply curves. Factors n and m shall be the remaining variables which describe behavioural relations with the aggregated surpluses. Further definition of these variables is omitted because they are not part of the analysis.

Some transformation costs are reduced over time because these costs have been aimed to be internalised by investment and employment guarantees as well as contractual investment agreements. These costs are (if not internalised) costs to society and these resources could have been used more efficiently. Once these transformation costs are transferred to the private level (i.e. accrue to the private owner of an enterprise), they enter the private production costs as part of a production function and are not to be born as public or opportunity costs by society.

It has been assumed that particular methods of privatisation internalised such transformation costs by for example incorporating infrastructure investment plans into the sales agreements. The transformation costs at any time t can thus be defined as the initial aggregated welfare-relevant public and social transformation costs (assumed to be known) minus the transformation costs which were internalised by truncated property rights (truncated by the centrally imposed conditions of investment guarantees and plans and employment guarantees (first-best solution)). Transformation costs over time can thus be written as:

$$T = T(t) - \int I(t)\,dt \qquad (7.9).$$

The present value of an investment plan and employment and investment guarantees (Ip) that the new owner and third investor are obliged to implement as part of the contract which assigns the property can be expressed as a discounted definite integral of the following form:

$$Ip = \int_{t=1}^{n} I(t)_e{}^{-rt}\,dt \qquad (7.10).$$

The effect of private costs (Ip) in potentially reducing the respective producer's economic rent via the investment outlay is welfare-neutral and shall thus be disregarded. This is part of the aggregated surplus values and the income and capacity effects can be assumed to offset the cost aspect. The contractual conditions increase national income (*ceteris paribus*) via the multiplier and accelerator effect. In addition potential output is increased as the capacity effect is such that the economy is now capable of producing more. The truncated property rights thus have two effects: a) a growth effect and b) an internalisation effect. The growth effect will not be further analysed but is used to exclude the effect of the guarantees and investment plans reducing the aggregated surpluses. Transformation cost internalisation has been effected through the sales contracts, i.e. by attaching certain behavioural conditions to the property ownership. (Investment into capital increases economic efficiency and competitiveness and will also reduce the cost of unemployment for example.)

7.7 Welfare and Property Value Relationship

The final assignment of the property (whether through new- or re-privatisation) follows the principle assignment to the highest bidding potential buyer. This assignment according to the property's value allowed the deduction of first and second-best solutions (section 4.2.2.2). The bidding price (P*) is not the exclusive factor of relevance. The offer of investment and job guarantees and investment plans (Ip) becomes part of the property's value (Vp) which is thus defined as:

$$Vp = Ip + P^* \qquad (7.11).$$

The present value of the property can be expressed as:

$$PVp = P^* + \int_{t=1}^{n} I(t)e^{-rt}\,dt \qquad (7.12).$$

The necessary degree of adjustment of the economy in order to complement the changed institutional framework and societal system determines the transformation costs. The less rigid behavioural factors are the faster is the adjustment to the new framework, and thus the more efficient will be the utilisation of economic resources. Market deficiencies D can be described as a function of the rigidity factor R (representing the behavioural adjustment deficiencies) determining the level of market deficiencies, and the state of the given economic infrastructure E. The cost of transformation can thus be written as a function of the market deficiencies D and the contractual conditions Ip:

$$T = T[D(R, E), Ip] \qquad (7.13).$$

The relationship between the transformation cost and the market deficiencies is positive whereas the one with the contractual conditions is negative:

$$T = zD^s - yIp \qquad \text{with } 0 \leq s \leq 1 \text{ and } z > y \qquad (7.14).$$

The costs of transformation are defined as the social costs of the market deficiencies D (the value of the market deficiencies is assumed to be measurable to demonstrate the analogous relationship) minus the internalised costs of transformation. The market deficiency D is expressed to the power of $0<s<1$ because the new system is a decentralised market economy and it can therefore not be expected that the government directly compensates for all temporal market adjustment delays by transfer payments. The factor s reflects that some costs resulting from the market deficiencies are expected to be carried by the private market and the relevant costs of deficiencies are here defined as the value which affects society, i.e. that is social. The factor z denotes the value that has been placed on the time sequence of adjustment and this factor is assumed to be close to unity in the German case because of the political situation which resulted from unification, i.e. it represents the incorporation and relevance of market deficiencies as transformation costs. The plans and guarantees Ip which are designed to internalise the cost of transformation can *per definitione* not be more than the costs resulting from the market deficiencies caused by the transformation D. The factor y describes the reducing impact the privately financed investment plans and guarantees have on transfer payments, i.e. the degree of internalisation of social costs. The factor y is positive because of the regulatory board checking the investment project for its social benefits but below unity assuming a rationally behaving investor.

A major problem of attaching investment and employment guarantees to privatisation is the existence of asymmetric information, i.e. the regulator does not know the value of the property as no efficient and functioning market has existed beforehand. The assignment to the highest bidder nevertheless is supposed to represent some market value as long as transparency of information is conditioned by the regulating institution making the availability of the property public. In the cases of the public bidding procedure this assumption can be assumed to be given so that the privatisation method of new privatisation can be identified as a first-best solution (chapter 4, section 4.4.4). It must on the other hand be surmised that the restitution of property does not necessarily reduce transformation costs as it does not attach any contractual conditions to the property assignment so that the assignment to a third investor who is contractually confined to realising the suggested investment plan can also be identified as a first-best solution. (However, it was argued in chapter 6, section 6.3 that restitutive privatisation might have reduced some of the behavioural adjustment deficiencies.) Once a market that functions well has been established the former owner can resell his property. But it should be expected that a potential private purchaser will only pay the market property price without the necessity of further granting any internalisation of transformation costs. The welfare and property value relationship is presented in the following figure.

Figure 7.3: Welfare and Property Value Relationship

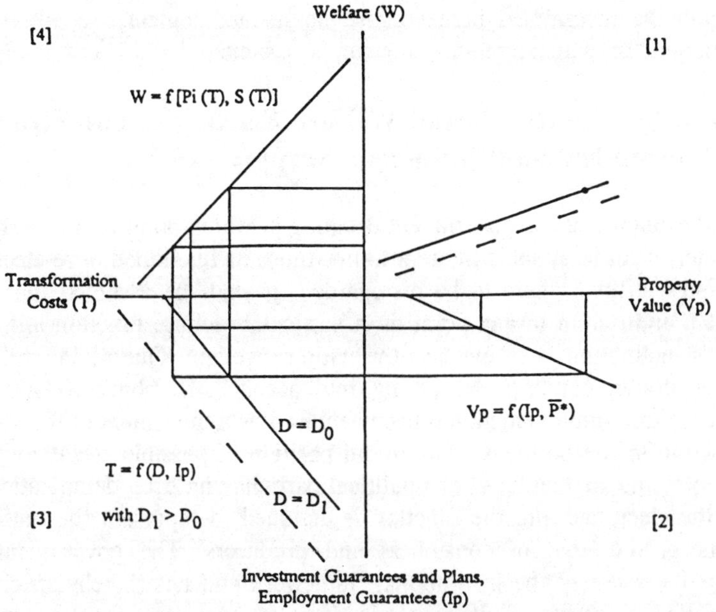

The figure 7.3 below (which is based in particular on the equations 7.3, 7.8, 7.11.and 7.13) represents that the higher the present value of the property (i.e. truncated property right) the higher the welfare attainment. The second quadrant represents the relationship between the value of the property right and the contractual sales agreement in the form of investment plans and employment and investment guarantees. The relationship is positive in that the value is the higher the higher the contractual agreements are for a given property price P*. The third quadrant reflects the impact the contractual agreements have on the internalisation of transformation costs for some given z, s and y. The greater the agreement to guarantees or investment plans the larger is the effect of internalising costs of transformation, i.e. the lower are the remaining ones. The reduction of public and social costs of transformation by their private internalisation has been described as increasing social welfare by their effect on producers' and consumers' surplus (third quadrant). The three relationships lead to the derivation of the welfare and property value relationship which is positive.

Figure 7.3 also describes the relation between adjustment rigidity - partly determining the magnitude of the market deficiencies D - and welfare besides the welfare implication of the property value. The more rigid the adjustment process the higher the value of the market deficiencies, and the higher the value of the property has to be in order to attain a particular welfare level. In other words the more rigid the adjustment process the higher will be the transformation costs and the lower will be the attained welfare level. Alternative distributional implications (between consumers' and producers' surplus) of each privatisation method cannot be determined here because no methodological and empirical basis can be found on which a relationship can be assumed.

7.8 Welfare Ambiguity: Partial Welfare Elasticities and Growth Rates of Consumers' and Producers' Surplus

The political economy of the government deciding at which point on the welfare function society shall be situated in order to maximise its likelihood of re-election and politician's utility is here to be disregarded. It shall be assumed that the government is indifferent to any point on a particular welfare function and the government's inclination is to increase the nation's welfare. One social welfare function was drawn out of a set taking into account the above axioms. A comparative welfare improvement has been achieved by a movement of the social welfare function to the northeast. The initial position of possible social welfare functions represents a situation of one political party having been democratically elected by the electorate and the function is assumed to represent the nation's welfare concept, i.e. that of consumers and producers. The government is conceived as the setter of the institutional framework and has thereby specified particular welfare objectives. A difference in shape of the welfare function would therefore represent a political change.

The above welfare and property value relationship represents a positive behavioural relationship between the aggregated surpluses and the internalisation of transformation costs. As it is assumed that society's welfare is to be increased the growth (both in producers' surplus as well as consumers' surplus) has to be positive unless re-distributive instruments are applied in order to suffice a welfare improvement according the Scitovsky criterion (section 7.3).

The growth rate of welfare is determined by the growth rates of consumer's and producer's surplus according to the partial welfare elasticities c and d. The chosen approach which has been modelled is too general and disregards two fundamental issues: 1.) the social welfare function depicts an aggregated *German* social welfare function rather than an *East German* one, and 2.) behavioural adjustment deficiencies influence growth rates of consumer's and producer's surplus. These issues allow an elaboration of various welfare criteria according to Rawls (1973), Kaldor (1939), Hicks (1939) and Scitovsky (1942).

Although the transformational process was limited to the East German economic region with regard to the introduction of structural change the social welfare function was conceptually designed for the entire German economic region. It is necessary to split surplus rates according their regional distribution which leads to the following form of welfare function where consumers' and producers' surplus are separated for East (e) and West Germany (w):

$$W = [bP_{ie}^{-p} + bP_{iw}^{-p} + aS_e^{-p} + aS_w^{-p}]^{-1/p} \qquad (7.15)$$

with $P_{ie} + P_{iw} = P_i$ and $S_e + S_w = S$.

The concentration of ownership and corporate control derived from the corporatisation and privatisation of former nationally owned property in West German companies (chapter 6, section 6.3.4) can be integrated into the amended welfare function in the form of the producers' surplus created by the transformational change being greater for West Germany than for East Germany. A majority share of economic rents produced in East Germany accrues to West German owners. It must however be noted that there is a positive relationship between transitional economic policies and the overall consumers' surplus. This arises because, for example, investment policies aiming at the adjustment of a particular macroeconomic aggregate as well as the internalisation of transformation costs (which moves the economy towards an efficient and competitive market economy) are assumed to increase consumers' surplus.[108] It is thereby not a question of the distributional parameters a and b reflecting the welfare shares of consumers and producers, it is a question of the share between East and West German owners. A privatisation strategy that alternatively had focused on the principle of restitution would have *ceteris paribus* increased the possibility of raising the East German producers' surplus. The consumer on the other hand can be assumed to have benefited from the applied privatisation strategy because of the input of managerial know-how and thereby a swifter real adjustment of the economy than otherwise might have been the case.

Since it was established to be methodologically wrong to compare welfare and utility before the societal change (i.e. compare the times of the GDR's existence with post-liberalisation situations) a qualitative judgement in the form of growth rates of producers' surplus cannot be used to derive implications for the distribution of welfare. A neoclassically defined producers' surplus as such conceptionally did not exist within the centrally planned economy with no private property rights. It would therefore be erroneous to deduct a welfare improvement from the creation of producers' surplus as such. However, it is possible to compare alternative scenarios of privatisation because the fundamental principles of market economics are applicable to either case. It can thus be stated that the partial welfare growth of producers' surplus in East Germany would have been greater if restitutional policies had been followed *ceteris paribus*. However the truncated property right strategy of privatisation can be concluded to satisfy the Scitovsky criterion because the increase in consumers' surplus would be eradicated or reduced if society moved from this situation back to a situation that would have alternatively been created by restitution. The sum total of welfare improvement can thus be expected to be higher in the applied approach because of the utilisation of managerial know-how (which otherwise would not have been available) and thereby the swifter adjustment of the real economy and their implications on growth of the aggregated surpluses. Here satisfying the Kaldor-Hicks criterion of a welfare improvement, the gainers of the welfare effect (i.e. the producers' surplus accruing to West Germans) are theoretically in a position to compensate by redistribution those who have lost the imaginary East German producers' surplus and still be better off than before: a net gain would still have been produced. However this movement is not equal in terms of net gain to a movement to a situation of restitution because the net welfare gain would have been lower. Therefore the applied transformation strategy suffices welfare improvements of the New Welfare Economics (Scitovsky, 1942).

The applied transformation approach thus caused welfare-ambiguous effects. It can be surmised that behavioural adjustment deficiencies found their way into the welfare function because they have affected the growth rates of consumers' and producers' surplus because of the real economic adjustment deficiencies. The effect of the institutionalised structural change is thereby twofold. The internalisation of social and public transformation costs is juxtaposed to the restricted identification of East German economic agents with decentralised behavioural authority. It has been suggested that the concentration of ownership and control in West German companies, the X-inefficient decentralisation and the externalisation of decision-making authority qualify as lowering the marginal product of system change (chapter 6, section 6.3). No basis exists to find empirical values for these opposite effects because of the specific circumstances of transformation. It must be noted that the East German case of economic transformation went with along the political unification and thereby limited the appropriateness of alternative approaches. The objectives were correctly set in aiming for a fast privatisation and institutionalisation of the structural changes in order not to create socially unacceptable situations. The chosen programme of transformation herewith classifies as pragmatic and successful in achieving its set aims but scope remains for criticism with regard to the distribution of welfare growth and the on-going existence of behavioural adjustment deficiencies. It has however been suggested that the concentration of ownership will disperse with time (Carlin, Mayer, 1995) and that some adjustment deficiencies will be corrected with an increase of acquired experience and the realisation of learning-curve effects (Arrow, 1962; Kaldor, 1957, 1962).

7.9 Conclusions

The East German privatisation method has been described and analysed within a static neoclassical welfare model. It was argued that a particular approach for privatising former nationally-owned property has been employed in line with a definition of a social welfare function. This function was modelled to consist of the aggregated producers' and consumers' surpluses. These aggregated surpluses were assumed to be affected by opportunity costs which resulted from the social and public costs of transformation. These costs were found to be potentially reduced by a privatisation policy which employs a selection function for the assignment of property which is to be privatised. Private property rights which are truncated by contractual agreements (to behave in a particular way in a set period of time) were suggested to reduce the public costs of transformation accruing to society. A relationship between costs of transformation and the value of the property right as a selection variable in the privatisation process was established. It appeared to be welfare improving in transitional periods during which market deficiencies exist to exercise regulatory policies aiming at the internalisation of social and public transformation costs. The conditioning of property contracts derives first-best solutions in the form of a) new privatisation with employment and investment guarantees and b) the assignment of the property to a third investor with investment plans. A second-best solution is identified as the assignment of the full bundle of property rights to the former owner in the form of restitution. A strong limitation of this model is its static and short-term nature. It can be even suggested that, once the contractual agreements expire, transformation costs which were initially internalised might then be externalised (for example by labour shedding once the employment guarantees expire). Furthermore it has been suggested that this particular privatisation approach causes welfare-ambiguous effects, in particular because the social welfare function was defined as a *German* rather than an East German one. Further conceptional problems of this welfare model were pointed out in the introduction to this chapter and further substantial limitations will be exposed and discussed in section 8.4 in the concluding chapter.

Chapter Eight
Synopsis and Conclusions

8.1 Relevance of the East German Case Study for Transformational Economics

It has been established that norm changes preceded the transformation of the East German society and its partial societal systems. The high grade of the former East German society's order implied a low reaction flexibility to external and environmental influences and prevented an adjustment to modified needs within the existing systems. This necessitated fundamental structural changes and these alterations can not be interpreted as evolutionary because no adaptation within the existing systems in the form of integrating new elements and features happened.

The norm change pressurised political institutions to take decisions which led to the political unification of the two German states and thus the demise of the former German Democratic Republic. This political unification implied considerable structural changes of the partial societal systems. The compatibility of these structural changes with the preceding norm changes and the compatibility of the changes within the partial systems resulted in a successful institutional transformation, i.e. a transfer of norm changes on to the level of institutional structures of societal systems.

The transformation of the economic system employed a particular policy of transformation which institutionalised the system change. This institutionalisation was achieved by the adoption of a legal framework which aimed at the inauguration of decentralised decision-making and deconcentrated market structures as well as the establishment and the safeguarding of private property right structures. Particular changes of the organisational framework and the corporate structures of the economic system were organised by the trust agency Treuhandanstalt which was established for this particular task of transformation. The transformation of the economic system itself was thus institutionalised in the form of one institution deconcentrating, separating, decentralising, restructuring and selling enterprises and enterprise parts. These features of transformation were theoretically based on system-theoretical elements and non-deterministic evolutionary economics (see chapter 2).

The institutional economic transformation was operationalised and carried out by a particular approach of transformation. This approach focused on transformation policies such as a) the incorporation of a behavioural selection function into the process of transformation and b) the introduction of pragmatic transitional follow-up policies. The implementation of these policies successfully achieved their objectives in the form of a swift institutional transformation (chapter 3) and influencing particular urgency factors of changing aggregated economic variables (section 5.3). The successful implementation of the chosen structures did however not imply a fast adjustment of economic behaviour which was analysed within the system-theoretical adjustment model (chapter 5, sections 5.2, 5.3.2, 5.4 and chapter 6).

It was concluded that despite classifying the East German societal change as a transformation this development is not characterised as a spontaneous evolution although the norm change can be classified as such. Structural features of the economic system were consciously designed and elements of the legal and political systems were adopted in forms which previously existed in West Germany. In particular the privatisation method selected the new private owners according to their expected economic behaviour in the short term, and the pragmatic introduction of separation laws indicates the institutional forming of particular economic structures. It was argued according to the findings in previous chapters (in particular the identification of a selection function) that the East German economic transformation pursued a particular welfare concept, which was described and analysed in chapter 7.

The institutionalisation went beyond liberalising economic interaction because it discriminated between individuals as being considered as potential owners and thereby identified predominantly West German companies as the new private owners of the formerly nationally-owned property. Despite this selection function having achieved its set aims of internalising some costs of transformation (and thereby speeding up the process of structural change) the economic process and outcome was influenced by this selection. Despite the successful introduction of decentralised decision-making, dispersed information and altered motivation and inventive structures, behavioural adjustment deficiencies have been identified as being inherent within the chosen form of transformation. These findings lead to the evaluation of the chosen method as pragmatic and also lead to the identification of general implications for transformational economics.

8.2 System Theory Restated and Refined

Chapter 2 identified the general system theory (Koopmans & Montias, 1973: Leipold, 1985; North, 1990) and non-deterministic evolutionary approaches (Smith, 1926; Coase, 1937, 1960; Hayek, 1945, 1949, 1963; Eucken, 1950, 1952; Alchian & Demsetz 1972, 1973) as relevant and applicable to the analysis of the transformation of economic systems. Systems were defined as the entity of elements and their characteristics which are interrelated, and as social systems of organised complexity which work in a mechanical way. The system theory is inherently confined to the traditional "institutional structure-conduct-performance" approach in that it assumes that the norm determines the elements which condition the system which then leads to a particular economic behaviour and thus outcome. Within the theory of the social and economic system two levels of the system's framework were distinguished: the institutional and the organisational framework.

8.2.1 The Adjustment Model as Modification of System Analysis

The institutional framework classifies the economic system according to a limited number of structural elements and defines the economic system as a partial social system. The comparative analysis of economic systems assumes that partial social systems are correlated and resources are allocated within the institutional framework in the course of economic process. The institutional arrangement of the structural elements is constituted according to a social goal function which defines the choice of economic objectives *inter alia*. The economic process is thereby assumed to be constrained by the societal institutional framework.

The adjustment model has been developed on the basis of these theoretical ideas and has aimed at adding a dynamic aspect to this comparative-static approach. The model depicts the relationship between norm and value changes, their incorporation into the institutional framework and the adjustment of economic behavioural functions to structural changes. In the tradition of system theory it is assumed that these behavioural functions determine economic process and performance, i.e. the outcome as the economic product. The model can be classified as dynamic because it identifies that the achievement of changed societal goals and desired economic objectives - which are preceded by norm changes - depend on a) the internalisation of norm changes into the institutional framework of the societal system, b) the compatibility of structural changes within partial societal systems and c) the "partial marginal products of system change" as adjustment elasticities, i.e. the degree to which the structural changes are internalised in behavioural functions. It was shown by applying the model to the East German case study that the model is valid in explaining transforming economic structures which result from changes in norms and values. The model demonstrates the advantages and limitations of the transformation approach of institutionalised change.

8.2.2 Organisational Framework and Identity of Rights Holders

The institutional characteristics of the economic system can be analysed according to the organisational structures within which economic agents plan and act. In particular the DIM-approach (Neuberger & Duffy, 1976) and the structure of coordinating economic plans (Hurwicz, 1969, 1970) have been identified to classify differences between economic systems, to set behavioural assumptions on the basis of these structures and to distinguish various forms of economic processes. The DIM-approach conceives of economic systems as differing according to the structures of decision-making, information and motivation. Structures of decision-making in its authority, origin, form and content are categorised as centralised and decentralised according to the respective distribution of authority. The distribution of decision-making is here defined as the degree to which superiors can influence and control actions of subordinates. The structure of information is supposed to determine the efficiency of resource allocation. The substitution of a mono-directed informational flow by multi-lateral purpose-oriented information channels which create dispersion of information thereby increases allocative efficiency. The motivational structure (which is highly correlated to the structures of decision-making and information) has been analysed according to Weber's *Zweckrationalitaet* and *Wertrationalitaet* as well as according to Leibenstein's X-inefficiency concept. Organisational structures can be differentiated according to the degree to which individual preferences and utility functions allow the identification with the structure of decision-making and as a result create mutually tolerable organisational objectives. This notion was further supplemented by Ellerman (1986, 1990, 1992) who suggests that the degree of mutual tolerance and X-efficiency depends on the identification of variables of individual utility functions with organisational objectives. He identifies X-inefficient structures in the division of ownership rights and contractual rights within conventional employment firms. Decentralisation of the decision-making structure, dispersion of information and complementarity between individual incentive and motivation structures and organisational objectives are supposed to increase allocative and economic efficiency by improving the proficiency by the organisation's participants.

The East German case study analysed structural change within organisations as the transformation of a centralised structure of decision, information and value-oriented motivation structures into a structure with decentralised decision-making, dispersion of information, purpose-related motivation structures and a coordination of individual economic plans by the market process. The DIM-approach restricts the analysis of the distribution of authority to the degree of centralisation and hierarchy within organisations. This structural decentralisation was found to have been established but the distribution of decision-making authority was at the same time confined to authority derived from ownership, in other words control from inside the firm. The analysis of behavioural adjustment deficiencies suggests that the "marginal product of system change" (section 6.3) could have been higher if structures had identified a larger participation of East Germans in the actual process of decentralised economic planning. It was argued that the adjustment elasticity would have been higher if the degree of authority distribution had been extended to those individual participants whose behaviour was expected to change. Instead decentralised decision-making authority concentrated in a corporate ownership form in West German companies which caused for example an externalisation of decision-making authority. Although it was acknowledged that a time-lag of behavioural adjustment exists it was suggested that the structural transformation as such did allow an efficient internalisation of the structural.

8.3 Evolutionary Approaches Restated and Refined

8.3.1 Applicability of the Ordo-Liberal Theory and Liberal Economics

8.3.1.1 Terminological Differentiation between Transformation and Evolution

The ordo-liberal theory of the economic system in terms of the morphological methodology (Eucken, 1950, 1952) identifies a limited number of pure forms of economic systems and analyses the course of economic action under the assumption that economic behaviour can be interpreted on the basis of the institutional framework. Structures and elements thereby define the room for economic behaviour by individual agents and the approach can be classified as dynamic because it recognises that the final outcome of the economic process can not be determined. A great variety of economic systems exists due to the unlimited number of combinations of different structures and elements. These notions have been found to be valid and an adjustment model was developed which depicts this concept within a general system-theoretical frame.

Eucken (1950, 1952) however did not consider the impact of societal norm changes and restricted his analysis to the historic differences of orders in their structural forms. The grade of the system's order is identified within the adjustment model (Chapter 2, section 2.8) to define the grade of evolutionary development, i.e. to what degree new structures and elements can be integrated within a system which continues to exist (within its general societal framework). This influence of external or environmental factors on the system classifies as evolutionary development in terms of non-deterministic approaches. The term "transformation" does not necessarily describe this form of development. Rather a development is classified as transformation if the grade of the system's order does not allow the input of evolutionary factors. This necessitates the demise of this system and this development becomes transformational if a new desired order exists and this is aimed to be established. The dominant terminological differentiation in Hayekian tradition is based on the degree of spontaneity in contrast to a consciously designed order. The present form of institutionalised change thereby implies non-evolutionary transformation and necessitates, due to the limited knowledge and information of institutionalised actions, pragmatic follow-up policies. This has been the transformational approach in East Germany. It must however be remembered that dynamic and evolutionary developments are not excluded but they are not the same as the structural change. They can be identified as coming into existence once the order has been set under the presumption that the grade of the system's order allows such development.

8.3.1.2 Refined "Institutional Structure-Conduct-Performance" Approach

Traditional system theory and ordo-liberal thought are based on the assumption that an economic system's structure defines economic behaviour according to the specific structures of decision-making, information and motivation. The adjustment model identifies the grade of the system's order to define the individual scope of economic action and the system's flexibility in reacting to influences and its grade of dynamism. In this respect the two approaches and the developed adjustment approach are synonymous. The analysis of the East German transformation has allowed a revision of this general assumption due to the identification of behavioural adjustment deficiencies. It has been established that the economic system was successfully transformed with regard to the decentralisation of economic decision-making, the dispersion of information and the forming of individual economic plans according to individually defined utility functions which identified specific motivational and incentive structures. Although this structural alteration allowed a general widening of the economic scope of action the adjustment of the real economy was concluded to materialise with a time-lag in comparison to the implemented institutional transformation. The adjustment of the real economy as a result is determined by the partial marginal product of the economic system change and the state of technology. The partial marginal product has been defined as the degree to which the structural change is internalised, i.e. is transformed into individual economic behavioural functions.

The rigidity of a system to structural alterations as such does not exclusively determine the degree to which norm and value changes are transferred on to the level of the economic outcome. Also the dispersion of the structural features has been identified to determine the degree by which economic agents can adjust to these structural changes and thereby influence the adjustment of behavioural patterns. The identification of economic agents who are allocated with the scope of action which transforms behavioural functions influences the value of the marginal product of structural change, i.e. the degree to which the change has been internalised. Although the above relationship where the structure determines economic behaviour which then conditions the economic process and outcome is accepted in principle, it must be extended by the distribution of rights derived from these structures.

The East German case study has shown that alongside the institutional transformation a concentration of derived rights was noticed. This is considered to have created behavioural adjustment deficiencies by reducing the adjustment elasticity (and resulting in a comparatively lower marginal product of system change). This interpretation is based on behavioural relations which were identified in the analysis of the organisational framework as part of the theory of social and economic systems (Weber, 1947, 1968; Leibenstein, 1966; Koopmanns

& Montias, 1973; Neuberger & Duffy, 1976) in Chapter 2 (section 2.2.2). However because of the low grade of the newly formed economic system's order it can be expected that these features might alter with time if they prove to be sub-optimal.

Organisational features such as a dispersed distribution of rights derived from the structures of decentralised decision-making and private property would have *ceteris paribus* improved the adjustment of the real economy as it can be assumed that these structures would have increased the adjustment elasticity and thus the partial marginal product of system change. This argument holds as long as one notices that the institutionalised transformation made use of a behavioural selection function with regard to the privatisation and the restructuring of enterprises. The market did not create the current concentration of West Germans holding property and control in East German companies, rather this structure was consciously designed and created by the Treuhandanstalt. The short-term effect of a smooth transformation which has *de facto* been created is therewith opposed to the alternative long-run effect of internalised structural changes. The traditional "institutional structure-conduct-performance" approach needs to be supplemented by the structure of authority distribution in form of the identity of the right holders. Economic decentralisation, private property rights and the coordination of individual plans via the market mechanism need not just be established in their constitutional form, a deconcentrated distribution in the form of the identity of rights holders is here suggested to create benefits in the form of increasing the marginal product of system change in transformational economies.

8.3.1.3 Economic-Ethical and Economic-Democratic Principles

Behavioural adjustment deficiencies were identified as having been created by the X-inefficient decentralisation of organisational structures, concentration of ownership and corporate control and externalisation of decision-making authority. These features represent a sub-optimal distributive structure of the identity of economic agents with regard to the rights which accrue from a decentralised structure of decision-making, a purpose-oriented motivation structure, a private property rights structure and multi-lateral information channels. Rights-based theories can be utilised to support an amendment of the applied approach. The "institutional structure-conduct-performance" approach was *de facto* adopted in its normative utilitarian form in establishing a consciously designed order. It thereby identified particular economic agents as being superior to others to create benefits to the transformational society. This approach is fundamentally rejected by rights-based thought. It also rejects the utilitarian-normative concept of modelling welfare effects of the transformation, which was presented in chapter 7. The employment of the selection function identifies individual economic agents as a means for achieving a particular economic action which is supposed to internalise social costs of transformation and thereby create benefits. This is strictly opposed by the Kantian principle of the categoric imperative (chapter 2, section 2.5.1.1). It follows that the chosen transformation approach is not just in Rawl's (1973) conception as the chosen structure is justified on utilitarian grounds but not on the Kantian principle. The transformational methodology discriminates in its treatment of human beings as it assumes that some individuals behave more rationally than others and attaches different weights to individuals' values. The initial legal right of restitution suffices the Kantian principle as it treats individuals equally in law. In contrast the identification of first-best and second-best situations discriminates between various property owners in order to achieve a set of objectives and ignores the equal status of individuals. This discrimination is not direct in that it treated individuals differently in law but the definition of a behavioural selection function sets presumptions which could only be met by a particular group of individuals because of their initial endowment position (with capital and knowledge). The concentration of ownership and corporate control must therefore be criticised on grounds of ethical principles because of the selection methodology applied and not because of its structure as such. Furthermore the X-inefficient decentralisation of organisational structure disregards the inalienable rights theory (chapter 2, section 2.5.1.4) and ignores the transformational option of implementing democratic principles in the continuation of the classic employment firm. The substitution of the conventional employment contract with the structures of the democratic firm is supposed to increase economic efficiency and productivity because it increases workers' incentives and motivation whilst stabilising the organisational structure (because property rights can not be sold to outsiders). These considerations are based on principles of the labour theory of property (Proudhon, 1966) and the inalienable rights theory (Ellermann, 1992). Although the merits of these amended structures according to the theory of economic democracy were discussed in Chapter 2 (section 5.2) the fact that the East German economic transformation went along the political social integration of this region into the existing structures of West Germany meant that these X-efficiency improving structures could not be implemented. It would have implied a fundamental change of existing West German organisational structures.

8.3.2 Applicability of the Property Rights Theory for Transformational Economics

The property rights theory (Coase 1937, 1960; Alchian & Demsetz 1973; Demsetz 1988) as a non-deterministic evolutionary approach perceives an eventual development of any communal property right structure into a system of private property rights because only the private structure ensures a full utilisation of resources. Under the assumption of negligible transaction costs a private rights structure is socially preferable because of the internalisation of externalities. The private ownership structure (under the assumption of negligible transaction costs) allows an allocation of resources which ensures their most valuable use. These theoretical suggestions were shown not to apply to the East German transformation. Within this case study it was identified that transaction costs were *de facto* positive and not negligible, they could only be considered as negligible because the potential owners did not have to bear these costs. Positive transaction costs were defined as social costs because they accrued to the privatising institution. The communal ownership structure did not evolve into a private property structure, the private right structure was institutionally established by an institution which itself had to bear the costs. Thereby the theoretical argument that the private ownership structure itself is stable because it internalises social costs can not be applied, rather the establishment of this structure has created social costs of transaction.

Social transaction costs are different from social and public costs of transformation which were aimed to be internalised by the amended approach of the property rights theory. Costs of transformation have resulted from structural economic deficiencies and were caused by the societal change. These costs have been positive. The conventional theory suggests that any private owner is as good as next one given the assumptions that private transaction costs are negligible and that a market property price exists. The value of the property (that was to be privatised) has substituted the price concept in the conventional form. Properties were allocated to the highest valuing bidders and this allocation has created a comparative Pareto-improvement according to a cost-benefit analysis (Chapter 4, section 4.4). The value concept (property price, investment plans, investment and employment guarantees) represents elements of the potential purchaser's or investor's utility function and pre-defines the future utilisation of the respective property according to the national production function in terms of the resource's capacity effect. The value concept implies a truncation of the property rights bundle and identifies a first-best solution in the transferral of the truncated property rights bundle to a new purchaser or an investor and a second-best solution in the case of the restitution of the full property rights bundle to the former owner. This ranking of property assignments is based on the *ex-ante* definition of the owner's future behaviour according to the contractual agreement which has been designed to internalise social transformation costs. Coase's assumption of a truncation of property rights lowering the property's value can thus not be applied, rather this assumption has been reversed in that the willingness to agree contractually to a certain behaviour increases the social value of the property (which can be assumed to be identical with the private value because of the market simulation by the Treuhand). In comparison to the restitution of the full property rights bundle the first-best solution of contractually truncated property rights is assumed to create a Pareto-superior situation during the transitional period of transformation which reflects a major incongruity between the property rights theory and the privatisation approach applied. Limitations of this method and the welfare concept which was suggested to have been applied (chapter 7) will be shown in the next section.

8.4 Limitations of the Analysis

The transformation from a socialist planned economy to a system of market economy has been characterised by a fundamental norm change and a corresponding change of the societal goal function. Conceptional limitations are imposed by the definition of any norm and social values. Throughout the thesis norms and values were assumed to exist because of individuals living within a society. Although this existence is here not doubted questions are raised with regard to identifying situations which characterise norm changes as being influential. The size of the affected group and the effect of creating a public crisis can only be classified as indicators for the existence and the effects of norm changes. The thesis did not attend to a sociological analysis of norms and values and neither aimed at studying political issues of decision-making and division of authority.

Clear limitations were imposed by the non-comparability of situations prior to transformation with situations since transformation. In accordance to v. Mises (1920) it could for example be assumed that the distribution of consumption goods in a system of planned economy is independent of the question of production and of its economic conditions due to the common nature of ownership of the means of production. Any concept of a welfare function at the time of pre-liberalisation places different weights on distribution of income. Neoclassical analysis generally assumes the nature of common ownership to imply allocative inefficiency which would lead to the assumption of the criterion "producer's surplus" being infinitesimal small. This kind of analogy has been rejected throughout the thesis because it would have implied a comparison of two situations with different assumptions and an employment of variables which were only operational in one situation. Furthermore, a welfare analysis of a socialist structure cannot be limited to consumer's and producer's surplus because the objectives of this form of society are inherently different and economic sub-objectives were politically collectively oriented and not individually aggregatedly constructed. The economic system of the GDR constituted a price system in which prices were officially set by planning authorities. The non-existence of free markets excludes the application of demand and supply curves or if a demand curve was theoretically constructed no information for such modelling is available. Economic calculations were hindered by information constraints and the information by official authorities regarding the production process. The producing units themselves were better informed than the authorities and this divided allocation of information and decision-making authority often resulted in the construction of soft plans (Kornai, 1986).

The comparative-static nature of the model in chapter 7 also imposes clear boundaries on the analysis of welfare implications. The contrasting assumptions and conditions of the two economic systems implied that the concept of producer's and consumer's surplus could only be applied restrictively in its conventional sense so that only considerations post-liberalisation have been pursued. Despite the obvious difficulty of reducing the social value to an individual level, Nemchinov (1963) attempted a transformation of the form of value. He defined the social value which is realised at the individual level of different production-consumption cells as the net income of society. Any central construction of an economic plan for all consuming and producing units has thus the effects of a) truncating the economic opportunity set which truncates the individual's consumption opportunity set (like rationing) and b) truncating the production opportunity curve not least because of the opportunity costs involved in socialist production (information cost, waste of resources, difficulty of monitoring etc). Furthermore the quality of consumption products has to be taken into consideration which can be expected to be lower in the case of socialist planning due to the lack of insight into consumer's preference and utility functions. This truncation of both the consumer's and the producer's opportunity sets imposes a social opportunity constraint on the economy *ceteris paribus*. It can thus be assumed that the truncation can be offset by liberalising the markets. The liberalisation of the markets is thereby assumed generally to create a Pareto-improvement. Nemchinov has thereby ignored the conceptional differences in values and this type of analysis has been rejected. The analysis concentrated on the circumstances of transformation and alternative privatisation methods, their effects within the structurally re-shaped system and could, due to the above given incompatibilities, only concentrate on a comparative-static analysis of alternative situations after the liberalisation of the East German society and economy. The neoclassical concept of welfare and utility disregards sociological factors which adds another major hindrance to the analysis of welfare effects of transformation. No information and knowledge exists on how one individual assesses the right of ownership and the right to act individually according to self-defined plans. It is therefore impossible to conclude welfare implications of any form of fundamental structural changes as these individual variables will remain unquantifiable and even their quality is only known by each individual economic agent. Furthermore the assumption that each private owner is making the best use of a property according to rational behaviour is far too general and only approximations about peoples' behaviour can be made based on a deductive methodology. It can thus merely be assumed that some individuals might gain welfare from the sheer right of being allowed to behave in an individually chosen way but it is not certain that they will behave accordingly and will gain welfare from this behaviour (in for example producing an economic rent). Also no knowledge exists on whether the identification of political and economic life in the realised form of the former German Democratic Republic did not create welfare for the individual, a welfare that is not measurable in economic terms and is not conceived by neoclassical economics. It follows that any transformational analysis is strictly limited to the known methodologies and only those issues which are known and are intended to be achieved can be analysed.

8.5 Institutionalised Transformation: The Right Approach?

Transformational economies which are characterised by preceding norm and value changes which made the existing system unsustainable are dominated in their development by the adjustment elasticity in the form of the marginal product of system change. Norm changes are assumed to lead to structural changes which need to be internalised in their specific forms to create the adjustment of economic behaviour. An institutionalised system transformation separates the levels of individual norm changes and the realisation of these changes with regard to the structure of societal systems. Assumptions are set with regard to behavioural implications of the consciously designed order which it is aimed to establish. These assumptions are deduced from ordo-liberal and property rights-theoretical approaches such that every change in the economic system brings about a change in economic behaviour and in the relationship between the structure of property rights and economic choice. The theoretically approved structure of decentralised planning and private property rights was successfully implemented but rights which derive from these structures were allocated in a discriminatory way. The separation of the structure-implementing and rights-allocating group from the eventual group of economic agents gave room for pragmatic economic policy under the assumption that some economic agents act more "economically and rationally" than others.

The analysis of the privatisation methodology led to the conclusion that a discriminatory selection function has been employed and that some owners will behave in a way that is more socially valuable than others. Despite the righteousness of this notion with regard to the neoclassical analysis of the welfare implications of the chosen approach, it has also been identified that this policy implied the creation of different transformational adjustment deficiencies. These adjustment deficiencies were argued to cause a comparatively lower marginal product of system change *ceteris paribus* due to the restricted identification of economic agents with rights accruing from the altered structures. It was argued that this specific method of transformation was applied to avoid socially unacceptable situations which were also aimed to be caught by transitional follow-up policies. The general situation of the economic transformation going along with fundamental political and societal changes can be identified to have implied the objective of a fast privatisation and establishment of the new system. This can be surmised to have been achieved by the discriminating selection method as those economic agents which were considered to create spill-over effects by their particular economic action and behaviour were assigned with respective authority.

Both types of first-best solutions - privatisation to third party investors and new privatisation - were identified to have positive partial welfare effects as they internalise transformation costs and reduce some adjustment deficiencies and potential public expenditure designed to speed up the process of transformation. The analysis has shown that the Coasian assumption of the non-existence of income and substitution effects in the case of private property transfer under the assumption of negligible transaction costs does not hold in the transitional period. A comparatively higher value of the property right and the pre-determination of the usage of the property by the truncation of the rights bundle create a Pareto-improvement as compared with a full transfer of the property in the case of restitution because of the internalisation of transformation costs. Not every private owner placing the same value on the property creates the same economic outcome which contradicts Coase. It can however be criticised that the function selecting the owner can be centrally pre-determined and that the information about the best usage of the property was known by the institution Treuhandanstalt. The best usage had been specified by investment and employment objectives but the process of economic transformation had nevertheless to be supplemented by public interventions. Since it can not be established by which magnitude the marginal product of system change would have altered otherwise and within which time period the intended economic behaviour had been realised it is room for ethical considerations whether the adopted approach is advantageous. The short-run benefit of a smooth transformation might be opposed to long-run deficiencies due to the method of selectively allocating rights to economic agents.

Any institutionalised transformation allows scope for the separation of the transforming institution and the identity of future rights holders. The identification of the transforming institutions can thus be accompanied by problems as to who nominates the institutions. If the norm and value changes are transferred onto the level of all partial social systems a compatibility of partial system changes can be assumed. If congruence of structural changes is given with regard to, for example, the legal and political system, it can be expected that the institution sets some correct assumptions about the desired changes. If the transforming institution is politically appointed, a realisation of norm changes can only be expected if the political constellation represents some form of social value. Here again clear limitations of the institutionalised approach are identified by questions of political theory. If one assumes that a democratic political structure forms a government that executes policies which represent some form of "common will", the government's appointment of the respective institutions can be assumed to follow the nation's preferences. As this assumption is here fundamentally rejected because of non-existence of any common will, the political institutions which nominate institutions or groups to transform the economy's structure can not be assumed to be in the position to know the relevant changes in individuals' preferences and to accordingly form a respective order. With regard to the developed adjustment model this notion imposes clear limitations as to how the institution can create an internalisation of value changes onto the level of the economic system. This institutional incapability can lead to the construction of structures which eventually prove to be not equivalent with the norm changes. This will cause the real economic adjustment to the structural change to be sub-optimal. These changes can not be internalised because they are not part of the individual economic agent's utility function.

The institutionalised transformation must be criticised, if Hayek's concept of spontaneous orders (chapter 2, section 2.3.1.3.2) is accepted. Any rational construction of an economic system's order is inherently limited by the assumption that the relevant data is given. The institutions constructing and establishing this order do not possess this information and knowledge because this data is only available to individuals. Institutionalised transformation is rejected by Hayekian thought because the construction of the framework goes beyond securing the best use of resources and individual knowledge. In particular the method of incorporating assumptions about certain individual's economic behavioural functions as the basis of the privatisation is impeded by the lack of such behavioural knowledge on the institutional level. The market simulation as such is not criticised because it proved to be an efficient way of selling nationally-owned property to new owners, but the truncation of the property rights bundle in order to internalise transformation costs sets assumptions about the society's welfare concept. As soon as the existence of such a social welfare concept is doubted, because of the un-quantifyability and un-qualifyability of preferences and utility, institutionalised transformation is conceptionally deemed to fail because it is denied a methodological basis. The existence of some transformational welfare concept which has been modelled above assumes knowledge about economic behaviour and the type of variables which are part of individual behavioural functions. As the ability of transforming institutions to acquire this information is limited the institutionalised transformation needs to be supported by transitional pragmatic follow-up policies. As was suggested by Hayek (1945) only those individuals who possess intimate knowledge about changing factors should take the decisions within the changing environment and this represents the fundamental limitation of any institutionalised transformation approach. The institutionalised transformation might have proven more successful if the economic agents in the East German region would have been assigned with more rights of economic action within the transformational period.

Footnotes

[1]During my time as a class teacher at the London School of Economics I came across a seminar question of the following form: "The optimal rate of murder is positive". This implied a cost-benefit analysis of murder detection and , yes, the optimal rate is positive. But it must be questioned which use this analysis bears if the outcome must be fundamentally rejected from any moral-ethical point of view.

[2]Economic theory also refers to this mechanical relationship between elements, so that unambiguous connections between the cause and the effect are created by using *ceteris-paribus* assumptions.

[3]These relations can easily be transferred to the economic order and the claim for economic freedom, defined as autonomous decisions and wide scopes of action of economic subjects, excludes the claim for a planned order of the economy which aims for a common purpose and objective. The definition of a system of order needs an appropriate relation between order and freedom.

[4]Since the economic environment is inherently dynamic, the use of the terminology "initial" or "original" situation, environment etc. are to be handled with caution and any system analysis which realises that systems are not static, approaches the problem of system comparatibility. The dynamic nature also increases the difficulty in distinguishing between endogeneous and exogeneous causes of any events, because apart from natural circumstances such as earthquakes, every development can be defined as human and thus as an endogenous part of the system ignoring a time specification of the system.

[5]Lausanne School: Walras and Pareto are its most important members.

[6]See Hensel (1977, p. 37) on coordination of individual plans in a centrally planned economy.

[7]The concept of the collective stable strategy is conjectured to be the same as the evolutionary stable strategy. See McLean, Williams (1985).

[8]The economic theory of bureaucracy states that power serves mainly the objective of maximising individual income, prestige, life without conflict etc. Weber (1921, p. 129) suggests that all power is necessarily and inevitably placed in the hands of the bureaucrats in a modern society.

[9]Neuberger and Duffy (1976, p. 34), define the main origins of decision-making authority as tradition, coercion, ownership and information. The aspect of tradition is here rejected since it does not apply to an important extent to modern industrial economics. The aspect of information is closely linked to the decision-making structure and thus does not define the authority itself.

[10]House of Lords as example for traditional decision-making authority.

[11]The assumption of homogeneous preferences should be negated in the case of group decisions and the coordination with underlying heterogeneous preferences can be analysed with a public choice application.

[12]By definition it is assumed that production along the production possibility frontier is possible. All factors of the production function are known.

[13]A major application of the ordo-liberal conception can be found in the economic framework within the FRG set by Ludwig Erhard.

[14]Communal rights are characterised by the absense of a market clearing system, i.e. prices, but rivalry still exists if government regulations define resources as free goods up

to a particular quantity. The limited quantity of a resource might also lead to rivalry on a "first-come-first-served basis".

[15]The derivation of demand functions for public goods from individual pseudo-demand functions which represent a willingness to pay has been neglected, because the existence of rivalry distorts this possibility. The behavioural differences between the cases with and without rivalry assuming non-exclusion are considerable. The demand function in the case of rivalry can rather be expressed as a function of the limited availability: the less is available the more will be individually demanded.

[16]According to Alchian and Demsetz, (1973, p. 21), a legal system excluding non-payers from using communal rights removes the problem of increased transaction costs.

[17]In the paper by Furubotn (1985) conclusions about productive efficiency within a framework of codetermination are derived from specific utility functions.

[18]See Coase (1960). A further study of the Coasian Theorem where all externalities are eliminated under market negotiations if transaction costs are zero is not part of this thesis.

[19]See Demsetz (1964). If transaction costs are positive an incongruity between the market value and the social value of the right of action is created.

[20]This only applies to communal rights which are owned by several individuals and any government regulation towards the legal structure and attempts to prevent the establishment of private property rights are absent in this particular case.

[21]See Coase (1937). Social costs are perceived high enough to considerably decrease or even eradicate the resources.

[22]In the case of restrictive attenuation of a property right the theory of the state suggests that the benefit loss has to be compensated for by the state. See Buchanan & Stubbleline (1962).

[23]Although human knowledge is assumed to be a factor of production, in the traditional case where a two input factor model is assumed, no production is possible with only human knowledge, since material input factors such as capital or land are rendered necessary for the production of goods. The supply of services is disregarded since the property rights theory mainly concentrates on the ownership of resources and the production of an output mix by the utilisation of these transferable resources. The transferability of human knowledge will later be criticised refering to the inalienable rights theory and its application certainly rules out any transfer of human knowledge and thus rules out any cases where individuals, without an original endowment with wealth, can participate in the transfer of resources that shall be assumed as necessary for the production. The employment of labour does certainly not qualify as proper participation because it does not involve the control and decision-making authority which ownership of material resources does.

[24]The aspect of moral self-control can also be found in the Kantian philosophy and will be elaborated further within the theory of the democratic firm.

[25]Schumpeter (1976) points out that only in cases of minor innovations and small disturbances to the existing market, the new equilibrium will be near or close to the competitive equilibrium.

[26]Schumpeter's terminology of "commercial theory" is replaced by "capitalist theory" here.

[27]See Aster (1932, p 326): "Dem Menschen ist gleichsam seine Aufgabe im Schosse der Zeit, der Konstellation, in die er hineingeboren wird, bereitet, er muss ihr Werkzeug werden und sie durchfuehren...der einzelne Mensch kann glauben, seinen ganz persoenlichen Zwecken, seinem Ehrgeiz etwa, zu dienen; in Wahrheit wirkt er im Dienste

hoeherer geschichtlicher Ziele, von denen er keine Ahnung hat, die aber eben durch sein Tun ihrer Verwirklichung naehergefuehrt werden".

[28]Oakley (1984, p. 189) states in a section referring to Grundrisse that "by exposing the sources of this fate in the immanent structure and operation of capitalism, Marx's idea was to reveal the revolutionary path which could lead to the establishment of a truly human socio-economic environment".

[29]Questionable remark about the feudalist structure in the Manifesto (1848, p. 36): "The bourgeoisie, wherever it has got the upper hand, has put an end to all feudal, patriachial, idyllic relations. It has pitilessly torn under the motley feudal ties that bound man to his natural superiors."

[30]The overproduction of commodities relative to the effective demand was the heart of the crisis and vehemently contradicts Say and Mill. Marx states in Grundrisse: Foundations of the Critique of Political Economy: "The nonsense about the impossibility of overproduction (in other words, the assertion of the immediate identity of capital's process of production and its process of realisation) has been expressed...by James Mill..." His conception of the crisis was that its extent would increase rather than resolve itself and finally lead to - like Oakley (1984, p. 222) states - "an expansion of the increasingly alienated and unemployed proletariat".

[31]Popkin and Stroll (1986) interpret Marx's thesis in the following way: All class relationships areindependent of human wills and are in fact really determined by the prevailing economic system.

[32]It should nevertheless be noted that those costs might differ essentially since the motives of the private and state owner are inherently different.

[33]The analysis by Furubotn (1985) misses the point that the bundle of property rights is reduced by the employees' control rights. Although this positive motivation analysis is helpful, the concept has to be modified.

[34]The positive relationship between investment and growth in GDP was analysed and confirmed by Barro (1991).

[35]Utilitarian normative theory - offering prescriptions or recommendations based onwelfare economics and its Pareto-concept - will not be further detailed since it is considered to be particularised in any standard economics textbook. However in this section, notions which are rejected by the rights-based theory, will be restated.

[36]This distinction betwen positive and negative control rights is not applicable to stages where slavery and ownership of human beings were allowed. Here clearly no employment contract is necessary and positive control rights are assigned through the ownership itself.

[37]This formulation follows the Marxist labour theory of value applied to the labour theory of property if Marx's terminology of value is neglected.

[38]Collective internal capital accounts are often implemented in socialist worker-owned firms since the internal capital endowment is raised by governments and thus no individual capital accounts are in existence. Collective accounts are also used in order to self-ensure the corporation against the risk of paying out individual capital accounts. Often only a majority share of the actual capital account value is paid out and the remaining value is credited on the collective account. The proportion put into this collective reserve account at Mondragon used to be 12.5 per cent (Oakeshott, 1975).

[39]Ellerman proposed in 1990 a movement from physical lease to financial lease - moving from a worker lease-out to a worker buy-out of state sector firms - and this proposal was put into reality by Dr. Rutgaizer in the former Soviet Union (Moscow Experimental Plant, Khljupin Building Materials Plant).

[40]This production function explains system relations and their effects on the economic output. It has to be noted that the elements of the political and economic system are not necessarily homogeneous but since the partial production elasticities are not analysed in any further detail the production function of the Cobb Douglas type is applied. The same approach has been followed in dynamic growth theory, where use is made of the linear-homogeneous production function in the case of technical progress and certainly technical progress can not be identified as homogeneous. See Rose, 1987, p. 169.
[41]Constitution of the GDR 1968 (version 1974) cited in: Rytlewski, R. (1985).
[42]Verordnung ueber die volkseigenen Kombinate, Kombinatsbetriebe und volkseigenen Betriebe vom 8.11.1979 in GBL DDR, I, 1979.
[43]Verordnung ueber die volkseigenen Kombinate, Kombinatsbetriebe und volkseigenen Betriebe vom 8.11.1979, GBL DDR, I, 1979.
[44]Bericht des Zentralkommittees der Sozialistischen Einheitspartei Deutschlands an den X. Parteitag der SED (11.-16.4.1981), Berichterstatter Honecker.
[45]The main objective of the first five-year-plan was the restructuring of the economy and the expansion of the primary industry (Grundstoffindustrie).
[46]In 1971 Walter Ulbricht was replaced as General Secretary of the SED by Erich Honecker.
[47]Westermann (1993) describes the expropriations of industrial enterprises in 1972 as illegal and concludes that the former property owners have to be reinstated.
[48]Combines replaced VEBs in 1978 and are characterised by the horizontal and vertical integration of several VEBs of industrial and material production into one economic concern.
[49]In cases where the agricultural cooperatives did not meet minimum earnings the state intervened with economic and financial subsidies.
[50]The planning period was extended in 1959 to a seven-year-plan in accordance with the Soviet practice. The plan covering the period 1959-1965 was not carried out entirely and was abandoned in 1962 and more flexible reform plans were introduced (NES).
[51]The state planning commission continued to be responsible for the preparation of long-term plans and the general outlook but was supported by the Institute for Economic Research (established in 1960) and the Advisory Committee for Economic Research (established in 1963). The Economic Council (established 1961) was responsible for the preparation of the one-year-plan for the industry.
[52]Mittagsche Selbstversorgungsideologie
[53]Beschluss ueber die Grundsatzregelung fuer komplexe Massnahmen zur weiteren Gestaltung des oekonomischen Systems des Sozialismus in der Planung und Wirtschaftsfuehrung fuer die Jahre 1969 und 1970, GBL DDR, II, 1968, Nr. 68, S. 433. See Ulbricht (1969).
[54]Hans Modrow was elected President by the Peoples' Chamber on 13th November 1989 and the Cabinet started governing on 18th November 1989.
[55]Beschluss zur Gruendung der Treuhandanstalt, Verordnung zur Umwandlung von volkseigenen Kombinaten und Betrieben und Einrichtungen in Kapitalgesellschaften, GBL DDR, Part I, Nr. 14, 8.3.1990.
[56]The shares of companies with limited liability which were originally subordinated to combines -tranformed into AGs - became property of the stock company. It had to offer the shares to the TH-stock companies for an appropriate price (Paragraph 12 Clauses 2 and 3 THG).
[57]Anlage Treuhand Satzung.

[58]The first supervisory board was constituted to consist of 23 members according to the Unification Treaty which amended the original consistence of the TH supervisory board in that federal and local representatives replaced the originally 16 appointed East German members, seven from the Council of Ministers and nine from the People's Chamber (Pargr. 4 Clause 2 THG, Art. 25 Clause 2 UT).

[59]Deconcentration and newly-created company structure are to be interpreted as the creation of market foundations, the structures are not static and within a dynamic economic process they are likely to change in time and even further conglomeration can be expected.

[60]Gesetz zur Spaltung der von der Treuhandanstalt verwalteten Unternehmen vom 5. April 1991, BGBL, Teil I, S. 854.

[61]The term division includes both kinds of deconcentration, i.e. splitting-up and separation.

[62]Deutsche Presseagentur, 14.3.1990.

[63]Gesetz zur Aenderung und Ergaenzung der Verfassung der Deutschen Demokratischen Republik, Verfassungsgrundsaetze vom 17. Juni 1990, GBL DDR, 1990, Teil I, Nr. 33, 22.6.1990.

[64]Article 23 of the Basic Law was abolished under Article 4, Section 2 of the Unification Treaty.

[65]Dritte Durchfuehrungsverordnung zum Treuhandgestz vom 29. August 1990, GBL, I S. 1333.

[66]The initial property law (VermG) had been valid since the validation of the UT on 3.10.90. It was amended by the Law to Eliminate Hindrances of Privatisation (Hemmnisbeseitigungsgesetz, BGBL, 1991, S. 766, 22.3.1991) and the later amendment and revision of both laws in the Second Amendment of the Property Law (Zweites Vermoegensrechtsaenderungsgesetz BGBL, 1992, Teil I, S. 1268) dated 14.7.1992.

[67]Gemeinsame Erklearung der Regierungen... 15. Juni 1990. The joint declaration is part of the Unification Treaty (Article 41 Clauses 1, 3 UT) and binds the German government not to issue legal regulations which contradict this declaration. This enables the new German Laender to enforce rights derived from the announced benchmarks. Article 41 UT does neverthelss not imply that the declarartion can not be changed, an amendment is possible with the consent of both parties. Deviations were indeed enfoeced, e.g. the introduction of the law to abolish investment impediments (Hemmnisbeseitigungsgesetz, March 1991).

[68]See Vertrag zwischen der Bundesrepublik Deutschland und der Deutschen Demokratischen Republik ueber die Herstellung der Einheit Deutschlands - Einigungsvertrag-, BGBL, Jahrgang 1990, Teil II, Nr. 35, 28. 9.1990; Gemeinsame Ereklaerung der Regierungen der Bundesrepublik Deutschland und der Deutschen Demokratischen Republik zur Regelung offener Vermoegensfragen, BGBL, Jahrgang 1990, Teil II, Nr. 35, 28. 9.1990.

[69]Gesetz ueber die Entschaedigung nach dem Gesetz zur Regelung offener Vermoegensfragen und ueber staatliche Ausgleichsleistungen fuer Enteignungen auf besatzungsrechtlicher oder besatzungshoheitlicher Grundlage (EAGL), 27. September 1994, BGBL, 1994, Teil I, S. 2624.

[70]The number of managed enterprises comprises completely privatised enterprises, enterprises returned to local authorities, vesting orders and liquidations (completed and still to be completed).

[71]Gesetz ueber die Eroeffnungsbilanz in Deutscher Mark und die Kapitalneufestsetzung (D-Markbilanzgesetz), in der Fassung der Bekanntmachung vom 18. April 1991 (BGBL. I, S. 971).

[72]Announcement by the former chair of the board of directors D.K. Rohwedder to the Federal Chamber in Vienna, Meldung der Nachrichtenagentur ADN vom 19. Oktober 1990.

[73]Claims and applications for property restitution had to be filed by 31st December 1992 (Zweites Vermoegensrechtsaenderungsgesetz).

[74]They were dealt with by the Aemter und Landesaemter zur Regelung offener Vermoegensfragen. The decision-making authority of property administrative authorities was later supplemented by the Law in order to Eliminate Hindrances of Privatisation which expressed the possibility of decisions by the court of arbitration (Schiedsgericht). Furthermore mutual agreements between the holder of the right of disposal and the former owner became regular decisions which only had to be supported by the property administrative office.

[75]Compulsory administration has been invalidated under Paragraph 11VermG.

[76]BGBL I, S. 766, 22.3.1991, and BGBL I, S. 1257, 14. 7. 1992.

[77]Gesetz ueber den Vorrang von Investitionen bei Rueckuebertragungsanspruechen nach dem Vermoegensgesetz (InVorG), vom 14.7.1992, BGBL I, S. 1268.

[78]The formal and legal procedure was not necessary and the affected persons, i.e. the rightful owner, the investor and the holder of the right of disposal had the possibility to come to an agreement without using legal provisions. The obvious difficulty was the non-transparent circle of persons, the lack of knowledge and the high uncertainty.

[79]This could only have been initiated until 31st December 1995 and the investment has had to be implemented and been carried out within a specified period of time (Paragr. 13 InVorG). Similar to the original Paragraph 3a VermG (super regulation) the investment measures in enterprises and land property have had to be carried out within this time period.

[80]The holder of the right of disposal could also submit different applications for alternative investment plans for the same real estate.

[81]Document supplied by Herrn Konrad, BVS, Investitionsvorrangentscheidungen und Grundstuecksgenehmigungen, Berlin, 27.2.1995.

[82]This possibility of a real property market was rejected due the political urgency to fasten up the process of structural adjustment, migration etc. which was expected to have been prolonged by restituting first and then assigning the right to the highest bidder.

[83]Vertrag ueber die Schaffung einer Wirtschafts-, Waehrungs- und Sozialunion zwischen der Bundesrepublik Deutschland und der Deutschen Demokratischen Republik.

[84]The monetary aggregate M3 contains currency in circulation, sight deposits, time deposits, savings deposits and foreign currency held by domestic investors at banks in Germany.

[85]The discount rate is the rate at which the central bank buys bills from commercial banks. The highest rate pre-unification was achieved in the early 1980s when the rate reached a level of 7.5%. The lombard rate is normally 1% above the discount rate and it is the rate for the lending of securities.

[86]Contract managment is carried out by the organisation succeeding the Treuhand, the BVS, and the materialisation of guarantees is supervised.

[87]The tax free investment allowance as well as the special depreciation allowance have been an instrument of economic policy employed in West Germany for many decades.

Prior to unification it had been made use of predominantly for subsidising the German border area with an allowance of 10% (*Zonenrandfoerderung*). The depreciation allowance has also been employed as a means of economic policy to support the *Mittelstand* in West German states.

[88]An investment allowance of 12% had been granted for investment projects which started after 31.12.1990 and were finished before 1.7.1992. The level was reduced to 8% for investments which started before 1.1.1993 and were finished before 1.1.1995 and after 30.6.1992. An investment allowance of also 8% was granted for projects which started after 31.12.92 and before 30.6.1994 and will be finished before 1.1.97. A sectoral investment allowance of 10% is granted for investment which started before 30.6.1994 as long as the basis of the valuation does not exceed DM 5 m.

[89]According to calculations carried out by the Commissioner of Audits (Bundesrechnungshof, Drucksache 12/894, S. 139 ff) DM 1 bn were allocated as allowances under false circumstances. These were mainly assigned for old assets, for claiming the same costs twice, for leasing-cases etc. (BMWi, 1995).

[90]The suggestions made by Ludewig were instigated by and were a reply to the public debate of the waste of public resources within the process of economic recovery and subsidisation in the new German states.

[91]24. und 25. Rahmenplan der Gemeinschaftsaufgabe zur Foerderung der regionalen Wirtschaftsstruktur.

[92]These regional structural programmes have been supplemented by projects by the federal states (e.g. Atlas). Individual states choose enterprises which are considered significant for the regional structure. As long as the Treuhand classified the enterprises as viable for restructuring a joint restructuring between the state and the Treuhand was chosen. If the Treuhand classified the enterprises as not viable for restructuring the enterprise continued its existence with financial help from the particular federal state. In any case the subsidisation was designed to be temporary and it was planned that the enterprises were to be privatised. The federal states hoped to use financial resources of the GA-funds.

[93]Commercial companies within the following sectors are excluded: the mining industry, construction industry, retailing, wholesale trade in consumer goods, energy and water supply, agriculture and forestry, hospitals and sanatoriums and transport and storage.

[94]This general maximum can be exceeded by for small and medium sized companies (42%), for start up businesses 48% and other exceptions 75% (DIW Wochenbericht, 12. Bericht, 3/95).

[95]The European Union has participated financially with ECU 1567.2 m out of the Eurpoean Fund for Regional Development (EFRE) during 1991 - 1993 in East German regional development. Those resources have been prodominantly employed within the GA and purposes defined within this support scheme.

[96]About 20 different loan programmes exist of which only the dominant ones are analysed. Other programmes by the European Investment Bank and the KfW exist which focus on Eastern Europe (*Darlehen der Europaeischen Investitionsbank, KfW - Mittelstandsprogramm - Ausland und Osteuropa*).

[97]A survey with regard to the economic situation of the German "*Mittelstand*" was carried out by the Verband der Vereine Creditreform (1995) which surmised that insolvency is predominantly caused by low equity capital which makes companies economically vulnerable when liabilities are lost. This pattern was considerably recognised in the new states and an increase of 50% in the number of insolvencies was forecast for 1995. Only

one in two companies holds equity capital in excess of 10% and more than one third of the companies loose liabilities of more than 1% of the sales revenue. An average of 17.3% of all companies within the manufacturing industry (10.6% of the building sector, 11.5% of the trading and service sector) hold equity capital of more than 30% that is assessed as economically sound.

[98]The financial support of the KfW / Treuhand Programme is generally subject to EU acceptance and projects can be rejected according to Articles 85, 86 and 92 of the Treaties of Rome. Applicants in the iron and steel sector for this support programme must register their intention according to Article 54 of the European Iron and Steel Treaty. Subsidisation of industrial companies which have proved difficult to privatise can best be exemplified by the EKO Stahl AG and the Deutsche Waggonbau AG. Here the European Commission approved financial support of this programme.

[99]Initially the Treuhand has supported these programs financially with a contribution of 10% of the total costs and by granting interest free loans.

[100]Arbeitsfoerderungsgesetz (AFG), vom 25. Juni 1969, in der Fassung vom 5.10.1994, BGBL, Teil I., S. 2911. Paragraph 249h was changed by law on 21.12.1993 and came into force on 1.1.1994. It also includes the support of sport, culture and the preservation of historical monuments. Since August 1994 this regulation has been adopted as Paragraph 249s in West Germany too.

[101]The Federal Labour Office financially supports people employed within the scope of job-creating measures and those who can claim short-time payment.

[102]The maximum share supported is 75% of the investment costs; per newly created job a loan of max. ECU 30 000 (DM 57 600) is supported - up to a maximum of 27 jobs (DM 1 555 200). The jobs have to have been created after 28.4.1994 and have to exist for at least 6 months.

[103]It is here assumed that such basic social objectives exist and this assumption is based on the belief that a rejection of anarchy necessitates the acceptance of some fundamental political principles by individuals within the society. As long as a particular form of society is sustained by the society's members, keeping the definition of a system in a dynamic form in mind, and no considerable pressures for changes exist this form of acceptance must be presumed.

[104]The paper suggests that the market for corporate control is not as closely associated with the correction of managerial failure as has traditionally been assumed. Furthermore the intercorporate ownership in Germany is not similar to the one of Japan, where corporate ownership is frequent in cases of trading or production complementarities.

[105]The data published by the mergers commissions covers only registered mergers. According to German mergers law (*Kartellgesetz*, Paragraphs 23 I, II and 24) the commission has to be notified of the merger if a) the fusion established a market share of at least 20% or if b) both enterprises have at any time during the last commercial year employed more than 10 000 people or achieved a turnover of more than DM 500 m.

[106]In accordance with the CES-production function.

[107]$W = [bPi^{-p} + aS^{-p}]^{-1/p}$, $dW/dPi = -1/p\,[bPi^{-p} + aS^{-p}]^{-1/p-1} \cdot (-pbPi)^{-p-1}$, $dW/dPi = b\,[bPi^{-p} + aS^{-p}]^{-1/p-1} \cdot Pi^{-p-1}$, inserting (7.4a and 7.4b): $dW/dPi = bW^{1+p} \cdot Pi^{-1-p}$, $dW/dPi = bW^{1+p} \cdot 1/Pi^{1+p}$, $dW/dPi = b(W/Pi)^{1+p}$ and $dW/dS = a\,(W/S)^{1+p}$.

[108]The structural change in East Germany and the implementation of transitional economic policies has also had effects on the West German consumer surplus. For example has the imposition of the solidarity contribution had a negative income effect as it

has reduced the purchasing power of consumers in East and West Germany ceteris paribus. Similar welfare effects are neglected because the thesis has aimed at the analysis of the East German transformation which was defined in its pre-unification borders and fiscal political implications for the West German economy were thus not part of the analysis.

Abbreviations

ABM, ABS	Arbeitsbeschaffungsmassnahme (job-creating measure)
ACZ	Agrochemisches Zentrum (agro-chemical centre)
AFG	Arbeitsfoerderungsgesetz (law for labour development)
AFO	Contract Research and Development East
AG	Aktiengesellschaft (public stock company)
AIF	Arbeitsgemeinschaft industrieller Forschungsvereinigungen e.V. (working group of industrial research associations)
AktG	Aktiengesetz (corporate law for stock companies)
AWO	Contract Research and Development West-East
BAROV	Bundesanstalt zur Regelung offener Vermoegen fragen (federal office for open property issues)
BfA	Bundesanstalt fuer Arbeit (federal office for labour)
BIP	Bruttoinlandsprodukt (gross national product)
BL	Grundgesetz (German basic law)
BMFT	Bundesministerium fuer Forschung und Technologie (federal ministry for research and technology)
BMWi	Bundesministerium fuer Wirtschaft (federal ministry for economy)
Bund	Federation
BVVG	Bodenverwertungs- und -verwaltungsgesellschaft mbH (TH-corporation handling land)
BVS	Bundesanstalt fuer vereinigungsbedingte Sonderaufgaben (institution succeedung the TH)
CBM	Central Bank Money
CDU	Christlich Demokratische Union (christian democrats)
Co KG	Kommanditgesellschaft (corporate form of limited partnership)
DDRV	Verfassung der Deutschen Demokratischen Republik (constitution of the German Democratic Republic)
DIW	Deutsches Institut fuer Wirtschaftsforschung
DM	Deutschemark
EAGL	Gesetz ueber die Entschaedigung (compensation law)
EFRE	Europaeischer Fonds fuer regionale Entwicklung (European Fund for Regional Development)
EG	East Germany
EKP	Equity Capital Assistance Programme
ERP	European Recovery Programme
ESS	Economic System of Socialism
EU	European Union
FDGB	Der Freie Deutsche Gewerkschaftsbund (head trade union organisation)

FDJ	Die Freie Deutsche Jugend (youth organisation)
FRG	Federal Republic of Germany
GA	Gemeinschaftsaufgabe "Verbesserung der regionalen Wirtschaftsstruktur"
GDR	German Democratic Republic
GEMSU	German Economic, Monetary and Social Union
GmbH	Gesellschaft mit beschraenkter Haftung (company with limited liability)
GPG	Gaertnerische Produktionsgenossenschaft (gardening co-operative)
IAB	Institut der Arbeits- und Berufsforschung der Bundesanstalt fuer Arbeit
IMF	International Monetary Fund
InvG=BInvG	Gesetz ueber besondere Investitionen -Investitionsgesetz- (law for special investment)
InVorG	Investititonsvoranggesetz (investment precedence law)
KfW	Kreditanstalt fuer Wiederaufbau
KG	Kapitalgesellschaft (joint stock company)
LPG	Landwirtschaftliche Produktionsgenossenschaft (agricultural production co-operative)
MBI	Management-Buy-In
MBO	Managemant-Buy-Out
NES	New Economic System
NSDAP	Nationalsozialistische Deutsche Arbeiterpartei
Paragr.	Paragraph (paragraph)
PGH	Produktionsgenossenschaft des Handwerks (trade production co-operative)
SED	Sozialistische Einheitspartei (socialist unity party)
SME	Mittelstand (small and medium-sized enterprises)
SpG	Spaltungsgesetz (separation law)
TBG	Technologie-Beteiligungsgesellschaft mbH (technology participation)
THA, TH	Treuhandanstalt (trust agency)
THG	Treuhandgesetz (Treuhand law, law on the THA and the TH-corporations)
TLG	Treuhandliegenschaftsgesellschaft mbH (TH-corporation handling real estate)
TOU	Setting Up Technology-Oriented Enterprises
UT	Einigungsvertrag (Unification Treaty)
VEB	Volkseigener Betrieb (enterprise owned by the people)
VEG	Volkseigenes Gut (agricultural production unit owned by the people)
VermG	Vermoegensgesetz (law for the regulation of open property issues)

VVB	Verband Volkseigener Betriebe (conglomeration of VEBs)
WG	West Germany

List of Tables, Figures and Diagrams

Chapter 5:

Chapter 6:

Chapter 7:

Bibliography

-**Alchian, A.** (1950) Uncertainty, Evolution and Economic Theory, *Journal of Political Economy*, vol. 58, no. 3.

-**Alchian, A., Demsetz, H.** (1972) Production, Information Cost, and the Economic Organisation, *The American Economic Review*, vol. 62, no. 5.

-**Alchian, A., Demsetz, H.** (1973) The Property Rights Paradigm, *Journal of Economic History*, vol. 31, no. 1.

-**Allen, R.G.D., Hicks, J.R.** (1934) A Reconsideration of the Theory of Value (parts I and II), *Economica,* vol. 1, no.1 and no. 2.

-**Angresano, J.** (1991) Comparative Economics, London.

-**Apel, E., Mittag, G**. (1964) Oekonomische Gesetze des Sozialismus und neues oekonomisches System der Planung und Leitung der Volkswirtschaft, Berlin.

-**Apel, E., Mittag, G.** (1965) Fragen der Anwendung des neuen oekonomischen Systems der Planung und Leitung der Volkswirtschaft bei der Vorbereitung und Durchfuehrung von Investititonen, Berlin.

-**Arrow, K.J.** (1962), The Economic Implications of Learning by Doing, *The Review of Economic Studies*, vol. 29.

-**Arrow, K.J., Chenery, H.B., Minhas, B.S., Solow, R.M.** (1961) Capital-Labour Substitution and Economic Efficiency, *Review of Economics and Statistics*, vol. 43.

-**Arrow, K.J., Debreu, G.** (1954) Existence of an Equilibrium for a Competitive Economy, *Econometrica*, vol. 22, no. 3.

-**Ashby, W.R.** (1956) An Introduction to Cybernetics, London.

-**Aster, E. von** (1980) Geschichte der Philosophie, 17th ed., Stuttgart.

-**Axelrod, R.** (1984) The Evolution of Co-operation, London.

-**Balassa, B.** (1962), The Theory of Economic Integration, 4th edition, Amsterdam 1973.

-**Barro, R.J.** (1991) Economic Growth in a Cross-Selection of Countries, *Quarterly Journal of Economics*, vol. 106, pp. 406 - 443.

-**Baumgart, E., Krengel, R., Moritz, W.** (1960) Die Finanzierung der industriellen Expansion in der Bundesrepublik Deutschland waehrend der Jahre des Wiederaufbaus, Berlin.

-**Baumol, W.J.** (1952) Welfare Economics and the Theory of the State, London.

-**Beise, M.** (1995) Hat die Ordnungspolitik ausgedient?, *Handelsblatt*, 7.8.1995.

-**Bender, D. et al** (ed.) (1985) Vahlens Kompendium der Wirtschaftstheorie und Wirtschaftspolitik, Muenchen.

-**Bentley, R**. (1992) Research and Technology in the Former German Democratic Republic, Oxford.

-**Bergson, A.** (1938) Social Welfare Function, in: Samuelson (1948).

-**Bergson, A.** (1966) Essays in Normative Economics, Cambridge.

-**Bethkenhagen, J., Cornelsen, D., et al** (1981) DDR und Osteuropa - Wirtschaftssystem, Wirtschaftspolitik, Lebensstandard - Ein Handbuch, Opladen.

-**Beyer, H.J.** (1995) Mittelstandsfoerderung in den neuen Bundeslaendern, Koeln (Deutscher Instituts Verlag).

-**Blaich, F.** (ed.) (1971) Wirtschaftsysteme zwischen Zwangslaeufigkeit und Entscheidung, Stuttgart.

-**Blaug, M.** (1980) The Methodology of Economics. Or How Economists Explain?, Cambridge.

-**Brennan, G., Tollison, R.** (eds.) (1979) What Should Economists Do?, Indianapolis.

-**Brockhaus, F.A.** (ed.) (1991) Der neue Brockhaus, German Encyclopedia, 6th edition, Mannheim.

-**Buchanan, J.M.** (1979) What Should Economists Do? in: Brennan, G., Tollison, R. (1979).

-**Buchanan, J.M., Stubbleline, W.C.** (1962) Externality, *Econometrica*, vol. 29.

-**Bundesanstalt fuer Arbeit** (1994a) Strukturanalyse 1993, Bestaende sowie Zu- und Abgaenge an Arbeitslosen und offenen Stellen, Nuernberg.

-**Bundesanstalt fuer Arbeit** (1994b) Amtliche Nachrichten der Bundesanstalt fuer Arbeit, Arbeitsmarkt 1993, Nuernberg.

-**Bundesanstalt fuer Arbeit** (1995a) Presseinformationen: Der Arbeitsmarkt im Februar 1995, no. 14/1995, 7.3.1995 and current issues.

-**Bundesanstalt fuer Arbeit** (1995) Amtliche Nachrichten der Bundesanstalt fuer Arbeit, Arbeitsmarkt 1994, Nuernberg.

-**Bundesanstalt fuer Arbeit** (1996) Presseinformationen: Der Arbeitsmarkt im Oktober 1996, no. 52/1996, 7.11.1996 and previous issues.

-**Bundeskabinett** (1991) Bericht zur Taetigkeit der Treuhandanstalt, vom 18. Oktober 1991, Bonn.

-**Bundesministerium fuer innerdeutsche Beziehungen** (1984) DDR Handbuch, Bonn.

-**Bundesministerium fuer innerdeutsche Beziehungen** (ed.) (1985) DDR-Handbuch, Cologne.

-**Bundesanstalt zur Regelung offener Vermoegensfragen** (1994) Pressemitteilung, 31.12.1994, Berlin.

-**Busse, C.** (1995) Kein Kompromiss ohne Bundesbeteiligung, *Handelsblatt*, 30.8.1995.

-**Carlin, W.** (1994) Privatisation and Deindustrialisation in East Germany, in: Estrin (1994).

-**Carlin, W., Mayer, C**. (1992) The Treuhandanstalt: Privatisation by State and Market, paper presented at the *NBER Conference on Industrial Restructuring in Eastern Europe*, Cambridge Mass., 19.-26.2.1992.

-**Carlin, W., Mayer, C.** (1995) Structure and Ownership in East German Enterprises, paper presented for the *Economics of Transition, CEPR-NBER-TCER Conference*, Tokyo 6./7.1.1995 (December draft paper).

-**Christ, P., Neubauer, P.**, (1991) Kolonie im eigenen Land, Berlin.

-**Claessen, D., Kloenne, A., Tschoepe, A.** (1989) Sozialkunde der Bundesrepublik Deutschland, Hamburg

-**Coase, R.** (1937) The Nature of the Firm, *Econometrica*, vol. 4.

-**Coase, R.** (1960) The Problem of Social Cost. The Distinction Between Private and Social Benefit and Costs, *Journal of Law and Economics*, vol. 3.

-**Cornelsen, D.** (1981) Die Wirtschaft der DDR, in: Bethkenhagen et al (1981).

-**Cornelsen, D.** (1991) Privatisation - The Example of East Germany, paper presented at the *WEFA Group: International Economic Outlook Conference on Eastern Europe and the Soviet Union*, Berlin 22.-26.4.1991.

-**Cox, H**. (1990) Entflechtung und Privatisierung in der DDR, Diskussionsbeitraege zur oeffentlichen Wirtschaft, Nr. 26, University of Duisburg 1990.

-**De Meza, D., Osborne, M.** (1980), Problems in Price Theory, Oxford.

-**Delhaes, K. von** (1971) Stadien wirtschaftlichen Wachstums nach W.W. Rostow, in: Blaich (1971).

-**Demsetz, H**. (1964) The Exchange and Enforcement of Property Rights, *Journal of Law and Economics*, vol. 7.

-**Demsetz, H.** (1988) Ownership, Control and the Firm. The Organisation of Economic Activity, Volume I, Oxford.

-**Deutsche Bundesbank** (1996) Monatsberichte, November 1996 and previous issues, Frankfurt.

-**Deutsches Institut fuer Wirtschaftsforschung, Institut fuer Weltwirtschaft, Institut fuer Wirtschaftsforschung in Halle** (1991-1995) Gesamtwirtschaftliche und unternehmerische Anpassungsfortschritte in Ostdeutschland, Erster - Zwoelfter Bericht, *DIW-Wochenbericht*, vol. 58-62, various numbers.

-**Deutsches Institut fuer Wirtschaftsforschung** (1992a) Zur Politik der Treuhandanstalt - Eine Zwischenbilanz, *DIW-Wochenbericht*, vol. 59, no. 7.

-**Deutsches Institut fuer Wirtschaftsforschung** (1992b) Strukturwandel im Prozess der deutschen Einigung, DIW-Wochenbericht, vol. 58, no. 48.

-**Deutsches Institut fuer Wirtschaftsforschung** (1994) Volkswirtschaftliche Gesamtrechnung des Deutschen Instituts fuer Wirtschaftsforschung, April/Juli 1994, Berlin.

-**DiLorenzo, T.L.** (1988) Property Rights, Information Costs and the Economics of Rent Seeking, *Journal of Institutional and Theoretical Economics*, vol. 144.

-**Domar, E.D.** (1946) Capital Expansion, Rate of Growth and Employment, *Econometrica*, vol. 14.

-**Downs, A**. (1957) An Economic Theory of Democracy, New York.

-**DTV (Deutscher Taschenbuch Verlag)** (ed.) (1994) Vermoegensgesetz, 5th edition, Muenchen.

-**Dunleavy, P.** (1991) Democracy, Bureaucracy and Public Choice, London.

-**Easterby-Smith, M., Thorpe, R., Lowe, A.** (1991) Management Research. An Introduction, London.

-**Eckstein, A.** (ed.) (1973) Comparison of Economic Systems: Theoretical and Methodoligical Approaches, Berkeley (University of California Press).

-**Eggertsson, T.** (1990) Economic Institutions and Behaviour, Cambridge.

-Ellerman, D. (1986) Horizon Problems and Property Rights in Labour-Managed Firms, *Journal of Comparative Economics*, vol. 10.

-Ellerman, D. (1988) The Kantian Person/Thing Principle in Political Economy, *Journal of Economic Issues*, vol. 22, no. 4.

-Ellerman, D. (1990) The Democratic Worker-Owned Firm, A New Model for the East and for the West, London.

-Ellerman, D. (1992) Property and Contracts in Economics, Oxford.

-Engels, F. (1884) Origins of Family, Private Property and State, in: Marx, Engels (1962).

-Estrin, S. (1994) (ed.) Privatisation in Central and Eastern Europe, London.

-Eucken, W. (1950) The Foundations of Economics - History and Theory of the Analysis of Economic Reality, London.

-Eucken, W. (1952) Grundzuege der Wirtschaftspolitik, Tuebingen.

-Federal Office for Foreign Trade (1991) Information - Doing Business in Germany's New Federal States, Berlin.

-Federal Mergers Commission Bundeskartellamt (1994) Bericht des Bundeskartellamtes ueber seine Taetigkeit in den Jahren 1992/93 sowie ueber die Lage und Entwicklung auf seinem Aufgabengebiet, Berlin.

-Federal Ministry of Economics BMWi (1994a) Economic Incentives in Germany's New Federal States: An Overview, Bonn.

-Federal Ministry of Economics BMWi (1994b) Jahreswirtschaftsbericht 1994, Bonn.

-Federal Ministry of Economics BMWi (1994c) Wirtschaftliche Foerderung in den neuen Bundeslaendern, Bonn.

-Federal Ministry of Economics BMWi (1994d) Forschung, Entwicklung und Innovation in der ostdeutschen Wirtschaft, *Dokumentation*, no. 353, 2nd ed.

-Federal Ministry of Economics BMWi (1995) Verwendung von Foedergeldern in den neuen Laendern, *Dokumentation*, no. 367.

-Fieberg, G., Reichenbach, H. (1994) Einfuehrung, in: DTV (1994).

-Fischer, W., Hax, H., Schneider, H.K. (eds.) (1993) Treuhandanstalt. Das Unmoegliche wagen, Berlin.

-Franks, J., Mayer, C. (1994a) Ownership and Control, paper presented at the *International Workshop at the Kiel Institute*, June 1994.

-Franks, J., Mayer, C. (1994b) The Ownership and Control of German Corporations.

-Friedman, M. (1962) Capitalism and Freedom, Chicago.

-Friedman, M., Schwartz, A.J. (1982) Monetary Trends in the United States and the United Kingdom, Chicago.

-Friedrich, W. (1992) Management-Buy-Outs and Management-Buy-In. Untersuchung im Auftrag des Bundesministers fuer Wirtschaft, Koeln.

-Friedrich-Ebert Stiftung (ed.) (1992) Finanzierung der deutschen Einheit. Ansaetze zur Neuordnung des Finanzausgleichs und zur Verbesserung der Politik der Treuhandanstalt, *Reihe Wirtschaftspolitische Diskurse*, no. 26, Bonn.

-**Friedrich-Ebert Stiftung** (ed.) (1993) Finanzierung der deutschen Einheit. Grundlagen und Perspektiven, Bonn.
-**Frisch, T.** (1993) Unternehmenszusammenschluesse in den neuen Bundeslaendern, HWWA Report Nr. 119, Hamburg.
-**Furubotn, E.G**. (1985) Codetermination, Productivity Gains and the Economics of the Firm, *Oxford Economic Papers*, vol. 37.
-**Furubotn, E.G.** (1988) Codetermination and the Modern Theory of the Firm: A Property Rights Analysis, *Journal of Business*, vol. 61, no. 2.
-**Furubotn, E.G., Pejovich, S.** (1972) Property Rights and Economic Theory: A Survey of Recent Literature, *Journal of Economic Literature*, vol. 10, no. 4.
-**Gabler-Verlag** (ed.) (1984) Wirtschaftslexikon, Wiesbaden.
-**Galbraith, K**. (1972) The New Industrial State, 2nd edition, Middlesex.
-**Gesamtdeutsches Institut** (ed.) (1984) Bestimmungen der DDR zu Eigentumsfragen und Enteignung, Bonn.
-**Goerzig, B., Gornig, M., Schulz, F.** (1994) Quantitative Szenarien zur Bevoelkerungs- und Wirtschaftsentwicklung in Deutschland bis zum Jahr 2000, *Beitraege zur Strukturforschung*, no. 150, pp. 55.
-**Haase, H.H.** (1990) Das Wirtschaftssystem der DDR. Eine Einfuehrung, Berlin.
-**Haertel, H.H., Krueger, R., Seeler, J., Weinhold, M.** (1992) Institutionelle Ursachen von Wettbewerbsverzerrungen in den neuen Bundeslaendern, HWWA Report, Nr. 92, Hamburg.
-**Handelsblatt**, Duesseldorf, various issues.
-**Harrod, R.F.** (1938) Scope and Methods in Economics, *The Economic Journal*, vol. 48..
-**Harrod, R.F.** (1939) An Essay in Dynamic Theory, *The Economic Journal*, vol. 49.
-**Harrod, R.F.** (1948) Towards a Dynamic Economics, Some Recent Developments of Economic Theory and Their Applications to Policy, London 1956.
-**Hayek, F.A.** (ed.) (1935) Collectivist Economic Planning, Clifton 1975.
-**Hayek., F.A.** (1945) The Use of Knowledge in Society, *The American Economic Review*, vol. 35, no.4.
-**Hayek, F. A.** (1949) Individualism and Economic Order, London.
-**Hayek, F.A.** (1963) Arten der Ordnung, *Ordo*, vol. 14.
-**Hayek, F.A.** (1969) Freiburger Studien - Gesammelte Aufsaetze, Tuebingen.
-**Hayek, F.A.** (1976) Law, Legislation and Liberty, Vol. III, Chicago.
-**Heimpold, G., Kroll, H., Wilhelm, M.**, (1991) Privatisierung in den neuen Laendern, Berlin.
-**Hensel, K.P.** (1977) Systemvergleich als Aufgabe, Stuttgart.
-**Hesselberger, D**. (1990) Das Grundgestz. Kommentar fuer die politische Bildung, Bonn.
-**Hicks, J.R.** (1939) The Foundation of Welfare Economics, *The Economic Journal*, vol. 49.
-**Hobbes, T.** (1651) Leviathan, London 1968.

-Hodgkin, T. (1832) The Nature and the Artificial Right of Property Contrasted, Clifton 1973.
-Hollander, S (1985) The economics of John Stuart Mill, Vol. I, II, Oxford.
-Hume, D. (1739) A Treatise of Human Nature, 2nd ed., Oxford 1978.
-Hurwicz, L. (1969) Centralisation and Decentralisation in Economic Systems, *The American Economic Review*, vol. 59, no. 2.
-Hurwicz, L. (1973) Centralisation and Decentralisation in Economic Process, in Eckstein (1973).
-Institut fuer Arbeit- und Berufsforschung der Bundesanstalt fuer Arbeit IAB (1995) Neue Bundeslaender: Lohnkostenzuschuesse nach Paragraph 249h AFG: Die investive Komponente steht im Vordergrund, *IAB Kurzbericht*, no. 2, 17.3.1995.
-Ifo-Institut fuer Wirtschasftsforschung et al (ed.) (1994) Die Effizienz der finanzpolitischen Foerdermassnahmen in den neuen Bundeslaendern, Muenchen.
-Jaeckel, P. (1994) Neue Bundeslaender: Weiterer Anstieg der Industrieinvestitionen, *ifo-Schnelldienst,* no. 24.
-Jensen, M., Meckling, W. (1979) Rights and Production Functions: An Application to Labour-Managed Firms and Codetermination, *Journal of Business*, vol. 52, no. 4.
-Jones, D.C., Svejnar, J. (eds.) (1982) Participatory and Self-Managed Firms, Toronto.
-Kaldor, N. (1939) Welfare Propositions in Economics, *The Economic Journal*, vol. 49.
-Kaldor, N. (1957) A Model of Economic Growth, *The Economic Journal*, vol. 67.
-Kaldor, N., Mirrless, J.A. (1962) A Model of Economic Growth, *The Review of Economic Studies*, vol. 29, 1962.
-Kant, I. (1781) Kritik der praktischen Vernunft, reprint of 9th edition (1929), Hamburg 1967.
-Kelso, L., Hatter, P. (1976) Two-Factor Theory: The Economics of Reality, New York.
-Keynes, J.M. (1936) The General Theory of Employment, Interest and Money, London.
-Kornai, J. (1986) The Hungarian Reform Process: Visions, Hopes, and Reality, *Journal of Economic Literature*, vol. 24.
-Koopmans, T.C., Montias, J.M. (1970) On the Description and Comparison of Economic Systems, in: Eckein (1970).
-Kuhn, K. (1962) The Structure of Scientific Revolution, 2nd edition, Chicago.
-Leibenstein, H. (1966) Allocative Efficiency vs. X-Efficiency, *The American Economic Review*, vol. 56.
-Leipold, H. (1985) Wirtschafts- und Gesellschaftssysteme im Vergleich, Grundzuege einer Theorie der Wirtschaftssysteme, Stuttgart.
-Levine, H.S. (1973) On Comparing Planned Economies (A Methodological Inquiry), in: Eckstein (1973).

-Lichtblau, K. (1994) Investitionsfoerderung in den neuen Lanedern, in: Ifo et al (1994).

-Lipschitz, L. (1990) Introduction and Overview, in: Lipschitz, L., McDonald, D. (1990).

-Lipschitz, L., McDonald, D. (eds.) (1990) German Unification. Economic Issues, IMF Washington.

-Littlechilds, S.C. (1981) Misleading Calculations of the Social Cost of Monopoly Power, *Economic Review*, vol. 91.

-Luft, C. (1992) Treuhandreport: Werden, Wachsen und Vergehen einer deutschen Behoerde, Berlin.

-Ludz, H.P., Ludz, U. (1985) Marxismus-Leninismus, in: Bundesministerium fuer innerdeutsche Zusammenarbeit (1985).

-Mann, G. (1991) Politische Entwicklung Europas und Amerikas 1815-1871, in: Propylaen (1991).

-Marx, K. (1845) Theses on Feuerbach, in: Marx, Engels (1962).

-Marx, K. (1859) Preface to the Critique of Political Economy, in: Marx, Engels (1962).

-Marx, K. (1867) Das Kapital, Stuttgart 1957.

-Marx, K. (1867) Preface to the First German Edition of Capital, in: Marx, Engels (1962).

-Marx, K. (1875) Critique of the Gotha Programme, in: Marx, Engels (1962).

-Marx, K., Engels, F. (1884) Manifesto of the Communist Party, in: Marx, Engels (1962).

-Marx, K., Engels, F. (1962) Selected Works, Volumes I & II, Moscow 1962.

-Mayer, T. (1992) Aspects of Monetary Policy in the Unified Germany, *Goldmann Sachs paper*, 29.1.1992.

-McKinsey and Company (1991) Ueberlegungen zur kurzfristigen Stabilisierung und langfristigen Steigerung der Wirtschaftskraft in den neuen Bundeslaendern, Duesseldorf.

-McLean, I, Williams, M.E. (1985) Axelrod's Evolution of Cooperation: A Critique. Paper presented to the *Institute for Research at the Social Science Conference on Public Choice*, York.

-Mill, J.S. (1843) System of Logic, Ratiocinative and Inductive, extracts in: Hollander (1985).

-Mises, v. L. (1920) Economic Calculation in the Socialist Commonwealth in: Hayek, F.A. (1935).

-Mises, v. L. (1949) Human Action: A Treatise on Economics, New Haven.

-Mueller, J. (1993a) Strukturelle Auswirkungen der Privatisierung durch die Treuhandanstalt: in Hax et al (1993).

-Mueller, J. (1993b), Managementtransfers in die neuen Bundeslaender, Schwerpunktthemen zum Gutachten: Gesamtwirtschaftliche Anpassungsprozesse im Gebiet der frueheren DDR, Berlin Juli 1993.

-Myrdal, G. (1970) Objectivity in Social Research, London.

-Naegele, F. (1994) Strukturpolitik wider Willen? Die regionalpolitischen Dimensionen der Treuhandpolitik, Aus Politik und Zeitgeschichte, *Beilage zur Wochenzeitung Das Parlament*, B 43-44/94, Bonn 28.10.1994.
-Nemchinov, V. (1972) Basic Elements of a Model of Planned Price Formation, in: Nove & Nuti (1972).
-Neuberger, E., Duffy, W.J. (1976) Comparative Economic Systems: A Decision-Theoretic Approach, Boston.
-Nolte, D. (1993) Zwischen Privatisierung und Sanierung: Die Arbeit der Treuhandanstalt. Bilanz und Perspektive aus gewerkschaftlicher Sicht, *WSI-Materialien*, no. 32, Duesseldorf.
-North, D. (1990) Institutions, Institutional Change and Economic Performance, Cambridge.
-North, D., Thomas, R. (1974) The Rise and Fall of the Manorial System: A Theoretical Model, *Journal of Economic History*, vol. 31, December.
-Norzick, R. (1974) Anarchy, State and Utopia, New York.
-Nove, A., Nuti, D.M. (1972) Socialist Economics, Middlesex.
-Nove, A. (1983) The Economics of Feasible Socialism, London.
-Oakley, A. (1984) Marx's Critique of Political Economy, Intellectual Sources and Evolution, Volume I, London.
-Oakshott, R. (1975) Mondragon: Spain's Oasis of Democracy, in: Vanek (1975).
-Oakeshott, R., Wiener, H. (1987) Worker-Owners, Mondragon Revisited, Anglo-German Foundation, London.
-Oberhauser, A. (1993) Mehr selbstverantwortliche Finanzpolitik in den neuen Bundeslaendern durch die Neuregelung des Finanzausgleichs, in: Friedrich-Ebert Stiftung (1993).
-Olson, M. (1977) The Logic of Collective Action, Cambridge/Mass.
-Pejovich, S. (1987) Freedom, Property Rights and Innovation in Socialism, *Kyklos*, vol. 40, no. 4.
-Pohl, R. (1995) Die Investitionsfoerderung ist nicht effizient genug, *Handelsblatt*, 20.4.1995.
-Popkin, R.H., Stroll, A. (1986) Philosophy, 2nd ed., Oxford.
-Popper, K (1957) The Poverty of Historicism, London.
-Popper, K. (1959) The Logic of Scientific Discovery, reprint from 1965, New York.
-Propylaen der Weltgeschichte, Das 18. Jahrhundert, Band 8, Berlin.
-Proudhon, P.J. (1966) What is Property?, New York.
-Pryor, F.L. (1973) Property and Industrial Organisation in Communist and Capitalist Nations, Bloomington.
-Rawls, J. (1973) A Theory of Justice, Oxford.
-Recktenwald, H.C. (1985) Ethik, Wirtschaft und Staat, Adam Smiths politische Oekonomie heute, Darmstadt.
-Robbins, L.C. (1938) Interpersonal Comparisons of Utility: A Comment, *The Economic Journal*, vol. 48.

-Roesler, J. (1990) Zwischen Plan und Markt. Die Wirtschaftsreform in der DDR zwischen 1963 und 1970, Berlin.

-Romer, P. (1986) Increasing Returns and Long-Run Growth, *Journal of Political Economy*, vol. 94.

-Rose, K. (1987) Grundlagen der Wachstumstheorie, 5th ed., Goettingen.

-Rostow, W.W. (1971) Stages of Economic Growth, 2nd ed., Cambridge.

-Rytlewski, R. (1985) Wirtschaft, in: Bundesministerium fuer innerdeutsche Beziehungen (1986).

-Sachverstaendigenrat zur Begutachtung der gesamtwirtschaftlichen Entwicklung (1991a) Die wirtschaftliche Integration in Deutschland. Perspektiven-Wege-Risiken, Jahresgutachten 1991/1992, Stuttgart.

-Sachverstaendigenrat zur Begutachtung der gesamtwirtschaftlichen Entwicklung (1991b) Marktwirtschaftlichen Kurs halten. Zur Wirtschaftspolitik fuer die neuen Bundeslaender, Sondergutachten, Stuttgart.

-Sachverstaendigenrat zur Begutachtung der gesamtwirtschaftlichen Entwicklung (1994) Jahresgutachten 1994/95, Stuttgart.

-Samuelson, P.A. (1948) Foundations of Economic Analysis, Cambridge.

-Samuelson, P.A. (1962) The Gains from International Trade Once Again, *The Economic Journal,* vol. 72.

-Samuelson, P.A. (1976) Economics, 10th ed., New York.

-Schwalbach, J. (1993) Begleitung sanierungsfaehiger Unternehmen auf dem Weg zur Sanierung, in: Hax et al (1993).

-Schotter, A. (1981) The Economic Theory of Social Institutions, Cambridge.

-Schroeder, G. (1988) Property Rights Issues in Economic Reforms in Socialist Countries, *Studies of Comparative Communism*, vol. 21, no 2.

-Schumpeter, J.A. (1926) Theorie der wirtschaftlichen Entwicklung: eine Untersuchung ueber Unternehmensgewinn, Kapital, Zins und den Konjunkturzyklus, 2nd ed., Muenchen 1964.

-Schumpeter, J.A. (1939) Business Cycles, A Theoretical, Historical, and Statistical Analysis of the Capitalist Process, New York.

-Schumpeter, J.A. (1976) Capitalism, Socialism and Democracy, 10th edition, London.

-Scitovsky, T. (1942) A Reconsideration of the Theory of Tariffs, *Review of Economic Studies*, vol. 9.

-Scully, G.W. (1987) The Choice of Law and the Extent of Liberty, *Journal of Institutional and Theoretical Economics*, vol. 143.

-Scully, G.W . (1988) The Institutional Framework and Economic Development, *Journal of Political Economy*, vol. 96, no. 3.

-SED (1976) Manifest der Sozialistischen Einheitspartei Deutschlands, Berlin.

-Siebert, H (1991) German Unification, in: *Economic Policy*, October 1991.

-Siebert, H. (1992) Das Wagnis der Einheit. Eine wirtschaftspolitische Therapie, Stuttgart.

-Sinn, G., Sinn, H.W. (1992) Kaltstart, Tuebingen.

-Smith, A. (1926) Theorie der ethischen Gefuehle, Hamburg 1977.

-**Smith A.** (1776) The Wealth of Nations, New York 1937.

-**Spoerr, W.** (1993) Treuhandanstalt und Treuhandunternehmen zwischen Verfassungs-, Verwaltungs- und Gesellschaftsrecht, Koeln.

-**Staatliche Zentralverwaltung fuer Statistik**, Statistisches Jahrbuch der DDR, various issues, Berlin.

-**Statistisches Bundesamt**, Fachserie 4, Reihe 2.1, current issues, Wiesbaden.

-**Statistisches Bundesamt**, Statistische Jahrbuecher der Bundesrepublik Deutschland, current issues, Wiesbaden.

-**Statistisches Bundesamt** (1990) DDR 1990, Zahlen und Fakten, Wiesbaden.

-**Svejnar, J.** (1982) Codetermination and Productivity: Empirical Evidence from the Federal Republic of Germany, in: Jones, Svejnar (1982).

-**Thieme, H.J.** (1984) Wirtschaftssysteme, in: Thieme, Cassel et al (1984).

-**Thieme, H.J., Cassel, D., et al** (1984) Vahlens Kompendium der Wirtschaftstheorie and Wirtschaftspolitik, Muenchen.

-**Thompson, W.** (1824) An Inquiry into the Principles of the Distribution of Wealth, New York 1963.

-**Tobin, J.** (1970) On Limiting the Domain of Inequality, *Journal of Law and Economics*, vol. 13.

-**Torstensson, J.** (1994) Property Rights and Economic Growth: An Empirical Study, *Kyklos*, vol. 47, no. 2.

-**Treuhandanstalt** (1990), DM-Opening Balance, 1.7.1990, Berlin.

-**Treuhandanstalt**(a), Monatsinformationen, current issues 9/1991 - 9/1994, Berlin.

-**Treuhandanstalt**(b), Informationen, current issues 9/1991 - 12/1994, Berlin.

-**Treuhandanstalt**(c), Privatisierung, current issues 9/1991 - 12/1994, Berlin.

-**Treuhandanstalt** (1992) Fragen und Antworten zur Privatisierung, Berlin.

-**Treuhandanstalt** (1994) Daten und Fakten zur Aufgabenerfuellung der Treuhandanstalt, DIW-Arbeitsmarktbilanz, August.

-**Ulbricht, W.** (1969) Zum oekonomischen System des Sozialismus in der Deutschen Demokratischen Republik, Berlin.

-**Vanek, J.** (1971) The Basic Theory of Financing of Participatory Firms, in: Vanek (1975).

-**Vanek, J.** (1975) Self-Management: Economic Liberation of Man, Baltimore.

-**Verband der Vereine Creditreform** (1995) Wirtschaftslage im Mittelstand Fruehjahr 1995, Neuss.

-**Vickers, J., Yarrow, G.** (1989) Privatisation. An Economic Analysis, London.

-**Vogt, H.** (1984) Einheitliches sozialistisches Bildungssystem, in: Bundesministerium fuer innerdeutsche Beziehungen (1984).

Watrin, C. (1991) Treuhandanstalt: Transformator im Prozess der Systemaenderung in: *Wirtschaftsdienst*, vol. 71, no 4.

-**Weber, H.** (1991) DDR - Grundriss der Geschichte 1945-1990, Hannover.

-**Weber, M.** (1921) Parlament und Regierung im neugeordneten Deutschland, in: Weber, M. (1921) Gesammelte Schriften, Muenchen.

-**Weber, M.** (1947) The Theory of Social and Economic Organisation, London.

-**Weber, M.** (1968) Economy and Society, Volume I, New York.
-**Weber, R.** (1995) Hohe Foerdermittel fuer Gewerbe-Investitionen, *Handelsblatt,* 20.4.1995.
-**Wegner, M.** (1991) Mezziogiorno im Osten, *Wirtschaftwoche*, no. 15, 5.4.1991.
-**Weidenfeld, W., Zimmermann, H.** (1989) Deutschland - Handbuch. Eine doppelte Bilanz 1949-1989, Muenchen.
-**Westermann, H.P**. (1993) Der rechtliche Rahmen und seine Veraenderung, in: Hax et al (1993).
-**Wiles, P.J.D.** (1977) Economic Institutions Compared, Oxford.
-**Williamson, O.** (1979) Transaction-Cost Economics: The Governance of Contractual Relations, in: *Journal of Law and Economics*, vol 22.
-**Willms, M.** (1985) Strukturpolitik, in: Bender et al (1985).
-**Yeager, L.B.** (1976) Economics and Principles, *Southern Economic Journal*, vol. 42, no. 4.

Legal References
(Listed per Date of Issue)

-**Grundegesetz fuer die Bundesrepublik Deutschland** (Basic Law of the Federal Republic of Germany), 23.5.1945.

-**Montanmitbestimmungsgesetz**, Gesetz ueber die Mitbestimmung der Arbeitnehmer in den Aufsichtsraeten und Vorstaenden der Unternehmen des Bergbaus und der Eisen und Stahl erzeugenden Industrie vom 21.5.1951, BGBL, 1951, Teil I, S. 347.

-**Betriebsverfassungsgesetz** vom 11.10.1952, BGBL, 1952, Teil I, S. 681.

-**Verfassung der Deutschen Demokratischen Republik** vom 6. April 1968 in der Fassung des Gesetzes zur Ergaenzung und Aenderung der Verfassung der Deutschen Demokratischen Republik vom 7. Oktober 1974, in: Sartorius III, Verwaltungsgesetze, Ergaenzungsband fuer die neuen Bundeslaender (vormals DDR-Sartorius), Textausgabe hrsg. von Dr. Ronald Brachmann, Oktober 1994, C.H. Beck'sche Verlagsbuchhandlung, Muenchen.

-**Beschluss ueber die Grundsatzregelungen** fuer komplexe Massnahmen zur weiteren Gestaltung des oekonomischen Systems des Sozialismus in der Planung und Wirtschaftsfuehrung fuer die Jahre 1969 und 1970, GBL DDR, II, 1969, Nr. 68.

-**Betriebsverfassungsgesetz** vom 15.1.1972, BGBL, 1972, Teil I, S.13.

-**Programm der Sozialistischen Einheitspartei**, Berlin 1976.

-**Mitbestimmungsgesetz** (MitbestG) vom 4.5.1976, BGBL, 1976, Teil I, S. 1153.

-**Verordnung ueber die volkseigenen Kombinate, Kombinatsbetriebe und volkseigenen Betriebe** vom 8.11.1979, GBL DDR, I, 1979.

-**Vertrag ueber die Schaffung einer Wirtschafts-, Waehrungs- und Sozialunion** zwischen der Bundesrepublik Deutschland und der Deutschen Demokratischen Republik, BGBL, 1990, Teil II, S. 518, 29.6.1990.

-**Treuhand Satzung** (TH-statutes), 18.7.1990.

-**Beschluss zur Gruendung der Treuhandanstalt,** Verordnung zur Umwandlung von volkseigenen Betrieben und Einrichtungen in Kapitalgesellschaften, GBL DDR, I, Nr. 14, 8.3.1990.

-**Gemeinsame Erklaerung der Regierungen zur Regelung offener Vermoegensfragen** dated 15.6.1990 (part of Unification Treaty) BGBL, 1990, Teil II, Nr. 35, 28.9.1990.

-**Gesetz zur Aenderung und Ergaenzung der Verfassung der Deutschen Demokratischen Republik**, Verfassungsaenderungsgesetze vom 17. Juni 1990, GBL DDR, I, 1990, Nr. 33, 22.6.1990.

-**Dritte Durchfuehrungsverordnung zum Treuhandgesetz** vom 29. August 1990, GBL DDR, I, 1990, S. 1333.

-Vertrag zwischen der Bundesrepublik Deutschland und der Deutschen Demokratischen Republik ueber die Herstellung der Einheit Deutschlands (Einigungsvertrag), BGBL, 1990, Teil III, Nr. 35, 28.9.1990.
-Hemmnisbeseitigungsgesetz, BGBL, 1991, S. 766, 22.3.1991.
-Gesetz zur Spaltung der von der Treuhandanstalt verwalteten Unternehmen vom 5. April 1991, BGBL, 1991, Teil I, S. 854.
-Gesetz ueber die Eroeffnungsbilanz in Deutscher Mark und die Kapitalneufestsetzung (D-Markbilanzgesetz, DM Opening Balance), in der Fassung der Bekanntmachung vom 18. 4. 1991, BGBL, 1991, Teil I, S. 971.
-Gesetz ueber besondere Investitionen -Investitionsgesetz- (InvG), BGBL, 1991, Teil I, 26.4.1991.
-Gesetz zur Regelung offener Vermoegensfragen, BGBL, 1991, Teil I, 25.4.1991.
-Zweites Vermoegensrechtsaenderungsgesetz, BGBGL, 1992, Teil I, S. 1268, 14.7.1992.
-Gesetz ueber den Vorrang von Investitionen bei Rueckuebertragungs-anspruechen nach dem Vermoegensgesetz (InVorG), BGBL, 1992, Teil I, S. 1268, 14.7.1992.
-Gesetz zur Regelung offener Vermoegensfragen (VermG), BGBL, 1992, Teil I, S. 1446, 3.8.1992.
-Gesetz zur Umsetzung des Foederalen Konsolodierungsprogramms, BGBL, 1993, 23.6.1993.
-Gesetz ueber die Entschaedigung nach dem Gesetz zur Regelung offener Vermoegensfragen und ueber staatliche Ausgleichsleistungen fuer Enteignungen auf besatzungsrechtlicher oder besatzungshoheitlicher Grundlage (EAGL), BGBL, 1994, Teil I, S. 2624, 27.9.1994.
-Arbeitsfoerderungsgesetz (AFG), vom 25. Juni 1969, in der Fassung vom 5.10.1994, BGBL, 1994, Teil I, S. 2911. Paragraph 249h was changed by law dated 21.12.1993 and came back into force on 1.1.1994.
-24. Rahmenplan der Gemeinschaftsaufgabe zur Foerderung der regionalen Wirtschaftsstruktur. Fuer den Zeitraum 1995-1998, Kurzfassung des Teil II des Rahmenplans veroeffentlicht im Bundesanzeiger Nr. 53, 16.3.1995.

Druck: Strauss Offsetdruck, Mörlenbach
Verarbeitung: Schäffer, Grünstadt